RIFT VALLEY FEVER
A BRITISH VET IN AFRICA

HUGH CRAN

MERLIN UNWIN BOOKS

First published in Great Britain by Merlin Unwin Books Ltd 2024

Text © Hugh Cran 2024
Cover and illustrations © Merlin Unwin

Merlin Unwin Books Ltd
Palmers House
Ludlow
Shropshire SY8 1DB
UK
www.merlinunwin.co.uk

The author asserts his moral right to be identified with this work.
ISBN 978 1 913159 68 9
Designed, edited and typeset in 11.5 point Minion Pro by
Merlin Unwin Books
Printed by CPI Group (UK) Ltd

*'Dedicated to the memory of Kim, and to all friends,
black, white and brown, in Africa, and beyond'*

Contents

DOCTOR'S ORDERS

'Right, Mr Cran, I'll operate tomorrow.'

Professor Renato Ruberti knew his onions. He had all but diagnosed my problem by phone and it only required confirmation by CT scan to prove he was right.

'You've got a massive chronic post-traumatic subdural hygroma, fluid has collected between the skull and the brain. I have to do a craniotomy and drain it off. If this had gone on any longer you would have started blacking out, or you might have suffered brain damage.'

Being a vet in private practice in Kenya, I knew what he was talking about. Two months previously I had been involved in a car accident and this was the result.

'OK,' I said, 'Thanks very much. Soonest done, soonest mended, eh?'

'Indeed. Right, get yourself checked in and I'll see you in the morning.'

Chapter One

ROAD RAGE
29TH OCTOBER 1991

The bay gelding was big, very big. About seventeen hands, I estimated. I raised the heavy rasp. The syce grasped the horse's tongue and held it to one side of the mouth. Behind me stood my African assistant Moses. My arms and shoulders were aching. I had just rasped the teeth of twelve horses at the Mt. Kenya Safari Club. Above us loomed the great jagged mountain which dominated the whole area, and after which the club was named.

This was the last horse. A baker's dozen. Number thirteen. Was that unlucky? The horse's name was Viper. There was a brass plate to that effect on the stable door. I had noticed that as we pushed our way in.

I would have preferred a nice friendly name, like Topper or Dobbin. The reptilian overtones of Viper were not friendly.

The syce gave me due warning. 'This horse,' he said, 'eh, he is kali (fierce), kama nyoka!'(like a snake!) 'Great,' I thought. 'There's always one.'

'Right, Viper,' I said, in my most soothing tones, 'open your mouth like a good boy and let's get this job finished.'

Viper was having none of it. As soon as I introduced the rasp into his mouth he seized it with his huge yellow teeth and shook his massive head, worrying it like a terrier with a rat. I held on grimly while Viper did his best to bisect the titanium rasp, grinding it noisily between his enormous molars.

'Moses,' I said, 'get me the twitch from the car.'

Our attempts to attach the twitch to Viper's nose were met with an infantile exhibition of petulant equine outrage. Viper reared, grunted and struck out with his fore hooves. He jumped up and down like a demented kangaroo. He lashed out with his hind legs. The trouble was that Viper was no infant, but a fully-fledged adult, albeit a castrato. After one iron-shod hoof almost de-eared me I decided that it was time to resort to drugs.

I prepared a Viper-stunning syringe-full of Xylazine, guaranteed to bring the strongest charger to his knees. By the time I returned to the scene of the fray, another syce, alerted by the sounds of Viper's uncooperative behaviour, had arrived at the stable door. I welcomed arap Ruto, a lean, sharp-eyed, vigorous man of about 40, shaking his dry, leathery hand.

'Jambo, daktari, he said. 'Leave him to me. I know how to handle him.'

Very quietly he pushed open the stable door and stepped inside. Viper snorted. Arap Ruto paid no attention. 'Wacha kichwa,' he said to the other syce. 'Leave his head.' The syce dropped the head rope. Arap Ruto turned his back on Viper and sat down, cross legged, on the stable floor. Viper snorted again. Then he fell silent, staring at the small figure, squatting motionless before him. He moved closer, lowered his head and sniffed at arap Ruto's shaven ebony poll. Arap Ruto lowered *his* head, as though in prayer, then slowly raised his right hand. Viper nuzzled the black fingers and mouthed the pink palm. Arap Ruto gently rubbed the horse's muzzle.

We stood silently watching and, as we watched, arap Ruto, like an uncoiling spring, rose gently to his feet, still with his back to the horse. With infinite patience he pivoted on the balls of his feet, rotating until he was facing the horse. He blew into Viper's nostrils, rubbed the muscular neck and laid his own sinewy arm across the thick, black mane.

Viper stood motionless, breathing stilled, head drooping.

Arap Ruto spoke: 'Come,' he said, 'you can inject him with the tranquilizer now. He will be fine.'

And so he was. A slight shiver as I pushed the needle into his raised jugular vein, but that was all.

Fifteen minutes later I was cleaning my rasps and shaking arap Ruto by the hand as I prepared to depart and embark on the 120 mile return drive to Nakuru, in the Rift Valley, where I was based.

Late afternoon clouds were obscuring the mountain as we departed the hallowed precincts of the Club. A uniformed askari saluted smartly as we drove through the massive wrought iron gates and down the hill and back into the real world.

About a month previously I had had a go of one of those intestinal maladies which periodically afflict those foolish or unfortunate individuals who live in the tropics. I took myself to Nairobi to get myself checked out. The medico, grizzled and stooped from years of peering at suffering humanity, diagnosed a combination of giardia and a surfeit of roundworms.

For some reason he seemed to think that the stress of driving might have been a contributory factor and advised that on long journeys I get my assistant, the faithful Moses, to share the load.

Accordingly, as this was a long journey, I took the sage sawbones at his word and asked Moses to take the wheel for the first stretch, which was all tarmac. After about 20 miles there was a right turn onto a dirt road leading to the august Aberdare Country Club, the township of Mweiga and the main road to Nakuru. At this point I would resume command.

I sat in the back of my Peugeot 504 saloon, on the left side, trying to read an improving, if incredibly boring, veterinary journal. The scientific jargon had its effect. I nodded off. I came to as we passed a lorry heavily laden with timber. Before us was a long hill, near the bottom of which the near moribund railway line from Nairobi to Nanyuki crossed the road. There was no level crossing, but, as the number of trains plying this route had dwindled almost to vanishing point, the risk of an unequal collision was minimal. On the right stood a match factory and a little further on, also on the right, was our turn off to the Aberdare Country Club, Mweiga and home.

I put down my stultifying periodical, removed my spectacles, and prepared to unclip my seat belt in preparation to getting back behind the wheel.

Moses turned right.

There was an ear-splitting bang, the car was propelled brutally backwards, and we were now 200 yards beyond our turn off point, facing the way we had come, and behind us, in the ditch, was a lorry, minus a front wheel. Visibility was minimal. For a moment I thought I was partially blind, but it was just dormant dust and debris from within the car, stirred violently into action by the impact, which was clouding my vision.

I shook my head. I felt my limbs. All appeared to be intact.

'Moses!' I asked. 'Moses! What happened?'

He remained silent, crouched behind the wheel.

I opened my door and stepped out onto the tarmac.

People, peasants from their fields, came running towards the car. There seemed to be an awful lot of them, until I realized I was seeing double. I shook my head again and things stabilized. I stood my ground. I knew that if I didn't the car was liable to be looted. Car accident victims were an easy prey, frequently robbed and stripped of all their possessions as they lay bleeding and insensible. The dead were the most vulnerable, with watches and rings torn from stiffening wrists and fingers, necklaces yanked from lifeless throats, even shoes prised from feet that would walk no more. Seeing that I was neither unconscious nor dead the mob slowed, then stopped, staring at me. I wondered why, until I glanced at an unbroken car window and saw a reflection of myself – hair like a tornadoed haystack, face bloodied and eyes glaring. I frightened myself.

The left side of the car, from which I had emerged, appeared to be intact. But the right side, which had borne the brunt of the broadside collision, was mangled beyond repair. Both doors were crushed, the rear right suspension was collapsed and the tyre burst – split open like an over-ripe pawpaw – and the boot was concertinaed. The right rear window was broken and it was the blast of shattered glass from this which had peppered my face.

As I stood surveying the wreckage, a car driven by Africans drew up. They offered to take Moses to Nyeri Hospital, which was not far distant. Moses was a Kikuyu and Nyeri was his home town so this was fortuitous. He still sat dazed and wordless. I knew that no ambulance was likely to turn up, so I agreed. He was lifted from his seat, placed in the car and off he went.

Had he been struck dumb and speechless by the shock of the impact? Or, was he overcome by guilt, knowing that he had neither looked in his mirror, nor indicated his intention to turn right? I had no time to ponder on these possibilities. I was more concerned about defending the contents of my stricken steed. As I turned to see a woman trot down the road with my gum boots under one arm and a brace of towels under the other, out of the corner of my eye I saw a man lean into the car and remove the cigarette lighter from the dashboard. Another gent, wearing a black bomber jacket and a natty trilby, produced a screwdriver from his pocket and set to unscrewing one of the wing mirrors. As he bent to his task, a tourist Land Rover, driven by a uniformed chauffeur, drew up. The mob scattered as the vehicle stopped and the occupants emerged.

They were a French couple returning to Nairobi from the Samburu Game Reserve.

Exclamations of horror as they viewed the scene. 'Ooh la la! Mon Dieu! Sacre bleu! Votre pauvre visage! Il est couvert de sang! Et votre auto! Une bonne Peugeot, n'est-ce pas? Elle est morte! Finis, je crois!' 'Et le camion la bas….' I had forgotten about the lorry. I looked and saw the lorry driver sitting disconsolately beside his vehicle, a solitary and forlorn figure. A lorry laden with heavy timber had little to offer the opportunistic scavenger.

I looked back up the long hill, looking for skid marks. There were none. So had the lorry driver been free-wheeling down the hill, minus his servo-assisted brakes, in order to save fuel? Then, when Moses had suddenly made his indicator-less turn, the lorry, without effective brakes, had ploughed into us amidships. Both individuals would deny it, but this was the undoubted truth.

The large chauffeur, imposing in his black, brass-buttoned jacket, had found a large stick and was laying into the circling sharks and jackals. His name, according to the tag on his lapel, was Oluoch, indicating that he was an uncircumcised Jaluo, and by default no friend of the circumcised Kikuyu, scuttling out of range of his whirling baton.

I asked the French couple if they would report the accident to Kiganjo Police Station, a few miles further down the road, and to phone my wife, Berna, in Nakuru, informing her that, although the car was a wreck, I was not. This they promised to do. Indeed, they did more. They returned to tell me that they had got through, and that Berna was on her way to pick me up. This would take about three hours.

As the tricolour and the entente cordiale departed towards Nairobi, so it was replaced by the red, green, black and white of the less than cordial Kenya police, arrived to apportion blame, and, if possible, derive benefit from other's misfortune. They were soon followed by a break-down truck, come to drag away the mortal remains of my car to the police station.

I hastened to remove my things – boxes of drugs, surgical instruments, tools, spare wheels – before they vanished, never to be seen again. By the time the gendarmerie had taken their measurements, examined my car and taken my statement, I had piled my chattels onto the verge. I said farewell to my Peugeot as it was jacked up and towed away. The police departed whence they came and I was left, feeling like the last man standing at Isandlwana, with the menacing impis closing in for the final assegai thrust.

The crowd edged closer, hungrily eyeing the tools of my trade.

'Any moment now,' I thought.

The noise of a vehicle. I looked up. A pick-up had stopped at the junction, coming from the direction of the Aberdare Country Club. A European was at behind the wheel. I recognized him. It was a friend, Mervyn Ward. I waved. He waved and drove over. The crowd drew back, muttering.

'Problem?' asked Mervyn.

I explained the situation.

'Right,' said Mervyn, 'let's get your stuff into the back of the pick-up and I'll drive you to the club.'

Cheated of their prey, the mob dispersed. Like hyenas bold enough to attack a lone buffalo, they retreated when another arrived on the scene.

We rattled along the rocky road to the club.

'Glad you came along when you did, Mervyn,' I said, 'or I don't know what might have happened.'

'They'd have cleaned you out, man, that's what,' he replied. 'Those Kukes there are a bad lot. Those bastards would steal the pennies off a dead man's eyes and the air out of your tyres if they could sell it. I'm always glad when I'm away from there and nearer Nanyuki. But hell, we'd better get you cleaned up before your missus sees you. You look a right old mess – bloody face, hair full of dust and eyes like piss holes in the snow.'

'I'm fine. Just the odd scratch. I didn't hit anything. I'll be fine'

We reached the club at about 6.30pm.

As we drove in from one direction, so Berna, accompanied by two of our daughters, Sophie and Kim, drove in from the other.

More cries of alarm – contralto, treble and soprano.

'Don't worry,' I said. 'A little water clears us of this deed!'

And so it did. I had a Coke, we left a little after 7pm, in the dark, and by 9.45pm we were home.

Chapter Two

GIN AND GONADS

The weeks following the accident were not restful.

For much of this time I was without the services of my Man Friday, assistant Moses, who had suffered bruised ribs and whiplash injury to his neck. If the lorry driver had not swerved at the last moment, thereby hitting the rear side of the car, instead of the front, Moses would almost certainly have been killed, or at the very least, seriously injured. When he did eventually reappear, he was unable to do much more than creep around like a geriatric tortoise, neck encased in an orthopaedic support.

I felt sorry for him. I would have felt rather more sorry if he had shown any inkling of remorse or regret for what had happened. But he never, ever, expressed any concern for the loss of my vehicle, nor for the major resulting inconvenience. It all smacked of suppressed feelings of guilt.

Meanwhile the work of the practice had to continue, come what may.

Things could not be held up by a mere traffic accident. Nor that shortly before that accident we had sold our gas-guzzling , three gear, Toyota Land Cruiser and were now down to one vehicle, whereas previously we had three – one practice Peugeot 504, another 504 for

Berna, and the Toyota for safaris and emergencies. No indeed.

Three vehicles sounds extravagant, but with both parents working, with no available safe public transport, living miles from the nearest town and having to ferry children 40 miles to school, possessing more than one car was less of an extravagance than a necessity. Rona, our first born, was aged seven, and a weekly boarder at St. Mungo's Preparatory School, an hour and a half drive away on the bracing heights of the Rift Valley, near Molo.

St. Mungo's was the polar opposite to Dotheboys Hall. It was a caring, ecclesiastical sort of place, and many of the teachers were of a missionary bent. The head was no Wackford Squeers. He was a quiet-spoken chap, who never raised his voice and who preached in chapel on Sundays. This was all well and good, but it allowed strong personalities and natural gang leaders, like Rona, free rein. More than one young, idealistic teacher was brought to the edge of a nervous breakdown by Rona and her team, whose cunning, low key tactics were so subtle that their luckless victims were only dimly aware that they were being targeted by a junior Moriarty.

Sophie, our number two, when she duly arrived at the school, adopted the role of the mild innocent, assuming a butter-wouldn't-melt-in-her-mouth attitude which left teachers baffled and confused.

Kim, the youngest, who seemed to know the answers to most questions before they were even asked, regarded many of her teachers with barely concealed scorn. Those who failed to meet her own exemplary standards were given the cool, blue-eyed, withering, drop-dead look, a look which left many apprehensive and on edge. One head went so far as to say that he had nightmares about coming back to the school as a junior teacher and finding to his dismay and horror that Kim was in charge as the new head.

But all three did well, amassing prizes and emerging with the wherewithal to move on to further spheres of higher education.

All this lay in the future. In the meantime I grappled with the aftermath of the accident.

While Berna ran her own small private school for infants, including Sophie and Kim, I was run off my feet dealing with a multitude of problems, not all animal related. As Honorary Correspondent for the British High Commission in Nairobi, an unpaid sinecure, I was expected to deal with any difficulties involving British Citizens in my area – an area extending from Mau Narok, 30 miles to the south, to the Ethiopian border, several hundred miles to the north.

And the problems were not slow in coming. An Ancient Briton, called Herbert Allen, took up a great deal of my time. Destitute, bed ridden, with heart problems, he seemed to appear out of nowhere. He told me that he had worked for many years in Uganda, had fallen on hard times, his heart began to give up the struggle, here he was and could I help him? I did, exceeding both his and my wildest expectations, and more importantly from her point of view, those of his African lady companion. By dint of making innumerable phone calls, and writing countless letters, I obtained for him not only a monthly stipend and rent payments from the British Legion and the East African Women's League, but also a British old age pension, despite the fact, that as far as I could ascertain, he had made zero contributions. Herbert's co-hab was over the moon with avaricious joy. She made a point of coming to the surgery on an almost daily basis, usually when I was in the midst of a particularly tricky diagnostic challenge, seeking, and demanding, information on the next financial instalment.

Eventually, with Mr Allen's ticker beginning its terminal countdown, I arranged for him to be moved to the Cottage Hospital at Nanyuki, hard by the Mt. Kenya Safari Club. Here he lived out his last few months in more comfort that he had known in years, before being called to the Final Reckoning. But not before he had made an Honest Woman of his dusky companion, who, as the sorrowing widow of a British Citizen, promptly applied for, and was granted, permission to settle in the Mother Country, to which favoured isle her extended family soon followed, there to batten on the largesse of a state, to which neither her death-bed husband, nor she, had contributed a penny.

⛨✕⛨✕⛨✕

Coincidence! Is there a rational explanation to the phenomenon, or was it a random throw of Fate's dice that decreed that Felicity Drudge's pet giant rat and the Stock Theft Unit's prize colt should both suffer testicular trauma on the same day?

The Stock Theft Unit beat Mrs. Drudge to the phone.

'Harro? Dr Cran? Inspector Kiptanui here.' Ah, Inspector Kiptanui, former star of the show jumping arena, whose bright comet blazed briefly across the fickle world of dressage, cross-country and three day events. Then he was slim, naturally dark and very handsome. A veritable African centaur, his proud entry into the ring caused many a female heart to go pit-a-pat. Now, instead of the saddle, he spent most of his time in his padded swivel office chair and it showed. The buttons of his uniform strained to contain his swelling paunch, below his moon face his triple chins flowed over his collar and at the back of his head there was a crease like a tectonic continental crack.

'Yes, inspector, what's the problem?' I inquired. 'It's Imotep.' 'Imotep?' 'Yes Imotep, our best young stallion. He tried to mount one of our mares and she kicked him and one of his testicles is damaged. Doesn't look too good. Can you come?'

The Stock Theft Unit's head quarters was at Gilgil, about 30 miles away. I jumped into the 504 and sped to the scene of the crime. As I swerved to avoid an aberrant donkey strolling across the highway I mused on the choice of name for the stallion. Obviously the powers that be at the Stock Theft Unit had been watching too many episodes of The Mummy. But some films have that effect on people. The Jensens at Kampi ya Moto, for example. Their children must have been born when Dr Zhivago was all the rage and names with a Russian whiff were vogue. Otherwise why would they have chosen to bestow the names Ivan and Tanya on their son and daughter?

I was now abreast of Lake Elementaita, its blue waters shimmering in the sun. Drifts of white pelicans were circling, spiralling upwards on the thermals rising from the shoreline flats. A rim of pink at the water's edge showed where greater flamingos were feeding in the soupy, algae-rich water. On the other side of the lake strange volcanic cones peppered the plain, while in the background rose the dark outline of the Mau Escarpment, formerly thickly forested, now thickly sown with a multitude of corrugated iron shacks, the forest gone, along with the shy bushbuck, the sad faced colobus monkeys and the elusive Dorobo hunters.

The road swerved past the Kariandusi Prehistoric Site and the nearby diatomite factory, spewing out white smoke as it rendered down the remains of the hard-shelled microscopic algae to soft abrasive siliceous powder. Then it was down and across a small stream, past the rustic Church of Good Will on the left and up a small rocky escarpment. A troop of baboons sat on boulders beside the road, eyeing the passing traffic, waiting for some vehicular vandal to throw an empty milk tetrapak or crisp packet out of a window. The prize would be seized and borne away for close inspection and any remnants of contents consumed. The unlovely township of Gilgil lay on top of the escarpment. An army barracks, a bank or two, breeze block buildings, a neglected railway station, a row of dukas, a police station, and one thanked one's lucky stars not to live there. The Stock Theft Unit lay a few miles outside Gilgil. The Unit comprised many horses and a few camels. These in the past had been used in the pursuit and apprehension of cattle rustlers. With the advent of mechanization this role became subservient to nominal appearances in agricultural shows and in crowd control at times of periodic unrest.

An askari opened the gate and I rumbled down the hill to the stables on the other side of a small river. A jodhpured askari directed me to a stable. I stopped the car and stepped out. A trail of drops of blood on the concrete led to the stable door. I looked at the askari and raised my eyebrows. He opened the door. A grey colt stood in the centre of the stable. Both hind legs were soaked in blood, which was dripping from his right testicle which was partially exposed and hanging from a ragged hole in the scrotum.

Two more men had appeared. I turned to them. 'Right,' I said, 'We've got to take him out and knock him out. That testicle has had it. It looks ruptured to me. We've got to remove it before he loses any more blood. With a bit of luck the other one will be OK.'

'I sincerely hope so,' said a voice behind me. I turned. It was Inspector Kiptanui, rather larger than I remembered him. Normally his round face was wreathed in smiles. He wasn't smiling now. 'This is our best young stallion, cost us a fortune and if the other testicle goes then he's a dead loss to us.'

I had to be careful. The horse had lost a lot of blood and he was also apprehensive and nervous. How would he react to the anaesthetic? Well, there was only one way to find out.

I asked for a bale of hay, prepared my instruments, including plenty of artery forceps and catgut and laid the lot on a clean towel.

'Right, chaps,' I said, 'hold up his head while I slip this dose of Xylazine into his jugular.' Slowly, slowly, draw back on the syringe, take your time, he's lost a lot of blood, watch his reaction, check your watch, do this over two minutes. Giving an injection over two minutes seems to take forever. But at the end of two minutes the stallion's head was down by his knees, his hind legs were crossed and he was staggering to one side.

Now for the ketamine. A computed bolus, also given into the jugular. Doing this job under sedation alone was not an option. If things went wrong I, and the horse, would be up the creek. And being bent double below a horse's hind legs for half an hour did not appeal.

The ketamine had to be given as a job lot, not trickled in slowly as was the case with the xylazine. In it went. I stood back and waited for the reaction. The stallion stood to all intents unmoved, blood still dripping in an unceasing stream from his groin. At my side Kiptanui also watched in an ominous silence. Come on, come on! Is it never going to work? Then Imotep swayed slowly to his right and collapsed onto his side. I dragged the bale across and investigated the damage. The right gonad had to all intents and purposes been bisected and the two parts were connected by a merest thread. Half was hanging outside the scrotum and the other half was still inside. So a modicum of care would be required in order to remove the lot and not leave remnants behind. I swabbed the area and with scissors carefully enlarged the hole caused by the mare's hoof. Blood was still running from the area. It was like working at the bottom of an inkwell. Kiptanui hovering at my shoulder spoke. 'Dr Cran, is he still breathing?' I looked up, and looked at Imotep's chest. Sure enough there was no movement. Nothing. My heart sank. Had I killed him? But I also knew that the xylazine/ketamine combo sometimes caused long unnerving periods of apnoea, when the patient appeared to hold his breath for worryingly long periods of time and when the surgeon at one end would anxiously enquire of his assistant at the other whether the patient was still breathing at his end. After what seemed like an age Imotep took a deep breath. I did the same and continued with my investigation.

The most important thing was to stop the bleeding – arrest the haemorrhage as the text books would have it. 'Moses,' I said, 'Can you bring...' But of course there was no Moses. I reached over and grabbed the largest pair of artery forceps I could see. The spermatic artery must have been torn. I had to find the bleeding end and clamp it off, or Imotep was going to pretty soon exsanguinate, in other words bleed to death. I extended the incision. I had to see what I was doing. I shoved in a wad of cotton wool and when I removed it I caught a glimpse of the responsible spouter and clamped the artery forceps onto it. Normally when castrating a colt I would have clamped an emasculator round the spermatic cord crushing all the blood vessels therein. In the present situation that was impossible and getting a ligature onto the artery looked equally unlikely. The alternative was to leave the artery forceps attached for 24 hours to enable clotting to take place. 'OK, Inspector,' I said, 'I'm going to remove the remains of this testicle, leave the artery forceps in situ for 24 hours, and come back tomorrow and take them off. The other testicle looks fine so he should be all right as a breeder. Shit!....' Imotep lashed out with a hind leg. One moment he appeared to be slipping away, the next he was trying to get up. I grabbed the bottle of Ketamine and gave him a half dose into his jugular.

Imotep was sweating. So was I. I stood up to rest my back and wait for the second shot to take effect, before returning to the fray. Finally, satisfied that the ravaged gonad had been removed in its entirety and that all bleeding had stopped, I cleaned the area, gave an injection of tetanus antitoxin and antibiotic and waited for Imotep to recover from the anaesthetic.

When you top up an anaesthetic it inevitably delays the recovery period. But at long last the stallion staggered to his feet. I checked the wound, the artery forceps were still in place and I was able to leave with a relatively clear conscience.

As I turned the corner into Club Lane, in which my surgery was sited, I saw a grey Renault Roho parked opposite the door. The word lane suggests something leafy, rural and tranquil, where the refugee from life's strife may find peace and solace. Club Lane may have been like that 30 years previously. Now it was a pandemonium of hawkers, beggars, motor bikes, mendicants, pedestrians, wandering musicians and pedlars selling mounds of everything from second hand brassieres to heaps of battered, sad looking teddy bears. There was little peace and tranquillity to be found here. I recognized the Renault as one belonging to Felicity Drudge. Felicity was not my favourite person and I was almost tempted to drive on past, in the hope that she might be gone when I returned. She was the sort of person who liked to think that she knew everything, gave no credit to anyone and was quite devoid of humour. This would have been bad enough if she had been a raving beauty, but she was not. Far from it. At some time in her distant past Felicity had been a paramedic in the British army and she never hesitated to let you know it.

Felicity Drudge was a walking advertisement on what happens to you if you have been on a daily diet of beer and cigarettes for 40 years, and don't wear a hat. She coughed incessantly, her face was a mass of wrinkles, with the texture of a much used washboard, she was pencil thin, with legs and arms resembling twigs of blackened teak and whatever sex appeal she once might have had, had long since withered on the vine. She was only 50 but looked about 80. Physically she was one of the least attractive women I had ever met.

I parked the car and pushed open the swing door into the surgery. Felicity rose to meet me. 'Ah, Hugh,' she shrilled, 'you're back – at last. I've been waiting here for hours and hours for you. What on earth were you doing at Gilgil that took you so long?' None of your bloody business,

I thought. 'Well,' I said, 'I was doing a hemi-castration of a colt. Not a swift job and Gilgil is not exactly round the corner.' 'Nonsense,' she barked, 'I can drive there in twenty minutes.' 'How can I help you,' I said, trying to remain calm. Out of the corner of my eye I could see my Goan receptionist, Miss. D'Souza, trying to conceal a smirk.

'It's Oscar, our tame giant rat. He's been in a fight with a wild rat and, well, one of his, er, testicles is not quite right.' I thought – isn't it just like Felicity to have a rat, weighing two kilograms, as a pet.

'Really?' I said. 'It's been a bad ball day today!' Felicity seemed to regard such levity as ill placed. Her thin lips pursed until they resembled the patient's puckered fundament.

'Right then,' I said, 'let's have a look at the damage.'

Felicity turned Oscar onto his back. 'Gosh!' I exclaimed, 'almost a carbon copy of the horse at Gilgil. What an amazing coincidence!' Just like the colt, one testicle was exposed and lacerated, while the adjacent area had been rent and torn by the opponent's teeth.

Felicity was less interested in coincidences than in what I was going to do to repair the damage to Oscar's vitals.

I did some rapid thinking. The xylazine/ketamine combo worked well enough in cats and dogs and it was safe. I had used it in non-domestic species including lions. It was time to put it to the test on Oscar.

With a confidence I did not entirely feel I turned to Felicity. 'I'm going to give Oscar an anaesthetic, remove that ravaged gonad and repair the other damage. With a bit of luck his manhood should be unimpaired. Like a twin-engined plane he can easily function on one.'

Felicity had a nose rather similar to that of a dik dik. In other words it was more of a trunk than a nose and it had a peculiar ability to twitch from side to side when the owner was agitated. Felicity was agitated now. 'Very well, but I want to stay and watch. I have had medical training as you know and if I had the drugs I would have dealt with this myself. As it is I suppose I will have to pay you to do something I could easily have done myself.'

Felicity's efforts to treat her animals had not been an unalloyed success. On more than one occasion I had had to re-suture wounds, re-treat mis-diagnosed illnesses and euthanase those unfortunates botched beyond redemption.

So I kept my peace and said nothing, knowing full well that if anything went wrong I would never hear the end of it. I decided to use the canine dosage, on the premise that the creature had more in common with a small dog than a cat. The dose was very small and the needle very fine, but Oscar did not appreciate being injected and gave his mistress a sharp nip as the needle went in.

Felicity uttered an unladylike word and her nose twitched sharply to the left.

Ten minutes later Oscar was out for the count.

In order to see more clearly what I had to do I donned my loupe, a sort of magnifying glass strapped to my head. Now what I was seeing looked almost as big as that of the colt at Gilgil. Luckily there was no bleeding and my task was that much easier. In no time I had removed the exposed testicle, cleaned the wounds and inserted the required stitches. I gave Oscar an injection of antibiotic and stood up.

Felicity spoke. 'Well, that wasn't much was it? *I* could have done that if I had had the drugs. Now I suppose you're going to charge me a massive bill.' I looked at her. Her nose gave a convulsive twitch to the right. '*Massive?*' I said. 'The correct adjective is *reasonable.* Now I suggest you leave Oscar with me for an hour or so to monitor his recovery from the anaesthetic while you go to the bank and draw out the sum which the lovely Miss D'Souza will request you to pay.' Felicity's jaw dropped. She spun on her heel and marched out, swinging her handbag like a sling shot. Not for the first time, I reminded myself that 'the female of the species is more deadly than the male.' Forewarned is forearmed.

By the time Felicity returned, Oscar was awake and his owner had calmed down. She paid her bill.

Next day I drove back to Gilgil and removed the artery forceps from Imotep's scrotum. He made an uneventful recovery and went on to sire many foals.

⊗⊩⊗⊩⊗⊩⊗⊩⊗

About two weeks after the accident I became aware of a hissing in my left ear. I consulted a local medico, one Dr Gokani, giving him the whole history of the incident. Thinking that it might be caused by the Deep Heat spray with which I had applied to my various aches he suggested that I stop using it. I did. The hissing continued.

Moses was advised by *his* medical attendant to take ten days off work. As he was, in his present predicament, unable to assist me in any material fashion, I gave permission gladly.

The hunt for another vehicle continued, as did the flow of work. A horse kicked in the face, resulting in a damaged frontal sinus. Bitches to spay. Cattle with bloat. Dogs with tick fever. Dogs bitten by puff adders. Cows to pregnancy test. Pups with parvovirus disease. Lame horses.

A message from the British High Commission in Nairobi. Would we arrange a lunch reception for 150 people, please, at our house? On the 24th of November. At twelve noon. 'The 24th of November?' I repeated, mentally working out how soon that was. Berna's mother, Eve, I knew, was coming to Kenya on the 25th. Good timing. 'Yes' the voice continued, 'but we'll bring all the spirits and wine and send out the invitations. All you'll have to do is to contact a caterer to supply a variety of attractive foodstuffs, bring chairs and tables, ensure there are enough plates and glasses, several crates of beer and soft drinks, beer mugs, hay bales, ice, sunshades, marquee, awnings and oh, don't forget a few teetotal waiters. I'm told that you hosted an evening reception for our previous High Commissioner, Sir John Johnson, and by the end of it all the waiters were reeling drunk and several guests were little better. One chap even tried to pinch a bottle of Chivas Regal. We don't want a repetition, do we?' Before I had time to reply, I heard a click as the diplomatic phone was put down. I was about to say something undiplomatic, when the phone rang again. It was the man from the High Comm again. 'Sorry, old chap, forgot to tell you. All the replies will be coming to your post office box number. What did you say it was?' I hadn't, but I told him. Box 958.

A few days later we received an invitation to a Reception to be hosted by His Excellency the British High Commissioner to be held at the residence of Mr and Mrs. H R Cran. How nice, we thought. Please reply to – wait a minute – PO Box 758, Nakuru! What the renter of PO Box 758 thought of all those replies to His Excellency is not recorded.

A visit to an ear, nose and throat specialist in Nairobi re the hissing auricle brought temporary relief. I reeled out the whole rigmarole again and Dr D'Cruz prescribed a course of drugs which seemed to work while I took them. When I stopped the hissing returned.

The day of the reception dawned wet, cold and overcast. The day before there had been a massive hailstorm and the marquee erected in the garden was almost blown down. The meteorological omens did not look good. The grass was waterlogged. The bales were soggy. 'Let's hope they bring plenty of booze to narcotize the guests,' I said to Berna. 'You haven't forgotten that my mother arrives tomorrow,' she said. I hadn't. 'I've arranged to stay with the deputy consul at her house at Lavington in Nairobi. I'll drive down with Sophie and Kim after the party and collect her tomorrow.' 'Chris Orme-Smith is coming to the party,' I said, 'and has offered us his Suzuki until we manage to get another car.' 'Wonderful!' 'Well, if Murphy's Law holds, as I expect it will, someone is bound to phone up when you have left and without a car, I'm snookered.'

The diplomatic entourage duly arrived bearing the essential wine, whisky and gin. At noon the first of the invitees arrived and within a very short time we had 150 people benefiting from Her Majesty's government's largesse. I had warned people that there would be a cut-off time when the noble party would depart for Nairobi taking away the vital spirits so carpe diem should be the watch word. I had been at Queen's Birthday bashes in Nairobi and when the cut-off time arrived the band would play God Save the Queen ad infinitum until the penny dropped and the last few of the hard core staggered away.

The rain held off, the food was deemed to be excellent, the drinks were unlimited and the High Commissioner thought we were all jolly fine chaps. The barmen, including myself, remained visibly sober, and, apart from the fact that our lawn had received one mortal blow after another as vehicles had churned across it, all seemed to be in order.

At 2-30 the phone rang. It was from the Gilgil Polo Ground. A horse had colic. It was bad, very bad, and could I come asap. 'Shit!' I thought as I put the phone down and returned to my post behind the bar. 'Another gin and tonic, madam? Certainly. And you sir? Two large Tuskers. There you go.' A low-slung saloon, bedaubed with mud, was coming up the drive. A late arrival? Nothing unusual in that. I frequently arrived at parties, wedding and receptions as the first guests were leaving. We were busy people in Kenya and to arrive bang on time was regarded as unmannerly, indeed as a sign of social desperation.

Out of the car emerged Jill Evans of Rumuruti, some 85 miles to the north. In her arms she bore a dachshund and as she approached it became evident that it was a female and in advanced pregnancy. 'Hello Hugh,' said Jill, 'so sorry to barge in like this. I see you're having a bit of a thrash.' I wondered where the High Commissioner was. Then I saw him, talking to Chris Orme-Smith, glass in hand, head back and laughing like a kookaburra. That's all right then. I must remember to see Chris about his Suzuki I thought.

'What's the problem, Jill?' I said. 'It's Panya,' she replied. (Panya is Swahili for rat) 'She's being trying to have pups since last night without success.' 'Right, bring her into the kitchen and let's have a look at her.' Panya's belly was so heavy that it almost touched the floor, which is where I examined her, in the chaos of the kitchen. 'She's got uterine inertia,' I told Jill, 'the cervix is open, but the uterine muscle is stretched so much it's almost incapable of contracting. I'll give her a shot of oxytocin and hope that that will do the trick. If not we may have to do a Caesar.' 'I hope not,' said a voice. It was the High Commissioner. 'Sorry, I have to fly. A Minister is flying in from London and I have to meet the plane. No rest for the wicked what! Thank you for everything.' And he was gone. As his underlings entered to collect all the undrunk bottles, opened and unopened, I gave Panya her injection.

I heaved myself to my feet and realized that I had had nothing to eat. Too late! The table was bare. People seemed reluctant to leave but I had work to do and Berna had to get to Nairobi.

Chris Orme-Smith's Suzuki was small, yellow, very metallic and very box-like. 'There you are,' said Chris, 'don't break the speed limit now!' The vehicle's top speed was little more than 40mph. Behind his sardonic exterior Chris had a heart of gold. With his high cheek bones, dark swept-back hair and his red-brown complexion he resembled a detribalized North American Indian. He lived with his wife Teresa, two daughters and a son at Rongai at the foot of Mt. Loldiani. We had spent many holidays at their delightful coast house at Vipingo, north of Mombasa.

Telling Jill to join the party and that I would be back in an hour or so, depending on how fast the Suzuki went, I loaded up, said goodbye to Berna and set off for Gilgil.

To say that the vehicle was uncomfortable would be a gross understatement. I suppose it did have springs and shock absorbers. It just felt as though there were none. Every time the Suzuki hit an irregularity in the road it leapt into the air like a startled impala, and came down with a crash like a lead balloon. This was bad enough on the tarmac but when I hit the murram and the rocks and the potholes I was thankful that I was insured for things like spinal surgery and pelvic replacement. But I was motoring and moving, that was the important thing and for that I had to thank Chris, who, like so many up-country residents, had come up trumps.

The horse, a bay polo pony, was in a bad way. He was pouring with sweat and continually pawing the ground with a fore hoof. Abrasions above his eyes showed where he had rolled on the ground in his agony. His heart rate was 85 beats per minute, his conjunctival colour was a horrid reddish purple, and his capillary refill time had lengthened from a normal two seconds to a life-threatening six. I sounded his abdomen. An ominous silence. I passed a stomach tube up his left nostril. I lowered the tube and two litres of sour smelling fluid drained out. I soaped my arm and did a rectal examination. The tract was dry and tacky and I could feel tense distended loops of intestine. The wretched animal groaned as I palpated them.

The horse's owner stood nervously at my elbow. He was new to polo and this was his best horse. He was young and pale and a dark lick of hair fell over his forehead. I turned to him. 'I'm sorry,' I said, 'this is bad, very bad. From his symptoms he has got an intestinal catastrophe, probably torsion of the small intestine, perhaps an intussusception or possibly a rupture of the stomach. Either way the outlook is very grave, probably hopeless.' 'Can anything be done?' he asked. 'We can give him xylazine to sedate him and relieve the pain, give an antispasmodic to try to lessen abnormal gut activity, and give drugs to counteract the inevitable toxaemia which occurs in these cases, but....' 'Please try,' he said. 'Very well,' I said, 'we'll try, but if there is no improvement by first light the only humane answer is euthanasia.' He gulped and nodded. The xylazine worked quickly. The horse's head drooped and he no longer pawed the ground. His heart rate decreased to 70 beats per minute and he stood quietly. But I feared the worst, although as always hoping for the best, remembering another horse with colic, writhing in agony and with a heart rate of 120. That horse had recovered.

As I drove home I recalled yet another horse showing signs of extreme ungovernable colic. Drugs had no effect and so I shot the horse. A post mortem revealed no cause for the colic. Mind churning, I reached home. A few revellers still remained, slumped on the verandah in various stages of inebriation. 'Harro, Hugh,' shaid one, 'well, how did it go then?' accompanied by a loud hiccup. 'Bloody awful,' I said, 'where's Jill?' I was in no mood for conversation. 'She's in the lounge with her bitch and shree puppies.' Thank God for that, I thought. And so she was. Mother and babies all fit and well. After I had examined them and confirmed that there were no more pups remaining within Panya, Jill departed, not to distant Rumuruti, but to relations at Rongai.

The polo pony died during the night. I did a post mortem and found a complete torsion of the small intestine, whose inner surface resembled black velvet.

Chapter Three

BRAIN DRAIN

Many Kenyans, especially Kikuyus, experience difficulty in differentiating the letter L from the letter R. The Njoro River becomes the Njoro Liver, 'hello my friend' transmutes into 'harro my flend,' and so on.

I was spaying a bitch one afternoon when attractive blonde and buxom Australian Heidi Rust came into the surgery. My door was partially open as my regular receptionist, Miss D'Souza, was away and her place was being taken by Kikuyu odd job man Bernard, whose social skills were not of a high order. As I carefully lifted the left ovary out of the abdomen I heard Heidi ask Bernard for worm tablets for her dogs. Bernard's English was limited. 'Bwana doing opelation,' he said, 'prease can you give name and will ret him know.' I clamped off the ovary and prepared to ligate the associated blood vessels. 'OK,' said Heidi, 'my name is Rust. The doctor will know who I am. Write that down.' There was a pregnant pause. Then.. 'No no no! The name is Rust! Not Lust! Do you understand?' 'Ah, Lust, rook, I have litten.' 'Yes and you have written Lust! Rook, I mean look, let me do it! R.U.S.T.' 'Ah yes,' said Bernard, 'Lust, just as I wlote.' There was an Antipodean expostulation, the scrape of high heels, the bang of the swing door as it was burst open and Heidi was gone.

Breathing deeply I continued with the operation. After I had finished I phoned Heidi to apologise. In a way one had to give Bernard the benefit of the doubt. Heidi was so attractive and eye catching that my minion's clanger was not so inappropriate.

As I replaced the receiver a sudden spasm of pain stabbed my left temple, and was gone, leaving my left ear to hiss as before.

Berna's mother had now arrived, to participate in the daily trials which afflict all those who dwell south of the Mediterranean littoral – the regular power failures, the sudden and unexplained lack of water in the taps, the influx of flies, bees, ants and mosquitoes, the routine crash of smashed crockery in the kitchen. Fortunately she had spent time in Egypt and Tanzania during her matrimonial career and was to a certain extent acclimatized to such vicissitudes.

What she wasn't used to was the almost casual way that Death removed members of society on an almost daily basis. In Tanzania, thieves and villains were almost apologetic for their crimes. Not so in Kenya, where gratuitous violence was the norm. Our good friend, Hobo Swift, talented artist and farmer, was brutally attacked for no apparent reason while working in his studio. Hacked with an axe, slashed with a panga, losing an eye, part of his nose, cut on his head, neck and hands, I received a frantic call from Hobo's servant to say that he had collapsed. I phoned AMREF, the Flying Doctors. Hobo was flown to Nairobi and rushed to the theatre and into intensive care. He died two weeks later.

Another call from the High Commission. No parties this time. A British tourist had been found comatose in his hotel room, dying 20 minutes after admission to hospital. My services were required. A combination of anti-depressant tablets and vodka was the cause of death. On the 6th of November he had been given 90 tablets. When he was found on the 3rd of December there were only two left. The diagnosis was the easy part. Moving the body to the mortuary, dealing with the police, collecting the belongings, liaising with the funeral 'directors', was the difficult part.

Then there was the evening when a tourist truck overturned near the Elementaita turn-off. A mixed bag of Brits, Aussies,

Americans and Kiwis, they had sustained a wide variety of injuries – a broken patella, broken vertebrae, a dislocated shoulder, lacerations, a torn ear – and the patients were scattered among several different hospitals. So we did our evening rounds, phoned the High Commission, contacted the tour company, phoned relatives, arranged for the injured to be transferred to Nairobi and did our best to make them feel that we cared for their welfare and that they were not alone. Apart from us, no one, least of all from the embassies, visited them in hospital, either in Nakuru or Nairobi. So our appearance was received with touching gratitude. One American girl with a fractured patella, when we told her who we were, sobbed 'Oh, thank God for the British!' We wished we could have said the same for the British consul, whose main response was to tick Berna off for phoning the UK-based mother of one girl to tell her that her daughter was coming home.

Berna's widowed mother, Eve, hailed from Northern Ireland, and possessed the accent and couthie character peculiar to that valiant province. Having spent much of her expatriate life au bord de la mer, in Alexandria and in Dar-es-Salaam, Eve was keen to spend some time at the water's edge and definitely not amid the terrors of the bush. So we drove to Msambweni on the south coast and spent a few soporific days amid the palms and mango trees, inhaling the warm, dense atmosphere and making desultory excursions to immerse ourselves in the Indian Ocean. The kids loved it. On our return we collected Berna's sister, Gerry, from the airport. Gerry, like her mama, was not a fan of Wild Africa. But both seemed to be drawn to water and Eve, having sampled the salt, now wished to cast her eyes on the fresh, in the form of Lake Victoria. The search for a replacement for my deceased 504 finally bore fruit in the form of a second-hand Peugeot 505 station wagon, an impressive seven seater, with a cast iron bonnet, the raising of which could only be achieved by strong men and determined women. We tossed for it. Berna won and I took over her somewhat smaller car.

The hissing in my ears continued unabated. But there was work to be done, not to be postponed by mere auricular irritants. Horses with colic, dogs with tick fever, a cat whose leg required amputation – in the owner's garden of all places – cows stuck calving, bitches to spay, mares to pregnancy test.

Things were no less eventful in the country at large – a tour leader taken by a crocodile in Lake Rudolf, British tourists attacked in the Maasai Mara Game Reserve, eight German visitors killed when their plane hit a vulture, a horrific bus accident killing 23 passengers and injuring many more, a clash between police and political demonstrators involving the use of tear gas and live ammunition. Situation normal, I informed my disbelieving mother-in-law.

Christmas came and went. Now I had headaches and partial deafness. I consulted Dr D'Cruz in Nairobi, who shone powerful lights down my ears and found nothing of consequence. Then there was eminent surgeon Mr D'Cunha of Nakuru who said my eustachian tubes were infected and prescribed various antibiotics. None had any beneficial effect.

It was time for our trip to the Great Lake. Mother-in-law was excited. Our goal was Mbita Point, opposite Rusinga Island, birthplace of the charismatic politician Tom Mboya, gunned down in Nairobi in 1969, one of several such in Kenya who met, and continue to meet, violent ends. We rose betimes and were on the road by 7am. It was fortunate that we were travelling in the new seven seater. We were seven, and had we been crammed into the Peugeot saloon, infantile and in-law friction would have been the inevitable result.

Our route took us through the tea estates of Kericho, past the neat, hedged homesteads of the Kipsigis and into the territory of the Kisii, where it seemed that every square inch of the lush green land was farmed and occupied. The seemingly endless approaches and exits to the town were blighted by an interminable succession of humps, designed to slow speeding drivers and to drive Irish mothers-in-law into fits of high pitched whoopings of distress as the car lurched over the umpteenth obstacle. The road wound downwards to Luo-land and to the somewhat ominously named Homa Bay – Fever Bay – a charmless conglomeration of characterless buildings and dusty streets, lined with fly-blown kiosks and breeze block dukas.

We were now close to the Lake. We could feel its massive presence. It was hot and humid. I felt hot and humid, head muzzy, ears singing, pain behind the eyes. The land was dry and sere, the maize withered and drooping. Small humped cattle driven by tall, black, gap-toothed Luos wandered along the road, which was no longer tarmac, but rutted murram. Pipe-smoking women squatted by the roadside beside mounds of bananas, sugar cane, mangos and pineapples.

We turned a corner and there, ahead, after five hours driving from Nakuru, was the humped outline of Rusinga Island. Mbita Point was little more than a few buildings and a jetty, overlooking the narrow channel between the mainland and the island. Large canoes paddled by strong young men were ferrying passengers across the swift-flowing passage. To our right the vast waters of the largest lake in the world stretched to the horizon. Before we could stop them the kids had dashed down to the shore and were in the water before we could shout 'bilharzia!' But here the current was strong so the risk was minimal. After 20 minutes to allow Eve to absorb the view and the atmosphere, we left for the long return journey. But it was worth it. We saw it as it was and is no more. Now the road to Mbita Point is tarmacked and there is a causeway across the channel to the island. Now cars speed along the highway and are on the island in a matter of minutes, radios blaring, drivers and passengers chattering into their mobiles, peering at their incoming text messages and fondling and stroking their smart phones. No longer do canoes make the journey from the mainland to what is an island no longer, and the stone umbilical cord has blocked the current and prevented fish from accessing the Kisumu part of the lake.

Two days later and it was New Year's Eve and we were at a party, hosted by George and Janet Manuel. George had a mop of unmanageable hair. No matter what he did, it stuck out at all angles of the compass, as well as vertically. Normally George's locks were reasonably static, but tonight as I looked at them they took on a life of their own, until they resembled a mass of writhing snakes and George metamorphosed before my eyes into a male Medusa. I shook my head. George was now his normal self, but was I? I felt very odd, as though my head was detached from my body. I stood up to get a Coke and a sudden blinding headache rooted me to the spot. I was unable to move. 'Are you all right?' asked Berna. The headache dissipated. 'Yes, fine,' I said with typical British understatement, but I felt very muzzy, as though I was sleepwalking underwater. The evening passed in a sort of blur and we left early.

The headaches returned that night and in the morning I was almost incapacitated. Happy New Year! We drove to Nairobi Hospital, taking all the things needed for a stay in hospital. I was sure I would be admitted. I gave Dr Ndele full chapter and verse, telling him all about the accident, as I had to all the other learned medicos, describing the symptoms and how they had developed. He checked for malaria, blood glucose levels and other parameters and came to no positive conclusions, just like all of his honourable colleagues. I was given various symptomatic drugs and sent on my way.

Very early the following morning, after a night of precious little slumber and considerable cerebral discomfort, I was summoned from my rumpled sheets by a call from Jo Mills. Jo and his wife Janet bred racehorses on their farm near the township of Mogotio. Regardless of the situation, whether the barometer indicated conditions to be sunny, fair, stormy or cyclonic, Jo was invariably cheery and full of the joys of spring. As he was now. 'That you Hugh? How *are* you?' 'Great, just great,' I groaned. 'So sorry to trouble you at this early hour. You weren't in bed I hope?' I glanced at my watch – 5.45am – where the shoot did he expect me to be for crying out loud? 'Right then. Good. One of our mares has just foaled. Nice big colt foal. But during the foaling process he shoved a hoof through his mummy's vagina into the rectum. Can you please come and sort her out?'

I dragged myself out of bed, mumbled to Berna where I was going, and drove to the farm, getting there just as the sun was rising over the rim of Menengai Crater, shedding a benign light over the wakening world. Jo was standing in the stable yard as I drove in, looking obscenely cheerful, grinning his gap-toothed grin and wearing his old sweat-stained hat. 'Right, Hugh,' he said as I exited my car, 'here she is,' pointing to a large bay mare, held by a syce, a large gangling foal nuzzling her udder. 'We had to assist her during the foaling and half way through she stood up and that's when it happened.'

'Right,' I said 'let's put her in the stocks and I'll put a hand in and assess the damage.'

As I followed Jo and the mare towards the stocks a sudden spasm shot through my skull, rooting me to the spot. It felt like having a red hot needle shoved through the top of my head. Jo turned. 'You ok?' he inquired with a look of concern. 'Yes,' I answered, 'a bit of a twinge, that's all. It'll pass.' It did and I soaped my trusty left arm prior to inserting it carefully into the mare's vagina. I found what I expected – a hole approximating the diameter of the foal's hoof in the roof of the vagina, extending through the floor of the rectum. I turned to Jo. 'The hole is about four inches inside the vagina and there's another one through into the rectum. Most authorities suggest leaving things for up to six weeks before operating but I've never had much success doing it as late as that as the edges of the holes becomes hard and fibrous so I prefer doing it right away. You can't stitch them from the inside so we have to dissect between the vagina and rectum, close the holes and then stitch the layers together. Got that?' 'Sort of, but you're the expert so go ahead!'

Not feeling like an expert at all, I did.

First, knowing that the sedative I was going to use, Xylazine, would take only two minutes to take effect, I prepared my kit. It's no use giving the animal a sedative which works in two minutes and then taking 20 to get ready. By the time you are, the stuff is wearing off. Common sense really, but a commodity strangely lacking in today's digital world.

Strong, absorbable suture material, scissors, retractors, tissue forceps, all things which are normally carried in the car of a British vet in Africa, I was ready to begin.

I gave the mare her dose of Xylazine intravenously. 'I've given her a big dose,' I said to Jo. 'not enough to make her lie down but I want her really relaxed so that her vulva flops open and gives us good access to the scene of destruction.' 'Good idea,' replied Jo.

The mare sagged and drooped, her vulva likewise I was glad to see. I could see the hole now, gaping like the mouth of an oversized goldfish. Using a fine-needled syringe I injected local anaesthetic around the area. 'Right,' I said to Jo who was hovering at my right elbow, holding a tray bearing my implements, 'this is the tricky bit'. I made a horizontal incision between the anal ring and the vulva and carefully cut forwards until the anus and rectum were separated from the vulva and the vestibule of the vagina. I clamped forceps onto the upper layer of skin and asked Jo to hold on to them and lift in order to allow me to see into the cavity. The lower vulva was still sagging nicely. Now I could see the two fistulae, one upper communicating with the rectum and one lower leading into the vagina. Now all I had to do was to stitch them closed! Easier said than done. I tackled the rectal repair first. Luckily the mare's dung was firm and so far nothing had dropped through the hole. Transverse inverting sutures, being careful to place them into the submucosa of the rectum and not through into the lumen where they might act as a wick for infection or cause the mare to strain. The strain was beginning to tell on me. This was not the sort of job where you could stop for a break for a cup of tea or even straighten up. 'Please! Not another headache!' I prayed. Now for the vaginal fistula. Time had passed. The mare was beginning to fidget. Nip round to the front and give her a half-shot of Xylazine. Back to her rear end. More transverse sutures inverting the fistula margin into the vagina and the hole was closed. Carefully I checked both suture lines to ensure that they were secure and then turned my attention to closing the area between the rectal and vaginal tissue to obliterate any dead space. That done, all that remained was to suture the skin.

'Right, Jo,' I said, 'that's it. Let's take her out so that her foal can suckle her. Give her a soft, laxative diet, molasses, or liquid paraffin if necessary. We don't want her breaking any stitches, do we?' 'No indeed,' said Jo. 'Stitches out in 14 days?' 'Yes' I replied. 'Restrict her exercise. Oh and I'll just give her a shot of penicillin. We don't want her getting tetanus after all that. Are her vaccinations up to date?' 'Yes, I think so. Come along to the office and have a cup of coffee while I check.'

As we stepped into the office the phone rang. Jo lifted the receiver to his ear.

'It's for you,' he said. It was the surgery. Berna must have phoned them to tell them where I was. I glanced at my watch. Nine thirty. My, doesn't time fly when you're having a good time!

'Hello, Mr Cran. Miss D'Souza here. Sorry to trouble you. A dog has just been brought in by the Police Dog Section. It's in a bad way, having fits or something. Can't stand and it's panting really fast. Can you come?'

'Sorry Jo,' I said, 'better go. That sounds serious.' By the time I reached the surgery the headaches were back. I shoved my way through the batwing doors and strode into the surgery. A large German Shepherd dog lay on the table, jerking and twitching, gasping and hyperventilating. My assistant Moses and a uniformed constable stood by.

Quickly I asked questions. She was a three-year-old bitch. She had whelped ten pups three weeks previously. I checked her teats. Full of milk. I took her temperature, and whistled – 110°F. I listened to her heart – the rate was so fast it was barely countable. She had eclampsia, hypocalcaemia, due to loss of calcium into the milk and from inadequate dietary calcium intake. The tetanic muscle spasms were due to the hypocalcaemia having an excitatory effect on nerve and muscle cells, resulting in repetitive firing of motor nerve fibres.

'Moses! Get me a bottle of calcium borogluconate. Fast!' He did. This was a 40% solution for treating milk fever in cattle. Give this intravenously to a dog and its heart would stop – dead. It had to be 10%, so quickly I withdrew 5ml and added 15ml of sterile water. Now raise the cephalic vein on the forearm, slip in the needle, and slowly, *very slowly*, inject the solution, check the pulse, watch the breathing, 'hold that leg, Moses! I know she's jerking, but we've got to get this in or she'll die.' As the solution trickled in, the German Shepherd's breathing slowed and the twitching lessened. But we were not out of the woods. Her body, and more particularly, her brain temperature, was dangerously high. Her cerebral cells were at risk of being cooked, resulting in permanent damage. We had to lower that temperature and fast.

'Quick!' I said to Moses, 'we need ice to pack round her head. Get the ice cubes and ice blocks out of the fridge while I give the last of the injection.' As I slowly depressed the plunger of the syringe a sudden headache rooted me to the spot. Again I felt a red hot needle being shoved through the top of my skull. I was unable to move, standing rigid, motionless, afraid that any movement might worsen the agony. I was now the one in need of ice around my head. Slowly the spasm passed and I gave the final few drops of calcium into the vein.

We poured a mass of cubes into a long plastic bag and surrounded the bitch's head with an ice barrier. Every ten minutes I checked her temperature. Slowly it fell, until after half an hour it was down to 104.

She was out of danger. But was I?

The bitch was now sitting up, looking rather perky. I gave her the same volume of the calcium solution, under her skin to potentiate that given intravenously. 'Right,' I said to the constable, 'I want you to remove the pups for the next 24 hours and to give her calcium powder in her food until she has weaned the pups – OK?' He nodded. I gave him a pot of Calcium Phosphate powder and he departed with a refreshingly alive patient.

For myself, I felt decidedly less fresh than the patient. To date I had consulted four learned members of the medical fraternity, all had been apprised of my recent history of being all but trashed in a motor accident, all had subjected me to their professional scrutiny, but here I was, worse than ever, suffering from excruciating headaches, general malaise and my ears hissing like the Flying Scotsman building up a head of steam. That evening as I lay comatose on my couch, the phone rang. It was Petre Barclay. Petre did explain once why his name was pronounced Peter but spelt in this odd way, but the reasoning was so complex that it went right over my head. Especially now when I feared that the content of my throbbing skull was like a pot of bubbling porridge. Berna took the call. Petre was a local aristo and landowner, a highly skilled farmer with extensive acres on the fertile slopes of Menengai Crater. In a British setting he would have been the lord of the manor, the laird of the glen, attended by panting retrievers, fawning ostlers and forelock tugging gillies. His accent and build conformed to this pedigreed impression, the former being patrician, the latter strapping and stately, with a chest like a pouter pigeon and an abdomen to match. One of the retrievers was lame. Berna relayed the symptoms and I croaked out a few words of veterinary wisdom. During the conversation Berna mentioned my cerebral symptoms. It appeared that Petre's wife, Carol, had recently had an ear problem and had consulted neurosurgeon Professor Renato Ruberti with gratifying results.

In the morning Berna phoned the professor, gave him chapter and verse, he responded with a few Tuscan monosyllables and within the hour we were on our way to his Nairobi suite. Thus it was, that on the 3rd January 1992, we found ourselves in the professorial sanctum and in the presence of an undoubted medical expert. The professor, although Italian, did not look or behave like one. For a start, he had ginger hair and his manner was far from what one expected of a southern European. He was brusque to the point of rudeness. He dismissed the opinions of the other doctors I had seen as those of a bunch of incompetent charlatans. After a thorough examination and after carefully listening to the history of the car accident he ordered me downstairs to the CT room to have my brain scanned. After a chilly and claustrophobic session in the CT tube, my fate was announced. 'Right, Mr Cran, I'll operate tomorrow. You've got a subdural hygroma and I have to do a craniotomy to drain off that fluid. Check yourself in!'

My first thoughts on hearing this news were not alarm and consternation at the prospect of having my skull opened up, but relief that a mere three days before the accident I had taken out a medical insurance policy with Africa Air Rescue, thereby saving me from bankruptcy on receiving Professor Ruberti's bill. I had come to Nairobi without so much as a toothbrush, far less items of minimal nightwear, having made so many abortive visits to members of the healing profession that I had given up all hope of getting to the bottom of my problem. I was checked into St. Luke's ward. 'Aha,' said Berna, 'a good sign. St. Luke was the beloved physician, and is the doctors' patron saint. All will be well.'

Still pyjama and toothbrush-less I settled into my room, while Berna shot off back to Nakuru to deal with the children, as well as her mother and sister, who were on the point of leaving to return to England.

My tenure as Honorary British Correspondent now paid dividends, when the Consul came in bearing welcome gifts in the form of toothbrush, razors and a pair of purple pjs. Having brought no reading material with me, as I lay abed that evening, I was able to give my imagination full rein. A few years previously I had, in the illustrious company of the previous British High Commissioner, Sir John Johnson, a keen mountaineer, climbed Nakugen, the highest summit of the Cheranganis, in north-west Kenya. The climb itself was little more than a moorland plod. Included in the company was an elderly Canadian doctor, who spent three months every year working in a hospital at Kapsowar, the nearest centre of civilization, where we were spending the night. The good doctor managed to get himself lost and separated from the rest of the party and I went back to look for him. Having found him, we got into conversation as we trudged down the track in the footsteps of those who had gone before. 'This is a funny area,' he said. 'Funny?' I said, 'what do you mean?' 'Well, the locals go in a lot for trepanning of the skull, to release the spirits trapped inside, for example, in cases of epilepsy, fits, cases of rabies and the like.' 'Gosh,' I said, 'how jolly interesting. Have you got any examples I can see?' 'Well, yes I have, and as you've been such a good chap in coming back to find me I'll show you a couple of cases in the morning.'

He was as good as his word. He had asked if anyone else in the group would like to join us, but curiously they all declined. I followed him into the ward. He led me to a child with an arm in plaster. 'Now,' he said, 'feel the right side of this young man's head.' I did as instructed. The boy's head was as smooth as a billiard ball. I ran my fingers over his shiny skull. Nothing. Aha, a round section, about an inch in diameter, here there was no bone, just skin. The child smiled. The doctor took me to see a woman. 'She's an epileptic, so they trepanned her.' 'How is it done?' I asked. 'Probably with a hammer and chisel, but I must show you our piece de la resistance. He's outside.'

Sitting on a green, grassy bank outside the hospital was a man dressed in a white institutional gown. He had a rather vacant look about him, staring blankly into the middle distance. He took no notice of us. 'Look at his head,' said my friend. I did. I was shocked. Instead of being convex, like a football, as most normal heads are, his was concave. The whole of his frontal bone was missing. 'When this chap was brought in,' the doctor said, 'he was unconscious, the wounds had been stitched with lengths of grass and there was pus oozing from his head. The people who accompanied him said that he had been suffering from seizures. Rather a drastic way to treat a condition treatable with tablets, eh? He is getting around, is eating and can communicate but is unable to speak. I'm surprised he's still alive with the brain damage he must have suffered.'

Later I heard that after three weeks this patient left the hospital and that three months later he died.

Such were the lurid images imprinting themselves on my brain as I lay abed on the evening before my own trepanning. That night I dreamt that I was imprisoned in a mud hut, lashed to a wooden frame with leather thongs, unable to move my head, which was held in some sort of primitive vice. A posse of witchdoctors, armed with an alarming array of blunt instruments, capered around my mortal remains. As in most nightmares of this sort I was paralyzed, incapable of any movement. The hideous medicine-men closed in, I could smell their reeking breath, they seized my skull with hands of iron. They raised their implements. I could feel them grating on my skull…

I woke up, trembling and drenched with sweat, wondering where I was and spent what remained of the night trying not to go to sleep.

In the morning I was wheeled into the theatre, and, after what seemed like a few minutes, was back in my bed. So does anaesthesia mercifully telescope the patient's time beneath the knife. There was an unbearably tight tourniquet around my skull. I tried to claw it off. Faces swam before my unfocussed eyes. Nausea and bile rose in my throat and I vomited violently into a bowl. Hands pushed me back onto pillows. As I slowly came back into the world of the living I realised that, emerging from the folds of my turban, and presumably from my skull, was a tube, draining fluid into a plastic bottle standing on a table beside my bed. In its colour and consistency the fluid resembled Coca Cola and already the bottle contained at least 300ml. Only Heaven and Ruberti knew how much came out when my skull was opened. Over the next day the volume decreased by about half, after which the good surgeon removed the tube in one unannounced yank, assuring me as he did so that the fluid would not recur. I was relieved to receive this assertion.

In 1968 I had had my right femur broken in five places by an outraged cow. In 1978 I had had my back broken in three places while on a safari to Lake Rudolf. It came to me that this present episode had merely been postponed by a couple of years. What would 1998 bring?

My sojourn in hospital was enlivened by a succession of concerned visitors, quite apart from Berna and our three girls. My bedside was even graced on one occasion by the British High Commissioner, Sir Roger Tomkys and his Consul. Berna's mother and sister came in on their way to the airport to catch their plane back to the UK. Both were suffering from vomiting and diarrhoea and their sufferings continued when their Air France plane failed to materialize, forcing them back to a city hotel for the night, where they received no food, and when their plane did finally take off on the morrow it did so minus the normal nutriments expected and, in some cases, anticipated, by fare-paying passengers. They arrived in London dehydrated, famished and exhausted, so much so that they were unable to face the coach journey to Birmingham and paid a vast sum to be conveyed there in moderate comfort by taxi. I felt in some way responsible, especially as my own sufferings were in abeyance.

Others were also suffering. Arriving at the hospital on the same day as myself was Dennis Rust, husband of the lovely Heidi. He was suffering from trigeminal neuralgia. He also had to have a brace of growths removed from his face. Released from my restraining tube, I walked along to Dennis's room. I opened the door and burst out laughing. Dennis was sitting in a chair. He looked at me and also burst out laughing. He looked like Scott of the Antarctic. One eye was covered with a piratical patch, his head was swathed in a heavy bandage and over all was a stockinette skull cap. About the only part of his face visible was his heavy grey Mexican moustache, one piercing blue eye and his eagle nose. 'Say, Dennis,' I said, 'why are there bars on your windows?' 'Well, I was told that a chap was brought in here some time ago. An up-country guy, European, apparently fell off his horse playing polo. Fell onto his head, and was concussed. Brought in here, and when he came round, went a bit ballistic and tried to throw himself out of the window.'

I dredged my memory, trying to recall the time, yes, yes, at Bwana Begg's at Gilgil, there was a melee, a scrimmage of horses and one stumbled and the rider was catapulted onto the rock-hard ground and it was.....

There was a knock on the door and Berna's head appeared. She looked at us both, before throwing back her head and letting rip with a full blown roar. 'You both look like a couple of detribalized Sikhs,' she gasped. 'And I've just been talking to the nurses – they're tickled pink that Mr Cran had come in for a craniotomy!'

My headaches had largely gone and apart from some hissing in my left ear, on the side where the good Ruberti had opened my skull, I felt in good form, and, with stitches removed, I was discharged.

Chapter Four

CHAOS UP THE COLON

There was no period of recuperation, no civilized breaking in, no gentle half-days, no quiet time pottering about the surgery examining the odd dog or cat. It was straight back to the trenches, still wearing my turban.

Not long after my return I was once again on the estancia of Jo Mills. It was strange how months, even years, would go by without ever receiving a call from a particular farm, and then, out of the blue one would be there, almost every second day. On this occasion I was pregnancy testing 84 of his Jerseys. The majority was in calf so Jo was pleased. 'Right,' said Jo, 'now I would like you to look at some foals – they've not been doing very well, they've lost weight, their coats are dry, despite being de-wormed and given vitamins.' The foals were wheeled out, one by one, by the usual leathery old syce. Number one gave a wheezing cough as he emerged from his stable, number two had a mucoid nasal discharge and number three was gasping for breath. I laid the bell of my stethoscope against their chests one after another and listened.

'Mmm,' I said, 'not a nice sound. Lots of interesting rasping and scraping. Let's check their temperatures.' All were elevated to a moderate degree. 'Right Jo,' I said, 'this is most probably *Rhodococcus equi* pneumonia.' 'Rhodo what?' queried Jo. 'It's a bug which lives in the soil and foals get it by either breathing it in or by swallowing it. Usually affects foals between one and six months and rarely affects adult horses.' 'OK and how do we treat it?' 'Well, this pneumonia is quite nasty in that abscesses form in the lungs and most antibiotics are ineffective in that they can't penetrate the abscesses. But the good news is that there are a couple which can – erythromycin and rifampicin. The bad news is that they have to be given by mouth over a pretty long period – four to twelve weeks, but it works.' 'Right,' said Jo, 'so can you get the stuff, with directions, please.'

'No probs,' I replied and made a move towards my car.

'Not so fast, not so fast, we're not done yet,' Jo laughed and stopped me before I'd moved a yard.

'We've got a mare here, just come from Segera Ranch, and she's a bit dowdy and hasn't passed any dung since she got here three days ago.

Segera Ranch was not close to Nakuru and base camp. The ranch was situated on the windswept plains of Laikipia, some one hundred miles away. Black cotton soil and uncountable acres of whistling thorn were the predominant features on the dead flat prairie. Here there were no landmarks or helpful signposts to guide the uncertain traveller to his destination and as he rattled interminably along increasingly rutted tracks he would scan the sky with nervous apprehension, knowing that the first shower would in all probability direct him with heart-sinking finality into the nearest ditch.

It had taken 13 hours for the truck carrying the mare to get to Jo's broad acres and by the time it arrived she was exhausted and probably dehydrated to boot. I examined her. She was nibbling hay but she was depressed. Heart rate was elevated at 50 beats per minute, but when I listened to her abdomen, instead of the usual reassuring bubbling borborygmi I was met with an ominous silence.

'Can I have a bucket of water and some soap, please,' I asked Jo.

The water duly arrived and it was pleasantly warm and was accompanied by a bar of fragrant bath soap, the sort of thing that ladies use to make themselves attractive and supple. This was more like it. I expressed my sincere gratitude to the bearer. Usually I was presented with a bucket of icy water and something resembling a curiously coloured fossil, which, when applied to the skin, felt like emery paper and certainly raised no lather.

This bar, which was cunningly formed to fit the soft feminine hand, I now applied to my bared left arm. A pleasing lather was formed. 'Right, Jo,' I said, 'on the assumption that this mare is not going to kick my head in, would you please have her turned round and have the syce hold her tail to one side. I want to do a rectal examination.' When a horse is unwell usually it will not react violently to having an arm shoved up its rear end, but a modicum of care is always advisable. People have been injured, sometimes seriously, even killed, by non-compliant horses. Mature, experienced animals are less likely to lash out than younger, hyperactive individuals. By keeping as close to the horse's backside as possible the impact, should it come, should theoretically be lessened. Being at the end of a full blown kick from an adult horse is something to be avoided at all costs. But usually there is some warning. A horse leaning backwards on the bar at the back of a crush is often an indication that at any moment there is going to be an explosive or convulsive reaction and that is it time to move aside and out of the line of fire.

This mare showed no objection to my intervention and I found what I expected. The rectum was dry and tacky, devoid of dung, and projecting backwards into the pelvic cavity I could feel the firm, doughy mass of an impacted large colon. 'Right, Jo,' I said, 'she's got an impaction of the large bowel and in order to shift it we'll have to give her a gallon or so of liquid paraffin by stomach tube. I assume that it's due to her having been trucked all that way from Segera and getting dehydrated en route. I don't routinely carry containers of liquid paraffin in the car so I'll nip back to the surgery and be back asap. In the meantime put her in a stable, take out every scrap of feed and leave her with plenty of water, nothing else. We don't want any more mass added to what already feels like solidified cement.'

I was back within the hour.

'Now Jo,' I said, 'we, or rather, I, will attempt to pass this long stomach tube – or more correctly, naso-gastric tube, as it goes up the nose and then into the stomach – up the mare's right nostril. Some horses do not object to this procedure, others are not so accommodating. Bring the mare into a stable. Now I want the syce,' I looked at the ancient ostler holding the head rope – 'well, not our friend here, perhaps someone a bit younger, to climb up onto the manger to allow the liquid paraffin to flow in by gravity.' 'Sometimes,' I said, 'it's necessary to give a sedative, but the problem with that is that it can cause excessive relaxation which makes entry into the oesophagus more difficult. It's best to have a good swallowing reflex, so we'll dispense with that.'

I opened the five litre container and lubricated the business end of the tube and then carefully and slowly fed the tube up the nostril. The mare was not too keen about this bit, shook her head and started backwards, but, once the tube was located in her nose she relaxed. 'After about a foot and a half or so,' I said to Jo, 'we come to the pharynx where there is a junction. One route lies down the windpipe towards the lungs, the other down the gullet towards the stomach and that's the way we want to go. The trick is to persuade the horse to swallow the tube and then we can feed the tube where we want it to go.'

I had made a mark on the tube with a marking pencil so I knew when the tube would arrive at the pharynx. Sure enough when the mark reached the nostril there was an impasse. A gentle push, and the tube slid easily – too easily – forwards. I placed the end of the tube at my ear. A blast of air. I was in the windpipe. I withdrew the tube an inch or so and tried again. Again the tube slid into the windpipe. 'Jo,' I said, 'flex her neck.' He did so and I tried again. There was resistance and a firm feeling and now I could feel the tube advancing down the gullet. 'Check the left side of her neck, Jo. You should see the end of the tube moving down in the direction of her stomach.' 'Yes, there it is!' exclaimed Jo. Another mark on the tube indicated when I had gone far enough to start pouring the liquid paraffin in by gravity. But before I did so, I brought my end of the tube up to my ear and listened carefully. Sure enough, a gurgling, pot-boiling, bubbling sound indicated that the tube was in the right place. 'I always double check that I'm in the gullet,' I told Jo.

'I've read too many stories about vets pouring a gallon of liquid paraffin down a horse's windpipe and straight into the lungs and the horse dropping down stone dead. Owners are not too keen on that!' I handed the end of the tube to the waiting syce, perched on the manger. The elderly syce handed him up a funnel which he pushed into the tube and then started pouring the liquid paraffin into the funnel and down the tube. 'Some people,' I said to Jo, as I stood with the mare's head resting on my shoulder, holding the tube, 'like to use a stirrup pump and pump the paraffin down the oesophagus. It's quicker but I prefer the slower, gentler method. After all, it only takes a few minutes more this way.'

Soon all the liquid paraffin was gone to the mare's gastric regions. I took the end of the tube from the syce, blew down it, pushing the rest of the fluid into the stomach, stuck my finger into the tube to prevent any remnants leaking into the pharynx and trachea, and carefully drew it out of the mare's nostril. Carefully and slowly. Yanking it out is liable to result in bleeding as the end whips up and onto delicate vascular tissue. A sudden and alarming rush of blood from the nose, while not life-threatening, is the last thing you want in an already tense scenario.

'Now,' I said, 'I'm going to give her a small dose of flunixin iv. Two ml. The full dose of 10mls has antispasmodic properties, which is the very last thing you want in this situation. You want the gut to remain active to move things along, but the low dose acts against toxins in the intestine without acting on the gut muscle. Some unthinking, brain dead, horse owners, with access to antispasmodics like flunixin, when they have a horse with colic, shove it in regardless of the cause, and wonder why the horse gets worse. That is when they call in the vet to sort out the mess, usually at some unsocial hour.'

Jo gave a spasmodic cough. Funny, I hadn't noticed him coughing before. 'Right Jo,' I said, 'that's it. Put her into an empty stable. Take out every last vestige of anything edible, even off the floor. We don't want to add any more material to what's already in there, but provide plenty of water. It usually takes about 24 hours for the paraffin to reach the other end, but this may take longer than that to shift. Let me know how she is in the morning.' In the event I had to return the following day and give another five litres of liquid paraffin, following which the mare passed a massive amount of soft oily manure and recovered.

Three days later I was in Mweiga 100 miles away for work on Sangare Ranch, owned by the redoubtable Mike Prettejohn. Mike had been a professional hunter and had been on the receiving end of more than one sharp-horned, tusked, toothed and razor-clawed denizen of plain, bush or forest which had failed to behave as expected. Mike was as tough as old boots, even though the first flush of youth was now but a dim, receding memory. One night thugs broke into his house. During the fracas which ensued, one gang member seized a military sword, given to Mike by one of his fighting forbears and now hanging on his wall, and plunged it into his, fortunately substantial, abdomen. The thugs fled and Mike was rushed to Nyeri and there in the hospital underwent an operation to remove the debris introduced by the near-lethal blade. Miraculously no vital organ was pierced and Mike went on to make a full recovery and to continue his vital work on tracking, identifying and helping to protect the remnants of the highly endangered mountain bongo in the forests of Mt. Kenya, the Aberdares and elsewhere in Kenya.

I castrated three colts and swabbed four mares and as I was amputating a cat's leg on a table on the verandah, Mike's wife, Jane said, 'I hear that five horses have died on Segera Ranch and that another four are ill.' I pricked up my ears. Segera Ranch was where the recently, now recovered, constipated mare had come from.

Next day I was summoned to Ol Pejeta Ranch on the Laikipia plateau to deal with two sick horses. One had the protozoal disease, biliary fever, the other had broken wind. While there I was told that a rhino on Lewa Downs, near Isiolo had died of an impaction of the bowel. A rhino weighs about as much as several horses so the mechanics of delivering a proportionate volume of liquid paraffin to a rhino made the treatment of my impacted mare relatively straightforward.

In the early 1990s the volume of traffic on Kenya's roads was still relatively light. Daily mileages of several hundred miles were not unusual, something which would be impossible today due to the massive increase in traffic. So when I was asked to go to Naivasha 50 miles in one direction in the morning, and then 80 miles in the afternoon to Rongai and Sotik in the other, I didn't turn a hair. And getting back at 11pm was no problem either. Present-day night driving is an unpleasant form of Russian roulette. Unmarked roads, crumbling verges, vehicles with no lights, or only one light, drivers who fail to dip their lights, invisible dark-clad cyclists and an appalling standard of driving with zero consideration for other road users make Kenya's roads some of the most dangerous on the planet. Little wonder that some embassies in Nairobi forbid their personnel from driving at night. As a lowly unpaid *untermench* of the British High Commission I did not have that option.

Why there should have been a sudden spate of impactions and constipations in the animal world was something I had little time to ponder on as I was re-summoned by Brother Mills to attend to a puny new born foal, unable to pass its meconium, or foetal dung. As I expected the foal was a colt. The female has a wider pelvic diameter than the male, to allow for the passage of her offspring when the time for foaling is nigh. As a result retention of the meconium is uncommon in filly foals.

This particular foal was tiny, weak and wobbly on its feet, bent over, straining ineffectually to pass what it couldn't pass, abrasions on its head and hocks where it had been rolling and thrashing in pain.

'He's two weeks premature,' said Jo, 'but his mother won the Guineas so we're desperate to save him.'

He'll be lucky to last the night, if we don't shift this, I thought, as I carefully inserted a well-lubricated finger up his rectum. The pelvic diameter was narrower than my finger so that was definitely a no-go area. Palpation of the abdomen however revealed a hard solid sausage-like mass entering the anterior pelvis.

'Right, Jo,' I said, 'giving an enema to a weakling like this could well do some physical damage as well as doing no good, so before we indulge in heroic, last ditch surgery, I going to try to give liquid paraffin by stomach tube – yes, again! – and I've brought it with me.'

Jo gave a toothy grin. 'Go for it. What can we lose – except the foal?'

Over to me, I thought.

The foal was very small and so, luckily, was the stomach tube, designed for the very smallest of equine patients. 'Now,' I said, 'it's essential to hold the foal firmly while I feed this tube up his tiny nostril, so can you call your syce number one?'

Brawny but gentle arap Maina fitted the bill.

Slowly and gently I fed the tube up the foal's nose, listening, listening to the sounds coming down the pipe. Yes! We were there! In the oesophagus with a heartening bubble of gastric toil and trouble. Pour the liquid paraffin into the waiting funnel. Not too much now. We don't want to overload the stomach and cause a rupture do we? Three hundred ml should be enough.

I straightened up, easing out the cricks in the long suffering back. 'Right, that's that. Fingers crossed. Pray for a miracle. The prognosis is not good in view of the foal's fragility. Try to get him to suckle and, if he won't or can't, milk some of the colostrum from the mare and give that to him. That should help to stimulate gastrointestinal activity.'

After a welcome mug of coffee with Jo and his wife, Janet, I was on my way, hardly rejoicing, but knowing that the foal now at least had a fighting chance of recovery.

Which was more than could be said for a heifer owned by Mrs. Joshi, an Asian lady client, who phoned me in a panic that evening. Her staff, for reasons unknown had dosed the animal with a highly toxic insecticide. I arrived post haste, only to be told on arrival that ten minutes after infusion the animal had died. I was suitably impressed. On inquiry it appeared that it had been thought that the container in question had held a cattle dewormer. I looked at the lethal bottle. The vividly coloured label depicted an array of aggressive insects – cockroaches, mosquitos, spiders, centipedes – and the words 'SUMU – POISON' in red capital letters and the sinister warning – 'antidote – none.' I rolled my eyes and left.

Miracles do occasionally happen and to my astonishment next morning's bulletin informed me that the foal had done his duty during the night and was suckling furiously and in fine fettle.

But the impaction epidemic was far from over.

The following day was a Saturday and I was looking forward to Sunday and a Day of Rest, spent with Berna and our three girls, home from school.

I had just taken a first sip of my ice cold post-prandial Tusker when the phone rang. Not being fond of warm beer and not knowing how long the call might last I let it ring for six times while I gulped down several swallows of the life -giving fluid. Feeling rather better, I lifted the receiver. 'Jane Prettejohn here,' the voice at the other end declared. 'You remember those horses on Segera Ranch I told you about the other day?' 'Yes,' I replied. 'Well, things are no better. Worse in fact. No one seems to have any idea what's going on. The equine fraternity is in a flat spin. Panicking in fact. The head honcho at the Jockey Club is uncontactable and his female sidekick is completely foxed, as is a woman veterinary academic who came across from the other side of Laikipia. Can you come? Tomorrow?'

Great, I thought. They've been fiddling around for ages, accomplishing sweet fanny adams and now they ask me to travel over 300 kilometres – on a Sunday.

'OK,' I said.

'I knew you would, so, as the main road from Rumuruti is in bad shape with the recent rain I've asked Simon Barkas to meet you at the Ngobit turn-off with a Land Rover and he will drive you on a short cut through Suguroi and Ol Pejeta to Segera.'

Simon, stout chap, was waiting as I drove up next morning in my Peugeot 504. I had brought all the liquid paraffin at my disposal, hoping that it would suffice.

An askari was left to guard my car. Unguarded, it was quite likely to be found wheel-less and broken into on our return.

The track was rough and damp in places but we made it to the scene of crisis in an hour and a half.

I levered myself out of the Land Rover and looked around – a row of wooden stables in an open stretch of grass and an ominous silence. A personable young brunette emerged from one of the stables. 'Oh thank the Lord you've come,' she said. She had an attractive, smoky American accent – somewhere Deep South – and was clad in jeans cut off so high it was a wonder they were in one piece. 'My name's Roberta, and I'm just here on vacation from the States and my dad's away and I have no idea what's going on, and our poor horses! No one has been able to help and five have died so far and here we have *another* five in agony, all with colic, unable to pass dung and… well, come and look at them!' I did and there were two stallions, two mares and one yearling, straining like billy-o to pass what they obviously couldn't pass. As I watched, one stallion collapsed and rolled convulsively. One mare was pawing the ground.

By now a couple of syces had appeared on the scene and I rectally examined the horses. All had major impactions of the large colon. But why? The weather was not dry, there was plenty of grass and the horses had unlimited access to water. 'What are you feeding the horses?' I asked Roberta. 'Well,' she said, 'they're stabled at night and given hay and lucerne ad lib, pyrethrum mark and bran. And during the day they're out grazing.' And the grass is green, I thought. Could the pyrethrum be perhaps acting as a binding agent?

Whatever the cause, treatment was the first priority, and so I returned to the Land Rover to collect the stomach tubes, liquid paraffin and funnel. Simon had mysteriously disappeared. People either like horses or they don't. Simon, it seemed, belonged to the latter category. I stomach tubed all five horses, giving each five litres of liquid paraffin and two mls of flunixin to counteract possible toxaemia.

Two hours later and we were on our way back to the car. As we crossed the main dirt road to Nanyuki, Simon pointed out the spot where Segera's dairy head man had been killed by an elephant. Shortly afterwards two elephants materialized out of the bush. I wondered if one of these two was responsible.

Next day I was back on Segera. This time the journey was rather quicker as I was flown there by Mike Prettejohn in his Cessna. I stomach tubed another five horses, but was no nearer getting to the cause. Thanks to Mike I was back in Nakuru almost before I had left.

Before I laid my head on the pillow that night I prayed long and earnestly for a respite from any more stomach tubing.

Tuesday dawned overcast and damp, and I was soon made aware that my prayers had gone unanswered. Numerous vague phone calls and radio messages emerged from the far reaches of Laikipia, summoning me once again to the fields of equine suffering. But stocks of liquid paraffin had been reduced to precariously low levels so before we departed – by road alas – the town was scoured for more of the life-saving fluid. Pharmacies, supermarket (there was only one) groceries, feed merchants, all were drained of their meagre supplies until we had enough for our needs. Moses, my trusty assistant, loaded the car. A veterinary student had asked to come along and we shoehorned him in. There was other work to do and so it was late morning by the time we left on the 350 kilometres round trip. As we passed through the former Thomson's Falls, now renamed Nyahururu or 'waterfall' in Maasai, Joseph Thomson having been demoted – I noticed a garage above whose entrance reared a sign in big black letters – Colon Motors. Colon Motors! I shook my head. Was I seeing things? Yes, there it was. Was this someone's idea of a sick joke? No, it was just coincidence, that's all, I told myself. It's getting to you, you're getting jumpy. But as we drove along, I wondered. Back on the ranch I stomach tubed another five horses. At least those I had treated were on the road to recovery.

By the time we got back to base it was after dark and the student wished he had stayed at home.

For the next few days all was quiet on the colonic front, but I carried on wondering and pondering on what might be causing these symptoms. I extracted horses' teeth, I stitched up dogs attacked by monkeys, I removed tumours, I calved cows, I treated horses with colic, but all the time I had the question mark of why? at the back of my mind.

Then a few days later, Mike Prettejohn phoned up. 'Good evening, Hugh,' Mike began – Mike was always rather formal, there were none of your 'hi there' in his vocabulary – 'I have just learned that the watu (people) on Segera have been washing the horses in that new acaricide Triatix, which came out recently. There's nothing on the label to indicate that it can't be used on horses to get rid of ticks, but I just thought I'd let you know.'

'Thanks Mike,' I said, 'it's probably OK, but tell them anyway to stop using it.'

That evening and over the next few days I searched for evidence of adverse effects when using Triatix, or to use its chemical name, amitraz. The internet was in its infancy and we were infants when it came to using our new-fangled computer. Berna was better at trawling than I was and finally she found what we were looking for: a short article written in 1979 by a pair of Australians describing the toxic effects of amitraz when used on horses. They had found that it caused paralysis of the intestine, leading to large bowel stasis and consequent impaction and colic.

The mystery was solved. 'Hm,' grunted Berna, 'the drug manufacturers obviously didn't read this article before they released their product onto the market.'

'No indeed,' I said. 'But they've stopped using it on Segera so the crisis should be over.'

'We hope so,' she replied.

Five days later I was back on Laikipia, this time on Kifuku Ranch, owned by Clive Aggett. I was there to geld a colt. Clive, unlike the majority of ranch owners, did not tolerate wildlife on his land. Anything larger than a dik dik was given permanent marching orders. The same went for uninvited humans. Clive did not suffer fools, interlopers or bullshitters. He said it how it was, steel blue eyes flashing, his hard regimental voice rapping out orders or sardonic jokes. His Boran cattle were the best in the area and as a former member of Her Majesty's Armed Forces, he ran his ranch on military lines. As I removed the first testicle from the large bay colt, recumbent on a stretch of greenery near the airstrip, I heard the approaching buzz of a plane. 'Ah,' said Clive, 'that'll be Giles Prettejohn, Mike's son, come to fly you to Segera. I hear they've had a problem with their horses.' 'Tell me about it,' I said, and gave him a brief synopsis. 'Well at least I won't have to drive there. The road from Rumuruti was a bit damp. I had a bit of a struggle getting here.' Clive grunted. He didn't hold with wimps complaining about a bit of mud.

Giles' machine was an impressive six seater, a Dornier, with a massive radial engine and tail wheel, redolent of the past glory days of pioneer aviation.

The Dornier was not fast, but compared to a tedious journey along the mud-clogged road we were airborne and back on the ground within minutes, and I was examining a 28-year-old mare which had somehow slipped through the net. Having been ill for several days she was now thin and weak with very severe intestinal impaction. For good measure I gave her six litres of liquid paraffin by stomach tube, together with xylazine to control pain and flunixin to combat the concurrent toxaemia. All the other horses had recovered and were behaving normally. Then it was back into the plane and in no time we were back on Clive's ranch and into the car and back to Nakuru to complete the day's work.

Two days later, accompanied by eldest daughter Rona, I was flown back to Segera to tidy up the pieces. One final mare was awaiting my ministrations. In total 17 horses had been affected and I had stomach-tubed the lot. One horse had wandered off into the bush after treatment and had been eaten by a lion. Otherwise all had recovered. I knew that if I had been called at the outset, the first five horses would not have died. I phoned the supplier of the tick wash and told them what had happened. He expressed surprise and consternation, no doubt wondering if he was going to be sued for selling an unsafe product. Thereafter a warning was printed on all future consignments advising users not to use the wash on any horses, donkeys or mules – equids as they are called in today's strange, politically correct jargon.

That evening Berna spoke her mind. 'The whole episode,' she hotly declared, 'has been an unmitigated catalogue of incompetence, inefficiency, arrogance and carelessness, relieved only when you were called in.' 'Let's have a gin,' I said, 'a double. We deserve it.'

Chapter Five

IDIOCY ON THE ABERDARES

Not long after this episode I had cause to wonder if I did not have a touch of arrogance myself. It was now about three weeks since I had been discharged from hospital. I felt fine and was working full time. The Mountain Club had arranged a meet to climb Satima, the highest peak of the Aberdares, 13,120 feet high, and I was keen to go.

'Are you sure this is wise?' asked Berna. Of course it wasn't, but – 'you're just as stubborn as your mother, there's no point in my talking, you'll go anyway. But mark my words, there'll be consequences.' She was right of course.

Fourteen climbers met at the start of Wandare's Track above Mweiga on the eastern flank of the mountain. If there was a track it had long since disappeared. All that was left was the name of the mythical Wandare. Almost at once we were into a maze of waist-high tussocks. Thank God it was dry. Humping heavy packs, stumbling, falling, cursing, we staggered upwards into the zone of lobelia and giant groundsel, the air growing thinner and colder. Slowly the tussocks lessened in size, but by this time, for six climbers, enough was enough and they turned back. The unremarkable summit of Satima beckoned through a drift of rain and mist and after four hours of hard labour we were there, ineffectually trying to shelter from the icy wind sweeping over the desolate moorlands. Turning south we tramped along a broad, open ridge, to traverse a series of lesser peaks before descending to a col, where we pitched out tents, glad to shelter from the wind, which was increasing in ferocity. There was little sleep that night as the wind rose to gale force and the tent flapped and shook and tent pegs were torn from their moorings in the shallow turf. As dawn broke so the wind dropped and my spirits rose as the joyful sounds of birds, tiny and unseen, filled the air and the sun levitated gloriously and triumphantly over Mt. Kenya to the east. The tent was covered in ice and the surface of a nearby pool was frozen. The sky was blue, the air was still and expectant and Mt. Kenya, a jagged tooth, glaciers glinting amid black rock, hypnotized the eye. To the south the peak of the Kinangop, the most impressive of the Aberdare summits, beckoned. The name, meaning 'The Owners of the Land,' was bestowed by the Maasai, who were, before the arrival of the British, indeed the owners of the land.

Taking advantage of the superb weather a splinter group of three, including myself, set off for Castle Rock, a prominent feature halfway along a ridge overlooking the Rift Valley.

A 45 minute power scramble saw us on top, gazing down 6,000 feet at the mottled hide of the valley, pock marked with patches of forest, farms, rivers, lakes and the towns of Naivasha and Gilgil, all once the stamping ground of the wandering Maasai. 100 years ago they stood, leaning on their spears, their red cloaks fluttering in the hot wind, amid their flocks and herds, and watched as the Iron Snake of the Lunatic Line crept across their lands. Now the land was the place of other tribes, including the Wazungu, the Europeans, and they, the former owners, had been driven south to less favourable country, where they live to this day.

What goes up must come down, but descending a mountain is often as arduous as its ascent. Navigating tussock fields set at a sharp angle while toting a heavy rucksack, if done at speed, invariably ends in tears. Cries of anguish rent the limpid air as first one, then another, amateur mountaineer, went base over apex and vanished into the vegetation.

Two days later while removing a tumour from the flank of an Afghan hound, the fingers of my left hand went suddenly numb. The sensation disappeared after 30 minutes and, as I am right handed, it did not affect the progress of the operation.

In due course the lorry driver whose vehicle had rammed and destroyed my car was hauled before the judge in the old colonial courthouse in Nyeri. Both Moses and I were summoned to attend. The place was rather like a small, somnolent, ancient English church, with grey stone walls and stone benches surmounted by polished wood. Everything was spotlessly clean. Unlike most courts this one emanated an atmosphere of soothing calm and peace. As the magistrate entered I almost expected him to be robed in a surplice and wearing sandals and attended by a pair of altar boys.

The driver, one James Malinda, as expected, pleaded Not Guilty, My Lord, claiming that my car had been wrongly parked on the road when the accident happened. Evidence was given and he was found guilty and fined 6,000/- a modest sum in view of the consequences. But I knew, as did Moses, that although technically guilty, being the following driver, the fault was not entirely his. Ten days after the excursion up Satima, I experienced a numbness of the left side of my chest, my upper left arm, shoulder, fingers and the muscles of my back. 'That's it,' I thought, 'I've had a stroke!' I saw myself in a wheelchair, career at an end, speechless and slobbering. In a panic I phoned Ruberti and described the symptoms. I explained my movements since I left hospital. He gave an unsympathetic Tuscan grunt. 'OK, you come to see me and I will look at you, but are you crazy? Going mountaineering only two weeks after leaving hospital? Mama mia!'

Ruberti minced no words as I entered his sanctum. 'So, I imagine you were carrying a heavy rucksack, no? You were at high altitude, no? You were exerting yourself much more than usual, no? OK, go to the x-ray department and ask for an x-ray of your cervical vertebrae and then come back here and I will do an EEG. Mama mia!' The x-ray was perfect in all respects. Leads were attached to various parts of my cranium and the machine was switched on. There was a long anxious wait while the technicians and Ruberti pored over the long length of paper as it was extruded from the machine. Finally they stood up and stared at me. By now I was ready for the worst – an intracranial haemorrhage, a blocked blood vessel, tissue necrosis, brain cavitation – too much knowledge lets the overheated mind run riot. Much better to remain in pleasurable ignorance.

'You are very lucky,' Ruberti told me. 'Everything is normal. The symptoms were probably due to damaged cervical nerves from carrying a too heavy rucksack, but, just in case it wasn't, I want you to report back to me after two weeks. That will be 1,850 shillings please!'

The symptoms gradually subsided. My left arm gave me trouble for a while and a flickering at the outer corner of my left eye was concerning, but that too eventually stopped.

Chapter Six

A BANG ON THE HEAD

Outside the surgery a blind woman was beating a drum, soliciting alms from passers-by. In this enterprise she was seldom successful, but she was nothing if not persistent and the drumming went on and on. It was getting on my nerves. From time to time I would go out and drop a shilling into her tin mug, in the hope that she would move along and torment someone else. Being blind her hearing was sharp and acute and she knew by the ring made by the dropping coin the value of the piece. It was no good trying to fool her with ten cents. Further up the street another sightless citizen was beating *his* drum to the accompaniment of an enormous ghetto blaster, which was tastefully shrouded with a crocheted cloth.

The two blind minstrels competed with each other, hammering away at their respective tom toms. All of a sudden a fusillade of gunfire rang out, there was the sound of confused shouting which grew louder and louder and within seconds the street, Club Lane, was filled with a mass of running, stampeding people, pelting towards me.

I ducked back into the surgery, but before I had time to close the door, a dozen frantic members of the crowd forced their way inside. Multi-partyism was in the air and opposition to the rule of the one party of Daniel arap Moi was growing, with regular demonstrations and violent confrontations with the forces of law and order. Deaths were frequent, gunshot wounds common, hundreds were arrested and riots were the order of the day. I hoped that the two blind drummers had escaped unhurt. This was a regular occurrence in Nakuru. Shops would be shuttered, the streets would empty and an ominous silence would descend until it was deemed safe to emerge. As a posse of heavily armed police pounded after the retreating mob and as the baying of the crowd faded to a distant mutter I heard the shrill call of the phone.

I cupped the receiver to my ear.

'Would that be you now, Hugh?' a soft Irish voice enquired.

'Indeed it is,' I replied.

'Well now Hugh, this is Thomas O'Leary here, so 'tis. I'm out here at Ginger Bell's farm at Kampi ya Moto, keepin' an eye on his horses while he's down at Mombasa at his butcherin' business.'

'Yes,' I said, 'I'd heard that his workers had gone on strike for better wages, so he's driven down to read the riot act.'

'Aye, well that's one problem, but we've got another one here, so we have.'

'Right, shoot.'

'Well said. That's what we might have to do to his best mare. We were tryin' to load Warrior Queen – ye'll have heard of her – to take her to the races in Nairobi. She refused point blank to go into the lorry. Well, to cut a long story short, she reared up, and went over backwards and hit her poll on the ground. Doesn't look good. You'd better bring a gun.'

As luck would have it, I had brought my humane killer to the surgery, hoping to take it to the Central Police Station for its annual inspection, a hope thwarted by the ongoing civil unrest.

Suitably armed, I drove past shuttered shops and through deserted streets and was soon on the narrow bitumen road leading to Kampi ya Moto and Ginger's farm. The road passed Kabarak, the farm and home of the president, Daniel arap Moi, around whose head the unwelcome winds of change blew.

An askari emerged, troll like, from his roadside hovel, and raised the barrier pole to allow me entry to the farm.

I passed Ginger's office, where dust and mildew lay deep on long-abandoned files and out-of-date bottles of antibiotic and forlorn items of machinery. I passed the farm workshop where ancient past-their-date tractors stood rusting and tyre-less, in rank uncut grass, and up the long track leading to the stables, at the end of which I could see a small knot of figures, clustered around what I assumed was the horse, lying on the ground.

I drew closer, cut the engine, and coasted to a halt.

As Thomas the Irishman had said, things did not look good.

Warrior Queen was lying flat on her side in the middle of the track, legs thrashing wildly. I nodded to Thomas and moved closer, the better to examine the mare.

She was pouring with sweat, so much so that a veritable torrent of epidermal fluid was running down the side of the track. Both eyeballs were darting madly from side to side in their sockets. And she was blind. There was no reaction when I batted my hand towards her eyes. I got a stethoscope from the car and listened to her heart. 80 beats per minute and rising. I pricked her hind legs and tail with a needle. No reaction.

I straightened up and turned to Thomas.

'This is hopeless,' I said. She's either fractured her neck, severed her spinal cord, or suffered an intracranial haemorrhage. Whatever, there's zero hope of recovery, and we'll have to give her the coup de grace. Now.'

Thomas nodded, as did the attendant syces and hovering camp followers.

'Dere's only one problem,' he said. 'She's insured, and before putting her down we have to get de go-ahead from de insurer or dey won't pay up.'

'OK, can you phone them up.'

'I have, and de head wallah is not available and his deputy has gone for lunch.'

I looked at my watch.

'It's a quarter to three,' I said, 'when is he expected back?'

'Indeed I asked dem dat.'

'And what did dey – sorry, they – say?'

'Dey just said 'sijui – I don't know'.'

I saw red.

'So, while this poxed-up, be-suited jackanapes is munching his chicken and chips, washed down no doubt with a cold Tusker, we have to wait on his pleasure, as the poor horse lies here thrashing her life away. I'll give him 15 minutes and if we've had no joy by then I'm going to shoot her.'

We drove back to the office and phoned. No reply. We stood and waited, fuming with exasperation. 'Right,' I said, 'it's two minutes to three. Let's go.'

The phone rang. It was the insurer. I gave him chapter and verse, not mincing my words. He gave the go-ahead. Back at the mare, I cocked the humane killer, placed it against her forehead and pulled the trigger. A loud bang, a convulsive shudder and her sufferings were over.

Back in Nakuru the streets were still deserted. A well-dressed man, hands in the air, was being frog marched down the middle of Kenyatta Avenue, with a cocked gun in the hands of a paramilitary policeman pointing at his back.

They turned a corner and were lost to view.

Chapter Seven

TROUBLE AT MILL

'Hugh? Is that you?' Bruce Nightingale was on the phone. 'Can you come up to the farm? Urgently! The Sercombes were here this morning and they cut that big colt of theirs.' The Sercombes, husband and wife John and Patsy, were both vets from Nairobi, and this particular colt was stationed with Bruce, along with his other, numerous horses. 'The colt was pretty wild and the recovery from the anaesthetic, whatever that was, was rather violent. Anyway, now there's a long piece of something hanging down from where they made their incision. So I need you to come – now!'

'Right, I'm on my way.'

I knew that I might meet with trouble on the road to the farm, which was between Njoro and Elburgon, but I also knew that it would be unlikely to be directed at me personally. Sure enough, as I turned off the main highway onto the Njoro road, there, facing me, was an abandoned lorry, tilted at a precarious angle and blazing fiercely. The tarmac had already melted and as I drove past, the shimmering heat almost singed off my right eyebrow. No one was to be seen, which was odd and slightly sinister. Normally any such incident would have attracted a goggling mob of onlookers, but as I approached Njoro, boulders on the road alerted me to problems ahead. I slowed down.

No point in running into a situation and being unable to turn round. A small group of ragged-trousered men materialized, trotting along the verge. Two were carrying large wooden shields, another three toted spears, while the others brandished axes, bows and arrows, knobkerries and jembes (mattocks). I reduced gear. As I did so, they raised their fists above their heads and gave a hoarse primeval roar. This was a hunting party, Kikuyus on the warpath, searching for prey, their tribal foes, Kalenjin or Luos. If it were not for their tattered European attire, it might have been a scene from a past century and not the dying years of the 20th. I rocked over the railway tracks and turned a corner and onto Njoro's bumpy main street. I did not get far. Backed across the road were two trailers, used for carrying logs of timber. What looked like a telegraph pole was suspended between them. A mob of angry looking men was manning the barricade. But, as I approached, they raised the pole. One of their number gave me a smart salute. I saluted back. I was not their target. Two more barricades negotiated and the road was clear of obstacles.

As I vainly tried to avoid the numerous potholes and strategically-sited drainage ditches which made any excursion to Bruce's estancia a critical test for driver and vehicle, I hoped that whatever lay ahead would not extend into the hours of darkness. Meeting roving bands of hopped-up warriors in the gloaming when they would be unable to distinguish friend from foe was to be avoided if possible.

Bruce was waiting for me. Small and wiry and with that curious undulating gait known in Scotland as the ploughman's loup, Bruce ushered me into the stable where the patient awaited my attention. No mention was made of what appeared to be an impending peasant revolt outwith the premises. There was nothing either of us could do about that, and the equine crisis was of more immediate importance. Bruce was right. There was indeed something hanging down from the colt's groin. The colt was large and flighty and was stamping and kicking at the two foot length of omentum, the membrane which covers and protects the intestines, which had prolapsed through the inguinal (groin) canal. The hanging tissues were red in colour and bits of straw and grass were stuck to its surface.

'Right, Bruce,' I said 'what we have here is an omental prolapse. It's come down through the inguinal canal. The canal is possibly wider than normal and the violent recovery from the anaesthetic probably increased the abdominal pressure and forced the omentum through the aperture. The omentum will prevent anything else, like small intestine, from escaping, but we don't want to risk that happening when we correct the situation, so we will have to knock the horse out, turn him onto his back and do whatever we have to do.'

'Fine,' said Bruce.

'Can you bring me a tray on which to lay the instruments and then we can begin.'

Tools neatly arranged, I was on the point of giving the colt an intravenous injection of the sedative pre-med Xylazine when there was a sudden burst of gunfire from the main road about 400 yards away. The colt, nervous and skittish already, stampeded madly into a corner of the stable, knocking the attendant syce (groom) to the ground.

'What the dickens was that?' I said. 'My syce tells me that the miscreants had erected a barrier of rocks on the road along our boundary. That must be the police sorting them out.'

'Right then, let us proceed.'

The colt was now in a state of high anxiety, as was I. Applying a twitch to the colt's nose was out of the question. He would almost certainly go berserk. People, I thought, have been killed by animals just like this one. But a smooth, slow induction of anaesthesia was vital if the job was to be done properly. This, I could see, was not going to be easy. I returned to my car and soaked a pledget of cotton wool with local anaesthetic and re-entered the stable.

Very slowly I shuffled towards the patient. The colt shivered, his nostrils were dilated, his head was raised, his ears were laid back. Any moment now, I thought, he's going to erupt. For five minutes I just stood beside him, letting him get used to my proximity. Very carefully I laid a hand on his neck and began to scratch him with the ends of my fingers. Infinitely slowly he began to relax, but I knew that any sudden movement or sound would stimulate him into violent activity.

I changed the needle on the syringe to the finest consistent with the ability to inject the vital sedative.

Carefully I swabbed the area over the left jugular vein with the local anaesthetic in the hope that it would at least partially desensitize the skin, prior to the essential injection.

I waited for another two minutes.

'OK,' I said to the syce holding the halter, 'lift his head.'

I placed my left thumb in the jugular furrow. The vein swelled. I placed the needle against the skin and, infinitely slowly, began to push it into the vein, praying that this equine firebrand would play ball. In it went. I held my breath, and slowly, slowly the precious drug flowed into the vein.

I stepped back. 'Right,' I said. 'We wait for two minutes and then take him out into the paddock where the grass is fresh and clean.'

The horse's head began to droop. His hindquarters swayed. 'Right, let's take him out.' The long red rope of omentum swung to and fro. 'Jimmy,' I said to the syce, 'grab a handful of neck skin while I shove this ketamine into the vein. He may be sedated but he's still capable of antisocial behaviour.'

'Jimmy' did so. The colt bared his teeth and grunted to indicate his displeasure, but it was too late. The ketamine was within and it was just a matter of waiting for a few minutes before he hit the deck. He staggered to the left, he staggered to the right, and then down he went.

'Right,' I said, 'put that towel over his eyes. Not over his nose, you idiot, he's got to breathe! Now, roll him onto his back and let's have a shufti at the damage.'

Taking hold of the prolapsed omentum I gently pulled it until I could see normal tissue emerging from the abdomen. Next I applied Allis tissue forceps to spread the edges of the inguinal canal through which the omentum had inconveniently passed. Then, with my biggest pair of artery forceps I clamped the normal emerging omentum. 'I'm doing this,' I said to Bruce, 'as a precaution against bleeding. If there's none, we can let it slip back into the abdomen. Finally we have to twist the inguinal tunic into a pedicle in order to prevent this happening again, tie it off with a ligature and stitch it to the side of the canal and Bob's yer uncle.' I was halfway through this text book procedure when the colt showed signs of coming to. A hind leg flexed violently and a hoof shot past my right ear. Technicolour visions of more than omentum emerging from the abdomen flashed horridly before me. 'Bruce!' I said with some force, 'hold these forceps while I top up.' Bruce did as instructed. Nipping round to the front end I shot a half dose of xylazine and ketamine into the jugular, waited for two minutes and returned to the fray. Working fast I ligated and twisted and stitched and trimmed. 'All done,' I said as I stood up, 'I assume that the Sercombes gave antibiotic and a shot of tetanus antitoxin this morning, but there's no harm in repeating that. Now, we have to keep this horse down for as long as it takes. Keep those eyes covered and, Moses, kneel on his neck. This animal is a makorra – a ruffian – and when he gets up, he's going to get up in a hurry. I want him up smoothly, not staggering all over the place, falling down and getting up again and undoing all we have just done. So hold the bugger tight.'

They did, keeping his head covered. But you can't hold a good horse down forever. Finally, shaking off the towel and stretching out his forelegs he heaved himself to his feet and in one smooth movement stood. I checked the operation site for any bleeding. There was none.

'Put him into a stable for the night and let him out in the morning, make sure he gets some exercise to lessen any possible swelling and keep in touch. I must go while I can, while there's still some daylight. Vigilante roadblocks are bad enough in daylight. At night they could be lethal.'

As I negotiated my way back to the tarmac another incident involving an unannounced veterinary incursion on a different establishment came to mind. A vet, working for the Nairobi Jockey Club, came, castrated a colt, and left. I spent a considerable amount of time that night, which I would have preferred to have spent on more pleasurable pursuits, in stemming the life-threatening effusion of blood from the scrotal wound. The definition of an expert in Africa is 'one who goes in to find out, and gets out before he's found out.' Was there any difference in this case?

Africa is the stamping ground of the Experts. They flit in and they flit out. For the most part they live in luxury, they are chauffeured around in the largest and latest four wheel drives, though many never leave their tarmac comfort zone, and their salaries make a mockery of those they have come ostensibly to help. Their effect is short term and transitory. In the long run only the people on the ground will change things for the better.

The drive back to the surgery was incident-free but that could not be said for the state of affairs in Nakuru. As I drove along Kenyatta Avenue I could hear the sound of gunfire, the shops were shuttered and the streets empty. A helicopter clattered overhead. I made to turn into Club Lane and to my surgery, but a heavily armed policeman waved me away. I could see a crowd milling around in front of my premises. I parked in the car park of the adjacent Rift Valley Sports Club and walked to the surgery. I pushed my way through the mob which was standing around the body of a woman, dead, with a spreading pool of blood forming around her head. The blood, like a fat red snake, curled its way towards the gutter. 'Nani liua yeye? (Who killed her),' I asked an onlooker. He looked shifty, worried, glanced at the policeman, shook his head and remained silent. An ambulance roared up, the body was hoisted aboard. It drove off. The crowd drifted away and I entered the surgery.

'Ye Gods,' I thought, whatever next?' It was after five and the staff had all left, in a hurry perhaps.

Now it was time for me to leave, before anything else happened.

As I was carrying my things to the car, the phone rang. It was Tony Hughes, son of the late Mike of Men's Bar fame, phoning from Rongai.

'Hi Tony,' I said, 'how are things?'

'Well, not so good,' he replied, 'I've just come from Tegat Farm at Elburgon, where I was delivering hay and there's serious trouble there. Shirley Douglas-Dufresne is looking after the place which has been bought by a group of teachers from Kericho, all Kips, and the Kikuyus from Elburgon are marching on the farm, en masse, intending to attack it and I just got out in time. There was no way I could go back.

Those guys meant business. I know you're the British rep. so can you contact the High Commission, the cops and anyone else to see if Shirley's all right?'

'Thanks,' I said, 'I'll get onto that. The High Commission is shut after 3pm but there should be a duty officer I can speak to. Any other problems up there?'

'There certainly are. Up at Molo and towards Keringet the Kikuyus are being attacked by the Kalenjin and there's a mass exodus. They're moving out in large numbers. I hear that many people have been killed, houses burnt, cattle stolen, women raped. I hope Shirley's all right.'

'So do I. I'll get out of here and start phoning. I'll keep you posted.'

Back home Berna and I got onto the blower. 'Right,' I said, 'let's try the High Comm. first, and see if we can get any joy from the duty officer.'

The phone rang for a long time before – 'Yes, can I help you? And who are *you*?'

It was a woman's voice and she did not sound friendly. I explained the situation, that Shirley was a fully paid up British Citizen, I was the local rep, and that she was in mortal danger from the approaching impis. 'Very well, I will contact the consul,' and put the phone down. At least I assumed that's what she did. She might have slammed it down and uttered an expletive for being disturbed and gone back to her gin and tonic. 'Well,' I said to Berna, 'she's not a cuddly bunny. I wonder if the police are any better.'

Amazingly, they were. I phoned Nakuru Central Police Station, who said that reinforcements would be sent to deal with the problem. Encouraged, I next phoned Elburgon Police Station and again, *mirabili dictu*, they replied and told me that they would go to the farm and would report back to me later. This was nothing short of miraculous. We phoned a few other people – Col. Mutuku of the army, a bantam-sized officer with more get-up-and-go than others twice his size, Geoff Nightingale, whose ear was permanently glued to the ground, and Jean Chalcraft, an amateur radio ham whose living room was so full of batteries, antennae, receiving equipment, unidentifiable ironmongery and other paraphernalia that it resembled the navigation deck of the Titanic.

Then at 10.30 the phone rang – twice.

The first was from the British Consul in Nairobi, Alex Summers. The second was from the inspector at Elburgon Police Station to say that a contingent of his men had been to the farm and that Shirley was safe, but that much damage had been done and that people had been killed. But before I could ask any questions the phone went dead. Par for the course, but I felt lucky to have heard any news at all. Usually the line was either dead or there was no answer.

The following day, after clearing the list of waiting patients, I made my way to Tegat Farm. I seemed to be the only one moving in that direction. But coming towards me were vehicles laden with people and their belongings. As I got closer to Elburgon, herds of cattle and flocks of sheep appeared, driven along the road by their ragged owners, all fleeing from whatever was happening behind them. What that was I discovered when I drove up the track and into the farm.

The dairy, where I had not so long ago pregnancy-tested cattle, was in ashes. Of the cattle there was no sign. I hoped that they had escaped. More likely stolen, I thought. The manager's house was burnt to its foundations. Smoke rose into the still morning air. Apart from the drifting smoke nothing moved. The silence was almost palpable. Everyone had fled. A cape rook croaked from an unburnt tree.

I drove to the big, shingle-roofed house. It appeared to be deserted. A burnt out pick-up stood on the lawn, reduced to its bare, blackened, metallic skeleton. The nearby garage was no more, a mere pile of ash and charred timbers. I stared at the big, two storied colonial house. One corner had been set on fire and was still smouldering. Wisps of smoke rose from the shingled roof. All the hedges which formerly had surrounded the garden had been burnt down. From the skeletal twigs of one hedge protruded something which I hoped was not what I thought it was.

I got out of the car and walked to the front door, which as usual, in Kenya, was actually the back door. I rapped and shouted 'hodi?' meaning 'is there anyone at home?'

Through a window I could see someone. Then the door opened a crack, and a nervous head peeped out. A middle-aged African woman beckoned me to come in. I entered via the kitchen. The place smelt of smoke. 'Wapi Memsahib?' I asked: 'Where is madam?' 'Nakula breakfast,' came the reply.

I walked through into the dining room and there was Shirley, elbows squared, working her way through what looked like the full English. 'Come in, come on in!' she cried, 'sit down and join me. I'm so glad to see you! Betty! Lete chakula kwa bwana! Bring the bwana breakfast!' I was impressed. Despite what had obviously been a harrowing night, Shirley appeared unfazed. But I knew that most Kenyan up-country Europeans were like that. You took the almost hourly trials and tribulations in your stride. Get over it and get on with it was the norm. Keep calm and carry on. As Shirley was doing now.

And as she did some years later when she retired to her retreat on an island in Lake Baringo, when, while taking her morning bathe in the lake, she was attacked by a crocodile. One arm was almost severed and she sustained other life-threatening injuries. She survived, with the arm permanently deformed. But she never complained. She carried on.

Over the fried eggs and bacon she told me what had happened.

'A bloody great mob came swarming down from Elburgon, armed to the teeth with pangas, spears, rungus, I could hear them from here. Looking for any Kalenjin they could find. They set the dairy and the manager's house on fire – I suppose you saw that as you drove in.' 'I did.'

'They caught one chap at the dairy and hacked and slashed him to death. Then they came howling down here and tried to set the house on fire by throwing petrol bombs onto the roof. When that didn't work they burnt the garage down and incinerated the pick-up. Anyway I know that at least four people have been killed and there are eight missing and all the cattle are gone. One child was burnt to death and one old man is out there, dead, and stuck in the hedge.'

I looked through the bay window and across the lawn. The sky was a lovely light blue, the lawn was green, the birds were twittering, but the old man in the hedge could neither see nor hear anything of this.

'Well, the mob was all round the house for what seemed like hours, baying and whooping like a pack of hyenas on bhangi, smashing windows, throwing rocks, banging drums and I thought: any moment now the impi will break in. Isandlwana, Rorke's Drift and all that.'

'And no Michael Caine and Stanley Baker to hold them off!' Shirley laughed.

'Just as I thought that this was it I heard a vehicle. It was the police – at last. I was never so relieved. But those poor people who have been killed...' Her voice faltered. I cleared my plate. 'Right Shirley,' I said, 'many thanks for the breakfast, it's so good to see you alive and well. I'm going to go up to St. Mungo's to check on the situation there. The school's not open yet and I know that the expats get a bit jumpy when things get out of hand.'

'Well watch out when you go through Elburgon then. The mood up there is not good.'

It wasn't. All the shops on the main street were shut. Instead of the usual noise and bustle, the shouting of hawkers, the jaywalking sheep and goats, the blaring radios, the hooting matatu horns, the trundling donkey carts, the wandering pedestrians, there was silence. No women were to be seen. Knots of grim faced men, carrying spears and pangas stood glaring as I drove slowly past. On high banks sat other silent glowering groups, watching as I moved past. The menace was palpable, but no one moved to stop me.

Beyond the town a burnt-out lorry lay on its side and beyond that was a makeshift roadblock, manned by ragged youths, armed with clubs and machetes. Expecting the worst I slowed to a halt. A pair of villainous, yellow-eyed thugs slouched up to my window. Suddenly one gave me a huge grin. 'Jambo daktari!' he grinned, 'so, it is you! How is da job?' It was Samwell, the son of Peter Mwangi, a Kikuyu farmer in the area and whom I had visited recently when one of his cows had had difficulty giving birth. Samwell had hauled on one of the ropes when I delivered the calf. Here he now was, one of the panga-swinging vigilantes. 'Jambo Samwell,' I replied, 'how is the calf?' 'Oh it is doing fine, thanks to you. We were soo happy. And the mother, she has plenty of milk. Now, we have wok to do, as you can see. But, you, you may plocede. You are Mzungu, you are not Kalenjin, you are our flend, not our enemy.'

No I wasn't, but perhaps I might have been, 40 years before, in the dark days of Mau Mau. Then I might have been regarded much as these Kikuyus now looked at the Kalenjin – as the enemy.

I drove on and the road was now clogged with people driving their livestock – cattle, sheep and goats – heading away from the area of conflict, Molo. Women walked along the verge, holding their children by the hand, bundles on their heads, blankets and bedding on their backs. Donkey carts, piled high with beds, sofas, chairs, pots and pans, struggled up the steep inclines. Old men lay exhausted in the dust. Ancient pick-ups crammed with the internally displaced crawled past.

The refugees were all Kikuyus. When the Europeans who had farmed in the area were forced to sell at Independence, Jomo Kenyatta, Kenya's first president, had moved his people onto the vacated land. But this had never been a Kikuyu area. If anyone had owned the land it had been the nomadic, pastoral Maasai and the forest-dwelling hunter gatherers, the Okiek/Ndorobo. The place names showed that: Elburgon, Olenguruone etc. The European farms which displaced them had formed a buffer between the Kalenjin Kipsigis to the west and the encroaching Kikuyus, moving from their own overcrowded Central Province and other areas of the country. Now that buffer was gone and in the struggle for power and the mayhem over multipartyism, the ugly head of rampant tribalism had reared up, hissing like an angry cobra. I reached the school and saw the headmaster. Opening would be delayed by a week, or until the situation improved.

Following the example of the Three Wise Men, I returned to Nakuru by another way.

Chapter Eight

BUFFALO AND BHANG

Now began a season of strife and turmoil.

The forces of the president, Daniel arap Moi, aka L'etat est Moi, aka Donnez Moi, were arrayed against those favouring multipartyism. The president was a Tugen, a Kalenjin, of the same tribal grouping that was so intent on driving the Kikuyus from Molo. The multipartyism lot were mainly Kikuyus and their tribal allies. So the scene was set for a period of protracted conflict.

Every day helicopters clattered over Nakuru on their way to Molo to deal with the latest outbreak of unrest. Tension in the area was high. Arrests were frequent. Random killings and casual violence were common.

The economy of the country was affected. Foreign exchange dried up, financial remittances were forbidden, the cost of living rose, and there was a serious lack of drugs. There were continual power cuts, and fuel shortages became everyday occurrences. We bought a 40 gallon drum and slowly filled it with petrol as a safeguard against the day when all the pumps ran dry. But life and work had to continue.

The most prolific vegetation on Simba Farm on the western shore of Lake Naivasha was the leleshwa bush. The most prolific animal on Simba Farm was the buffalo. Large, black, dangerous buffalo, with their massive horns, bullet-proof bosses, armour plated hides and aggressive temperaments. I had treated young buffalo and they appeared to be made of concrete. Domestic cattle were jelly babies by comparison. No wonder the Maasai made their man-sized shields from buffalo hide, which, when dried and hardened, would deflect spears, arrows and even bullets.

Jack and Serena Rivett-Sykes ran the farm from their cliff top eyrie overlooking the lake. Jack was a gentleman and former professional hunter, later killed by a wounded buffalo, together with his gun bearer, almost within spitting distance from his house, when the Kenya Wildlife Services fell down on their job. Violent death seemed to be ever-present in Kenya.

Adjacent to the house was a line of stables where the lovely Serena kept her horses. Their life was a precarious one, sharing their paddock, as they did, with grazing buffalo. One pony was gored, disembowelled and died a miserable death. An old man, walking through the farm, was attacked by a buffalo bull and killed. One night, while escorting a guest to her car, Jack was charged by a bull grazing on his lawn, missing him by inches.

One of Serena's horses was a grey mare called 'Vixen.' She was well named. Whenever you walked past Vixen's stable, her ears would go back and she would make a lunge for your person, teeth bared, nostrils flared. I learned to skip sharply lakewards whenever I approached her stable. One day when I was on the farm, Serena appeared, sporting a large set of equine tooth marks on one shapely cheek. Vixen had struck again. Vixen was needle shy and whenever one entered her stable, syringe in hand, she went into immediate attack mode.

So when Serena phoned one day to advise me that Vixen had been gored by a buffalo and had sustained a serious chest wound, I knew that another adrenalin-draining experience lay ahead.

With Moses acting as ballast, tunny boy and right hand man I drove up the steep dirt track to the Rivetts' hilltop house and parked my car below the stables. Jack, wisely, had found more pressing matters to occupy his time. Like many Kenyan cattle farmers, he regarded horses as unpleasant, useless animals fit only for dog meat.

In the case of Vixen he was probably right. But here we were and so was Serena. I walked up to the stable and Vixen was standing moodily in a corner with her backside towards me. When she became aware of my presence she whirled round, teeth bared and ears flattened against her head. Now all too plainly I saw the huge wound across her right chest, 20 inches long at least, with red muscles gaping and a blanket of flayed skin hanging like a horrid curtain from the lower edge.

'Well,' I said to the hovering Serena, 'this is no five minute job. This is going to require a general anaesthetic, and then some, to repair, but first we have to get a needle into the vein' – I almost said 'bitch' but stopped myself just in time. 'Any suggestions? Can we put a twitch on her nose?'

'Heavens no! Not a chance. She'll hit the roof!'

'What about the syce? Can he hold her?'

'Not this one,' indicating a rotund, furtive individual lurking in the background, a sheen of anxious perspiration already reflected off his sable forehead. 'But wait a minute. There used to be an old Somali called Abdi in the camp who was an absolute wizard with horses. I don't know if he's still alive, but if he is, then he may be able to help. He was totally fearless and seemed to be able to deal with any horse. I'll pop down and see if he's still around.'

When the rattle and thump of Serena's Toyota had faded away I strolled to the edge of the rocky plinth overlooking the lake. Far out on the water I could see a tiny craft, a fishing canoe. I could imagine the men casting their nets, hoping to pull in a catch of tilapia or bass, perhaps even a catfish. The fishermen might have been legal. They might be poachers. But in either case the chances were that they were dirt poor, living from hand to mouth, trying to provide for a family on the equivalent of a couple of pounds a day. I often wondered just how such people survived. I had enough problems surviving myself. Their lot was much worse. The far shore of the lake, once covered with fever trees and whistling thorn, where lion once roared and where wandering Maasai had formerly grazed their cattle, was now covered with hectare upon hectare of polythene greenhouses, growing flowers and produce for the markets of Europe. Thousands of workers were employed in these vast soulless enterprises which crept inexorably over the former playgrounds of the Happy Valley set like some gargantuan budding amoeba, swallowing everything in its path. Behind this depressing sea of plastic, plumes of steam belched into the air from vertical pipes. Here geothermal activity was being tapped, in a vast complex of tubes and wells to provide electricity for the country's burgeoning population. Hell's Gate National Park, refuge for Kenya's last remaining lammergeyer, was under threat.

The few animals left were being forced into smaller and yet smaller areas. It was little wonder that human animal confrontations were on the increase. The larger animals had become accustomed to seeing people at close quarters, and with familiarity came, if not contempt, at least a certain of lack of fear. The hunting and shooting of game had been banned in the 70s. So the game, which in the past might have beaten a rapid retreat at the sight of a human, now showed none of their natural apprehension at the proximity of the world's top predator. An animal which loses its fear of humans is dangerous. This, combined with a shrinking habitat, led to numerous confrontations. People were gored by buffalo, bisected by hippo, clawed by leopards, even bitten by monkeys. The wretched animals were in a state of continuous high anxiety, so when humans intruded to within their diminishing comfort zone, such as it was, they went into attack mode. I could not blame them. I sometimes felt the same myself. And, let's face it, all human conflict boils down to the same thing, space, whether taking it or defending it. The unmistakable high pitched yelp of a fish eagle broke into my depressing musings. I could see the bird, snowy head thrown back, gliding effortlessly over the tall acacias which fringed the lake shore. A hippo grunted dyspeptically from the reed beds. A scarlet-chested sunbird flitted from flower to flower amid the vegetation growing in the rocks at my feet. None of these creatures were aware of the frightful mess humans were making of their planet. Lucky them, I thought.

I could hear Serena's Toyota grinding its way up the steep hill.

In the front passenger seat I could see a head topped by a white Islamic kofia, the embroidered brimless hat worn by followers of the Faith. The vehicle eased to a stop in a cloud of dust. A tall, thin, imperial figure stepped out and stalked across to me. That hooked nose, the hennaed beard, the humorous eyes, the grey knife scar across the ebony left cheek, surely this was the same Abdi who once worked for Andy Yakas on his sisal estate at Mogotio all those years ago. It was. 'Habari, effendi?' he greeted me, using the polite Turkish honorific, the equivalent of 'sir' or when addressing a professional. 'How are you, sir? The last time I saw you, you were a kijana (young man) on Bwana Yakas' shamba, treating his cattle. Now I am old, and you, you... are older.' I laughed as I shook his leathery hand. 'Abdi,' I said, 'I had no idea that you were a horseman?' 'Oh yes, when I was a kijana I was a duba, a tribal policeman, serving under Sir Gerald Reece, in the colonial Northern Frontier District, keeping the peace. Chasing bandits, tracking cattle thieves, protecting the people from the shifta. We wore blood red turbans and white togas like the Romans, ha! ha!, we carried rifles and we rode horses and camels. Oh, we were safi sana! (very smart!) All the girls loved us! We were afraid of nothing.'

I knew that. Somalis fear nothing. Death means nothing to them. Paradise is waiting when you will have all eternity to lie in the shade, sipping sherbet, chewing khat, sucking from your hookah, and being fondled by compliant virgins. Here on earth you had to act the man, pray five times a day, despise the softer slave tribes, follow your camels into the wilderness, kill your enemies and take offence from no man. Prickly but friendly, difficult and easy going, arrogant and proud, they were a mass of contradictions.

If any country in Africa should have evolved into a cohesive unit it should have been Somalia. All Somalis spoke the same language, all were Muslims, yet almost as soon as the colonial fetters had been struck off, the country degenerated into chaos, civil war and barbarism as clan fought clan over grazing rights, access to government and aid money until famine stalked the land. Hundreds of thousands died of starvation, the United Nations and the United States ineffectually and disastrously attempted to intervene, and Al Shabaab, like a malignant virus, grew out of the chaos, and spread across the country and south into Kenya, killing and mutilating as it went.

What had been British Somaliland broke away from the rest of Somalia, declaring itself to be the as yet unrecognised Republic of Somaliland, and, free from the shackles and shambles to the south, prospered and did well. I often wondered whether the fact that Italy, the former colonial ruler, with its own chaotic record of governance at home, had been in any way responsible for the mess that now prevailed in Somalia. The more prosaic and less flamboyant British had imposed a system of law and order in the territory which they had governed and which still prevailed.

'Sema bas (so tell me'), said Abdi, 'where's the horse?'

I led Abdi to Vixen's stable. Something about Abdi made her stop and stare. Perhaps it was his embroidered cap perched on his grizzled head or the purposeful way in which he pushed open the stable door and marched inside. He took no notice of her, but turned round, leaned on the stable door, took out a cigarette, lit it and puffed the smoke in my direction. It had a strange musky smell. 'What sort of tobacco is that?' I asked. 'We will find out,' replied Abdi, 'let her wonder for a few more minutes and then I may puff some up her nostrils.' Vixen inched towards Abdi's back. He paid no attention. She nuzzled his shirt, she nibbled at his cap. Abdi smoked on. He lit another cigarette. Again that mysterious, oriental aroma.

'Don't stand too near,' said Abdi, 'I'm not inhaling and nor should you.'

Slowly Abdi turned around and shot a plume of smoke in Vixen's direction, waited for a few more minutes and then puffed another whiff at her nostrils.

Slowly, slowly, as I watched, Vixen's head began to droop.

'What's he doing?' whispered Serena.

'Smoke and mirrors, I think,' I muttered.

'Sasa(now),' said Abdi, 'you can come in. She should be OK.'

Vixen seemed to be oblivious to my presence. I was astonished. What was in that tobacco? Hemp? Opium? Abdi would not say. He merely gave an enigmatic smile.

Using a fine needle, I gave needle-shy Vixen her pre-med injection. She accepted it without demur. We led her out of the stable onto a stretch of grass, waited for the requisite two minutes, and then I shot a dose of ketamine into her jugular and as she slowly collapsed, I made sure that her gored side was uppermost.

Abdi leaned against a post and watched the bloody proceedings. He was smoking another cigarette. Perhaps he was immune to its contents.

Vixen's wounds were not small. A great flap of skin hung from her right chest, exposing ribs, subcutaneous tissue, nerves, blood vessels and muscle. Miraculously the horn had not penetrated the chest wall or punctured a lung. It was a long job, two hours, on my long-suffering knees, stitching and clamping and tying and topping up the anaesthetic whenever Vixen showed signs of coming round. Moses threaded needles, handed me instruments, proffered me cotton wool, swabbed oozing blood vessels, fetched and carried and took my barked orders on the chin. In situations like these your assistant is as important as you are. Without him, or her, you are working with one hand tied behind your back. They are the unsung heroes of any enterprise like this – the squaddies and non-coms are just as important as the officers. And where would we have been without Abdi? These things are team efforts in which everyone plays a part.

The last stitch was inserted and I creaked painfully to my feet. I gave Vixen a shot to ward off tetanus and another of long-acting antibiotic. I looked round for Abdi. Flat on his back, neck propped against the stable timbers, mouth open and snoring like a grampus, he was fast asleep. Perhaps he had inhaled after all.

Chapter Nine

MADNESS AND MALARIA

'Gad, what a day!' I said to Berna. 'Non-bloody-stop all day! Barely time to draw breath! Started off with Dick Crawford rushing in from his kennels waving a labrador's ear! Said it happened when his kennel-man put five dogs together and there was the most almighty scrap. Took me two interminable hours to re-attach it. Then I had to go to Technology Farm to see a cow which had fallen over a cliff onto rocks by the Njoro River. Broke its back. Then to Rongai to Kurungu Farm to see a horse. The point of its pelvis had come through the skin, so I had to saw off a section of bone and then stitch the skin over it. Back to the surgery where the Police Dog Section cops were waiting with six pups with parvovirus disease, all vomiting and scouring blood. So I had to give all of them IV fluids and hope for the best. Took forever. As you know the mortality can be very high, up to 100%. Then a pup with severe demodectic mange, a dog with tick fever, a cat to spay, and a collie bitten on the nose by a puff adder. Finally I had to go to Naivasha to see a coughing horse owned by Mrs. Temporini. The highlight of the day! She showed me the bullet wounds in her leg where she had been shot when her car was ambushed near Limuru by four thugs. She told me that they had sub-machine guns. She gave me a cappuccino. The only sustenance I've had all day.'

'What was her leg like?' said Berna. There was a tiny touch of unwarranted steel to her voice, I thought. 'Not bad at all for a woman of her age. After all she must be 50 if she's a day. The scars add a touch of interest to an otherwise average female thigh.'

'Oh, so you went as high as that did you?'

'Well, that's where they shot her. She knew I'd have a detached medical interest.'

Berna snorted. 'Right, you must be starving. Esther has made a meat pie, followed by rhubarb crumble.' Esther was our house girl and cook, although the appellation 'girl' was hardly appropriate. When we first employed her, she was slim and attractive, but as the years went by the slow, cement-like accumulation of cellulite transformed a buxom maid into a vast shapeless matron. Was this a genetic metamorphosis, we wondered, or were we partially responsible in being too lax in overseeing the security of our western foodstuffs? She had a one flaw. Whatever could be broken, she broke. Or, according to Esther, 'it' broke, or fell, or smashed, as though an inanimate object had a capricious mind of its own. So, considerably before the advent of the infamous trio of Saddam Hussein, Blair and Bush we had our own personalized Weapon of Mass Destruction on the premises.

But this was a minor peccadillo. She was scrupulously honest and our daughters loved her. And her meat pies were beyond compare. I tucked in with gusto. The meal over, the dishes washed, we bade Esther good night.

Time for a nightcap, I thought. It had been a hard day.

There came a knocking on the door.

'Who is it?' I asked.

'It's me, Esther.'

'What is it?'

'It's the McIntyre's cook. He's very ill and needs to go to hospital. He can't stand and the McIntyres are away.'

I opened the door.

'Lead on,' I said.

The cook was lying on the kitchen floor, twitching, his eyes rolled back into his head, until only the whites were visible, only now they weren't white but an unpleasant shade of yellow, almost umber. He appeared to be semi-conscious.

I returned to the house.

'Berna,' I said, 'this chap's in a bad way. We'll have to take him to the General. But he can't walk so I'll need help.'

'I'll phone the Robinsons and see if Tony can help.'

The Robinsons were our next-door neighbours.

'Tony has had a couple of beers and as a result is in a suitably compliant mood,' said Berna as she put the phone down. 'He'll be round in a few minutes.' Tony duly appeared, a smile of light inebriation flickering across his pleasant features.

We drove round to the McIntyres' place, and, with the help of a Maasai friend of the cook, not without difficulty, loaded the patient into the back of the car.

On the way to the hospital the cook groaned and moaned, turning and twisting from side to side. The Maasai did his best to restrain him.

I drove into the car park and stopped the car.

A nurse stood at the entrance to the hospital, seemingly enjoying the balmy night air.

We lifted the cook out of the back of the car. He attempted to stand and promptly collapsed onto the concrete apron.

The nurse slowly turned her head and stared in our direction but made no move to help. I looked around for porters or for some able-bodied passers-by, but there were none.

I spotted a stretcher propped up against a wall, and, at the end of a gloomy half lit corridor, a trolley. I grabbed the stretcher and wheeled the trolley back to the car. We loaded the seemingly unconscious cook onto the stretcher and hoisted him onto the trolley. 'Wapi daktari?' ('Where's the doctor') I asked the oblivious nurse.

Mutely she gestured down the corridor and returned to contemplating her navel.

We trundled the gurney over the cracked and uneven tiles, scrutinizing each darkened doorway until we came to one where the door was half open, and the interior lit by an unshaded bulb.

'This must be it,' I muttered to Tony, and pushed the patient inside.

A bulky black gentleman was seated at a desk, writing in a large ledger. A garishly embossed plaque on the desk suggested that the writer was Dr Festus Odhiambo.

Dr Odhiambo did not look up, but continued to inscribe, his pen slowly scratching across the page. After a few minutes he directed an irritated stare in our direction.

At this point the patient had what looked like a convulsion, sitting up, lying down, jerking, head zapping from side to side like a demented metronome. This seemed to stimulate Dr Odhiambo into activity. Rising in slo-mo from his seat he strolled to the door, and in stentorian voice, summoned a technician. After about five minutes a fellow in a grubby white coat sauntered into the room and, in an interval between seizures, stabbed a needle into one of the patient's finger tips, and made a blood smear on a microscope slide and, after waving it in the air to dry it, strolled away – presumably to the lab.

Ten amazingly short minutes later he returned. The result was as we expected: cerebral malaria.

The patient now lay comatose on his gurney.

Dr Odhiambo spoke. 'Please take this man to room 14. Follow the corridor to the end, turn right into the ward, go through that into another corridor and it's the third door on the left. A doctor will be along shortly to insert a drip.'

The three of us, Tony, the Maasai neighbour and I, trundled the trolley on its wonky wheels along the uneven surface of the gloomy corridor and into the ward.

Almost at once a rancid, ammoniacal stench of urine, unwashed bodies and excrement assailed my questing nostrils. Tony gave a hollow gasp and the Maasai grunted in disgust.

Although the light was dim and crepuscular we could see the dirt on the floor and on the walls, the filthy curtains tied in knots, the discarded syringes and needles underneath the beds, the blood on the walls. Humped shapes lay on beds, muffled groans and sighs filled the stifling air.

Our pace quickened as we strove to leave this hellish antechamber to whatever lay ahead. Breaths held, hands over our noses, we shot into the maw of the waiting corridor, found room 14, and burst inside.

Almost at once the cook had a series of convulsions and fell onto the floor. We lifted him onto a couch, whose interior appeared to be mostly exterior, with cushions torn and stuffing hanging out. Twice more the cook convulsed and hit the deck. After that we held him down by main force, waiting for medical expertise to arrive.

After what seemed like an age, a nurse appeared, followed by a doctor. The latter indicated to the former that he wanted some equipment from a cupboard. Try as she might she was unable to open it. She shook the panelling, she beat the wood work, she tried one key after another. All in vain. In the meantime we were left pinioning the wretched cook, hoping that whatever might save his life was not imprisoned in the unopened cupboard.

Finally the doctor left, returning a few minutes later, carrying a drip set.

He spoke. 'First,' he said,' I'm going to give him 20mg valium IV to control his seizures and then IV Quinine.' Sounds good, I thought. At last we're getting somewhere.

The nurse held the patient's right arm. At the other end we held his legs and torso. The doctor applied a tourniquet, swabbed the crook of his elbow and inserted a needle into the now dilated vein. The touch of the needle was like the application of a red hot poker or a live electric wire. The cook gave an inarticulate roar and a convulsive jerk. The needle came out of the vein, a tidal wave of blood spread over his arm and a large haematoma swelled up before the tourniquet could be released.

Beside me I could hear Tony's breathing coming in short, irregular gasps. I glanced at him. He was pale and sweating, swallowing, gagging, trying not to vomit. He tried to speak, failed and staggered from the room, followed by the Maasai. 'Once more unto the breech,' I thought.

I looked up at the doctor and nodded.

'Right, let's try the other arm,' he said.

'Let me hold it this time,' I replied.

I held the cook's arm in what I hoped was a vice like grip. Using a finer needle the doctor hit oil without any reaction from his recipient, shot in 20mg of valium and whipped off the tourniquet. Together we waited for the cook to slump back into a soporific doze. For a few brief happy moments I thought we had the situation in hand. The doctor even gave me a confident thumbs up. This premature signal of success, the upraised digit, the raised eyebrows, the smug smile, seemed to act as a jump-start to galvanize the cook into a fresh cyclone of activity, until he resembled a human windmill, legs pumping like a pepped up Lance Armstrong. Physical control was impossible. Then suddenly he conked and collapsed. Our relief was palpable. The doctor attached a drip and ran in a dose of quinine.

'OK,' said the doctor, 'let's take him to the ward.'

Must we? I thought.

We wheeled him into the ward, with me holding my breath, and decanted him onto a filthy bed. The darkness hid most of the dirt but I could see that the sheets and bedding were grey and mottled, with what I dreaded to think.

The cook, thankfully, was unaware of his revolting surroundings. I made a mental note to try to get him transferred to a more salubrious establishment in the morning. Any more time spent in this place, I thought, might prove fatal. And not only to him, I thought, as I made my exit.

Tony and the Maasai were waiting outside by the car. 'God!' said Tony, 'that place stank! If I'd stayed a minute more I'd have thrown up.'

'Yes,' I said, 'you don't appreciate fresh air until you've been in a place like that.'

It was now 10.30 and the night air was chilly but we drove home with the windows wide open, savouring every lungful of the passing breeze.

Berna was waiting when I walked in.

'Well?' she asked, 'how was it?'

I paused.

'The great thing about living in Africa,' I said, 'is that you have the privilege of being able to experience at first-hand what it was like to live, for example, in the Stone Age, the Iron Age or the Middle Ages. Tonight I was taken back to the early eighteen-hundreds, to the period leading up to the Crimean War. Illuminating, if rather taxing on the ocular and olfactory systems.'

The following day we transferred the cook to the private War Memorial Hospital. His right arm was very swollen from the botched infusion, but he made a good recovery.

Chapter Ten

SEEING SPOTS

Waiting for the next patient, I glanced idly at the day's copy of *The Tropical Enquirer* which the last client had left behind. Normally I did not read the local papers, finding their contents boringly parochial, humourless and depressingly full of death and disaster. Today was no different. *'Outbreak of Yellow Fever – 500 dead in Baringo, Kabarnet and Elgeyo Marakwet.' 'More violence 50 dead at Njoro, hundreds of houses burnt down. Curfew from 9pm until 6am.' '100 people dead in Nairobi after drinking changaa* (a locally brewed spirit) *contaminated with methanol.' '140 people drowned when train washed away on the Nairobi/Mombasa line.' '106 killed in bus crash in Machakos.'* These bulletins of adversity and misfortune were not accorded front page status as might have been the case in more effete nations, but were instead consigned to the inner regions of the news-sheet, alongside reports of outbreaks of army worm, coffee berry disease, incest and cattle rustling. The front pages were given over to the latest pronouncements by the President, where he went, who he met, what he had for breakfast and so on.

Lesser calamities were often not given any news space at all. Such as the Asian family attacked by thugs in their house in Nakuru. The father was gravely wounded. Then, as the family escaped, they were shot by the police who thought they were the villains. There was the horrific incident on Ol Suswa Farm on the shore of Lake Naivasha, where I had gone to pregnancy test cattle. A worker was feeding cut maize into an unguarded silage cutting machine. His attention was distracted, he stepped forwards and his leg was dragged into the machine up to the thigh, where the razor sharp blades sliced through his leg and for good measure, emasculated him as well. Our cook/housekeeper, the burgeoning Esther, related, with grisly relish, the report of a dead baby thrown onto the municipal rubbish dump. This was bad enough, but there was more. A nutter, one of the freely roaming unhinged community, came along, spotted the tiny corpse, and started eating it.

I tossed the paper aside. Perhaps it was as well everything wasn't reported. Sufficient unto the day is the evil thereof. I had enough to deal with on a daily basis without morbidly studying such horrors. Once a week or a month perhaps, but a daily literary dose of such stuff was a recipe for terminal depression.

The rumble of wheels, the squeal of brakes and the diesel rasp of a 4WD engine told me that Daisy Lekupe and her pedigree Rhodesian ridgeback had arrived. Daisy was an American, married to a Samburu, and lived either in Maralal, at the foot of the Karisia Hills, 120 miles north of Nakuru or in Ngurinit at the foot of the Ndoto Mountains, another hundred miles away, in the home of her husband. She was nothing if not peripatetic. So she had come a long way and had spent the previous night with a friend in the town of Gilgil to the east of Nakuru.

Daisy was large and upstanding. She was built like an isosceles triangle, slender and beguiling north of the equator, Junoesque and Rubenesque to the south. Daisy eschewed the buttock hugging jeans and thigh clamping trousers favoured by her female counterparts and instead swathed herself from the waist downwards in an all-enveloping kaftan-like garment. Her sense of humour was as generous as her hips. She moved with a nautical gait, rather like a stately Elizabethan galleon ploughing its magisterial way through a heavy swell. On her feet she wore immense sandals, made from some impervious jute-like material, from which her large spatulate toes protruded like an advancing platoon of angry rodents.

Daisy had decided to have her year-old Rhodesian ridgeback, Tyson, gelded. Like his namesake, Tyson was a rampant male, cocking his leg on any object, animate or inanimate, which took his fancy. He was also a sex maniac, attempting to rape passing pedestrians, sofas, bales of hay, trees, boulders, and more importantly, as far as Daisy was concerned, Winkle, her small terrier bitch. If she survived penetration by Tyson, which was unlikely given the disparity in size, and became pregnant, Daisy knew that the chances of a normal delivery would be nil, and that, living in such a remote spot as Maralal, where veterinary assistance was limited to non-existent, that her chance of surviving emergence of Tysonesque puppies was likewise nil.

Hence Tyson's presence on my premises.

Despite his rampant sexuality, Tyson was much prized by his mistress. He was highly pedigreed, and a splendid specimen of his breed, hence Daisy's insistence that she be present during the operation, in order to keep close watch on the surgeon as he incised and ligatured and sutured.

Daisy heaved herself out of her mud-bespattered Toyota and dragged a reluctant Tyson through the batwing doors into the surgery.

'Right, Daisy,' I said, after the usual felicitations, 'let's put him on the scales.

'We need to know his weight so we can compute the required anaesthetic dose.'

Tyson wasn't keen on being weighed, so I summoned Moses to assist, and, after a brief struggle, got a reading of 88lb – 40kgs.

I calculated the dose of pre-med of Xylazine and drew it up into a syringe.

'Has Tyson had anything to eat during the past 12 hours?' I asked Daisy, 'Because, if he has, he may vomit after he's had the injection.'

'No problems there,' Daisy assured me. 'I spent last night with a friend in Gilgil, and he was with me – Tyson I mean,' she giggled, 'all night, in my bedroom, with no access to food or water. So his poor stomach must be completely empty.' She patted poor Tyson's head.

'Fine,' I said, and gave Tyson his injection into his right hind leg.

Daisy lowered her vast haunches onto a low stool while I checked that all required instruments were ready.

Five minutes after giving the injection Tyson gave the first indications that he was about to vomit. He began to drool and swallow convulsively. He lowered his head in preparation for imminent gastric evacuation. It came with considerable violence and a surprising volume of noise. Tyson gave a great yooaaaaah!, giving the impression that he was trying to turn his stomach inside out. Daisy looked concerned. Then, through Tyson's considerable jaws, there appeared what seemed to be the pelt of a large spotted cat, possibly a serval or an overgrown genet. Covered with slobber, it flopped slimily onto the floor like a mottled octopus. I regarded this phenomenon with some astonishment. Then Daisy gave a great hoot. 'So that's where they were! I looked everywhere for them! Searched high and low. Couldn't find them anywhere and I knew I had taken them off the night before.' *They* were Daisy's maxi-size leopard-spotted knickers! Tyson, deprived of his evening meal, and feeling a bit peckish, had snacked on his mistress's gargantuan underwear. Swallowed them whole.

Moses, lurking in the background, now appeared with a pair of tongs, and bore the offending garment away. I never did ask what became of it, but rumour had it that he had the knickers washed and then flogged them to a second-hand emporium for a modest sum.

The operation to deprive Tyson of his manhood went off without a hitch, but I never did ask what Daisy was, or was not, wearing beneath her kaftan.

Chapter Eleven

DEBTS AND DANCING

Late afternoon. Tristan Voorspuy was on the phone.

'Hugh, can you come out and deal with one of my safari horses? He ran into a tree and now there's something long and fleshy hanging out of his flank. Don't particularly like the look of it.'

'Right. I'm on my way.'

Tristan was a safari guide running horseback safaris in the Mara for well heeled guests, mostly from the UK and the US He was somewhat of a legend, having had numerous close encounters with hippo, elephant and lion as he led his entourage across the plains and through the thickets of the reserve. I had had one or two personal brushes with buffalo and elephant while scaling Kenya's mountains but I was a mere tyro compared to Tristan, who was in the professional league when it came to courting danger. His svelte and lissom wife Cindy was no better, forever diving into half empty swimming pools and being tossed off horses as she did battle on the polo field or tackling impossibly high fences on her hunter. To find one or other hobbling around on crutches or laid up with broken ribs raised no eyebrows.

Both were now somewhat lined and leathery from a surfeit of sun and alcohol.

Tristan had lost most of his hair and walked like a spavined nag with a short tripping gait, the legacy of a compound fracture of his tibia following a fall in the Mara. But once aboard his favourite steed he was a veritable centaur. He finally met his quietus when he and horse were shot dead by a Pokot bandit. Against sane advice he had set forth to investigate the burning of a house on his Laikipia ranch after it had been overrun by marauding invaders. Typical Tristan.

I was glad to leave the surgery. For the past hour or so I had been phoning clients who had not paid their bills, overall a fruitless and frustrating exercise.

Either they did not answer their phones – the majority – or they made promises they had no intention of keeping. One Simon Mwangi was a case in point – he had rushed his dog to the surgery one Saturday afternoon, telling me that it had had a confrontation with a larger dog. I was sitting in my car at the time, engine running, mind in neutral, looking forward to an hour or two of Egyptian p.t. after the rigours of the past week, aided by a beaker or three of cold Tusker. He brought the dog into the surgery, and placed it on the table. I gave the animal a casual, passing glance as he did so, noting without comment that it had only three legs. Mwangi returned to his car, which I had observed was a model considerably newer than mine, and came back carrying the dog's fourth leg, which by now was rather past its sell-by-date.

Closer examination revealed that the entire foreleg, from scapula downwards, had been torn off. By fortuitous chance the main artery was still intact. So, instead of reclining in semi soporific state in my hammock, I spent the next few hours repairing the massive wounds left when the leg was so untimely ripped from its normal attachment.

During the following weeks I dressed and treated the wounds and the dog made a near miraculous recovery. But this was a minor miracle compared with that required to extract money, *my* money, from Mr Mwangi who, though quick to rush his dog to me for treatment, was in no such hurry to pay his dues.

Neither was Lettice Grigoryan, one of the infernal legion of chancers who wormed their way into the country on the pretext of being experts in running an orphanage. What qualifications she had for such a position was debatable and what benefits her wretched charges derived from her ministrations even more so. She was from West Virginia, and was small, bubbly, dark haired and attractive. She had given birth to five children in rapid succession with ease and with no apparent effect on her curvaceous figure. Her husband was Armenian, swarthy, squat and monosyllabic. It was a case of Beauty and the Beast. Later, to public consternation and presumably also that of the Armenian, she declared herself to be a lesbian and had been so all the time.

On the small acreage of land which she shared with the Armenian, her five home-schooled offspring and a handful of orphans, was a stable and a pigsty wherein dwelt a brace of nondescript horses and a trio of pigs. One day I received a call from the lady of the manor to the effect that one of the horses was unwell and would I attend?

The road to the property was not a good one. But, in the interests of animal welfare, I did my best to ignore the cacophony of rattles and bangs as my tortured vehicle lurched from pothole to rut and back again.

The affected horse was large and bony and despite being ill was markedly antisocial. Added to this, the owner was terrified of it. She stood well back as I approached the animal, a gaunt, bay mare, held by a nervous looking syce. Of the Armenian, there was no sign.

As soon as I got within a few feet of the mare she laid her ears back and lunged at my person. Then she pivoted on her forelegs and lashed out with her hind legs, missing me by inches.

I turned to Mrs. Grigoryan. 'She's not very friendly, is she? Do you ride her?' She tittered. 'Oh no! Ah just lets her run wild, just like my children, Ah don't believe in restraint.'

I rolled my eyes but kept my peace. Diagnosis would be tricky if I was unable examine the patient. At this point the mare decided to lie down.

Could this be colic, I thought?

'Is she passing dung?' I asked the lady. 'Oh yes, plenty, she passed a big load this mornin.'

'Well, I want to do a rectal exam to check.' Mrs. Grigoryan gave a scornful laugh.

'Moses,' I said to my assistant, 'can you bring the twitch from the car?'

'Oh,' said Grigoryan, 'she's a head tosser, paranoid about needles and she cain't breathe through her left nostril. That's how Ah got her real cheap from Nairobi.'

Another strange Appalachian laugh. Any moment now I'll be hearing hill billy banjos.

Anything else you haven't told me? I thought.

Moses returned with the twitch. 'Sorry, Moses. We cain't – I mean – we can't put a twitch on this bitch's nose otherwise she'll fall down, unable to breathe, and she's a head tosser to boot. Can you get a bottle of xylazine. We're going to have to sedate her somehow.' I didn't add that I felt like putting a twitch on the Grigoryan nozzle and twisting hard, really hard.

'Right,' I said to the syce, 'take her into the stable.'

To Mrs. Grigoryan, 'Can I have a bucket of water please and some soap?'

'You want cold or cold? Cos we ain't got hot.' She seemed to regard this as excruciatingly funny and burst into hysterical laughter.

Hmm, I thought, we've got a right one here. Straight out of 'Deliverance.'

I filled the syringe with a moderate dose of the sedative. 'Now, Moses, grab a handful of neck skin while I try to get the twitch on her ear.' Moses did as instructed, the mare threw her head up but I grabbed her left ear and hung on grimly while she tried to turn and bite. I fed the loop of the twitch over my hand and turned the handle until it was good and tight.

The mare stood still, rigid and tense. But now was the critical moment – would she stand for the injection? I gave the handle of the twitch to Moses. 'Hold firm with both hands. If that gets loose and she shakes her head, someone, probably me, may get brained.'

I scratched the mare's neck. This scratching can quieten certain animals. I wasn't sure if it would work here, but any port in a storm. Carefully I raised the jugular and pushed a fine needle into the vein. To my astonishment the mare did nothing. I attached the syringe and fed in the sedative.

Moses removed the twitch and waited. Three minutes later the mare's head was drooping, we turned her round, I did a rectal and did not have to go in more than a few inches before I encountered a massive large bowel impaction.

I turned to Mrs. Grigoryan and gave her the diagnosis. 'Now,' I said, 'we have to give her a laxative in the form of liquid paraffin, by stomach tube, five litres, which I have in my car, in order to shift what's in there. The dung you saw must have by-passed the mass. Usually one lot of laxative does the trick, but if it doesn't I will have to come back and repeat the procedure.'

I could see her lips moving as she reckoned up the dollars and her eyes narrowing with backwoods cunning.

I fed the tube up the mare's right nostril and she accepted the procedure without objection, but I kept the twitch on her ear until all of the liquid paraffin had been poured into her stomach. Having got this far I did not want anything going wrong at this stage. As I withdrew the tube she reared and lashed out with her forelegs. But the job was done.

'OK,' I said, 'now, she must be stabled without any food until she passes lots of dung. No food, not even straw and no bedding on the floor which she might eat. Just plain water. Nothing else. And if she hasn't passed dung by tomorrow I need to know. I will have to come back and repeat what I've done today. What's in there is like concrete. This has happened because she hasn't been drinking enough. I know the weather's been dry but you must make sure she gets plenty of water. And once she has recovered add molasses and vegetable oil to her feed. She does get feed doesn't she?'

'Naw, we just lets 'em forage for themselves.'

'Well, cut some green grass and add some molasses to it. Because this may recur if you don't.'

As I left I saw a dark, furtive figure lurking by the pigsty. It was the Armenian.

Sure enough I had to return the following day and risk life and limb once again. And sure enough six weeks later the same tiresome scenario was repeated. On both occasions the mare recovered. Ten months later I still had not been paid.

Then there was Mr Silas Kaka, District Commissioner in Muranga, wearer of the post-colonial sola topee and the brass-buttoned tunic, the recipient of a princely salary and whose perquisites far exceeded anything I could aspire to and who sent in his German Shepherd bitch for my attention. Mr Kaka took the view that his exalted position demanded that, like a medieval robber baron, underlings and serfs such as myself, should toil on his behalf gratis, taking his cue from his political superiors who held similar opinions. The given history was that the dog had been unable to stand and, as she staggered into the surgery, I could see why. Hanging from her posterior abdomen was the largest mammary tumour it had ever been my misfortune to encounter. It was football sized. I looked at it and thought – there is no way to remove this monster. Thus I informed the subordinate who had brought the dog to my surgery. Mr Kaka in the meantime was lording it over his distant Muranga constituency. I phoned him and told him we either euthanase the dog or make what I assumed would be a futile attempt to excise the mass. He opted for surgery and asked how much the operation would cost. In the 'West' this would be of the order of several hundred guineas. Here in Africa, outside of the hallowed halls of the Aid Industry and Diplomacy, such sums would be regarded with a mixture of disbelief and derision. So I quoted a sum which, modest as it was by western standards, did not prevent Mr Kaka demanding a discount. If I had any sense I should have asked for double and then perhaps, perhaps, I might, just might, have been paid enough to cover my overheads.

Three hours of stress and strain, blood on the floor and on me and the grotesque mass was removed and the huge resulting wound closed.

The bitch recovered but I only received partial payment for my efforts. Some cynics might say – well Hugh, if you must live in a banana republic, expect bananas in payment.

I must have phoned Solomon Nderitu about twenty times. He was the proud possessor of a South African Boerboel attack dog, a canine of enormous size, strength and ferocity. Many countries have banned the import of this breed, for good reason. The dog had developed a large salivary cyst or mucocele, which hung unpleasantly below its left mandible. Due to its immense size Mr Nderitu was unable to transport the animal to my surgery and so I drove the eight miles to his place, anaesthetised the dog, loaded it into the back of my vehicle, and drove it back to my surgery, where I operated to excise the cyst, an exercise which taxed my knowledge of salivary gland anatomy to the limit. Dissection of the cyst lining and removal of the affected salivary glands is a tedious and lengthy business where close attention has to be taken to ensure damage is not inflicted on vital nerves and blood vessels.

When I was finished we re-loaded the sleepy patient into the rear of my vehicle and re-drove it home. Ten days later, after necessary tranquillization, I removed the sutures. The Boerboel, aptly named Chaka Zulu, made what the textbooks call an uneventful recovery. Would that all patients did the same.

Solomon, in his wisdom, paid half of his bill. Three years later, I was on the phone, in a fruitless endeavour to persuade him to settle the balance. I regarded such clients with justifiable contempt.

So it was with gritted teeth that I left the surgery and headed through town in the direction of Tristan's establishment at Rongai, some 35 kilometres away. Nakuru now had short stretches of dual carriageway on both sides of the town, constructed at the expense of the former lovely avenues of jacaranda trees, which had been ruthlessly hacked down in the name of progress. But at least, I thought, now one could motor in relative safety without the risk of meeting an oncoming vehicle with some power driven maniac hunched vengefully over the wheel. I pulled onto the highway. Unlike in Europe, in Nakuru it was normal to join the dual carriageway in the fast lane, the sort of thing which made driving in Kenya such high adventure. Before I could move into the slow lane a bus howled past, overtaking me on the left, bearing the slogan 'Royal Brains School.' Wow, I thought, fancy having that on your academic CV.

I overtook a tuk tuk – his slogan read 'I Was Born Intelligent But Education Has Ruined Me.' Perhaps he had attended the Royal Brains School. I passed 'Harmless City Boy' – fat chance I thought – when I saw something coming towards me at high speed. It looked like a great cloud of dust but it was moving in my direction – and fast. Out of the storm of dust appeared a car, but upside down and hurtling with colossal velocity straight at me. Time seemed to slow down. I glanced in my side mirror. There was a car behind me, but better to be hit from behind than face almost certain death from a head-on collision with this airborne unguided missile. I wrenched the steering wheel to the left as the inverted vehicle shot past me at head height and vanished, probably into Eternity. I looked to my left. The following car, which I had fully expected to ram me in the rear, had also taken violent evasive action, but, unlike me, had run out of road and had bounced at high speed down the grassy embankment and had come to a stop with the bemused and shaken occupants sitting like zombies in their seats.

I was more than a little shaken myself. The quick and the dead I thought. Whoever was in that car, which must have been travelling at tremendous speed in the opposite lane when it had hit the central reservation and had done a half barrel roll, was both quick and almost certainly dead – as I might have been.

As I pressed on at a psychologically enforced reduced pace, another similar incident sprang to mind. Coming back from Gilgil one day I was ascending a modest hill when I saw a large lorry approaching down the hill. Overtaking the lorry and bouncing ever higher in the air was one of its massive double rear wheels. Very soon it was way ahead of the lorry and making enormous and increasingly enormous bounds, until they were several times the height of my puny vehicle. I had heard of one luckless Asian youth who had been killed when a runaway lorry wheel crushed him and his car, and in my mind's eye I could see Charon beckoning me to the shores of the River Styx. But not yet. I yawed my car to right and to left but the wheel seemed magnetized to my machine and no matter which way I turned it seemed to be making a beeline for my windscreen. Its velocity was increasing the further down the hill it bounced, but so was the height of its bounces and, *mirabile dictu*, it gave one final colossal leap and cleared my car by several feet and, like the barrel-rolling roadster, vanished from my ken.

The track to Tristan's neck of the woods was drawing nigh and I dropped several gears in anticipation. On a good day it took 30 minutes to cover the 30 kilometres of tarmac to the start of rock and rut and another 30 minutes to complete the last three. But it was always worth it. The Voorspuys were hospitality personified. Their parties were legendary and whenever I had occasion to visit I would always be invited to partake of coffee, lunch, tiffin, or gin and tonic, depending on the time of day or night. If my car broke down they would lend me one of theirs. They were a wonderful throwback to an earlier more civilized era when there was time to converse in pleasant surroundings and no one was glaring fixedly at their smartphone or fondling and caressing their ipad. They had 80 riding horses on the land they leased from Deloraine Estate and as a result I was often called in to deal with a multitude of ailments. Lacerations, lion bites, colics, rabies, biliary fever, trypanosomiasis, castrations, lameness, fractures, tumours, and more, all had come my way. I trundled as fast as the road surface would allow towards the distant stables. I always thought that the Voorspuys left the road in this state in order to give their clients a small frisson of wild Africa before they met the real thing.

From the long hanging tendrils of an avenue of gum trees male weaver birds were hard at work nest building, frantically chattering and diving down to collect grass fronds to add to what they hoped would impress a receptive female. Suddenly they all fell silent. I looked up. A grey harrier hawk was slowly flapping through the trees, looking for nests to plunder. But he was too early. No eggs had as yet been laid. He would return. Meanwhile he went on his way, searching for other prey.

The road bent to the right and crossed below a small, reed fringed dam. In the shallows stood a heron, immobile, patient, watching, waiting. A pair of African pochard swam quietly in the shadow of the sedges. Dragonflies hovered above the pewter surface. A hammerkop pottered along the margin of the dam, probing and prodding. A small green snake slithered along a weedy ditch, reared a sharp-eyed head, and, startled by the car, vanished. The heron rose on great smoky wings, long thin neck bent into a sinuous reptilian curve, and with easy grace drifted to where he could contemplate the waters without being disturbed by noisy passing vehicles.

I pressed on, the track now more pothole than anything else. A last bouldery uphill section, tree-scattered paddocks to right and left, full of grazing horses, and then everything opened out and there, across acres of manicured lawn stood the most impressive colonial mansion in the Rift Valley. Deloraine House was built in the 1920s by Lord Francis Scott, an early pioneer, to accommodate himself, his wife and two daughters. It was a vast two-storey structure, brimming with en suite bedrooms, an enormous lounge with a fireplace big enough to roast an ox, a huge dining room whose walls were hung with grim portraits of ancient humourless ancestors, a verandah graced by a table long enough to seat twenty for lunch, and pleasantly lichened steps leading down to the croquet lawn. Imposing pillars supported an upper story verandah from which guests, gin and tonic in hand, could admire the view over the Rift Valley.

Behind the house rose the forested heights of Mt. Loltiani, once the haunt of rhino, bongo and buffalo, and still visited by the occasional elephant. Here rider clients could ride through the butterfly-strewn glades before venturing to the more exciting environs of the Maasai Mara or the plains of Laikipia.

After the death of Lord Francis, the house was lived in by his elder daughter Pam, who ran the estate, before selling most of the land to an African company, leaving her with the house and an acreage of land. After her death in 1992 the house lay empty. Colonial farm houses, whether large and opulent, as in this case, or small and functional, are not regarded as an asset by prospective African purchasers of the land on which they stand. It is the land itself which is valuable. So, in most instances, these dwellings of the former white masters and mistresses, were either left empty to moulder and decay, or were used to accommodate chickens, goats or squatters, when they also mouldered, only marginally less quickly. Such would have been the fate of Deloraine House had not Cindy and Tristan arrived on the scene with their innovative Offbeat Safaris, and peopled the premises with the rich and the famous, the bold and the beautiful. Without them Deloraine House would have been one with Nineveh and Tyre, relegated to the dustbin of colonial history.

So I gave silent thanks as I lurched past the croquet lawn and the proud buttresses and edged my way to the stables, where horse and owner were waiting.

The stables looked as though they had not been touched by the hand of man since they were built in the 1920s. Sided with wooden slabs and roofed with corrugated iron, they might not have passed muster in some countries but here they melded perfectly into the African environment.

Tristan, wearing a mustard-coloured shirt, which might have been a hand-down from Lord Francis himself, and a pair of corduroy bags of the sort favoured by Bertie Wooster, was standing on the uneven flagstones, holding a brown gelding, from whose left side was hanging a length of what resembled a bloodstained sheet.

'Afternoon Hugh,' said Tristan, 'glad to see you. Tom Tom here had a bit if a contretemps with a tree and as you can see something nasty is trying to get out.'

I peered at Tom Tom's flank as I exchanged pleasantries with his owner.

The eventrated material protruded from a hole between the last ribs. It hung about two feet from the exit. The gelding did not appear to be unduly concerned about having parts of his innards leaving the comfortable confines of his abdomen, but I knew that this length of tissue was like the Dutch boy's finger in the dyke, holding back the North Sea, and that it was preventing other more vital parts from exiting.

'This,' I said to Tristan, 'is part of the omentum, the covering of the guts. What we have to do is to trim it to a manageable size and push it back inside and stitch the hole before anything else comes out.'

'Right, I hope you can get that done soon. I'm expecting a group of clients out on an afternoon ride to rock up at any moment. Americans and excitable Spaniards. I don't want them milling around and seeing what I don't want them to see. We try to give the impression that we're in control.'

I thought this a bit rich, seeing that Tristan seemed to be permanently out of control and doing his utmost to court danger and possible injury at every turn. 'OK, I'll do my best. I'll put in some local and see how we get on.'

We didn't. I injected anaesthetic into the surrounding tissues and the base of the omentum and cut away a good length of tissue. But as I began to attempt to return what was left to the abdomen, Tom Tom lashed forwards with his left hind leg, hitting me an almighty crack on the knee.

An electric current of pain rushed up my leg, reached my brain and expressed itself in frank Anglo Saxon. 'OK, Tom Tom, you bastard, time for sedation.' I hobbled to the car, cursing myself for not having sedated the horse in the first place.

Before I had time to fill the syringe and return to the patient I heard the clip clop of hooves and in no time a posse of riders was on the scene, gasping and expostulating at the sight of Tom Tom with what looked like his entrails dangling from his abdomen.

'Madre mia,' exclaimed one swarthy hidalgo, and 'Waal ye just look at thaat,' from a sombreroed American. 'Oh I feel quite sick,' gasped a New World matron and 'I think I might faint,' from a tight-jodhpured blonde. By now Tom Tom and a jaw-clenched Tristan were surrounded by a goggle-eyed mob of voyeurs, eager, nay, desperate, to view a real life man and beast, life and death drama, in the heart of Darkest Africa. A Coliseum in miniature.

I limped manfully back to the fray, the crowd parted, and there was a moment of silence, a bit like that in the Plaza de Toros when the matador lines up to deliver the coup de grace on the waiting bull. Tom

Tom, to my relief, took his injection on the chin. A slight tremor, no more.

A few minutes later, his head drooped, his lower lip hung slackly open and he shifted slightly on a hind leg. I thought about shaving the area adjacent to the wound but decided that the risk of introducing hair into the abdomen was greater than swabbing and sterilizing unshaved skin and hair.

Now, with Tom Tom relaxed and, I hoped, compliant, it was fairly easy to return the truncated omentum whence it came. Stitching the wound was considerably more difficult. It lay between two ribs and was a deep and narrow cleft, bounded by hard bony walls and cornices of dense subcutaneous tissue. By the time I had finished the crowd of onlookers had drifted down to the house to fortify themselves with gins and tonics, and to discuss the peculiarities of life in the tropics.

I swabbed the wound and gave Tom Tom a shot of antibiotic and tetanus antitoxin.

'Why is it,' said Tristan, 'that this sort of thing always seems to happen when there are clients around?'

I recalled the time when I had been called out late one afternoon to examine a brain-damaged horse. One of many such incidents permanently etched in red letters on my own long suffering brain. As on this occasion a group of clients had gone out for a ride. They were returning as the sun was beginning to set. Riding into the sun their shadows stretched long and narrow behind them. They crossed a field, negotiated a gate and began the final uphill stretch of paddock to the stables, shading their eyes against the searchlight glare. At the top of the field a group of horses was grazing. Horses often tend to bond closely with others in their group and can become inseparable. One mare, being ridden by an English client, realizing that her friend, another mare, was in the same field, whinnied. The whinny was heard by the mare at the top of the field who set off at a full gallop towards the group of riders. Thundering down the field she had the sun behind her. Those at the bottom were blinded by the sun, unable to see clearly the approaching tornado.

The mare crashed at full speed, head to head with one of the ascending horses. The ridden horse was killed on the spot, the rider thrown, and lucky not to suffer injury. The other mare was severely concussed.

With luck and massive doses of intravenous steroids, she recovered, but it was a close-run thing.

I bade Tristan *bon soir* and set off for home.

That night one of his clients, medicated on Larium, a malaria prophylactic, and whose noxious effects on the central nervous system are now well-known, stepped out of an upstairs room, fell 25 feet onto a concreted patio, and suffered permanent neck-down paralysis.

Two months later Berna and I were invited by Cindy and Tristan to the Deloraine Hunt Ball. The theme was 'Leather, Feather, Fur or Spur.' Although this thematic conundrum taxed our imagination it seemed not to have been a problem for our hosts. Tristan appeared as an Argentinian gaucho, resplendent in leather chaps, poncho, boots and spurs. Whereas Tristan had up-dressed, Cindy, in typical fashion, had done the opposite, clad, if that is the correct terminology, in wisps of feathers and strategically sited tufts of fur, looking like a scantily-clad Queen of the Night. The ball was a tremendous success. A jazz band played, the food was sublime, the dance floor was packed with revellers arrayed in a fantastic display of outrageous costumes and the drinks flowed as though the Voorspuys had struck an alcoholic gusher in their garden.

Berna and I departed the still active bacchanalia at 4am. In those days one could bowl through the night on empty highways, unimpeded by rapacious police road blocks and homicidal tanker drivers. No more – the juggernaut of progress has now morphed driving on Kenya's roads into an unpleasant form of Russian roulette, where sudden death, injury and mutilation lurk with every passing mile.

The following morning those spending the night at Deloraine House and who were still capable of standing were encouraged to participate in the ritual Hunt. One woman fell off her horse before the Hunt had even begun, breaking her thumb, and was carted off unconscious. Hugo Johnstone, an amateur enthusiast, in a state of post-ball exuberance, rode into an unsuspecting tree, badly dislocating a knee and effectively terminating his riding career.

It seemed to me that, where the Voorspuys were concerned, it wasn't really necessary to go all the way to the Mara to get your kicks.

Chapter Twelve

A Picnic with the Pokot

Dick Crawford, the choleric proprietor of Blue Cross Kennels, stood at the surgery door, quietly grinding his teeth. Tooth grinding was something Dick did quite often. Short fused and impatient, it took little to send him into paroxysms of unbridled rage. The merest remark or action, especially by his African staff, would be enough to set Dick off into full blown, eye-popping fury.

'Hello, Dick,' I said, 'what's the problem…I say, what's happened to your ear?' For Dick's right ear, normally a prominent protruding organ, was now about three times its normal size, swollen, a horrid purple colour and was sticking out at right angles to his head like a chunk of badly sliced beetroot.

'Colbeck!' Dick bellowed, 'that poison dwarf Noel Colbeck! Brings in his pug for kennelling. He's got three of them. Brings in the bitch as she's on heat. Hands her to me. Doesn't say that she's partial to ears. Next thing I know she's latched onto my right ear like a bloody limpet, worrying it like a terrier with a rat. Colbeck just stood there, laughing. It's a miracle there's anything left!'

Later I heard that Dick had been somewhat elastic with the truth. Dick had taken the dog from Colbeck and, being Dick, who regarded dogs as more human than humans, had lifted it up for a friendly nuzzle. The pug, alarmed at this unwarranted display of affection, had snapped at the nearest protrusion, which happened to be Dick's ear.

'Very sorry about that, Dick,' I said, 'what can I do for you?'

'I've got old Ma Royston's basset hound, Boris, in the back of the pick-up. He's got a large swelling at the angle of his jaw and he's off his food.'

'Right,' I said, 'wheel him in.'

Boris was large and ill tempered. You could have tied his ears in a knot under his chin, but I refrained from doing so when he curled his lip and bared a large set of yellowing teeth. While Dick made soothing noises I prepared a sedative. Dick held Boris in a half-nelson while I shot the drug into the dog's ample hindquarters. We waited for the sedative to take effect. The phone rang.

'It's for you Dick,' I said, 'it's Sally. Something about a black labrador.'

Sally was Dick's right-hand woman at his kennels.

Dick lifted the receiver to his left ear. I could hear Sally's small tinny voice – high pitched and urgent, as though an infant was shouting down a very long narrow tube. 'What?' Dick roared, 'escaped? Speak up! How? When? Who?'

Sally squeaked a response.

Dick smashed the phone down. Later I found the bakelite to have sustained a notable war wound in the form of a long, life-threatening zig zag crack, yet another casualty in the service of animal-kind. 'Trouble, Dick?' I solicitously inquired. 'Trouble? Trouble? I'll say there's trouble! And there's going to be even more trouble for that arch moron, head kennel man Karau. A prize, pedigree black labrador has escaped! Came in last night from Nairobi. Put into a kennel behind three closed doors. So how many doors does that idiot leave open when he comes in to do the cleaning?'

'Three?' I asked.

'Yes, three!' Dick roared. 'Three!' 'Why?' I asked. 'I don't knoooow!' With that Dick leapt into the air, fists clenched, landing with a crash that rattled the bottles on their shelves and had the now somnolent Boris jerking in alarm.

'I'm sorry,' I said lamely. 'Not half as sorry as that bastard's going to be when I get my hands on him.'

But I knew that Dick would let him off with a slap on the wrist, especially when the escapee was re-captured. Dick never sacked any of his retinue of incompetent hangers-on. And later, when Dick joined the grim legion of those attacked by panga wielding thugs, was left brain damaged and unable to control his own affairs, his former servants were among the gathering ghouls who battened on his declining presence. Even following his demise the squabbling and fighting over Dick's land continued for years. Good deeds are never left unpunished. But at the moment Dick was hale and hearty and in full cry.

'OK, Dick, I think we're ready to deal with Boris,' I said, between threats of garrotting and bastinado to Karau's person.

Boris now lay prone, stretched out on his side. I examined the swelling, which was the size of a large grapefruit, round and tense. 'Probably an abscess,' I said to Dick, 'let's put a needle in and see what comes out.'

I shaved a small area where the swelling seemed to be coming to a head, swabbed it with spirit and injected a small bleb of local anaesthetic under the skin, waited for a few minutes and pushed a large needle into the centre of the mass.

Greenish yellow pus emerged from the hub of the needle. 'OK, we're going to now cut down into the abscess to allow drainage. I'll just do a bit more shaving and insert some more local and we're ready.'

The abscess was much denser than I expected. I had to cut my way through a good inch of solid muscle before I hit oil. And when I did it came out like a horizontal geyser and under the most impressive pressure. Unfortunately Dick was in the immediate line of fire and the evil smelling jet of bilious fluid hit him in mid short, soaking his crotch and trickling down his legs.

Dick uttered a great roar – aaarrgh! – and rushed out of the door and into the street where I could hear him vomiting into the gutter.

For years afterwards Dick would bring up this incident in conversation, implying that I had deliberately directed the pustular jet in his personal direction. Nothing would convince him that it was a mere accident.

❦❦❦❦❦

That evening as I lay in the bath, soaking in the chocolate coloured water, sipping a soothing beer, listening to the hum of mosquitos and to the rats stampeding across the ceiling, watching tadpoles and small fish emerging from the cold tap, I decided that it was time to do battle with Mother Nature for a change and not with such as Boris and Dick, guiltless though they were of any premeditated malice. A stress-free break was indicated, communing with the innocent elements and with the unsophisticated, friendly inhabitants of the hills and valleys.

To this end I phoned fellow mountaineer and Nimrod of the crags, the doughty Graeme Watson, in whose company much sweat and blood had been shed in pursuit of far flung summits across the length and breadth of the country. Graeme was stoutly built. More important was his stout resolve. No matter the odds, no matter the difficulty, the question of turning back never arose in Graeme's mind. While weaklings and those of a nervous disposition fell by the wayside, or turned back, Graeme would forge ahead. His rallying cry was always 'press on!'

Graeme suggested that we go for Tenus, a remote mountain in Kara Pokot, near the Uganda border. This was an area attractively untouched by modernity. A rugged range of summits, the Kara Suk hills, eight in number, stretched for 40 miles from south to north, parallel to the border. The inhabitants still clung to their ancient ways and tribal traditions, and were at odds with their neighbours, the Turkana to the north east and with the Sebei to the west in Uganda. The climate was warm and many of the people, apart from their weaponry and the accoutrements of the chase, went pleasingly unclad. It sounded idyllic, and I signed on the dotted line.

Accompanying us on our foray would be David Hirst, who worked at the British Council in Nairobi. David was a scholarly sort of chap, more used to the hushed, cerebral environs of pseudo-academia than to the rough and tumble, the beer and skittles, of up-country Kenya. But he was fit, friendly, active and as keen as mustard to break in his boots on virgin territory. We assured him that he was guaranteed to have an exciting time. Just how exciting even we could not imagine.

Graeme and David met at our house early one morning in time for breakfast into which they both tucked with gusto, having departed Nairobi with empty stomachs soon after dawn. Having satisfied the inner man, we bade Berna and the girls farewell and set off in Graeme's battle-hardened 4WD Trooper.

By mid-afternoon we had surmounted the western wall of the Rift Valley, had bowled across the Uasin Gishu plateau, former stamping ground of Afrikaner settlers, long since departed to Suid Afrika, crawled through the unlovely environs of the town of Eldoret and were now in Trans Nzoia, having crossed the Nzoia River by means of Moi's Bridge, so named after Kenya's second president. This always seemed a bit of a steal to me. The original name was Hoey's Bridge, named after Cecil Hoey, an early pioneer settler, who built a log bridge across the river so that he and his team of oxen could gain access to the fertile, untapped lands on the other side. As far as I could ascertain President Daniel arap Moi had built no bridges across the river.

Ahead of us now rose the huge bulk of Mt. Elgon, Ol Doinyo Ilgoon, the 'mountain shaped like a breast,' albeit one rather past its prime. At its base squatted Kitale, whose main claim to fame was its previous importance as an early staging post on the Arab slaving route between Uganda and Bagamoyo on the coast of Tanganyika, where dhows waited to ship the captives to Arabia and beyond. Being close to the border the slaves at this point were probably still in reasonable shape and liable to escape, so they were shackled at night in a ring around what is now the Kitale club. Once into the territory now called Kenya their chances of escape and survival diminished with every passing mile.

During the colonial era the area was intensively farmed, the soil being incredibly fertile, producing an amazing variety of crops, from apples and pears, to wheat and maize. Cattle grew fat and it was indeed a land of milk and honey. The settlers also flourished exceedingly and grew fat from the fruits of their labours and from the toil of the former owners of the land, who, having formerly lived a life of sunlit tribal harmony, now laboured beneath the iron heel of the white usurper. The settlers partied and drank in their clubs and mansions, exchanged wives and husbands and generally lived a life of high society. Then suddenly it was all over, the settlers, apart from a few sad hangers on, were no more and the land reverted to the tropical paradise it had been before the unwanted Arab and European invasion. Pondering upon these events we tarried not, but sped onwards, passing the Saiwa Swamp, where the near mythical sitatunga antelope lurked amid the reeds and rushes. With its elongated hooves it was reputed to be able, like the basilisk lizard of Central America, to walk on water. Whatever its aquatic capabilities, it lived up to its mythical reputation for we saw no sign of it.

Away to our right rose the distant mass of the Cheranganis, large, lumpy, mountains, forested at their base, rising to moorland at over 11,000 feet and peppered with Marakwet homesteads. To our left the land sloped down towards the valley of the river Suam, which flowed out of Uganda from that country's share of Mt. Elgon. The river's north easterly course brought it to the Turkwell Gorge after which it became the Turkwell river whose final destination was Lake Turkana. At the gorge a hydro-electric dam had been built. French-financed and mired in controversy over corruption and massive kick-backs, it failed dismally to live up to expectations, took years to fill up, deprived downstream residents of vital water and delivered a fraction of the power forecast by its Gallic constructors.

Once through the gorge the river was in Turkana territory, but to the west the land was occupied by their ancestral foes, the Pokot. Although to the casual observer the tribes appeared similar, in reality they differed considerably. Both were belligerent in nature. Both eschewed the effete European clothing worn by lesser tribes to the south, preferring either to stride forth as nature intended or to merely wear a short strip of black cloth around the loins. On both sides the men had no compunction about slaughtering men, women and children of the opposite tribe, using spears and guns to brutal effect. After all to kill women and children was to reduce the procreative potential of your enemy. They were like terrestrial Vikings, bent on rape and pillage.

Neither tribe grew crops and the people lived off their flocks of sheep and goats, and their herds of cattle and camels. The women wore tanned goat skins and braided their oiled hair into striking braids. Piled necklaces of blue beads were a feminine characteristic of both tribes. The men affected mud pack chignons. These were woven into their own hair and were often dyed red or purple with natural dyes. Into the dried mud were inserted cows' teats from which ostrich feathers jauntily waved. Lip plugs, wrist and finger knives for easy gouging completed the effect. Not for them were the beads, mirrors, and trinkets, the elaborate hair styles, the red ochre and striped football socks of the effeminate-looking Samburu and Maasai. The general effect was sombre and black was the predominant colour. Whatever they were, they were not dandies. The passage of the occasional tourist did not stimulate toothy smiles or friendly waves. Rather the opposite. Strangers were regarded with suspicion, ignored or regarded with studied scorn.

But despite their superficial similarities the Pokot – or Suk, as their northerly neighbours disparagingly called them – and the Turkana were different. The Pokot circumcised. The Turkana did not. The former spoke a form of Kalenjin. The latter spoke Turkana, a guttural tongue quite unlike the language of the Pokot. The Turkana were the more numerous tribe. Of the two, perhaps due to their geographical situation, the Pokot were on the whole probably the more aggressive, at odds with the Samburu to the east, the Njemps to the south, the Turkana to the north and even on occasion with their Marakwet and Elgeyo Kalenjin neighbours.

So any venture into Pokot land was accompanied by an understandable touch of apprehension.

For the moment however, we could relax and enjoy the passing scene, which was green and lush and easy on the eye. The maize stood ten feet high, the cobs were full, the peasantry smiling and content.

Weaver birds were hard at work nest building and chattering – at least the males were. The females observed and inspected and discussed the various merits of each nest and its builder. As fellow males we commiserated with their lot.

'Poor sods,' said David. 'Look at them. Sweating their little guts out while the females just sit back and pick and choose from the cream.'

'Still,' said Graeme, 'it's not as bad as that female spider which eats the male after copulation!'

'What a way to go,' I said.

'Yes,' said David, 'but only if it was a quick crunch and not a slow munch!'

'I read somewhere,' said Graeme, 'that the female octopus is 40,000 times bigger than the male.'

'I know people like that!' laughed David.

This vital subject absorbed our undivided attention for the next half an hour.

Makutano was drawing nigh, and the road which dropped steeply down into the land of the Pokot. Unseen to our right was the township of Kapenguria where Jomo Kenyatta, first president of the republic, together with close comrades, stood trial for offences against the colonial government.

I blinked, and Makutano, a collection of ramshackle wooden shacks and untidy hovels, with a few mamas selling produce beside the road, was behind us and Graeme was wrestling the Trooper into a sharp left hand bend and the start of the precipitous Kongelai escarpment. The road was steep shifting gravel, the sides thick green bush, alive with the birds for which the area was famous. Recent rain had cleared the air of dust. Far to the north-west, across the border in Uganda, the jagged ramparts of Kadam rose above a level sea of bush. To the west the huge mass of Mt. Elgon, half obscured by cloud, filled the landscape.

Directly to our north, 35 miles as the eagle flew, sharp and upright as a Crusader's blade, a vertical spear in the luminous air, stood the spire of Kapchoket. The highland equatorial light seemed to act like a magnifying glass so that objects, huts, hills and rivers ten miles away, looked almost close enough to touch. So it was with Kapchoket. From our vantage point on the Kongelai escarpment it seemed that we might reach it in half an hour. But it was almost two hours before we passed below its lofty pinnacle. This trick of light was all very well when one was snug, if not comfortable, inside a vehicle. It was not so when one was on foot, slogging across miles of endless plains, or slithering down interminable, boulder-strewn, knee crunching slopes, with the tiny tent of the far distant camp seeming to recede with every dry-mouthed, dehydrating step.

'That looks worth climbing,' I said.

'Yes,' said Graeme, 'I climbed it with Paul Clarke. 'Just about killed me. There's a dodgy exposed bit at the top where one false move and you would fall several hundred feet. We had no climbing rope so we used the tow rope from the Trooper instead. It's in the back there somewhere.'

'Will we need it tomorrow?' asked David nervously.

'I hope not,' laughed Graeme.

Our respect for Graeme edged up a notch. Bulky though he was, he was game.

Once his mind was set on an objective almost nothing would deter him.

Half way down the escarpment we stopped in order to take stock and to ease our straining bladders. Each chose a different vantage point. Mine was on a large flat rock, perched over a ravine and shaded by a convenient tree whose trunk was covered in antisocial spines. Many trees and shrubs in East Africa are protected from the unwanted attentions of livestock and other animals by an array of thorns and spikes of varying length and number. Younger, immature species often have more thorns than older, mature growths, in order to protect them while they are at the vulnerable growing stage.

I looked across the khaki-coloured bush towards Kadam. A dust devil, about a mile away, tall as a four storey building, spiralled slowly across the plains, twisting and turning, silent at this distance, until suddenly collapsing. Goat bells tinkled, the sound of children calling to each other, birdsong, the flutter of wings, the snap of a breaking twig, a swivel-eyed chameleon creeping infinitely slowly along a branch, a rustle in the undergrowth – I was surrounded by vivid life. A pair of augur buzzards circled high in the air, yelping conspiratorially to each other. I looked down. An orange-headed agama lizard lay motionless on a stone perhaps ten feet below me, enjoying an afternoon siesta. A well-directed jet of pent up urine, I thought, would enliven his reptilian torpor. But before I could take aim, with a flick of his tail he had vanished.

A yell of alarm broke this peaceful idyll. 'What the shoot?' I thought as I scrambled towards this unwanted auditory intrusion.

It was David, flies gaping, pointing towards a pile of stones, over which he had just sprayed the contents of his bladder. 'A snake, a snake,' he gasped. 'Long and green, and it stood up on end, mouth open, tongue darting in and out.'

'Probably just a harmless tree snake,' dismissed Graeme, who had silently materialized behind us. 'Nothing to be concerned about. There are no green mambas in this area. They are a coastal species. Let's see if we can flush it out, in the interests of science.'

'Good idea,' I said.

'Don't you think,' said David, 'that's...' – he hesitated – 'a bit risky?' I knew that he really meant to say 'stupid.'

'No, no, not at all, and anyway it's always nice to know what's in the area.'

So saying we – Graeme and I – started prodding at the rocks with bits of twig and fallen timber. After a few minutes of fruitless jabbing and thrusting we turned to go.

'Look out!' screamed David, as something like a brown hosepipe shot between Graeme's legs and disappeared into a thicket. 'What the hell was that?' I said. 'Didn't look very green to me,' said Graeme, 'Looked more black mamba than tree snake. You're not colour blind are you David?'

David just shook his head in disbelief.

'Must have been more than one snake in there,' mused Graeme, as we rattled off down the hill. 'Must have a word with Jim Ashe about that.' Jim Ashe was a renowned local herpetologist.

The temperature was rising and by the time we reached the plains I cast envious eyes on a sinewy Pokot, striding along the road, naked, except for his bandoliers, sandals, wooden neck rest and AK47. A white ostrich feather bobbed jauntily in his hair.

Ahead, I could see a line of green trees, green and inviting, which marked the course of the Suam, and a few buildings, the outskirts of Kongelai, the local metropolis. Kongelai, when we reached it, was little more than a collection of wooden shacks, a police post and a couple of dukas selling sugar, salt, chewing tobacco, cooking fat, tea and posho. But the place was humming. It was market day and the town plaza was full of people. Hundreds of goats and sheep stood in knots while their sellers and buyers haggled. Women, clad in tanned goat skins and laden with beads, squatted in the dust, selling fruit, vegetables, baskets, plastic jerry cans, and tins of kimbo. The air shimmered with heat. Black kites circled overhead. A stray dog limped across the road. Old men lay stretched out in the shade of a tree, heads propped up on their carved neck rests. Young men sat on their stools, chatting. The sheep and goats stood, heads together.

Graeme stopped the car. No one paid any attention to our presence. We might not have been there. No one approached, offering beads, necklaces or trinkets to sell, as would have been the case in Maasai-land or Samburu-land. These people were Pokot, and they were indifferent, if not actually hostile, to outsiders.

'God, I could do with a drink,' said David.

'We're not likely to get anything here,' replied Graeme.

I noticed a tall Somali, Moslem cap, hennaed beard, sandals, kikoi, checked shirt and waistcoat, standing outside what looked like a tea house.

'Let's try that place,' I said.

Graeme turned off the engine and we crossed the dusty road and pushed our way through a beaded curtain and into the dim interior. A couple of men, seated at a plastic table, glanced up at us as we entered, and turned back to their tea and talk.

We sat down. A young and elegant Somali woman, her face perfectly framed by her gauzy head scarf, drifted to our table. Her black eyes, ringed by kohl, were surmounted by stunningly matched eyebrows. She did not speak, but looked at each of us in turn, raising her eyebrows in mute interrogation, a faint smile playing over her slightly parted lips. A glimpse of snow white teeth, the fragrance of some exotic perfume.

'Chai kwa watu tatu, tafadhali,' I said. 'Tea for three, please.'

She nodded, and, on lightly sandalled feet, flowed towards the kitchen.

The tea, in a large Thermos flask, arrived in double quick time. We poured it out. It was hot and very spicy.

'May I join you?' It was the Somali gent we had seen in the street.

He told us he was Omar Yusuf Quaasim and he was from El Wak in Kenya's

North East Province. He, like many other Somalis, had replaced the Asians who had formerly been merchants and duka wallahs in these far-flung places, before being ousted by a presidential decree soon after independence.

'So,' he said, 'what are you doing in this God-forsaken dump?'

'We're on our way to climb Tenus,' said Graeme.

'Mmn,' said Omar, 'that's north of Kanyao, isn't it? Well, just be careful. The Pokot are a funny lot. All friends one moment, the next ready to stick a knife into you.' Rather like the Somalis, I thought, but kept quiet. 'They seem to a bit edgy at the moment. No idea why. No doubt you'll find out!' He laughed and fingered his Islamic rosary.

We paid and left. The woman watched us as we left, a beautiful sphinx, stranded in the wilderness.

The Suam was running high, between steep banks. The brown water rippled and burbled, twisted and turned, an adolescent stream enjoying itself, as though knowing that once through the Turkwell Gorge, it would, like a bride, shed its old name, and be obliged to settle down and adjust to a more settled way of life. Below the bridge a small tree with delicate, finger-like branches, overhung the water. On one of these sat a small bright blue kingfisher, studying the pool below. The bird could see something in the soupy swirl, which we could not, for it dropped, like a diving Stuka, and emerged with a tiny minnow-like fish in its beak. It knocked its prey on the branch to stun it, before swallowing it. I felt that I was being watched. I looked up and into the fixed gaze of a chestnut-eyed, blue-scrotumed monkey. It jerked its head from side to side, trying to intimidate me. In the distance, where the banks shelved and levelled to a ford, cattle with lowered heads were drinking.

Bees were coming and going. In the upper branches of the larger trees cylindrical log hives were suspended. They looked like wooden coffins. I studied them, knowing them for what they were, but half hoping to see a skeletal hand or foot drooping from one end. A bee flew into the car and David, agitated by its presence, urged Graeme to leave.

We crossed the bridge. On the other side was Kacheliba, so small as to be barely noticeable. The road, empty to the horizon, now ran through dense bush. Few vehicles came this way. At one time this was the main, the only, road to Lodwar, the biggest town in Turkana district. At Kanyao, the next settlement, the road branched off to Amudat, in Uganda, before returning to Kenya further north at a place with the memorable name of Kokodiangiro. From here it was a long uncertain way to Lodwar with no means of knowing if the road ahead was passable. There was one big river to cross, the Kosipirr, which, if in flood, might mean either a long wait until the water subsided or a lengthy retreat. So extra fuel carried in jerry cans was essential in all such ventures. Now the main road was to the east, running across the plains from the Marich Pass. As a result the area we were now in was a little-visited part of the country – which suited our purposes well.

This was not big game country. Hunger, spears, poisoned arrows and guns had long since seen to that. In this hard land there was little sentiment where wildlife was concerned. But there was wildlife. Ground squirrels raced across the road, dik dik darted though the scrub, goshawks perched on thorn trees, go away birds and hornbills dipped and swooped in front of the vehicle, eagles quartered the sky, huge skyscraper anthills reared out of the bush. The mesmerizing spire of Kapchoket was now to our right while ahead we could see the outline of the Kara Suk hills with their magical names – Sepich, Tarakwit, Lorosuk, Kapcholio – and Tenus, our objective. Distant blue hills, flat-topped thorn trees, red soil, coiling rivers edged by trees of almost unnatural greenery, an enormous sky, so vast it seemed to have no end; and that friend and enemy of all, the huge sun, lording it over the land.

Very many of the place names in the area began with the letter K. Of the eight Kara Suk hills, four began with the letter K – Kapiltugen, Kachalagalu, Kapchoket and Kapcholio. After passing the hamlet of Kanyao we pressed on until we came to Kiwawa and Kikosichautawala and turned off onto a track to Kauriong. Mostly these were not named on any map, being areas known only by the local inhabitants. If they were marked on a map and you assumed by seeing prominent lettering that you were approaching a significant settlement you were likely to be disappointed. A single shack selling posho and beans in this part of the world merited prominent geographical inclusion. Indeed, to many people living in the wilderness it was the centre of their universe, and even for us, rattling for hours across the bundu, over rocky hills, across sandy dry river beds, up and down escarpments, through forest and swamp, the distant sight of a single parody of a dwelling was enough to raise one's spirits and to suggest that we were now within the realm of safety and civilization.

We crossed a wide lugga, the Trooper wallowing in the deep sand, and climbed the opposite bank. We had been informed that there was a mission in the area, near the base of our mountain and that here a guide could be found. A small boy herding a flock of goats informed us that the mission was not far – 'si mbale.' I knew from bitter experience that 'si mbale' could mean anything from a couple of kilometres to five times that distance. Finally, after endless twisting and turning through the bush, scraping paint off the long-suffering Trooper, following what looked more like a goat path than a track, buildings appeared, tall green trees and signs of water. But of people there was no sign. The mission buildings were empty. There was a school, but no pupils. There was a chief's office but no chief. Graeme turned the engine off. A dove cooed in a nearby tree. Ants trekked across the sandy soil. The air was thick and heavy.

'Now what?' said David.

'We wait,' I said, 'Someone will appear. They always do.'

Sure enough a man clad in European clothing materialized as from nowhere. He was very black and wore spectacles. Smiling, he approached our vehicle. 'Good afternoon, gentlemen,' he greeted us. 'How can I help you?' We explained our purpose. 'I am the pastor here at this mission,' he told us, 'and my name is Emmanule Palonyang. You have come at a difficult time. The Turkana have raided one of our manyattas near the Turkwell, killed three of our people and stole many sheep, goats and cattle. Our moran threatened to retaliate but the Serikali (govt.) told us to stay quiet for five days while they returned our livestock. But three days have passed and nothing has happened. Our young men are angry. In two days they will go on the warpath. This is why you see no one here. But there is one man who can help you. His name is Kapkoyo and he knows the mountain well.'

This was disconcerting news, but we had come a long way and we were in no mind to turn back. We arranged for Kapkoyo to start walking at 6am.

We camped in the mission compound.

At 5am we struggled out of our tents into the warm, velvety dark, brewed up some tea and waited. Ten minutes before the appointed time Kapkoyo appeared and at 6.30 we set off.

Kapkoyo was lean and leathery with a skin the colour of dark teak. He was lightly clad. His only garment was a short strip of black cloth wrapped around his waist. Cow hide sandals protected his feet from thorns and stones. A pouch containing snuff, chewing tobacco and a small knife, a rungu (club) in his left hand and the ubiquitous AK47 over his right shoulder completed his equipment. We, on the other hand, were laden down like pack donkeys. Our rucksacks were bulging with water bottles, oranges, energy bars, chocolate, cameras, Swiss army knives and implements to remove stones from horses' hooves.

Trying to convince ourselves that Kapkoyo was merely going for a jaunt in his backyard didn't wash. His daily calorific intake was probably a fraction of ours, he was almost certainly a survivor of countless bouts of malaria and who knew what else, he slept on a skin bed and his possessions were minimal. I wondered what his Body Mass Index was. He didn't carry an ounce of fat. He was all tendon and finely tuned muscle. His legs were like thin, ebony pistons, carrying him effortlessly over the roughest terrain. As we set off I thought about the tortoise and the hare, and knew that that wouldn't wash either. This was more like the tortoise and the cheetah. But I also knew that Kapkoyo would not let us down. The bare-arsed brigade seldom do. It's the ones in pin striped suits and uniforms you've got to beware of.

We crossed a dry river bed and entered a thicket of wait-a-bit and wild sisal.

Almost at once Graeme's arm was punctured by a needle-sharp spine. First blood and we had barely left camp. The path ascended steeply. As far as Kapkoyo was concerned it might have been horizontal. In his wake we gasped and staggered, sweat-soaked and light-headed, but albeit looking forward to our second wind. An intestinal spasm had me rushing for cover. Unloaded, I stepped forward with renewed vigour. We were now climbing though dry, forested country and as we ascended a light, cool wind came gusting through the trees. The woods were full of birds, calling and singing.

After two hours, the incline lessened and a Pokot manyatta came into view. Normally it would have contained women and children, elders and gambolling lambs and kids. A small closely knit community. But it was deserted. The huts were empty, the ash in the fires cold. A few broken pots and gourds were all that remained. A pair of Egyptian vultures poking around in the cattle boma rose as we approached and flapped away.

Kapkoyo muttered something about the Turkana and spat into the dust.

We continued now up a steepening spur, the views expanding in all directions. Lorosuk, Kachagalau, and Kapcholio, blue and beckoning, rose above the ochre plains. Sand rivers coiled like serpents digesting their prey. The land below lay baking in the sun. Up here at 8,000 feet it was pleasantly cool. Above, fan tailed ravens were gliding, waiting for us to stop so that they could share our lunch on the summit, registering their impatience with a series of irritated croaks.

A pair of klipspringers perched on a jumble of rocks eyed us as we began our slithery descent down an alternative ridge. This turned out to be much steeper and longer than the one we had come up by. It was also more exposed to the sun which was now past its zenith. Half way down the ridge we came upon a Pokot shrine – a small wooden wigwam, and a circle of white stones with white pebbles inside. Kapkoyo said a few words, rather like an Austrian peasant passing an image of the Virgin Mary on an Alpine pass. We stepped carefully round it and continued our slippery descent.

At a dry waterfall we met some Pokot youths carrying bows and arrows. The arrows were wickedly barbed. One of those in your gut, I thought, if you weren't dead you would need major surgery to get it out. And what were they hunting? We had seen no game larger than the klipspringers near the summit. But the Pokot were a warrior race and, unlike other tribes, liked to keep their weapons sharply honed, just in case.

Our water all gone, our oranges sucked of all nutrients, our palates parched and panting for a beer, no matter what its temperature, we reached the dry river bed we had crossed soon after dawn that morning.

To our consternation we saw, on a stretch of hard-packed sand, squatting on their low stools, and obviously waiting for our arrival, a group of at least 20 Pokot elders.

'Oh, oh!' said Graeme.

The elders did not look friendly. All had long, thick wooden clubs in their hands. Off to one side, beside a cattle trough we had failed to notice in the early morning gloaming, lounged a gaggle of naked Pokot. One, having performed his ablutions, strapped on an enormous cartridge belt to accompany his AK47.

'What's the problem?' we whispered to Kapkoyo.

'They're upset that they weren't informed about strangers being in their area.'

'We thought that Emmanule would have told them.'

'Leo ni jumapili. Today's Easter Sunday and he's gone to church, he being the pastor. Your footprints were seen. The Turkana killed three of our people the other day and everyone is on edge.' All this is Swahili.

'Now what?'

'The elders will decide.'

We stood in a line, in front of the elders, feeling like naughty schoolboys in front of the headmaster, only here there were 20 headmasters.

The elders conferred. Ostrich feathers bobbed. Lip plugs wobbled. Every now and again they raised their clubs and smashed them onto the sand.

'What's that for?' we asked Kapkoyo. The elders only spoke Pokot.

'They're talking about sacrificial goats.'

And again?

'Now they're talking about ritual floggings.'

David swallowed and turned pale.

My throat was so dry I couldn't have swallowed if I wanted to. I had a stone in my shoe, the straps of my rucksack were biting into my shoulders and all I could think of was getting this business over and done with and rehydrating the person with a gallon of Tusker.

Finally, after what seemed like an age, but was more like 30 minutes, we got down to financial basics and agreed to a modest donation to the communal beer fund. Honour satisfied, hands were shaken all round and we staggered gratefully to our tents.

The moon rose, huge and orange, over the sleeping plains. But were they sleeping? In Africa you could never know. Jackals would be emerging from their dens. Owls would be quartering their territory. A leopard might be eyeing a boma in which sheep and goats were penned for the night. The mournful call of a distant hyena broke the stillness. And what of the most dangerous animals of all? Were they now, even now, armed with their AK47s, bows and arrows approaching some unsuspecting manyatta?

Bats hawked for insects, swooping and diving over our heads. Cicadas sawed in the darkness. The sky was brilliant with stars. There was no light pollution here. In fact, apart from our flickering tilly lantern there was no light.

We were not alone in the darkness. Our every move was scrutinized by a small posse of Pokot, seated on their stools. Every mouthful we took was commented on. An empty tin of beans was commandeered and set aside for later use. Water containers were seized upon. My red Swiss army knife was a source of endless fascination. One man in particular was mesmerized by it. He kept on picking it up and opening the blades. I gave him some oranges and he sat there, spitting the pips across my soup, staring at the knife. In the end I gave it to him.

In the morning we paid off Kapkoyo and Emmanule. As we left we were presented with gifts: a walking stick for David, a bracelet for Graeme and a stool-cum-neckrest for me. We felt this to be a rare honour from such a warlike people.

We headed back towards Kongelai but taking an alternative route we followed an old road running close to the foot of Kapchoket and crossed the dry Kanyangereng river. We passed three naked Pokot, one with his AK47 over his shoulder. This was now the fourth day since the attack and we wondered whether they were on their way to retaliate against the Turkana.

We re-crossed the Suam and instead of turning south, drove north, heading for Ptoyo. This was wonderful country. Mountains, wide sand rivers, masses of birds, vast views of the Cheranganis to the south, Kadam to the west and the great mass of Sekerr to the north. There were people here, the women in skins, naked to the waist, hair in braids and tufts, a young man with a splendid ivory bracelet on his left wrist, old men with lip plugs, young men with guns, bows and arrows, wearing nothing but their native pride, which, being Pokot, was considerable.

The Chesara river was, to our relief, dry, as it was half a mile wide at this point. The road rose steeply, cut into the side of the hills, huge drops to one side. It was rarely used – perhaps one or two vehicles a month. Up the Kabombo Escarpment, the peak of Taptolim to our left, our eyes drawn to it, brains mentally calculating the approach, the final ridge, the summit. A few more rocky luggas, then it was down into the wide bowl of Ptoyo, filled with euphorbia trees and tiny patches of maize.

Here we camped amid friendly people. Old men sat in the shade, chewing the fat. Children stood watching us, arms around each other. Giggling girls peeped at us. Young men passed, herding cattle, sheep and goats. The Turkana threat seemed not to bother them.

As the sun declined, the land was bathed in a soft golden haze. Shadows lengthened, the old men rose and slowly drifted away, birds settled in the trees, a lamb bleated, an early owl floated on silent wings, the high pitched bark of a distant jackal broke the stillness, then the sudden equatorial dark, brilliant star lit skies, bats flitting.

Noon on the morrow saw us back at Kongelai, and opting to follow a track parallel to the Suam, and which, if the maps were correct, would eventually lead us back to Kitale.

Unlike the road to Ptoyo, this one was deserted. We saw no one. We found this odd, but we pressed on. We crossed a number of dry, sandy luggas, the road gradually rising, seemingly aiming for a prominent rocky hill called Cheptumet. On our right, across the border in Uganda, Mt. Riwa was a prominent feature.

It was now late afternoon and we looked for somewhere to camp. The adjacent bush was dense and uninviting. We passed a number of Pokot graves, regular mounds of rocks in an area where the bush had been roughly cleared. We counted three on the right hand side of the road and one on the left. We slowed down, but the thought of camping in a graveyard did not appeal. So we pressed on and on…

Still we saw no one and the bush remained solid, dense, uninhabited. No animals, no birds, just those deceased Pokot beneath their rocks.

The hour was late. We turned back.

Next to the graves was a flat area, below a tall tree, large enough to pitch our tents. On either side were a number of deep, narrow watercourses. The whole area was decidedly spooky. The bush was silent. No birds twittered, no goat bells tinkled, no friendly locals came to investigate our presence.

Dead wood was in abundance, so we decided to build a fire. While dragging a log from a thicket I came across a curious, round flat stone, about three feet in diameter, engraved with radiating lines, like the rays of the sun. Or a bloodshot eye with the dark pupil in the centre. It all added to the strangeness of the place.

Behind our graveyard campsite rose the hill of Cheptumet, dark and forbidding, the rocks black and overhanging.

'This place gives me the creeps,' said David, as we sat round the fire, sipping our beers. It was 7.30 in the evening and it was still and windless. Dark clouds obscured the moon. I sniffed the air. It felt like rain.

'Well,' I said cheerily, 'it's only for one night. We'll be off in the morning.'

At that moment three shots of automatic gunfire rang out – dat! dat! dat! About half a kilometre away. The sound echoed off the hill behind us.

We looked at each other with wild surmise.

'Perhaps,' said Graeme, 'it might be best if we didn't have a fire after all.'

We quickly doused the warming flames and sat awhile listening.

Nothing.

Below in the valley a hyena whooped. Then another, closer.

Light rain began to fall.

'Time for bed,' I said. We packed our things into the Trooper and retired to our respective tents.

I woke with a start. Soft rain was pattering on the tent. But it wasn't the rain which roused me from fitful slumber. It was the whoops of hyenas. As I listened it seemed to me that they were getting closer – and closer. Soon I could hear them laughing and giggling and cackling. Then the crunching of bones, mere yards from where I lay. There must have been dozens of them and every time they let rip with a full throated whoop or giggle the sound was magnified manifold as it reverberated back from the hill above us.

The racket went on for hours. The brutes were having a full blown party in the dry watercourses beside our tents. Every now and again some would scuttle from one debauch to another, feet from where we lay, apparently making sure they hadn't missed a piece of the action .

At about four in the morning David's nerve snapped. Waiting for a lull in the proceedings, he burst out of his tent and made a dash for the vehicle and locked himself in.

I had pitched my tent on a slope and now the rain was beginning to seep into my boudoir. What with this and the non-stop caterwauling, sleep was impossible. 'To hell with this,' I thought. I looked at my watch – 5.30 am. Soon it would be light. I dragged myself out of my sopping tent, set up a camp chair and waited for the dawn. The hyenas were still hard at it, but as the first faint fingers of pallid chiaroscuro crept across the sky their infernal vocalizing lessened and finally stopped. They had gone.

David emerged from the vehicle, looking pale and shaken. 'Whose bloody idea was it to come back this way?' He glared at us accusingly. Graeme looked at me. I looked at Graeme.

The area around our tents, damp from the overnight rain, was covered in hyena pug marks. We investigated the gullies where the bacchanalia had taken place. The Pokot, we assumed, must have been in the habit of burying their dead here for decades, and for decades the hyenas had been coming here to tidy things up.

We took down our sodden tents, packed them away, and, over breakfast decided that, as we were here anyway, we might as well nip up Cheptumet.

We sipped our tea and ate our Weetabix, waiting for the sun to warm us up.

Then, two single shots rang out from the valley below, the crack of each retort volleying back from over our heads. More wild surmise. Now, should we climb the hill or not, leaving the vehicle at the possible mercy of whoever was pulling the trigger?

We climbed the hill. The ascent was steep and sweaty. The rocks appeared to be some peculiar ironstone which accounted for the extraordinary echo.

We reached the summit and looked down. The valley was filled with cloud. Everything was deadly still. Not a sound.

Not a breath of wind.

We tiptoed down the hill and to our relief the Trooper was still intact, untouched. The road rose steeply up an escarpment, the bush now thinning out. Here was good grazing, but no livestock. In the distance antelope bounded away. We followed an unused track, which led to a stream and here we met the first people we had seen since leaving Kongelai – an old man carrying a bow and arrows and a young man with a Lee Enfield 303.

We stopped to ask the way.

'What are you doing here?' they asked in Swahili. 'This area is very unsafe. The Sebei from Uganda are constantly invading and attacking with guns and other weapons. Ahh, they are very bad people! So everyone has moved away from the border. No one lives on this side anymore.'

We thanked them, they gave us direction to the village of Kanyarkwat from where there was a road to Kitale and we went on our way, wiser than we had been, relieved at our good fortune and rejoicing in our shared experiences.

⚔⚔⚔⚔⚔

Two months later David came to stay.

The girls were away at school. Berna was teaching at St. Mungo's and wouldn't be in until late. So after dinner David and I sat chatting and having a drink in the lounge.

At about 10pm Berna arrived and we had another drink and some more chat.

At 11pm we were aroused from our conversation by the sound of loud wailing emanating from the dwelling of our house help, the ever-faithful Esther, followed by the pounding of feet.

'What the heck?' I expostulated.

I went to investigate. Esther was the wailer. Behind her stood her nubile daughter, who was adding to the cacophony. Together they sounded like the sirens of an approaching Presidential motorcade. Esther's vast bosoms were rising and falling like an angry Pacific swell, and she was gasping like a beached salmon. Esther's daughter was also heaving and panting, like a racehorse at the finish of the Grand National.

'For God's sake, Esther,' I said, 'would you please stop making that horrible noise and tell us what's going on!'

'There was a man.' She paused to catch her breath, 'A man, he ran past our window. We saw him, we heard him!'

Esther was about twice the size of any ordinary man, but one read about elephants being terrified of mice, buffalo stampeding at the sight or smell of a honey badger, so I kept my peace. 'Right,' I said, 'I'll muster the troops.'

I returned to the lounge and informed Berna and David that we had an intruder on the premises and that we had to flush him out. So we pressed the siren alarm button, released the dogs, and roused the night askari from his slumbers. We circled the house, we tramped round the lawns, we thrashed our way through the flower beds, we peered up trees, we climbed onto the roof. The dogs ran around, sniffing, cocking their legs, wagging their tails. Of the uninvited visitor there was no sign.

We went back into the lounge to regroup and take stock.

'So, where the hell can he be?' I asked. 'Perhaps he went back the way he came in,' said Berna. 'Well,' I said, 'the only way in is over that old pepper tree that's fallen down over the cactus hedge, and if he came that way his backside must be more full of spines than a porcupine. Let's have one more look around the garden.' 'I'll stay here, if you don't mind,' said David. 'OK,' we said, 'see you shortly.'

Our second search was as fruitless as the first, and, puzzled and frustrated, we went back inside, to be met by David, finger pressed to pursed lips. 'I think he's in there,' he whispered, pointing to Kim and Sophie's room. During our unproductive survey of the property David had wandered round the house, including venturing into our daughters' bedroom. The walls were covered with pre-pubescent posters of horses, ponies and tightly jodhpured riders. The girls were at that stage of life when quadrupeds featured more prominently in their personal firmament than mere humans. David was intrigued and spent some time examining portraits of proud stallions, noble mares and imperious equestriennes. Being of an mildly eccentric nature, he had speech with himself and commented aloud on what he saw – 'Mmm, what a lovely animal.' 'What a splendid rider.' 'What sort of pony is that, I wonder?' – and so on. Imagine his consternation when a reply came back from below one of the beds. His retreat was rapid and he met us as we entered.

Quickly we manned all exits and summoned the now primed askari.

With stun gun and rungu in hand, we entered the bedroom and identified the bed below which our guest was taking his ease. We each seized a corner and at the word of command executed a swift lift. Below Sophie's bunk lay an African man, clad only in red underpants. He expressed some irritation at being so disturbed and indicated that a degree of retaliation was on his mind. This was quickly scotched by the askari who gave him a few biffs with his truncheon. I felt like giving him a couple of zaps with my stun gun but contented myself with pressing the trigger and when the fellow heard the worrying crackle and saw the purple spark leaping from one electrode to another he calmed down. We dragged him out and trussed him up with my skipping rope, which was now being out to good use. Until now it had been a mere expression of my best intentions. Berna phoned Harry Blunt, of Night Guards, and advised him of the situation.

We marched our prisoner outside to await Harry's arrival. With his hands tied behind his back we sat the man, who was obviously a lunatic, on the ground. Then, out of the stygian darkness, surged the frightening form of Esther's daughter, panga in hand. I saw the upraised arm, the glint of bared teeth, the outline of the blade, and envisioned blood, and worse, on the grass, perhaps viral spread as well. At the last moment she turned the edge and struck the captive with the flat of the weapon. There was a horrid thunk. The man made no sound and at that moment Harry Blunt roared up the drive in his pickup, waving a revolver out of his open window.

We loaded the intruder into the back of the pick-up and, guarded by the askari, he was driven away to the police station.

The following morning David still seemed to be somewhat stunned by the experience. Together with our recent encounters in the lands of the Pokot, I had the distinct impression that he regarded me as some sort of attractant or magnet for this sort of thing. Over bacon and eggs we impressed upon him that he was most welcome to come back at any time. We waved him off. The next we heard of him was that he had accepted a new posting to South Korea, almost as far from Africa as it was possible to be.

I drove to the police station to enquire about our other visitor. Inspector Lucy was on duty and she took me to the holding cell. There, backed into a corner like a flock of chickens facing a fox, was a group of terrified prisoners while the lunatic, now stark naked and apparently barking mad, occupied the rest of the cell.

Inspector Lucy asked if I wished to press charges. I did not.

Chapter Thirteen

DEATH OF DAMPNESS

In Africa the tenets of Gray's Elegy did not apply. The 'madding crowd' was ever-present. There was no 'noiseless tenor' here. Continual power cuts, fuel shortages, lack of foreign exchange, bank strikes, absence of drugs, riots, phones out of order, no water in the taps, potholed roads, you name it, we had it. In 1994, in Rwanda, close to a million Tutsis and moderate Hutus were slaughtered by Hutu extremists, unhindered by perfidious France and a supine United Nations.

In 1998 the American embassy in Nairobi was bombed by Al Qaeda and its affiliates, with over 200 Kenyans and 12 Americans killed, a bizarre dichotomy to my mind. Next-door to my surgery in Club Lane was a small enterprise run by an African Moslem convert, where he sold second hand cars. He was a jolly, rotund figure in his embroidered kofia (Moslem cap) and white kanzu (robe). Friendly and helpful, he struck me as an innocuous individual. In the weeks leading up to the embassy bombing, a pair of Afghans or tribal Pathans appeared and frequented his premises. Wearing baggy beige shalwar kameez, typical rolled down headgear, sandals and sporting long beards, they were an incongruous and conspicuous sight in Club Lane. They came and went, always together. Then the embassy was bombed and they vanished and were seen no more. I reported this to the authorities and to the British High Commission in Nairobi. I heard nothing back from either. Soon afterwards my neighbour closed down and left. Yet another mystery hanging unsatisfactorily in the Rift Valley air. Were they innocent imams or sinister anarchists?

100 people died in Nairobi after drinking changaa, a locally brewed spirit, laced with methanol. 270 passengers drowned when a ferry capsized off Mombasa. 106 people were killed in a bus crash near Machakos. 140 men, women and children drowned when a train was washed away on the Mombasa/Nairobi line. Death and disaster were always lurking in the wings. In the UK if a person was killed on the road the police might close the road for hours while investigations were carried out. In Africa, the body would, in all likelihood, be dragged to one side to allow the speeding traffic to proceed unhindered.

In the West television viewers might watch these scenes of misfortune with feelings of fleeting dismay before switching impatiently to the latest soap.

So when I saw a logo on a lorry stating that 'the vulture is a patient bird,' it seemed to encapsulate an attitude of mind prevalent in the continent and elsewhere. Was this fatalism, indifference, apathy, callousness? Or was it that as one disaster succeeded yet another, people were just overcome by disaster fatigue?

After a long spell of dry weather the rains were eagerly anticipated. Farmers had prepared their land, seed was ready to be planted, women and children were busy in their fields with their hoes and mattocks, getting everything ready for the first welcome showers. The country was biscuit brown and bone dry, gasping for water. Grass broke and crunched underfoot with a hungry crackle. Cattle stood listless in the baking heat, thin and exhausted, their udders empty. Dogs panted in the shade, tongues lolling. Streams had long since dried to sand and boulders. Dust rose in the air. The sky was an inverted bowl of glaring sheet metal across which the tyrant sun moved with ponderous indifference.

Two months later prelates, divines and the faithful were offering up prayers to the Almighty for relief from the incessant rain which lashed the country. El Nino had arrived and the effect was disastrous. Bridges were washed away, roads collapsed, crops were destroyed, people drowned, schools were closed, traffic was disrupted. But for some species of life the moist humid conditions were ideal for them to go forth and multiply. Insects and certain forms of bacteria flourished exceedingly as the humidity and water table rose.

Many years earlier, mosquitos infected with the virus which causes Rift Valley Fever had deposited their drought-resistant eggs in shallow forest edge depressions known as dambos. Here they lay, quiet and undisturbed, buried beneath a layer of soft featherbed soil. Seasons came and went, the sun rose and set, animals and people walked over their resting place, and they bided their time, waiting. Years passed, and still they waited. Finally El Nino came, the water table rose until it reached the waiting eggs and, like the creature in the film 'Alien,' they hatched; and the emerged mosquitos, bearing the virulent virus, went forth to infect and kill.

Soon I was receiving alarming reports from farmers that their cows and sheep were aborting and that lambs and young calves were dying. Further north camels were also aborting in huge numbers. The rains continued and the entire country was saturated. I spent much time taking samples from affected animals and sending them to the government laboratory in Nairobi. The livers of deceased lambs and calves were bright yellow and soon I could diagnose the condition immediately the abdomen was opened.

I had not seen this disease before but the combination of heavy continuous rain and widespread abortions suggested to my mind what this might be and this was soon confirmed by the government lab – Rift Valley Fever. There was a vaccine but due to the fact that the disease only occurs at protracted intervals – up to 20 years in some instances – few farmers vaccinated on a regular basis. Now there was a rush to vaccinate but in most cases it was too late, in fact counterproductive as some of those animals were already infected. So unless the farmer used a separate needle for every animal injected he was likely to spread the disease throughout the herd, acting like a human mosquito. In the north almost every pregnant camel aborted. These animals would now be immune to further infection but as the next outbreak might not occur for another five to 20 years when they would almost certainly all be dead, this was an academic benefit in most cases.

Human cases began to occur, especially in the normally desiccated eastern and north-east provinces. Here nomadic pastoralists depended on their livestock for survival. Most cases affected young men, probably because they were the ones doing the herding and handling of their animals. And when animals died, they were eaten. Several Maasai moran, partaking in a ceremony in southern Kenya, died, after consuming infected meat. People who were malnourished or infested with intestinal parasites, such as hookworms, and whose immune systems were already under stress, were more likely to succumb to infection. By the time the outbreak was over, more than 150 people in Kenya had died and tens of thousands of cattle, sheep and camels had aborted and their offspring had been killed by the virus. Then the disease moved into southern Sudan and Somalia where yet more people died and more animals aborted.

In the meantime in my neck of the Kenyan woods I battled away vaccinating unprotected stock, taking samples, doing post mortems and doling out advice. And still the rain thundered down.

I had spent the morning with Kim, our youngest, vaccinating cattle, and was on my way back to the surgery. Halfway down a long hill, Lake Nakuru ahead, Menengai Crater to our left, I glanced in my rear mirror. A white saloon was behind me, moving at speed. Its trajectory seemed to be rather erratic. Before I could pull over, there was a loud bang, the vehicle collided with my right flank, tore off my wing mirror, swerved and accelerated ahead. I wasn't having that. By now the white saloon had a 500 yard advantage. I crowded on the canvas and set forth in hot pursuit. 'Go get 'em! Dad!' yelled Kim. But the saloon was faster and growing smaller. The driver obviously could see that I was after him and had his foot to the floor. Then, he suddenly turned left onto a dirt road.

What he didn't know, but I did, was that the track was a dead end. I slowed down. There was no hurry now. What I didn't know was how the occupants, if there was more than one, might react. The track was narrow and winding so my arrival was totally unexpected. The car was stopped up a grassy dead-end. The driver was standing beside the car, a broad grin on his face, talking to two other men slumped in the back seat. When he saw me he whirled round, his features crumpled, he grabbed the ignition keys, hurled them into an adjacent field and legged it. He cleared a fence like a startled impala and was gone. I got out and approached warily. There was no need to have worried. The reek of alcohol reached me before I had taken more than a few paces. The men in the back were paralytic, legless and almost incapable of speech. With Kim as an impartial observer I engaged the inebriated duo in a one-sided pre-pubescent conversation. With some difficulty I persuaded one of the men to part with his ID card. The other, with even more difficulty, told me that the driver, Kinyanjui, the owner of the jalopy, lived in London. London? London was the name of a foetid slum area next to Nakuru's main rubbish dump. What, I wondered, would the Britannic City Fathers think of this arbitrary acquisition of their proud capital's name? Kim wrote down the number of the car and we left the pair to sleep it off, telling them, with more confidence than I felt, that I would be visiting London later that day, to see Kinyanjui and to press for funds to repair the damage inflicted on my innocent auto.

Luck was with us. Sitting in the surgery as we entered, waiting for a supply of Rift Valley Fever vaccine, resplendent in khaki, gold braid and epaulettes, was an inspector of police, from western Kenya. I gave him a modest discount and recounted our experience on the road. 'Leave it to me,' he said. 'Go to London. If they give any trouble, let me know and I will send some men to sort them out.' That was the sort of talking I liked to hear.

Leaving Kim behind, I summoned Moses and drove to London. A rubbish-strewn road led into the slum. I turned the car, in case we had to make a speedy exit. In these situations one should always be prepared for the unexpected.

Word had spread that we were coming. How, was beyond my comprehension. News travels swiftly in Africa. A crowd gathered and quickly grew to worrying proportions.

'Wapi Kinyanjui?' we asked – where was Kinyanjui? No one answered. 'Ona ghari yangu,' I said, gesticulating at the amputated wing mirror and the dent in the side of the car. The crowd bayed with laughter and moved closer and began banging on the paintwork. Then they started rocking the car from side to side. 'Time to make a move I think,' I said to Moses, who was displaying signs of acute anxiety. I blew the horn and drove slowly into the mob which reluctantly parted. A small stone hit the rear window. People shouted abuse.

'Bladdy muzungu!,' I heard, – bloody European! 'Kwenda kufa! Rudi nyumbani!' – drop dead! Go home!' Well, I thought, racism is alive and thriving in Kenya.

Back at the surgery, the phone rang. It was the elusive Kinyanjui. He must have heard that the police might intervene if he did not take action. I named a figure to cover the cost of repairs. He named a meeting place. The following day we met at an agreed rendezvous, and Kinyanjui, a shifty Kikuyu with red eyes and a tufty beard, gave me an envelope. I opened it and counted the notes, held them up to the light and counted them again, nodded and drove away.

Angus Simpson, the livestock manager of Italian owned Marula Estate in Naivasha was on the blower. I had known Angus since my first faltering steps on the Dark Continent, when he was an assistant farm manager on an estate close to the ramshackle cottage I rented at the entrance to the Solai valley. Single European women were in short supply in Kenya. Angus solved this problem rather neatly by cuckolding his boss, the irascible Reg, and commandeering his wife, the blonde and bubbly Jill. Needless to say there was a price to pay in the form of his job, which came to an abrupt end. 'Hi Hugh, Angus here. We seem to have a bit of a problem in our milking Friesians. Can't make it out. They're fidgeting and stamping their feet, milk yield is down and in a couple the milk is a pink colour. A few have aborted. And they don't seem to like being in the sun – not that there's much sun these days! It never stops raining! The place is under water!'

I cudgelled what was left of my stressed brain, dredging and sifting memories of past bovine calamities, in which I had been a ministering participant. Although there were similarities, this did not seem like Rift Valley Fever. Back in 1977, on the estancia of the then-President, Jomo Kenyatta, there had been a massive outbreak of Leptospirosis, a bacterial infection, causing hepatitis, jaundice, photosensitization, abortions and death. I was just about to go on some much-needed leave, not having been out of the country since I had arrived some eleven years earlier. But I diagnosed the problem, gave advice re treatment, saw animals under my care recover, and departed with a song on my lips, blithely trusting that by example during my absence my words of wisdom would be followed. When I returned it was to find that all of my modest precepts had been ignored. Others, mightier than me, a mere practitioner, had decided that this was not Leptospirosis at all but a tick-borne disease, Babesiosis. In this decision they had exhausted the country's entire supply of this ailment's antidote, all to no avail. Meanwhile the disease had spread far and wide and countless animals had been infected, aborted or died.

So it was with a degree of concern that I set off for Naivasha. Being in a hurry I swept past 'Injury Time' and 'Born to Fish, Forced to Work,' but slowed down when the driver of an approaching matatu, whose own slogan was hidden beneath a tasteful patina of mud, signalled by pointing at the tarmac with his index finger that a police speed check lay ahead. It helped to be aware of the meaning of these abstruse masonic type gestures. It might save you from being pressed to contribute to the Fund for Distressed Constables, a fine, or worse. As I rounded a tree-screened bend in 3rd gear, there, drawn into the verge was a wretched Indian, being harassed by a pair of rotund flatfeet. He obviously was not aware of the meaning of the downward pointing digit.

Angus was on hand when I arrived. We drove to the dairy along a road which was a river of glutinous mud, interspersed with pools of brown, viscid water, which fountained spectacularly on either side of the car as we slalomed along. The car, which was white when I left, was now an unpleasant earthy colour. 'How far to the dairy?' I asked

Angus, wondering when we were going to slither terminally into the nearest ditch.

'Only another couple of kilometres, beneath those big fever trees you can see in the far distance.' 'Let's hope we don't have to walk,' I muttered.

We slid to an uncontrolled halt at a wooden crush with a mobile dairy nearby.

I dismounted from my chariot and stepped into about six inches of mud. The air was hot and humid. Biting flies swarmed around us. The huge, ominously-named fever trees, towered above us. Pools of green-scummed stagnant water lay beneath them.

Waiting for us were a couple of farm hands, perched well above mud-level on the side of the crush. A group of Friesian cattle was huddled in a group in the crush boma.

'Right,' I said, 'let's see the cows first, in the dairy. Leave the heifers in the crush.'

As they walked out one arched her back, lifted her tail and let forth a stream of port wine coloured urine. As it hit the ground it rose into a heap of yellowish froth. I examined her first. As I was taking her temperature I noted that her vulva was a reddish/purple shade. I opened the lips to check her membranes – yellow. Temperature was up. I looked at her teats – again that reddish/purple hue – no wonder she might have been stamping her feet. Her muzzle also had the same unpleasant tinge.

I moved from cow to cow, checking, looking, examining. All, had, to a greater or lesser degree, the same symptoms. A couple had a soft, flabby mastitis, with bloody, thickened milk.

We persuaded the heifers to enter the crush. Some were symptom-less, others were similar to the cows.

I turned to Angus. 'Well... .' But before I could begin my peroration there was a shout of alarm behind us. 'What the...?' One of the workers had backed away from the crush and was pointing at the top bar. There, moving along in typical, jerky, slow motion was a large, dark brown chameleon. Chameleons are regarded by many Africans with disfavour. It swivelled its independently-moving eyes in our direction before continuing its journey. 'Kinyonga ni shaitani,' muttered the man. ('Chameleons are devils') Why chameleons, along with owls, have got such a bad name in Africa is open to debate. Is it to do with their extraordinary pyramidal eyes, with each able to look in different directions at the same time, their ability to change their skin colour and to merge into whatever background they find themselves, their strange clockwork gait on straggled legs, their tongues one and a half times their own length, and the fact that, unlike most reptiles, they don't move off at high speed when a human being intrudes into their territory, but either stand their ground, open their gaping mouths and hiss, or ignore them with what appears to be a studied indifference.

'As I was about to say,' I said to Angus, 'this is almost certainly leptospirosis.'

Once again I was interrupted. No sooner were the words out of my mouth before a man appeared on a mud spattered motor bike. 'Pole, bwana,' he said to Angus, 'ngombe likufa.' ('Sorry bwana, a cow has died.') 'Wapi?' 'Where?' said Angus. 'Huko,' 'There,' replied the man, pointing with his chin towards a distant clump of trees. 'OK,' I said to Angus, 'let's go and have a look and do a post mortem.'

After a good deal of backing and forwarding, heaving and shoving, we emerged
    from the mire. Men had already begun to skin the animal and at a distance of a couple of hundred yards I could see that the carcase was an impressively bright yellow colour. 'Look at that,' I said. 'Severe jaundice. More or less confirms the diagnosis. But let's take some samples and then some blood from the animals we've just examined.'

As we drove along I could see many field mice scuttling into cover. 'That's part of the problem,' I said, 'along with the humidity, the standing water and the warmth. Those rodents will be carriers, they pee into the water, the cattle come along and get infected, those that recover become carriers in their turn, pee into water and so it goes on. We'll send serum samples to South Africa and try to get hold of a vaccine.'

'What about treatment?' asked Angus.'

'In my experience 5g of Streptomycin Sulphate for three days by injection is best. I'll get it for you. Another thing – this disease can infect humans so alert the workers to avoid contact with urine, mastitic milk, any aborted foetuses, and wear gloves when dealing with any dead animals. You will have noticed the reddish brown muzzle, teats and vulva. Photosensitization due to liver damage. And those animals which recover –if they have any areas of white skin the surface almost invariably will be affected and go dry and hard and then slowly slough off. And as these animals are Friesians that's what to expect.'

'Bloody hell,' said Angus. 'It all sounds pretty dire.' 'It sure is,' I replied.

From the dead animal I took samples of liver and kidney. From the affected cows and heifers I took blood samples. The results, when they eventually came, indicated a mixed infected with Leptospira pomona, hardjo and grippotyphosa. Angus treated the affected animals and most survived. The vaccine, when we finally received it, was administered. But thereafter annual vaccination was required and even then new outbreaks occurred. The disease was now endemic on the property.

><

The rain continued. When would it ever end? I was sick of forever grinding through the mud and sloshing around in gumboots. Major Day owned a large ranch on the Laikipia plateau, called P and D. I was never sure what the P stood for but the D stood for Day. The Major had a short fuse and had no time for fools, shirkers and most of humanity. So when he requested that I attend to his sheep one Sunday I agreed, having no wish to be included on his list of undesirables.

Major Day's ranch was the best part of 100 miles from Nakuru and I had hoped to be able to fly there in the Super Cub in which I had a half share, so saving time and avoiding the mud and the mire which I knew I would encounter should I go by road. But the Cub was hors de combat so by road it was. The entrance to the Major's ranch was marked by two stone pillars, standing stark and alone beside the road which led to Maralal and the north. They were not connected to a gate or to a fence. They just stood there as though suggesting that further in there might be more architectural marvels waiting to be revealed. A bit like the trunkless legs of Ozymandias. Here we had arranged to meet. I arrived betimes, my car panting and bedaubed from base to apex with the various components which made up the Nakuru/Maralal turnpike. I turned off the engine and stepped out in order to stretch my legs and to relieve my straining bladder. As is usual in Africa you are not alone for long.

You may think that you are in an uninhabited howling wilderness, but just as you are about to perform some innocent personal task, out from behind a bush or rock will pop a local denizen, keen to inspect the arriving stranger. Usually there is nothing sinister in this examination, but just beyond where I had stopped there was a rocky decline, bordered by thickets of thorn and euphorbia, called, for good reason, Bandit Corner. Here, footpads and highwaymen were wont to waylay, with gun and pistol, passing travellers. So when, just as I was about to unburden myself, an armed man appeared, I paused to consider my situation. But he was a Home Guard, authorized by the government to carry a rifle to protect the local community. We exchanged pleasantries and he passed on his way. No sooner had he bade farewell than a pair of Samburu women appeared, festooned with beads and ochre, who must needs beg for alms from the mud bespattered wayfarer. As I rooted around in my pockets for something appropriate to the occasion I heard the distant growl of an approaching vehicle. The women looked alarmed and, without waiting for my modest offerings, scuttled away, muttering something about Bwana Kuchizi – the Mad Master. By now my bladder had reached the point of imminent rupture so Mad Master or no, bent almost double, I hirpled to the verge and with frantic haste, uncocked the valve and released the pent-up flood. To my irritation the vehicle stopped mere feet from where I was thus engaged.

I turned my head. Staring at me from the cab of an ancient Land Rover was a pair of polar blue eyes glaring out from below huge hairy cornices, which passed for eyebrows in this part of the world.

'Major Day?' I politely inquired.

'Major Day,' he barked. 'I assume you're Cran?'

'I am,' I replied. I noted that great tufts of rank foliage sprouted from his nostrils, and from his ears, that his nose was a delicate shade of mauve, he had a turkey dewlap, and that he wore a most un-officer-like travesty of a hat on his head. All this I noted in a flash, even as I was vainly trying to complete the process of micturition. You know how it is. You're in mid-flow and some stranger steps up beside you and that's it. The tap is closed. It's different if you're in a communal latrine on the motorway, with water flowing, soft music playing and everyone bent to the same task. But out in the open it's another matter. Some sort of atavistic protective mechanism from caveman days. Pee in the open with your furry flies open and you're likely to be set upon by a sabre toothed tiger. Always get into cover before you open up. Anyway it was too late. 'Finished?' the major asked with unnecessary irony. I wasn't. I still had half a tank, but it was too late. The ball cock had come down. 'Follow me,' he said, 'we'll go to the first boma and see what we can find. All my field men are Pokot. Pretty basic chaps, but sound, sound.'

I hoped so.

We set off, slithering across a wide plain of black cotton soil. We were all over the place. There appeared to be no road and we just aimed for areas which appeared to be less glutinous than the rest. That's the trouble with black cotton. When it's wet it's like driving through super glue. It's impossibly slippery and sticky, adhering to the underside of your vehicle until you're carrying hundredweights of unwanted cargo. It's noisy too, clattering against the chassis and sending gobbets of mud high into the air. It's the only mud which is noisy, so if you hit a stretch of damp unsurfaced track and you hear the tell-tale sound of black cotton rattling against the underneath of your car, get out of there, fast. When dry, it sets like concrete.

Zigzagging between thin copses of whistling thorn, we aimed for a distant boma, a circular laager wherein the sheep should, at least theoretically, be penned, awaiting our arrival. When we did arrive it was to be met with silence. A few birds twittered. In the distance a lone gazelle raised its head, and gazed at us, before returning its attention to the greensward. The boma was empty, sheep-less.

The major was displeased. He tooted his horn, clambered out of his Land Rover, banged the door shut with some violence and clumped across to the boma, gathering several pounds of mud to his boots as he went.

I followed him. 'Where the hell is the bloody muchungaji?' [shepherd] he shouted. 'He was supposed to be here, on parade, ready and correct, so that you can inspect the sheep. They're smacking their lips, some of their lips are swollen, some are lame, some are drooling and a few have died. So where is the bastard and where are the sheep?'

Answer came there none. We stood in tense silence. The damp plains steamed in the heat. Crickets chirped, a pair of augur buzzards circled overhead, calling plaintively to each other, a scuttling as a lizard rustled through the grass. The major seemed to expand and inflate as he stood there, chest heaving, nostrils dilated, muttering under his breath. Leaving him to formulate whatever plans he had in mind regarding the future of the muchungaji, I wandered round the perimeter of the boma. It was well constructed, with great branches, bristling with inch-long thorns, facing outwards. It was hard to believe that any predator, two or four legged, could penetrate such a barrier. At the outer side of the boma I came across a tiny structure, like a sort of primitive dog kennel, roofed with corrugated iron, with wooden walls upon which were stuck faded posters indicating that the occupant, or occupants, were fans of Manchester United football club. Projecting from the entrance of this rustic wigwam were two large and extremely dirty feet and from within came the rasp and snort of an unquiet sleeper. I bent, the better to peer within, and was almost asphyxiated by the combined stench of alcohol and body odour.

'I say, Major,' I shouted, 'I may have found your man!'

The major hobbled round the boma, muttering and cursing under his breath.

'What is it? What have you found,' he fumigated as he came nearer. I pointed at the emergent feet. The major said nothing. He turned and picked up a large stick lying on the ground. Raising it above his head, he brought it down onto the corrugated iron roof of the wigwam with a fearful crash. He proceeded to hammer the tin for all he was worth. The noise was stupendous, echoing across the plains. The distant gazelle took to its heels. The stick broke. The major picked up another and went for the roof hammer and tongs. 'Bloody, idle, drunken bastard!' he shouted. 'I pay you to look after my sheep, not to booze in my time. Out! Out, you lazy sot!' I thought he was going to have a heart attack. The feet stirred and slowly the legs to which they were attached moved out into the open. Then they stopped.

The major wasn't having this. He resumed his assault on the roof. 'Raus! Raus!' he bellowed. The pelvis, torso and finally the remainder of the bog eyed inhabitant came unpleasantly into view. He blinked owlishly at us, trying to focus in the harsh light. I noted with a degree of objective distaste that the whites of his eyes were an unattractive vermilion colour.

The muchungaji dragged himself to his feet and gave the major a ragged salute. This drove the major into fresh paroxysms of fury. 'Stand up straight, you scoundrel! Drunk on duty eh? Sackable offence. Report to my office in the morning. Get out of my sight before I do something I regret.'

The muchungaji protested. 'Mimi si mlevi. Mimi nachoka tu.' I'm not drunk, I'm just tired. He swayed on his feet, put out his hand to support himself on the ridge of his wigwam, missed it and fell into the mud.

The major gave a cry of disgust and turned away.

'Let's try the next boma and see if we have any luck there.'

The major set off at a great rate, gunning his Land Rover through the wallows and sloughs at full speed, great walls of mud and water fountaining out on either side of his furious steed. The major was obviously in a tearing rage. Heaven help the next muchungaji, I thought, as I tried to follow him, if he isn't on the ball.

A pair of Thomson's gazelle skittered across the bows of my Peugeot. A stately giraffe stared down in surprise as I passed. A late morning jackal trotted through the skeletal bush, turning its head to note my glutinous passage.

In the far distance I could see the major's vehicle careering from side to side like a deranged dodgem. Well, I think, if the muchungaji at the next boma sees that mad idiot coming, if he's got any sense, he'll light out of there and move smartly in the opposite direction. I topped a low rise and there, far below me, in a wide valley, I could see the sheep boma with a tiny Land Rover stopped beside it. I stopped as well and turned the engine off. Better finish that pee now that the old bastard was otherwise engaged. I selected a spindly shrub in obvious need of urgent nourishment and gave its roots a good watering. The lone and level plains stretched far away. To the north the blue-forested Karisia Hills etched the horizon. The sky was blue. The air was fresh and limpid. Peace laid its kindly benison upon the quiet land.

Distant shouting broke in upon that peace. Once again Bishop Heber's words about 'pleasing prospects' and 'only man is vile' were brought to mind.

'What do you mean, you can't speak Swahili? I don't expect you to be able to converse in the Queen's English, but Swahili's the country's official language for God's sake!'

More shouting and yelling. From my vantage point I could see two small figures standing in the middle of the boma, surrounded by sheep. One, presumably the Major, was waving its arms and bellowing, and the other, a small black figure, looking rather like one of L. S. Lowry's stick men, seemed to be standing on one leg, and taking all this abuse on the chin. I noticed another thing. The entrance to the boma was now wide open. The large half-grown thorn tree which normally closed it, had been dragged to one side, presumably by that frizzy eye-browed lunatic when he burst his way in. I could see a couple of sheep making their way towards it. Others, presumably sensing freedom, were following. I view hallooed to no avail. The officer corps was now in full cry, deafened by its own exuberance. I jumped into my car and shot down the hill. But it was too late. By the time I reached the boma the sheep had gone, the enclosure was empty and the Major had his hands round the muchungaji's neck.

'Major!' I shouted. He dropped his hands and the muchungaji just stood there, a sneering grin on his finely curved lips.

'Where the hell were you? If you'd been here this wouldn't have happened!'

Well, stone me, I thought. Isn't that just typical of these pumped-up nabobs, to blame the workers and the *untermenchen* for their gross incompetence.

'Sorry, Major, you're such a good driver, I just couldn't keep up with you.'

'Humph! Well, there's one more sheep boma so we'd better make sure of that one when we reach it.'

We'd better, you purple-nosed buffoon, I thought. Spending my Sunday haring across waterlogged African plains in the wake of a certifiable maniac in pursuit of elusive sheep when I could be sitting at my ease cradling a cold Tusker or my beloved, or coining it in suburban Surrey or Surbiton, made me wonder why on earth I was here. As I fought my way out of yet another marsh, wheels spinning, clutch burning, I had another feeling. Yes, I was glad to be here, in Africa, where life was a continual challenge, where nothing was predictable, where the monetary rewards were negligible, but where feelings of personal satisfaction could outweigh everything else. No I thought, apart from missing the cold Tusker and my own proud beauty back at base, I would not exchange this for a soft affluent life back in the Home Counties, where the vets probably earned more in a day than I did in a month.

This is what I came for – Africa, and Kenya in particular, with its plains, deserts, mountains, sea, its people, animals and more exotic diseases than you could shake a stick at – whatever that was supposed to mean. And of countries in Africa, East was probably the best bet. West – civil war, the White Man's Grave, even more corruption than here. North – more civil war and general destitution. No hope there. South – socialism, xenophobia, Afrikaner hairy-backs, and more civil wars. And the countries which were relatively stable, like Zambia and Botswana, and which might offer some employment opportunities, were tame, flat and lacking in the spark which made Kenya such an exciting place. Certainly there were problems – local unrest, corruption, poverty, crime, tribalism, police harassment, heinous taxation – but Kenyans are, on the whole, friendly and hospitable, and provided you don't poke them in the eye, you are made welcome.

The final sheep boma appeared on the horizon.

'At last!' I thought.

I could see ahead the Major standing beside a picturesque figure clad in tribal regalia. Compared to this paragon of Pokot manhood, the Major looked like a drab, monochromatic scarecrow. Encircling the sheep guardian's sinewy waist was a broad leather belt adorned with beads and cowrie shells. A short sword, a handy club and a curved dagger suggested that here was someone prepared to defend his woolly charges to the limit. His attire was limited to a short wrap around extending from waist to mid-thigh, so in the event of an emergency there would be none of the impediments emanating from obstructive clothing. In his hair a perky ostrich feather bobbed in the Laikipia breeze. His feet were shod with workman-like cow hide sandals. He eschewed the striped socks so much favoured by the ever more effete Maasai to the south.

The sheep, I was glad to observe were all standing to attention within their quarters.

'Right, Major,' I briskly said, 'so what does your man here have to report?'

'Report? Report?' the Major replied between gritted teeth, 'he's has nothing to report. Why? Because he's deaf and dumb! That's why!'

'Ah,' I said, 'well, at least both he and the sheep are here, he's able-bodied, so let's get on and do what I came for and examine the animals.'

Which is what we did and the shepherd, like most deaf and dumb people everywhere, was a splendid chap, willing and able, catching the sheep for my inspection, running to and fro and doing the work of ten men. He was worth his weight in gold.

It very soon became evident to me that the sheep were suffering from Bluetongue, a viral disease carried and spread by Culicoides midges, and exacerbated by the violent El Nino rains of recent weeks.

Many of the sheep had swollen tender lips which bled when touched. Gums were ulcerated. Some sheep had a clear nasal discharge, in others it was mucopurulent. Many animals were salivating profusely and licking their lips. If my lips were like that, I thought, I too would be salivating.

I watched the sheep as they moved around the boma. Some, I noticed, were stiff and lame, with a stilted, hobbling gait, rather like the Major in action. The Pokot seized affected animals so that I could examine them more closely. Around the junction between the skin and hoof there was a reddish purplish band.

The shepherd made curious grunting sounds as he grabbed the sheep, pointing and gesticulating. He knew intuitively what was required.

'Well, Major,' I said, 'this is almost certainly Bluetongue. Too late for vaccination now that you've got it. Carried by midges. As it's a viral infection there's no treatment apart from symptomatic, If you've got any higher land than these plains, move the sheep there. There might be fewer midges. Smoky fires at night will help, and another thing, it's been found that midges prefer ngombe blood to that of sheep, heaven knows why – so if you can boma sheep and cattle together, that will also help. Cattle rarely show symptoms but act as carriers.'

'What about vaccination?'

'Yes, there is a vaccine, and vaccinating unaffected sheep may help but in your present situation your seemingly unaffected sheep may be already incubating the disease and it may do more harm than good. But if you do, do not vaccinate any pregnant animals.'

As may be imagined the old buffer was none too overjoyed by this news. By now the afternoon was well advanced, the light was fading and I was keen to vacate his marsh and get back to terra firma before the evening rains rendered the roads impassable.

Already, heavy, plum-coloured clouds were massing above my homeward route and the first weighty gobbets of rain were splattering themselves on the windscreen of my Peugeot.

Under such meteorological circumstances most landowners would have offered succour and shelter from the approaching storm. Not so this dewlapped, heather-eye-browed, ex-army misery guts. Personally I would rather have dossed down with our mute Pokot, whose hand

I shook as I took my leave. I waved to the Major. 'Take heart, Major. Mortality rarely exceeds 20%!'

He did not wave back.

As I slithered back across the plains to the road, an early evening jackal trotted in front of the car, turning its head to look at me as it did so. It was the same one I had passed in the morning.

The outbreak spread with the migrating midges and for weeks I was inundated by Maasai from the highlands of the Western Rift and beyond, desperate for vaccine to protect their flocks.

🛖✕🛖✕🛖✕

El Nino was not done with us yet.

The rains continued and now we had deaths in dogs, cattle, chickens, ducks, even farmed fish. Some died quickly, others lingered, getting weaker by the day until they too, succumbed. Dogs had enlarged livers, some had bloody diarrhoea, those that survived longer often showed signs of jaundice. The one thing all had in common was having been fed maize in one form or another. I sent samples to the Government Chemist for analysis and as I suspected the results indicated that the deaths were due to Aflatoxicosis. When conditions are warm and moist as they had been lately, the mould Aspergillus flavus proliferates on maize, and when harvested, maize is unable as a result to be properly dried under controlled conditions and the result is an outbreak of Aflatoxicosis, not only in animals, but humans as well. After all, maize is the staple diet of most people in East Africa. The liver is the main organ targeted and apart from symptomatic therapy and change of diet there was no treatment. So once again frustration and a feeling of powerlessness, something all too familiar in the African context, ruled supreme for the next couple of months.

About half-way through the latest biblical plague I awoke one morning feeling somewhat diminished. The symptoms were 'flu like – a hot clammy forehead, a slight rise in temperature, muscular aches, lowered appetite – in other words, nothing to write home about.

But the symptoms persisted. 'Go and see a doctor,' my beloved exhorted me. 'Don't be ridiculous!' was my stock response. And I carried on working. When you're self-employed, unless you're a wimp or hospitalized or on holiday, you don't go running to a quack whenever you feel a tad below par.

About two weeks later we had occasion to go to Nairobi – the Big Shitty as we called it. Why anyone would want to live there was beyond our comprehension. Some, of course, had no choice. But the horrendous traffic, the pollution, the dense crowds of people and the overarching atmosphere of mendacious rapacity made it, for us at least, an undesirable destination.

Anyway, as we were there, and as I was still not quite myself, we decided to visit an Asian sawbones who had rooms in the Nairobi Hospital. The short-skirted African nail-polisher at the front desk bade us be seated while she alerted Dr Patel of our arrival. After about 30 minutes of wall staring we were ushered into the Presence. Dr Patel was seated behind a large expensive-looking desk. His head was bowed as though in prayer, until I realised he was studying what looked like a scientific paper laid on his vast desk 'Probably actually the Kama Sutra,' I thought, 'trying to cultivate an air of cerebral sanctity in order to impress us.'

Dr Patel's head remained bowed. Then he suddenly looked up, as though surprised to see two strangers in his sanctum. 'Yes?' he said, 'and what can I do for you?' He steepled his manicured fingers. I could see that this was a man who did not get his hands dirty very often.

I gave him chapter and verse, relayed the symptoms, told him that I had been dealing with insect transmissible and water borne animal disease and that, in my opinion, humble or otherwise, what I had was either Leptospirosis or Rift Valley Fever.

Dr Patel smiled benignly, as though indulging the idle whim of an unlettered peasant.

'Let me decide,' he said.

After a cursory examination he informed me that no tests were currently available for Rift Valley Fever and that only in Germany could tests be done for Leptospirosis and that would take up to six weeks. So we remained none the wiser as to the cause of my disorder.

'Please pay at reception on your way out,' were Dr Patel's parting words.

But I knew that if the medical authorities in Kenya were unable to provide a diagnosis, the veterinary ones might, as at Muguga, a research institute on the outskirts of the city, Rift Valley Fever testing on animals was being carried out. And I was also aware that the Americans had been working on Rift Valley Fever in Kenya with a view to using it as a biological weapon. Such being the case, surely they must have some means of testing for the disease in humans.

Back home in Nakuru I selected a 5ml syringe and a suitable blood sample tube, tied a tourniquet around my upper left arm and drew off 4ml of non-patrician Pictish blood.

The following day I dispatched it by courier to the veterinary laboratory with an accompanying explanatory note.

Three weeks later, I had just walked into the surgery after a testing time dealing with an uncooperative male ostrich which had prolapsed its penis, when the phone rang.

'Is that Dr Cran?' said an American voice. 'That's me,' I replied. 'I'm a researcher at Muguga,' came the reply. 'Your sample proved positive for Rift Valley Fever. How're ye doin'?' 'Fine now,' I said. 'Well that's good, and the best news is that now you're immune so should the disease rear its ugly head again, you don't need to worry.'

And I didn't when a year or so later a particularly virulent haemorrhagic form drifted up from Southern Africa and once again I had to delve and burrow into infected carcases.

Another tropical ailment to add to all the others which had invaded my person since I arrived on the Dark Continent.

Chapter Fourteen

DUTCH COURAGE

Hendrick Goosens lived with his African wife on a small farm on the high Kinangop plateau about 40k from Naivasha.

'Mr Cran,' he said in his strong Dutch accent, 'I vont you to come to my farm to vaccinate my 13 dogs unt seven cats against rabies, ja. But the road is not so gut in the last part so I vill send a Land Rover to pick you up from the Caltex petrol station at the junction. There you can be leaving your car.'

'That's very kind of you,' I replied. A Land Rover eh? imagining a spanking, air conditioned, super sprung, window-tinted, four-wheel-driven space mobile. Should only take us half an hour to get to the farm. Great! I parked the Peugeot at the petrol station as directed and assigned a wall-eyed youth the task of assuring its safety until I returned. Assistant Moses moved into the shade to rest after the rigours of the journey from Nakuru. I made sure the cool box had sufficient syringes, needles and vaccine. Vehicles came and went. There was a police road block a few hundred yards away, with the gendarmerie hard at work harassing motorists. A pot-bellied constable strolled into the station to slake his thirst on a quart of Coca Cola and to count the morning's takings. While idly watching this corpulent leech scratching himself and yawning in fiscal self-satisfaction, a clapped-out old canvas sided Land Rover, belching smoke, back fired into the forecourt.

'Surely,' I thought, 'he's going to book the driver of that travesty of a vehicle. It shouldn't be on the road. The thing is coming apart at the seams.'

The policeman did nothing. He could recognize as well as I that here the likelihood of monetary gain was remote indeed.

The driver of the Land Rover stepped out and looked around. He seemed to be looking for someone. Then he glanced questioningly at me and I realised with dismay that this must be the Goosens driver.

A bulky middle-aged ruffian, clad in filthy oil stained dungarees, he gave me a yellow-toothed grin and slouched towards me.

'Jambo bwana,' he said, 'mimi ni Kamau, dereva ya Bwana Goosens. Tapeleka wewe paka pahali yake' 'I'm Kamau, Mr Goosens' driver and I'm here to take you to his place.' He could see me looking askance at his conveyance. 'The gari! Ha! Slow but sure, old is gold! No worries!' He cackled like a laying hen. Another man appeared, younger, thinner, but with the same air of genetic shiftiness. 'Huyu ni tunny boy!' exclaimed Kamau, 'ta saidia kama gari nakwama!' 'He's the tunny boy. He will help if the vehicle breaks down!' 'Say jambo, Ezekiel!' Ezekiel said jambo and we shook hands. Watch your back pocket here, I thought.

Summoning Moses, I climbed into the front passenger seat, noting the bald tyres, worn down to the canvas, and the cracked windscreen devoid of both road licence and insurance discs. My seat was innocent of such luxury items as upholstery which had been replaced by a pair of gunny sacks. I banged the door three times until it closed.

Kamau got in beside me, but before he did so he signalled to the pump attendants who were obviously used to this sort of thing. 'Battery likufa!' Kamau laughed, 'the battery has croaked!' Kamau engaged first gear, the pump attendants pushed and with a great roar the engine started, belching dense clouds of choking smoke out of the exhaust and into the cabin. The tunny boy leapt aboard and we ground our way onto the uphill road leading to the Kinangop.

The first section was tarmac, but we moved incredibly slowly. Kamau explained that gear number three was missing and that if he tried to get into fourth the engine would stall. And of course with no battery.... Our snail like progress was not silent.

The fearful clattering noise which accompanied our passage had pedestrians and livestock a mile ahead turning their heads in understandable concern. Goats and sheep stampeded for cover as we approached. None of the dashboard dials, which were thickly encrusted with dust and dirt, appeared to be working. My gunny sacks did not afford my gluteals with more than a modicum of cushioning and soon I felt that I was seated on bare metal.

From the dusty windscreen I lowered my gaze to the floor, through whose holes I could see the road approaching and receding in a peculiarly hypnotic manner. At least we were going uphill so risk to life and limb at this stage in the proceedings was minimal.

We came to an escarpment whose angle would have been a stern test of any vehicle in tip top condition, far less one teetering on the brink of terminal senility. With a horrid crunch Kamau crashed into first gear. Thick clouds of acrid smoke vomited from the frail trembling exhaust pipe, and we inched our way up the steepening incline.

At the top, the tarmac ended with brutal finality and we were on rock hard, corrugated, unsurfaced washboard. The Land Rover, and I, did not appreciate this.

Neither, I assumed, did the other members of the crew. Under normal conditions there would have been non-stop chat, laughter, badinage, and regular whooping. Now there was none of that, just a grim silence punctuated by the rhythmic thump and crash as our jalopy met the road head-on. Everyone seemed to be waiting for something to happen. We didn't have to wait for long. As we approached the singularly unattractive settlement of North Kinangop, the Land Rover lurched into a deep sided cavity, there was an unpleasant metallic clang, and the back of the vehicle swerved violently to the left. The engine stalled. With weary resignation everyone piled out to inspect the damage. The U bolt supporting the left main leaf spring had sheared, the suspension had collapsed and the chassis was now resting on the wheel. Forward progress was now at a standstill.

Luckily Kamau had anticipated such an event. Together with Ezekiel he dragged out a couple of jacks, cleared the ground below the rear axle and raised the vehicle. Fitting a U bolt in a garage or workshop is not easy. Doing the same job on a frightful African road is another matter altogether. But Kamau and Ezekiel managed. It took time but they knew what they were doing and after about an hour and a half we were ready to push start and get moving. African mechanics are a breed apart. You will see lorries, buses and saloon cars collapsed at the roadside, their innards spread out in the open, covered in oil and grease, while a gang of mechanics tinker with the bits and pieces. Two days later the vehicle has gone, repaired, put back together and back on the road. Repairing the repairable is what is done in Africa. This is not a throwaway society. This has always been the way in poor countries like Kenya. But now vehicles come crammed with sensors and mini computers. If you break down anywhere, in the bush or on the highway, no one can help you. Your vehicle has to be carted away to be hooked up to the 'mother computer' in order to diagnose the problem. This is not helpful if you are halfway across the Chalbi Desert or ploughing across a mile-wide lugga. And if your car has an automatic gear box, a push start is out of the question. In the bush a bog standard vehicle is what is best. Something repairable by a good bush mechanic. Reliability is what counts, not speed. The chauffeured diplomats and aid mandarins who throng Nairobi in their gleaming computerized passion wagons seldom leave the tarmac and have little idea what really constitutes life in Kenya. Most would not even know how to engage four wheel drive and would certainly never need to use it.

By the time we were U bolted, a small knot of ragged tatterdemalions had gathered to watch the proceedings. A pair of yellow eyed goats joined the crowd. A gaunt cow peered over a rusty barbed wire fence. The sky was blue, the air crisp, a pair of augur buzzards circled above, yelping at each other. I enjoyed sitting on a rock, surrounded by a mob of undemanding African peasants, watching others toil. I knew that my turn would come. It was just a different sort of toil.

We were ready to go. Kamau got into the driver's seat, engaged rear gear and we pushed him backwards to gain momentum down the hill. The engine caught and we all got back in.

Half an hour later we crawled into the Goosens' yard. It had taken two and a half hours to cover 40k.

Hendrik was tall and angular, fair haired and red faced. Mrs. Goosens was small, demure and sweet. She was Kikuyu. A couple of golden skinned children watched shyly from a distance as I vaccinated the dogs and cats. Hendrik grew roses for export to Holland. Like many of his compatriots he was a rather solemn and serious individual, decent, conscientious and hard-working, but lacking in the humour, self-deprecation and irreverence so often found in people of British descent. But in Kenya even this was in sad decline. New arrivals came burdened with a baggage of post-colonial guilt, seeing the Empire as a gigantic old boys' club, built and designed with the express purpose of screwing every last penny out of the downtrodden natives. As a result conversation with such holier-than-thou, po-faced, left-wing do-gooders could be hard work. Most Africans were more liberal in their views and easier to discuss such matters than many European and American apologists. The hypocrisy of some of the latter could be particularly nauseating. I gave a lift once to an American Peace Corps volunteer, called Caleb.

When I mentioned that the farms we were passing had all been British once but were now owned by African farmers, he crowed in triumph. 'Of course! It was theirs anyway! The land was stolen by the colonists, racist rich white settlers who paid nothing for it, flogged the poor Africans with hippo hide whips and lived in Happy Valley with their mistresses.' When I replied that at least Kenya was now back fully in the hands of the legitimate owners of the land while this was hardly the case in the Land of the Free and Home of the Brave, he went silent. When independence was seized from their British masters in 1776, the authors of the famous Declaration described the Native Americans, rightful owners of the land, as being 'merciless Indian savages,' which hardly gelled with the lofty guff about 'all men being created equal.' Some were seemingly created less equal than others as Orwell later observed. They also blamed King George for inciting American slaves to insurrection. In fact, as I pointed out to my hitchhiking friend, the Declaration was a means of reinforcing slavery in the American colonies, encouraging a westward invasion of Native American lands and the beginning of a genocide of the indigenous people. I decided to rub it in. America, I said, was built on stolen lands by the labour of enslaved people.

In other words, mate, take the beam out of your own eye before taking the mote out of others.

He was from the Bible Belt and was familiar with Jesus' exhortation to the disciples in the Book of Matthew.

He laughed – 'judge not lest ye be judged' eh?

'Exactly,' I said, 'know your history before you start to condemn and point the finger.'

Caleb was not a fanatic, just a brain-washed, tow-headed ignoramus from the uncultured wastelands of backwoods America. We parted on good terms.

Hendrik gave me a mug of coffee and boosted Moses with heavily sugared tea.

'So!' he said,' my gari served you well?' 'Well,' I replied, 'we got here.' No point in complaining. Now all we had to do was to get back. Should be simple, I thought. All downhill from here on. Should be a doddle compared to the uphill Sisyphean odyssey.

'Let me see you off,' said Hendrik.

We walked outside. Kamau and Ezekiel were doing something with long strips of leather. 'What's the matter Kamau?' asked Hendrik. 'The chassis is broken, Bwana, so we're just tying it together.' Indeed they were. In effect they were putting a huge bandage around the whole chassis.

I had read somewhere about how, in the 1920s, when a safari wagon, possibly carrying some trigger-happy aristos such as the Prince of Wales, or knickerbockered Americans like Theodore Roosevelt, broke a main leaf spring, it was similarly cobbled together. Wet rawhide reins, preferably made of buffalo hide, were lashed around the spring, holding it fast and in position. When they dried, they shortened and hardened and the journey could continue.

I felt as though I was watching history in action.

We set off, and apart from the expected vehicular cacophony all went well until we reached the tarmac and the steep declivity of the escarpment. Here Kamau began to show signs of strain and tension. I could soon see why. The Land Rover, to all intents and purposes, which were pretty vital, had no effective brakes.

Kamau was frantically pumping the middle pedal. Great drops of sweat beaded his brow and his teeth were bared like those of a wild animal. My own brow began to feel similarly moist as we tore downhill. At the bottom I knew that there was a narrow bridge on a corner. Kamau desperately tried to reduce gear. Each time he attempted to move the stick there was a horrific grating of metal on metal. His right leg was going up and down like a demented piston. This is it, I thought, seeing myself propelled head first through the windscreen and mashed against the rocks below the bridge, fragments of my mauled carcase washed downstream into Lake Naivasha. An easy exit. The Land Rover had no seat belts.

The sky was still blue, the air still crisp, I could hear fragments of bird song, and thought 'This is not a good day to die.'

I could see the bridge now. 'Ye gods!' I thought, 'it's damned narrow. He'll never make it.' Flowers were growing beside the approaches, pretty yellow and red flowers, and the bridge was like one of those old stone affairs you see spanning mountain streams in the Highlands of Scotland. It had a hump in the middle. How quaint, I thought.

Now I could see the moss growing on the stonework. Soft greenish moss, probably with a lovely velvety texture. Funny the things which go through your mind as death approaches.

One hundred yards, fifty yards, then, with a monstrous crunch, Kamau, eyes bulging from his sockets, rammed the gear stick into first. The Land Rover almost stood on its head and I was slammed against the dashboard. I could hear Moses and Ezekiel threshing about in the back, yelling and calling on the Almighty for salvation. We had slowed, but only enough for Kamau to turn the corner without overturning. We hit the hump on the bridge and the ancient crock leapt into the air, returning to earth with a fearful crash, enough to sunder every U bolt ever made. As we hit the deck all four of us were propelled vertically and if it were not for the fact that the roof was made of moth-eaten canvas we would undoubtedly have been brained. More painful was our return to our seats. Being dropped from a height of two feet onto irregular metal promoted more loud vocalizing, most of it of an impolite nature.

But we were alive and gave due thanks to Kamau and to our Maker. I slapped Kamau on his ragged back. 'Well done, my friend. You saved our bacon there. I was sure we were done for.' 'So did I,' he said, 'the Lord was with us.' I agreed.

We cruised gently down the rest of the road to the Caltex service station, breathing slowly and carefully, not quite sure that we had made it.

On arrival we made for the plastic-themed eaterie to regroup and debrief. A sullen greasy waitress slouched across to our table, still littered with the revolting remains left by previous customers. As she bent to wipe the surface with a cloth which looked as though it had last been used to clean the drains, her sagging unfettered bosoms swayed to and fro like a pair of huge pendulums. 'Sasa?' (Now then?) she asked in a bored voice. She took my order of samosas, chips and Cokes and as she shambled back to the kitchen her vast buttocks grappled with each other like a pair of wrestling pumpkins locked inside a gunny bag. Kamau and Ezekiel regarded her with lascivious leers, the terrors of our downhill rush lost in a tsunami of pheromones. The samosas, dense and leathery, arrived, slapped down on the table with a hearty plebeian flourish. The Cokes were tepid but welcome. Soon we were joined by large numbers of flies, which enjoyed the taste of the samosas rather more than I did. Then I noticed the fleshy cop of the morning, sidling in our direction. This could only mean one thing. When a policeman stops you in Africa you know that he is not stopping you to inquire after your health, but after the contents of your wallet.

It was time to leave. Bidding Kamau and Ezekiel bon voyage on their return journey Moses and I made a rapid exit, inhaling the rancid reek of beer fumes as we passed the swaying Arm of the Law and the Servant of All.

I had had enough. Up to here and brimming over. What the hell was I doing here? Risking my life in this clapped out country for probably no payment?

By the time I reached home I didn't feel so bad, and Berna, thank God, was on hand with warm arms, soothing words and a beaker of Gilbey's. Tomorrow would be a better day.

Chapter Fifteen

'WHILE TIMOROUS KNOWLEDGE STANDS CONSIDERING, AUDACIOUS IGNORANCE HATH DONE THE DEED'

Macduff was from his mother's womb untimely ripp'd. Caesarean sections in the bitch and cat were generally straightforward operations and devoid of complications. Occasionally one might find the gravid uterus to have ruptured in which case one might have to remove the whole mess including the dead pups or kittens, or one might find a torsion or an anti-social perforation, but on the whole one felt in control of the situation. The patients were of a satisfactory manoeuvrable size, generally compliant, and amenable to anaesthesia.

When patients of alternative species, other than the cow, presented themselves with difficulties in parturition, it was time to scratch the poll and reach for the textbooks.

Andy Yakas, former White Hunter and sisal plantation manager, was a splendid and charming Anglicized Greek. A rugby forward, strong as an ox and built like a brick shit house, he exuded confidence and friendliness in equal measure. He stood for no nonsense. Once, when driving to the plantation, having collected the workers' wages in cash, his vehicle was held up on the Solai Majani Mingi road by two gunmen. What the gunmen did not know was that Andy had his own gun in the glove box of his car. He drew it and shot one dead and winged the other who later died of his wounds. The judge later congratulated Andy for having 'rid Kenya of two despicable vermin.' He had been a hunter of the old school, hunting a desirable target for perhaps weeks, on foot. He showed me the tusks of a bull elephant he had shot in the dry, withered waterless bush country of Eastern Province. 'Tracked him for 15 days. Damned near killed me. And all the time we were in shifta Somali bandit land. Felt we were also being hunted. Had this unpleasant feeling we were being watched all the time.' The tusks were huge, well over six feet long, beautifully tapered, weighing 95 and 91lbs. Worth a king's ransom these days.

Now Andy was retired both from hunting and from sisal farming and had a small property in the Solai Valley where he ran a small herd of Jersey cows and about 20 breeding sows and gilts.

I had farrowed many sows and gilts in my time. You got down on your hands and knees on the concrete – or straw if you were lucky – lubricated your arm – like a good Muslim I always used my left – said a quick prayer, and inserted your hand through the vulva and into the vagina and hoped to find a wriggling piglet in the waiting room. My hopes were more than often dashed. The presenting offspring was frequently dead and oversized, blocking the way forwards – or backwards – for the queue behind. But usually once I had winkled out the offending individual, shoved my arm in as far as it would go, removed as many occupants as possible and then gave the mother a strong dose of oxytocin to contract the uterus to expel the rest, I could depart, job done.

So when Andy phoned up late one Saturday afternoon to say that he had a gilt in obstetrical difficulties I rocked up, expecting the usual quick job, followed by a restorative beer or two and a fund of hunting stories.

Andy led the way to the piggery. In the UK this would probably be a sanitized structure where you would have to don overboots, surgical mask and be sprayed with a powerful disinfectant before being allowed entry. Here there was nothing like that. Andy pushed open the wooden door into a corrugated-roofed structure where there were a number of parallel sties housing the porcine inhabitants.

The patient was lying on her side on a bed of straw, her distended belly rising and falling gently. 'She was due to farrow two days ago,' said Andy, 'she's got milk in her teats but nothing has happened. She's not even straining. And she's stopped eating.'

'OK,' let's put a hand in and see what's going on.' While Andy went to bring some warm water I examined the pig, whose weight I estimated to be about 200lbs, that of an overweight human. Still, not as much as an average horse which bulks in at about 1,000lbs. Andy returned and I soaped my hand and arm. Immediately I knew we were in trouble. My hand is pretty small, perhaps not as small as Donald Trump's, but smaller than average. But even so I could barely get my hand through the vulva. This did not look good. As I moved further north it looked even worse. I reached the cervix, which was open, so indicating that the patient was ready and willing. The problem was her pelvic diameter, which was so narrow that there was no way that anything larger than a mouse could wriggle through. I managed to push my index finger through the canal and a friendly piglet on the other side gave me a welcoming nip. But I knew that without a caesar he – or she – was baby bacon, and the mother was pork.

I stood up and gave Andy the bad news. 'She's got live piglets in there but there is no way they can come out the normal route. The birth canal and her pelvis are far too narrow. She's not straining because the piglet is still behind the cervix. And there's no point in giving oxytocin to make the uterus contract. It won't do any good and might even result in a ruptured uterus. So it's either slaughter or a caesar, which I've never done in a pig before.'

'Well,' said Andy, 'if we slaughter her I'll get very little for her, what with her being pregnant. If we wait until morning she'll probably die, so we've got nothing to lose by trying and everything to gain if she lives. So go ahead and give it your best shot.'

My best shot? A quick shot from Andy's elephant gun would solve my problems, if not that of the labouring gilt, and release me from a host of mental and physical conundrums, one of which was how to anaesthetize the beast, a task which I had never been called on before to perform on a porker of this magnitude. I had castrated innumerable piglets and excised loads of irreducible rectal prolapses and by dropping a wad of cotton wool soaked in ether down a wellington boot and persuading the squealing patient to inhale deeply while being held in the inverted position was able to perform such interventions relatively easily. But this was rather different.

I cudgelled my overstressed brain. In my surgical bag I had a bottle of Stresnil, azeperone, which I had on occasion used to sedate antelope. I had read somewhere that if you gave this intramuscularly to pigs it would knock them out. But would it be enough to allow me to open the abdomen and keep the patient anaesthetised long enough for me to remove the piglets from the uterus, and then stitch everything up? I felt like taking a shot of the appropriately named Stresnil myself. But what if I added another pair of drugs, Xylazine and Ketamine, once the swine was down and out? After all I had to be both surgeon and anaesthetist simultaneously. Once I was armpit deep in unknown territory I did not want the patient suddenly deciding that it was time to go walkabout.

I explained all this to Andy, telling him that I would in effect be working in the dark and that I would be doing so literally unless he brought some powerful torches to lighten my way. While he departed to bring the required illumination I prepared myself for battle. Night falls suddenly in the tropics. Here there is no soft northern crepuscular gloaming lasting for several soothing hours. One moment it's light, the next you are plunged into stygian Nubian darkness. Hence my haste to get things ready while there was still a glimmer of some streaks of day.

While Andy was off searching for lanterns I prepared a tray of all the instruments I might need, piling on every haemostat, forceps, needle holder and suture material I possessed, in the sure and certain knowledge that ten times too many was better than one too few at a moment of crisis, something which I pressed on absent Moses at every possible opportunity, to no avail. No matter how many times I abjured him to ensure that all instruments and sutures were prepared, it was to find him rushing off halfway through the procedure to fetch some vital piece of equipment he had forgotten to lay out.

The funny thing was that he seemed to accept this as normal, he never ever apologized for his failures, and numerous well-deserved bollockings had zero effect. Now I was on my own and I made doubly sure that everything I might need was on hand. One missing instrument might be the difference between life and death. Trying to stop a big slippery spouting artery with your fingers was the stuff of nightmares.

The good thing was that I could give all drugs into the muscles of the hind leg. Giving intravenous injections to pigs is not easy and to be avoided if at all possible. Accessing the jugular through an inch or so of blubber is not to be contemplated and so the veins on the outside of the ear are the ones usually used. But pigs are not, on the whole, particularly cooperative animals and resent being restrained, voicing their opinion with ear splitting high pitched squealing, the only advantage being that when doing so their blood pressure rises and their ear veins distend, making an IV injection feasible. But by that time, unless you are wearing ear muffs you are probably partially deafened for life. As this young porcine was in labour I was reluctant to subject her and my hearing to such trauma. So I opted for the softly softly approach. First I gently massaged her distended mammaries. She grunted with obvious pleasure and satisfaction at the touch of my soothing hand and shifted to a more comfortable position on her side.

'Right, Andy,' I said, 'Can you carry on doing this while I shove the first injection into her hind leg.'

Andy did as instructed. I really had no idea what to expect. I had used xylazine and ketamine in dogs, cats and horses to good effect. It was safe and I just hoped that it would be equally safe and effective in the pig and that the results would be sufficient to do the job. And I added in the Stresnil for good measure.

A large shape loomed behind me and shone a brilliant beam of light onto the waiting rump. It was Elim, Andy's gofer man. Andy had rescued him from Marsabit prison where he had been incarcerated for a spot of cattle rustling. His father, a villainous looking Turkana, had worked for Andy as a gun-bearer. Andy had taken him on as a favour to his father for services rendered – always a major mistake in Africa. Elim was lean and ferrety with an ingratiating grin. Elim's grasp of Swahili was meagre, even worse than mine, which was Swahili ya jikoni na shamba – kitchen and farm Swahili – but I indicated that the light was to be directed onto the pig's backside and nowhere else. Elim got the message. I glanced at my watch. 7pm. I was in luck. If I had arrived any later Elim would almost certainly have departed to the local tavern and be incapable of any speech, far less execrable Swahili.

I rubbed some local anaesthetic onto the gilt's backside, waited for a couple of minutes and then slowly pushed in the dose of Stresnil and stood back, hoping that it would give a degree of sedation before I added the next cocktail. Ten minutes later she was indeed nicely drowsy so I gave her what I hoped was the correct dose of xylazine and we stood back and watched and waited.

'Right,' I said to Andy, 'now for the ketamine. This is the anaesthetic. The others were sedatives. In animals other than primates you can't use ketamine on its own. You have to give a sedative first otherwise you will get seizures and convulsions which may be fatal.'

The gilt's breathing slowed, slowed, then stopped. Shit! Had I killed her?Perhaps I shouldn't have given the Stresnil. Bloody fool! I had overdosed her. For perhaps a minute her chest did not move and I turned to get a stethoscope to check her heart to find if it was still beating. Then she gave a gasp and began to take in air. Relief! Relief!

The gilt was now out cold, breathing slowly and steadily. Next for the op. What sort of incision should I make? Angular or vertical? I could see that the latter would be limited in length should I need to extend it so I opted for the former. Whatever option I went for, there would be a lot of fat and muscle to saw through before I entered the abdomen.

I used a clean towel as a makeshift drape and clipped it to the skin. The good thing about pigs is that they are virtually hairless so I could dispense with shaving the operative zone. I always envied human surgeons in this regard. Many animals are covered with a dense hairy pelt which has to be removed before anything can be done, which all adds to the length of the procedure.

Andy had brought a straw bale upon which my tray of instruments was laid. Telling Elim to re-direct his beam I grasped the skin with a pair of rat-toothed forceps. No reaction. Right, here we go. The bold sweeping incision so beloved of the authors of surgical textbooks. Had they ever done this sort of thing themselves, I often wondered? A mass of spouters along the incision line greeted me. I clipped the larger ones and left the smaller ones on the hopeful assumption that they would eventually stop by themselves. Now for the fat, white and about an inch thick. No blood vessels here, thank God. But below this lay muscle, well endowed with unseen arteries and veins. Well, here goes! No point in hanging around.

If you make the abdominal incision through the midline, by cutting carefully through the linea alba, the fibrous white line separating the ventral abdominal muscles, you can avoid depleting the patient of any of its vital fluids. But in order to do so you have to have the patient lying on her back, there is greater stress on the stitch line when the animal stands up and when the piglets, if any survive, start to suckle they may, in their eagerness to get to the milk bar, do harm to the stitches with their sharp toes and needle-like teeth. So through the flank it had to be.

Here the blood vessels were more numerous so by the time I was about to enter the abdomen both sides of the incision were festooned with dangling haemostats. Control of haemorrhage in such situations is vital. There is no one on hand to administer a blood transfusion. Into the abdomen, insert a potentially sterilized hand and root around. Ah! Here we are! A uterine-encased piglet, squirming under my fingers. Now to pull the left horn of the lengthy uterus out into, if not the light of day, then under Elim's searchlight. Drag as much out as possible and pull it forwards to access the main body so that I can incise it here and try to milk all the piglets down and out through one incision. Some pundits I had read about suggested making an incision on the other flank for easier access to the other horn. Stuff that, I thought. The sooner we get this over and done with the better. So cut through the uterine wall. Some bleeding, but ignore it and pull out piglet number one and hand it to Andy to clamp the umbilical cord and give a good rub with a handful of dry straw. Right, squeeze another down the tube and out into the open. And another and another. Now for the other horn. Get your arm right in and pull it out and gently massage those piglets down to the exit. Another four, all alive, *mirabile dictu*. So eight in total, not bad for a gilt.

I could hear them snuffling and squeaking behind me but that was Andy's job. I had to get a move on. No time to check the results. Make sure there are no piglets left inside. Grab the needle holders and get the uterus sown up. It had already begun to contract which was a good sign. When it remains flaccid and inert you know that things are not good. Inverted stitches here. OK, done. Now for the peritoneum. Everted stitches and get it closed. I had no idea how long the anaesthetic was going to last so I had to work fast. The last thing I wanted was an armful of pig guts spilling out of the wound. Quickly I stitched the muscle layers, closed the fat, and the subcutaneous tissue. As I began to deal with the skin there was a stirring at the front end. The patient was waking up and objecting to the sharp triangular needle being pushed through her sensitive epidermis. Holding down an adult pig is not something which can be done by mere human hands. Frantically I stitched, knotted, threaded and cut.

Behind me there was a cacophony of piglet piping and snuffling. Andy also had his hands full. Two more stitches to go. As I prepared the push the needle through the skin, the beam of light waned, wavered, then it was all over the place, on the roof, on the walls, on the floor. 'What the hell?' Then there was a groan, a crash, a thump and we were plunged into inky blackness.

The piglets were squeaking and Andy was swearing. 'Elim's fainted! God knows where he is! Can't see a damn thing. So much for the indomitable Turks! Bugger couldn't take the heat I suppose. It is a bit warm in here.'

'Well, I can't see my hand in front of my face. And the gilt's waking up and I still have a couple of stitches to put in.'

Then we could hear grunting, wheezing and whumping, a bit like an elephant seal making its way down a South Georgia beach towards the sea. Elim was waking up. We could hear him scrabbling around, presumably looking for his dropped torch, which I sincerely hoped was still functional. On the home front the patient was also waking up and doing her own scrabbling. The question was, who would be on their feet first? To my immense relief it was Elim. The glass of his torch was smashed but the bulb, throwing a feeble glow-worm light, sufficiently illuminated the struggling patient's flank to allow me to insert the final stitches before she staggered to her feet.

I rose to my own feet and turned to Andy who was piglet full. 'Right,' I said, 'that's that. I'll give her a shot of oxytocin now to contract the uterus and let down her milk, and give her some antibiotic and then we can give her the piglets and hope that she accepts them. Some do, some don't.'

The gilt gave a resigned grunt and lay down. The piglets staggered across to her, she rolled onto her side, and they got stuck in and began to suckle.

'Well,' said Andy, 'that looks good. Well done! Come up to the house to wash up and have a snort and I'll tell you about that buff which almost got me in the Loitas.' I accepted with alacrity.

Two weeks later I was back on the farm to remove the stitches. Andy was away, having gone to Tanzania, or TZ as it was often called by the local cognoscenti, to visit his brother Adam in Arusha. He had left the day following the op. He had told me the gilt was doing well and that the offspring were thriving. Elim was skulking furtively about the premises, looking shifty and evasive.

'Right, Elim,' I said, 'I've come to remove the stitches from the pig I operated on two weeks ago. How is she and how are the piglets?'

'Mama ni sawa, laikini yeye likula watato wote – the mother is fine but she ate all of the piglets.'

I said nothing. I entered her premises. They were filthy. She was rooting around at her trough, nosing at a mess of swill, composed, as far as I could see, of cabbages, potatoes and unidentifiable vegetable elements. She seemed glad to see me and gave me a welcoming grunt. I rubbed her ears and her belly and she lay down with a sad sort of sigh.

The operation site was healed and healthy and I removed the stitches as she lay there in the mire. 'So where are your babies?' I asked her. I knew what had happened. Once Andy had disappeared over the horizon, Elim had downed tools and gone on the booze. The sties had not been cleaned out, the animals had barely been fed and the piglets had sickened and one by one had died. Savage sows can cannibalize their young or crush them but signs of such behaviour are usually evident before they give birth. And this gilt was not such a candidate.

I knew that Elim was lying but I also knew that he would deny everything. Just like the house girl who stole some of Berna's jewellery and who also denied her actions. She was sacked but, now jobless, came skulking back later hoping to resume her duties. When Berna pointed out to her that she was wearing one of the stolen necklaces around her neck she expressed innocent surprise and outraged indignation and claimed that she had acquired the said item from a passing merchant. She was sent off with a flea in her ear.

I read the riot act to Elim. He listened in sullen silence. I had better things to do than watch this contemptible wretch clean out pigsties but I was determined to do so and waited until I was satisfied that all was up to the mark. Then I had him fill the troughs with pig food, the sacks of which looked as though they had not been opened since Andy had left. I told him that I would be back I in a few days to check on his handiwork. He glowered at me with his yellowed eyes. I departed, thankful that I was not in Turkanaland where he might have gone for me with a spear or a knife.

That was the only porcine Caesarean section I was called upon to do in Africa. And, like most things on that continent, it was, at best, a qualified success.

◎◎◎◎◎◎

Africans are very fond of the term 'field.' 'Oh,' underlings would cry, 'he's gone to the field,' as though *he* was working in arduous conditions in the Gobi Desert or somewhere east of Lake Baikal in Siberia. Even if he was a desk wallah such as a seat warming accountant. *He* was in the 'field' and therefore totally unreachable, when you knew that he was possibly only a few hundred yards away and probably slaking his thirst in a local tavern.

In my book 'field' meant just that – a grassy expanse, enclosed by fences, or preferably by neatly trimmed privet hedges.

Caesarean section in the mare, carried out under 'field' conditions, whether in the Gobi Desert, or east of Lake Baikal, or even in a grassy pasture, is something which few vets would regard with calm equanimity. In the so-called developed world, all, without exception, would, with speed, refer the animal to the nearest equine hospital or veterinary faculty, where all the required facilities and expertise would be on hand.

'That's that,' they would sigh with relief as the horse box disappeared over the horizon.

There was no such option in Kenya, or anywhere in East Africa.

Bruce Nightingale was, for once, stumped. Like the Chinese, he was an expert at moulding and mining the skills of others to his own ends. I had been going to his farm for years, decades even. Bruce was a quick learner and an assiduous note taker, and, over time, he was, from scratch, able to take blood samples, swab mares, give injections, and suture wounds. He was ready to try his slim and agile hand at almost anything. And for this I was, on the whole, grateful, as I was spared being called out at some unsocial hour to cobble together some trifling tear in skin or muscle. And besides, he was a good payer of bills, unlike many other residents of former British East. And he was a good friend and hospitable to a fault. But on this occasion he was obliged to lift the phone.

'Hugh, we have a mare here, quite a big mare, having difficulty foaling. Joseph, my head syce, has been trying for hours, and he's got nowhere. She's getting bit weak and exhausted and I don't want to lose her. Can you come out?'

On receipt of these less than glad tidings I felt the first creeping twinges of my very own personal exhaustion. I knew, from bitter experience, that when mares do not deliver as per rote, you, and they, are in big trouble. The foal's immensely long legs, the python-like neck and the size of the dam means that you need arms with muscles of steel, and several of them, yards long, in order to access and manipulate and extract. Here there is no easy winkling out. In the past I had had several life-and-death struggles with foaling mares and emerged bloody and bowed from the experience. The mares, on the whole, survived my interventions. Few of their foals did. Once a mare starts to give birth, if the foal is not delivered within about half an hour, survival is most unlikely. By the time I had arrived on the scene, and after prior amateur attempts at extraction had failed, the foal was, in almost every case, deceased. The expulsive efforts of a mare trying to expel her foetus, whether alive or dead, are without parallel in the domestic animal kingdom, and no mere mortal, far less I, is able to compete, without some form of chemical assistance.

So after a quick assessment of the situation I always sedated the mare before attempting to correct the problem. This may make the mare less willing to propel her infant into the outer world, but is preferable to the risks associated with dealing with a predicament potentially dangerous both to the mare, the vet and the foal, should it be still alive. If it was alive, then forced extraction, after correcting any mal-presentation, sometimes worked. But more often, with a dead foal in a position impossible to correct, I had to remove it in sections, using my trusty embryotome, threading the cutting wire around neck or leg and removing manageable portions until everything was out. Sounds gruesome but in my view less stressful to the mare than 'Toyota traction' or a Caesar out in the open. But needs must when the devil drives. The main thing was to know when to decide what was the best course of action and which was best for the mare. There was no use in exhausting both yourself and the mare until both were so knackered that both were useless for any alternative.

I summoned Moses, checked that we had enough gear for every contingency, and tooled up to the farm to find Bruce and a squadron of African syces gathered like a conclave of undertakers around a mare of statuesque proportions. She did not look happy.

Head syce Joseph stood head and shoulders above the throng. He was a tall lean Samburu, he wore glasses and I knew him to be an excellent horse man, dependable and easy to deal with.

'So, Joseph,' I asked 'what's the problem?' 'Jambo daktari, siwezi pata mguu au kichwa.' 'I can't find a leg or head.' 'OK, let me have a feel.'

I soaped my left arm and he was right. All I could feel was the foal's back. The foal was lying transversely across the uterus. Try as I might, with my arm in past my straining armpit, I couldn't reach or even touch leg or head. As I was fossicking around, the mare suddenly, and without a word of warning, lay down. I whipped my arm out, just before it was caught on the wooden bar, laid behind her as a precaution against kicking.

As I did so I recalled in vivid Technicolour the case of the American vet who did not pull his arm out in time when the large beef cow he was pregnancy-testing also decided to lie down without informing him. He sustained a compound fracture of his arm, the bone fragment, sharp as a Somali dagger, pierced his skin and perforated the wall of the cow's rectum, effectively pinning him to the cow's rear end and with no means of withdrawal. He was trapped on the ground with his fractured arm impaled inside a soup of faecal material, blood and who knew what else, belonging to a very large cow. He just hoped she would not now decide to get up and make a run for it. The cow had to be slaughtered and her pelvis bisected with a saw before he was freed. He was lucky not to lose his arm.

I turned to Bruce, who waiting patiently in the wings. 'Right,' I said, 'the foal, which I assume is dead, is lying at right angles and there are only two options: shoot her; or do – correction – *attempt*, a Caesar. By the way, what's wrong with her feet?'

'She's pretty old but she's got a good pedigree and her foals have won many races, so if possible I would like to save her. She had laminitis when she was young and so never raced and was used for breeding. Her hooves have been like that for years.'

'OK. Well I'll try. This will be my number one, but first principals and all that. Anaesthesia may be an issue but let me get on with it.'

In the past, and even the present, doing a Caesar in the 'field' would not be contemplated due to the lack of adequate anaesthesia. Even now, due the time it would take to do the operation I would have to 'top up' by giving IV injections during the procedure. I would be both surgeon and anaesthetist! Something no vet in places such as the UK would consider. I sometimes wished I was back in the past, say in the 19th century. Then, you wouldn't be racking your brains and deepening your ulcer. You would just say, 'Sorry old girl,' take out your revolver and be back in your hansom cab and be off to your next patient or your mistress as the case might be. But here I was, in the 20th century, and had to make the best of it.

The mare had risen to her dilapidated feet. I had her led to a patch of relatively smooth greensward and girded my feverish loins for action. As far as I was concerned this was a do-or-die situation, so I did not intend to stint on the anaesthetic. I wanted her to be nice and deep, so that I had plenty of time to get in there and get the foal out before I had to do the inevitable top-up. So I gave her a slow IV dose of xylazine for her 1,400lb bodyweight plus another half dose for good measure. Two minutes later her head was drooping below her knees and I gave her a big bolus of ketamine to lay her down.

Bruce had summoned the troops so I was able to direct the men to support her so that she went down slowly and carefully. If she hit the ground with a crash that gravid, tense uterus might rupture. All went well and down she went.

'Right,' I said, 'now roll her onto her back and hold her there. Moses, bring water, soap and a razor blade so that I can shave her abdomen.' No smooth porcine skin here.

Shaved, and sterilized with spirit, I was ready to begin. A tray of instruments was laid on a bale of hay to my right. I seized the scalpel and carefully incised through the linea alba, the fibrous white line separating both sides of the lower abdominal muscles. Carefully, so that when the blade entered the abdomen it didn't cut something I didn't want it to cut, such as gut. Theoretically, with the mare on her back, organs such as intestine should fall down and be out of the way, but by so doing they, and especially the heavy uterus containing the foal, may compress the posterior vena cava (main vein), and, by impeding venous return, compromise the heart's ability to pump blood to the rest of the body. So no dawdling.

The incision had to be generously long so that removal of the foal did not involve any camel through the eye of a needle stuff involving wrenching and tugging. A smooth exit was the object. I glanced up at the men supporting the mare – Kikuyus, Turkanas, Kalenjin. I wondered if they would all stay the course. Or would one of them pass out? Often it was the big, brawny ones who would start swallowing and gagging before making their shameful excuses about the heat and humidity and staggering away, while their skinny colleagues sniggered and carried on.

I knew I was through and into the abdomen when there was an almost imperceptible hiss of gas and a relaxation of the muscular wall. Now get a hand inside and with scissors extend the incision northwards for about a foot or so. Root around inside and almost immediately feel the massive uterus. But where the shoot is a leg? Or the head?

All I can feel is what I assume is the foal's back. What I can also feel are the rivulets of anxious perspiration trickling down my back. Where the hell *are* the head and the legs? Time to get right inside. Up to the armpit. Ah, got a leg, grab it through the uterine wall and try to pull it up towards the open air. Shit! The anaesthesia is lightening. The mare's hind legs are moving. Grab the syringes pre-filled with dope and drop the foal's leg and shoot the drugs into the jugular. Wait for five minutes, relocate the leg and try again. Up to the abdominal incision, tilt the mare towards me so that when I make my incision into the uterus any unwanted fluids do not contaminate the abdominal cavity. This foal is dead after all and, unlike wine, does not improve over time. With a scalpel, cut over the hoof and extend the uterine incision along the line of the leg. I pull the leg out and up. 'Right, Moses,' I say, 'grab and hold that leg and do not let your unsterilized mitt go anywhere near the inside of the mare. I now have to locate the other leg. That's a hind leg, thank goodness, so the head should follow when we start to pull.'

Foal's legs are extremely long so though in theory it might seem simple that once you have got hold of one leg it should be a piece of cake to locate and re-correct the position of the other, in practice you need extendable robotic arms for the job. So I was seriously stretched as I ran my hand along the foal's rear end, discovering to my disgust that the other limb was extended beneath the abdomen. It might have been possible to extract the foal by traction on the one exteriorized hind leg but this might have resulted in uncontrolled tearing of the uterus and major haemorrhage. So I had to try to get my hand below the hock, flex the joint and then cup my hand below the hoof to prevent it from puncturing the uterine wall, before sliding it up, up and away. With a supreme effort I reached the hock, going light-headed with the strain. But try as I might I could not flex the joint. 'Get me a calving rope!' I croaked.

Moses rushed off to the car. I fed the thin looped rope along the leg until I was back where I had just been. Eyes popping, I tried to push the rope round the leg. Sounds simple. In the textbooks a picture of an immaculately-gowned academic with an air of supercilious swank on his finely curved lips demonstrates just how easy it is. Give me strength! I was in up to my armpit and beyond, fingers straining. I could feel the end of the thin cord. I stroked it with a desperate digit. Come on! Come on! Ah, gotcha! Draw it through and complete the loop and feed it down and below the joint, and tighten it on the leg. Now pull the hock upwards, now feed the loop below the fetlock joint. Cup my hand below the hoof. 'Joseph!' I barked, 'pull the rope, upwards, but carefully, no jerking or tugging.' All this in Swahili. 'Ndiyo, bwana.' Slowly, slowly, pressure on the uterine wall, keep that hand covering the pointy hoof which could so easily slip through the wall of the womb. Ah! Thar she blows! Now straighten the leg. Both legs out now, so time to extract the foal. But before we do, time for another top-up. OK. Done. Right, me hearties, all hands to the capstan bars and slowly, slowly and upwards and out she comes. Grab the sides of the uterine incision and clamp with tissue forceps before it vanishes into the abdomen. The foal is, as expected, dead, and dumped unceremoniously, without benefit of clergy, on the grass. There is a long wheezing sigh, like a far off approaching train whistle, and one of the Kikuyu gogglers is down and out cold, and laid beside the foal. I spare him a glance but my hands are full of equine uterus, so he'll just have to take his chance and lie there. I rather envy him.

The edges of the uterine incision are bleeding rather profusely, but I assume that this will stop once I have stitched the edges together, plus later a hefty shot of oxytocin. I hope so. The placenta has come out with the foal so that's one thing less to worry about.

A continuous double line of inverted stitches, check that it's all watertight, shove the uterus back into the cavity, squeeze in a few tubes of antibiotic cream and now for the abdominal wall. This bit is very important. It's got to be stitched such that the line will hold. The Thin Red Line comes to mind. Why am I thinking about the Crimea? Because if one section breaks, all is undone. The enemy, Russians or gut, will break through. So use very strong single polyglactin everted sutures, tying each knot carefully.

My back, broken in '78, is giving me stick, but I'm almost finished. This is no time for complacency however. Each muscle layer requires close attention until we reach the skin. Here I put in eversion stitches of monofilament nylon. Suddenly I have this weird feeling. I'm going deaf. I can hear no sound. I look up at a double row of slack-jawed, wide-eyed African faces staring at me. Under normal circs they would be gassing, chaffing and laughing. 'Karibu nakwisha,' I say. Almost finished. The ice is broken and they grin and smile and begin talking amongst each other.

Finished, we roll the mare onto her side, cover her upper eye with a towel. I stretch, glad that it's over and that she's alive, breathing slowly and steadily. I give her an injection of antibiotic and lean against a fence post, waiting for her to get up. Now I can hear birds chirping, crickets sawing, women nearby chattering, distant colobus monkeys hooting, things blocked out in those moments of concentration.

The mare is flicking her tail, indicating that the anaesthetic is lightening. A few minutes later she sits up, nibbles at the grass in front of her. Then, she heaves herself to her feet and stands, unsteadily. Men support her until, sooner than I expected, she is strong enough to walk to her stable.

To my surprise, and that of everyone else, the mare recovered well, with little or no after-effects. At three weeks I removed the sutures and she was put out to recuperate on grass. Alas, good times never last. Four months later there is a sudden storm of rain, thunder, a crack of lightning, a startled mare with dodgy hooves, slips, breaks a foreleg and has to be shot.

Yet another very qualified success.

Chapter Sixteen

NORTHERN EXCURSIONS

Moses, my right hand man, was getting old. He, together with office 'boy' Bernard had been with me for over 40 years. Before that both had worked for my predecessor, Welshman Owen-Jones of dubious memory, who had moonlight-flitted to the then-Rhodesia while I was recuperating after having had my right leg fractured by an overly anti-social bovine patient. Both were Kikuyus. Bernard had been a foot soldier in the Mau Mau insurrection against British rule. In this role he had taken part in the attack in 1953 on the Naivasha police station in which the raiders had got away with a large stash of weaponry, including rifles and sub-machine guns, which was later used to considerable effect in the struggle to overthrow the oppressive colonial yoke. He bore no grudge against his former overlords. After all, his side, in the final analysis, had won, along with that of all of his brothers and sisters across Africa. The British Empire was no more, leaving the palm to America and China, both also empires in all but name, and at least, if not more, despotic in their rule than the British version ever was. A majority government can subjugate a minority native population indefinitely. The reverse cannot.

Both Bernard and Moses were totally reliable and honest, invaluable assets in a land where both were rare commodities. Both cycled miles to work on their ancient push bikes. But now both were well over 70 and when I sent Bernard out on foot to do some chores in town I never knew when, or indeed, if, he might return. Sometimes he was gone for so long I was convinced he must have been run over by a bus. But then I would hear his characteristic soft shoe shuffle and he would push open the swing door and shamble into the surgery, a gap toothed grin on his amiable features. We always conversed in Swahili.

Bernard was not particularly bright but he never lapsed into the sullen state into which many Kikuyus tended to fall when they felt themselves slighted or hard done by. From time to time Moses would become morose and monosyllabic and I would wonder why. Was this some genetic throwback to the dark, secretive, introspective ways of his forest-dwelling agricultural forebears? I never came across this trait in pastoralists or nomads, people of the sunlit plains, followers of cattle and camels. But now Moses had even more reason to be less than chirpy. The poor fellow was afflicted by a trio of age-related abominations – diabetes, Parkinson's Disease and enlargement of the prostate. He struggled on but it became obvious that the time for retirement had come.

So it was mutually agreed, and after paying both faithful servants their well-earned dues we shook hands, bade farewell and another chapter was closed.

Bernard's successor was not a success. Francis Ng'anga was the son of our deputy house 'girl,' who, most unusually, was a member of the indigenous Holy Ghost Church of East Africa, which was founded in the 1920s and eschewed contact with Europeans and their ungodly ways. The church combined traditional Kikuyu beliefs with Christianity. Its adherents, mostly poor and uneducated, wore white robes and turbans as a sign of peace, drank no alcohol and ate no pork, met on the Sabbath to drum and sing hymns and tended not to mingle with non-members. They were immediately recognizable when you came across them, especially on a Sunday in the country, out in the open, with their hypnotic drumming and their jog trot as they followed their bearded deacons. They are called Akorinos, a name meaning 'people of God.'

Sadly, unbeknown to us and to his parent, Francis had, like the Prodigal Son, fallen into bad company, taken to drink and forsaken the tenets of his mother's church. But, unlike the Prodigal Son he had not returned home and when he was discovered breaking through the ceiling of the surgery to gain access to the till to acquire money to pursue his wicked ways, his probationary employment came to an abrupt end. Against my better judgement, and in a moment of weakness, Berna persuaded me to re-hire him on behalf of his toiling, impecunious mama. This was a fatal mistake. The leopard does not change his spots nor does the Aethiopian his dusky skin and neither did Francis change his evil ways. Moses was in the last throes of his employment and supervising his fellow tribesman in his duties and, probably due to his infirmities, one day gave Francis a sum of cash to be banked. Francis took the money and never returned.

It was time, I thought, for a change. Time for a change in tribe. Eric, the manager of a large dairy farm, near Nakuru, to whom I confided my problem, suggested a young man of his own tribe, which was Nandi. And what was more, he would guarantee his honesty, or money back. This was almost too good to be true. Which, of course it wasn't, as I found out, in the fullness of time.

The Nandi are part of the Kalenjin conglomeration of tribal groupings, from northwest Kenya, containing, also, the Kipsigis, the Elgeyo, the Marakwet, the Tugen, and our old friends, the Pokot. The Nandi, a warrior tribe, put up fierce resistance to the invasion of their lands by the British, much more so than the redoubtable Maasai, whose fearsome reputation collapsed like a pricked balloon as the pale invaders advanced. Not so the Nandi, who tore up railway lines, ripped down telegraph wires, attacked colonial outposts, decapitated quislings and wiped out uninvited intruders. They did not take the arrival of the imperial army lying down. So when Simeon Kipkorir, descendant of those doughty defenders, entered my employment I expected a lean, hawk-nosed, long-legged strider of the plains, with warrior blood surging through his aristocratic veins. Kip, as he preferred to be called, was moon-faced, a physical trait which, as time passed, incorporated other aspects of his anatomy, and, far from being a fearless warrior, was decidedly nervous when it came to close contact with animals which might do him mischief.

Soon after his arrival I had work to do in the Naivasha area. I took Kip with me in order to show him the ropes, although I would be the one hauling on the halyards, while he would be a mere supernumerary. I would be at the sharp end, he at the blunt stern, which was as it should be, despite my being more than double his age. We arrived at a property where I had to vaccinate a trio of boisterous labrador dogs. They were not aggressive in any way, just rather eager to greet any arrivals on their turf. I told Kip this and suggested he walk behind me. Sure enough, as soon as I opened the wicket gate and walked up to the house, out rushed the canine greeting party, as expected. What I did not expect was to have Kip leap onto my back and climb onto my shoulders as though I was a convenient tree. The dogs bounded around sniffing and licking while Kip shivered from a safe height. The lady of the house appeared and stared, open-mouthed.

Later, over a cup of tea, she said, 'Well, well, the roles appear to have been reversed! In the past it was the black man carrying the white bwana. Now it's the white man carrying his servant!'

'Yes,' I said, 'strange how times have changed! But I don't intend to make a habit of it.'

But Kip never got over his innate nervousness. He did his job well enough but while I got bitten, scratched, gored and kicked, he never allowed himself to get in harm's way. Pre-judgement of a set of people based on what you read or see in films leads one into a sea of false impressions. Few Americans these days look like Dirty Harry or Tom Cruise. More like Fatty Arbuckle or Oliver Hardy. It's the same with the Nandi. The lean, fearless warrior is a thing of the past. Western 'civilization' has seen to that.

The present never seems as good as the past, but not so long ago the past was the present, so get a grip and get on with it.

We were in the present now and it was a Sunday, another working day, if not for the 'workers' like Kip. We had left the charming Jasmina and her delicious French accent, her small farm near Nanyuki, her horses, her savage 'tame' zebra, and were on our way to Mogwooni

Ranch. Our real destination was Mpala Ranch, further on, across the Uwaso Nyiro river, managed by Mike 'Shrub' Littlewood, but we, Berna and I, had been diverted by a message from Mandy Kenyon, wife of Jackie, who owned Mogwooni. Could we check on a lame pony mare while we were passing? Indeed we could. No problem. The dirt road ran through the place and the stable was right there. Shouldn't take more than a few minutes would it?

Soon we had parked the Peugeot and were being introduced by Mandy to a medium-sized palomino-type pony. 'So glad you were around,' Mandy said, 'she's had this funny gait for about two weeks now. Very odd. Let me get the syce to trot her up.'

'Looks as though she's buggered her pelvis,' said a voice behind us. It was Jackie, big, black-haired, ebullient, jokey and friendly, a son of the savannah, one of Kenya's best.

The pony trotted with her hind legs straddled and awkward, stumbling. Odd, I thought. 'Has she ever fallen,' I asked, 'been knocked down by the other horses?' 'Not that I'm aware of,' replied Mandy. 'Right, bring her into the stable and let's have a closer look. Let me put a hand up and see if there's a pelvic fracture.'

'Damn,' I said, as I pushed my arm along the pony's rectum, 'there's a foal in her uterus and from what I can feel it's dead. Long dead.'

'Now what?' said Mandy.

'We try to winkle it out,' I grunted. 'Did you know she was pregnant?'

'We did not. She's not been near the stallion at any time that I know of.'

Another immaculate conception I thought. I soaped and scrubbed my arm and then for good measure swabbed it with spirit. Luckily the mare was a quiet, phlegmatic beast and I had no need to sedate her. It took me a full hour to open her cervix. First one finger, then another, finally, by opening and closing my fist, my whole hand. Now I had to insinuate my arm to make room for the removal of what was in there. Life had obviously been extinct for some considerable time. Sunken eyes, hairless, had to be careful here, must get everything out in one piece. Apply ropes, one on each leg, stainless steel hooks in eye sockets and slowly, very slowly out came something resembling a yellow pterodactyl. 'Ugh! How long has that thing been dead?' asked Jackie. 'A month, two months, hard to say, little wonder she walking the way she was, with that inside her. I'll just put in a couple of pessaries and give her some antibiotic and she should be fine.'

'Well, come inside for a beer and a spot of lunch, and meet the old folks.' I looked at my watch as I replaced it on my wrist. Five minutes had stretched into two and half hours! 'Don't worry about Shrub. He won't mind. This is Laikipia. One day is as much as another here. Put your watch away until you get back to Nakuru. Check the time by the sun. That's what we do here.'

So we had lunch, chewed the fat with Jackie's splendid parents, stalwart pioneer ranchers and hospitable to a fault, had a couple of beers, said our farewells and resumed our journey.

We crossed a small stream, drove up a hill and down the other side. At the bottom on our left a narrow track led to El Karama ranch, owned by legendary Guy Grant, one of a fast-dwindling band of unique individualists, who made Kenya such a special place. They don't make them like self-effacing gentleman Guy any more, with his snowshoe sandals, his bushy grey beard, his slow measured speech and his love for his camels, his Sahiwal cattle and his wildlife.

Up the hill and, on the right, in total contrast, the hyperbolic entrance to Ol Jogi Ranch, plaything of the supremely wealthy French/American Wildenstein family, now devoted to conservation and where to spend just one night in their luxurious lodge costs the equivalent of double the annual income of the average Kenyan. So, obviously, not aimed at the man, or woman, in the Kenyan street.

The setting of the lodge and its satellite buildings was beautiful beyond words, built at the base of a lovely timbered kopje, huge rounded rocks towering over the manicured lawns, the swimming pool, the game viewing tunnel, the stables, the airstrip.

This was luxury taken to its extreme limit. A French chef catered to the palates of the pampered palefaces who flew in to be squired around in custom-built 4-wheel drive passion wagons to view the elephant, the lions, the buffalo, the almost domesticated rhino and the Grevy's zebra. This was Africa at its most artificial and superficial. Far from being Africa of 20 years ago as it was promoted to be, this was Africa of the future, where game was confined within specified limits and access was denied to all but the rich and the well-connected.

I had been there on several occasions, usually by road, occasionally by air, flown in by no-nonsense, talk-from-hip, fire-first, ex-Marine George Aggett, to treat the Andalusian carriage horses and the wildlife. The former were under the care of Kob Johnstone, master saddler and another of Laikipia's numerous, notable eccentrics. I often wondered why it was that this area of Kenya seemed to spawn so many nonconformists. I supposed it was because here everyone was his, or her, own person, beholden to none. The area was very large, ranches were relatively isolated, allowing personal quirks and kinks to seed and flourish into full and, in some cases, luxuriant bloom.

One chap, on a farm we were visiting near Nanyuki, appeared, in mid-afternoon, clad in flannel pyjamas. When requested to bring to the dairy the cow I had come to examine in order to check her malfunctioning ovaries, I expected him, as was the norm, to summon a posse of subservient minions to drive the animal forth from the paddock in which she was peacefully grazing. Still in his nightwear and bedroom slippers, he raised his head, opened his mouth and let forth a shrill echoing cry, 'Ayeeeesha! Ayeeeeesha!' 300 yards away Ayesha raised her grazing head and immediately set out for the dairy, which she entered and obediently stood while I carried out my examination. Around the house also grazed a number of century-old giant tortoises, brought here decades ago from Mauritius by the slippered yodeller's father. The reptiles had been trained not to eat the roses, how we never discovered. The rest of the garden was ravaged.

Then there was the couple who were rather fond of chimps, overly so, we thought in retrospect.

We had gone to their mansion, nestled below Mt. Kenya, not to look at their chimps, thank goodness, but to deal with a terrier with an ear infection.

After a lengthy day, involving gelding colts at Mweiga, dehorning bulls and caesarean-sectioning a bitch on a kitchen table, we arrived at the residence at 5.30 in the afternoon. We assumed this would be convenient for both patient and owners, if not for us, as we would, after treating the terrier, face a three hour drive back to Nakuru, most of that in the dark.

The house appeared to be shuttered and closed, despite our having alerted the owners to our impending arrival.

After much hooting and belabouring of doors and windows, a young lady of mittel European extraction appeared, who informed us that she was a sort of au-pair.

And where were the owners, we politely inquired?

'Oh, zay are in bed!

'In bed?' we expostulated, looking at our watches.

'Oh ya, it's chimp bedtime, and ven the chimp, who is an alpha male, decides it's time to go to bed, ze owners have to comply. He is a very big chimp.'

'And where, pray, does the alpha male spend his sleeping hours?'

'Oh, in ze master bedroom vis his lord and lady!'

We dealt with the terrier, and departed in thoughtful mood.

When I visited Ol Jogi, there were still cattle on the ranch. Simon Barkas along with his lovely wife Lulu, were in charge, and the place ran like clockwork.

Around the kopje and built into the giant boulders was a mini zoo, housing, if that is the correct word, numerous exotic species, from spider monkeys to tigers, along with caracals, ferrets, leopards, and cheetahs. I was required to treat and vaccinate. On one occasion, we arrived with our three pre-teenage girls to vaccinate the tigers, and the other cats. As Berna and I climbed up the rocks, the tigers remained recumbent, somnolent and indifferent. But when the smaller persons clambered up behind us, the tigers immediately perked up, rose with alacrity, eyes gleaming with sinister carnivorous interest. Here was caviar and truffles. With their attention thus diverted, I pole-syringed the vaccine into their rumps. We did not linger.

But when we came to vaccinate a female leopard, which had been cruelly neutered and de-clawed by some misguided, mindless veterinarian, it struck home just how very wrong it was to imprison such beautiful non-endangered species, for the delectation of a few diamond-studded tourists.

We drove on. In the distance we could see Mukenya, a sharply conical peak, which lay within the distant confines of our destination, Mpala Ranch. With the help of the ever helpful Shrub, we had climbed this stunning viewpoint, and at its base we had seen, at close quarters, a pack of wild dogs, a species which had made a remarkable come-back after decades of near elimination, only to be virtually wiped out once again during the land invasions of 2017, when the domestic dogs of invading tribesmen introduced canine distemper.

On Mpala Ranch there was an American-funded conservation research station, investigating everything from insects to elephants. One group of students had been following the sheep on the ranch, observing their feeding habits, their preferred grasses and shrubs, when they ate, where they lay down and so on. Most people would think that sheep just ate grass, passed droppings, converted grass into mutton and that was it. Not so.

One of the students, after duly observing the sheep for several weeks, had returned to New York to collate her findings. But, before she could do this, she fell ill. She reported fever, chills, chest pains, lethargy, headache. When Shrub relayed these symptoms to me and also told that some of the pregnant ewes had aborted my first thought was, could this be Q Fever? We had come with plenty of blood sample bottles and because the disease was zoonotic and capable of infecting people, and because it also infected ruminants, I proposed also taking blood from the ranch's cattle and camels. But we had to be careful, for if it was Q Fever, we might also contract the disease. We had both had more than our share of tropical infections and were not keen on adding another to the list.

The ochre-red road led us over a broad whaleback and then steeply down to a bridge over the brown Uwaso Nyiru river. A family of warthogs trotted briskly across our bows, tails erect, big tusked dad leading the way, followed by mum and a quartet of hurrying hoglets. Rain had fallen recently and the bush was green and restful on the eye. Hornbills, with their curious dipping flight, were gliding from tree to tree. A pair of dik dik scampered across the road. A ground squirrel rushed along the verge before jinking into the undergrowth; and an impala ram ushered his harem of dewy-eyed does away from our unwanted passage.

The road zigzagged steeply down to the bridge. A black-headed heron, studying the water with avian intensity, rose into the air with evident irritation as we rumbled onto the wooden sleepers. A buffalo, knee-deep in the rust-coloured stream, looked up and glared at us with naked hostility, nose raised, big ears swivelled, huge black horns meeting in a massive iron-hard boss.

The bridge was called the Princess Hilda Bridge, a nomenclature which, like that of the Nairobi suburb Karen, commemorating the pioneering authoress Karen Blixen, recalled another woman who left her name on the map of Kenya.

Princess Hilda of Luxembourg was married to the ultra-wealthy Prince Adolph of Schwarzenberg, a Czech nobleman. In 1930 they came to Africa on a hunting trip. They travelled to the Sudan, the Congo and to Kenya. They fell in love with Kenya and three years later acquired a 999-year lease on a farm in Laikipia, which they had bought from the Wilmots, a British family. Hilda and Adolph named the estate Mpala Farm. They oversaw the construction of a dam, an irrigation system, a powerhouse and the bridge, now called the Princess Hilda Bridge, to connect the estate to the nearest town, Nanyuki. They spent a considerable amount of time on Mpala Farm with their relatives. Like Karen Blixen, they had no children of their own.

The war came. In Europe Hilda's husband's anti-Nazi stance did not endear him to the Master Race. He refused to replace his Czech workers with ethnic Germans. He welcomed Jews to his palace in Vienna, putting up slogans saying 'Jews Warmly Welcomed', in response to the more usual 'Jews Unwelcome', as seen in most locations. He refused to receive Hitler in any of his homes. The response was swift. All of his properties were seized by the Nazis. His 55,000 acres of land, his multiple castles, his art collection, his businesses, all were taken.

Adolph and Hilda fled to America. In 1945 they returned to Europe. Czechoslovakia was now under the heel of the Soviets and they, in their turn, also appropriated all of Adolph's properties.

Hilda and Adolph visited Mpala Farm for the last time in 1949, Adolph died the following year and two years later Hilda sold out to American Sam Small. Sam died in 1969, bequeathing Mpala to his brother George, dedicating the 48,000 acres of savannah, bush, plain, river and rock to wildlife conservation and research. George, an alumnus of Princeton, approached his old university about establishing a research centre on the ranch. Today the renowned Mpala Research Centre is jointly under the aegis of Princeton, the Smithsonian Institution, the Kenya Wildlife Service and the National Museums of Kenya.

But it was also a working ranch and that was why I was there.

We crossed the bridge, hoping that its aristocratic appellation would not fall prey to the current mania for re-labelling anything with a whiff of colonialism, rank or otherwise. A track to the left led to the buildings of the research centre. We bore right, following the river.'What's the time?' I asked Berna. Berna scanned her timepiece. 'Almost 4.30.'

'Hell, I told Shrub we'd be here by 10.30 at the latest. He'll be frothing at the mouth by now and there's been no phone signal since we left Mogwooni.'

It was cooler now and animals were emerging from the shade, drifting through the bush towards the river to drink. A troop of olive baboons was enjoying the cooling air, the youngsters playing and cavorting in the dust on the road. The males, barrel-chested, arrogant, with icepick-sized canines, sat, like hairy Buddhas, hands dangling, forearms on their knees, dark eyes watching us from under their jutting Neanderthal brows. A baby rode jockey style on a mother's back.

'What's very big, grey and's got a long nose?' asked Berna, 'because there's one just about to cross the road.' I looked and, sure enough, an elephant, a cow, was emerging from the bush on our left, followed by a small calf. Surprised by our closeness, she shook her great head, flapped her ears, trumpeted and made a determined move in our direction. I braked, reversed with some alacrity. 'Hang on!' yelled Berna, 'there's another one behind us!' For the next 20 minutes we sat, engine off, while the members of the herd slowly and, fortunately, sedately, made their unhurried way down to the river.

As the sun declined a warm golden glow lay over the land. Dust hung in the air. The light was luminous and soft and gentle, not like the harsh brazen glare of midday. Quick moving shadows – vultures heading for their distant cliff-side roosts. A pair of Egyptian geese rushed overhead, honking, circling before landing on a stretch of riverside shingle and a silver backed jackal trotted through the bush, gearing up for the evening hunt.

Round a corner, a thick patch of greenery on our left, and there, regarding us with calm equanimity from a pair of magnificent brown eyes, was a male greater kudu. With his double spiralled horns, huge rounded ears, white chevroned face and bearded neck, he was a noble beast. We looked at each other. If he was impressed, as we were, he did not show it. One moment he was there, the next he was gone.

We continued on our way. The distant thumping of a generator advised us that we were close to chez Shrub and that we were almost a day late. We parked at the rear of the small square house. In Kenya one rarely, if ever, entered by the front door. It was always in by the 'servants' entrance'. Shrub, some way past the first flush and not quite as handsome as the kudu, grinning his customary sardonic grin, appeared. 'Hello there, you two. You're early. I was expecting you tomorrow!' We looked at each other. I was certain that today was the day, or was this another instance of 'Laikipia Time'? 'No matter, come on in, have a beer, have a gin, have a whisky. Juma! Lete bilauri tatu na Whitecap. Tengeneza kitanda. Iko maji moto? Juma! Bring three mugs and Whitecap. Make up a bed. Is there hot water?'

This was rural up-country hospitality. Stranger or friend, no one was turned away. If you came across a stationary vehicle on the road you always stopped to inquire if help was needed. It was not done to pass by on the other side. If someone asked for water you gave it. The land was unforgiving and the next time it might be you doing the asking.

Beyond the house was a plain with a waterhole and beyond the waterhole rose a large bouldery kopje. From the summit of the kopje the house looked like a matchbox, tiny and insignificant, dwarfed by the immensity of its surroundings. The kopje was only a few hundred feet high but up here the air was fresh and cool, there was a breeze and one could look back clearly to the mountain, rising from its mantle of dark tangled forests to its crown of jagged spires of rock and ice. Below the kopje, to the north, at its base, flowed the brown river, twisting its way westwards to join the Ewaso Narok, before turning north and then eastwards through Samburu-land to die in the mosquito-infested wastes of the Lorian Swamp. The kopje was a world unto itself. Here dwelt the rock hyrax, the klipspringer with its rubbery hooves, the leopard and soaring above them all, the fan-tailed raven. All looked down at the plain and the little house, and at the waterhole, where the reticulated giraffe, the oryx and the Grevy's zebra came to drink. Encountering on foot such animals and birds in their home environment, is infinitely more memorable and rewarding than observing them from an open-hatched Land Cruiser, or through the dusty windscreen of a safari vehicle. The vast majority of tourists, sadly, miss that experience.

Animals seen from a vehicle are quickly forgotten, even if beautifully photographed. But, when you meet them on foot they remain a vivid reminder that you are a transient, an uninvited guest. If you go on foot, as you must to appreciate the 'real Africa,' you must go in company with not more than two or three individuals, and preferably with a local of the area. If you take two they will talk and laugh to keep their spirits up and scare away all the lurking animals. But take only one and he will gravitate toward you and show you various medicinal plants and herbs and leaves and many things you would miss. The forest, or mountain, is his backyard and he knows it well.

If you take pack animals, a donkey or two are best. Camels are fine but only on the plains. They are no good in the mountains or forests. An expensive up-market trek with a train of camels, with trinketed tribesmen, tarbooshed servants, pre-laid camps and chilled champagne, is a fine romantic way to move through 'wild Africa' but you are travelling in a bubble, an artificial shield. You may tone up your leg muscles, but predictability is more likely than risk or chance encounter with capricious locals or dangerous wildlife. A sprained ankle is probably your worst fear.

Climbing Ol Doinyo Orok – the Black Mountain – above Namanga, hearing buffalo crashing through the forests, meeting elephant on the summit of Longido in northern Tanzania, walking to a bush and unzipping my flies in readiness to lower bladder pressure and finding a lioness glaring at me from the other side, trekking with donkeys down the Nguruman escarpment and encountering a cheetah standing in the fork of a tree, all these unphotographed episodes resonated more than any visit to a national park.

Shrub did not stint on the wining and dining, even though our arrival was, to a certain degree, unexpected. Although it was evening and he was at home, he was not idle and the constant chatter of his two way radio gave him little peace – a lion had attempted to get into the camel boma, four cattle were unaccounted for, two possible poachers had been apprehended, cattle grazing illegally on the ranch had been impounded. 'Par for the course,' he grinned.

Before we retired we went out onto the verandah. A full moon – a rustlers' moon, growled Shrub – was rising over the kopje. Bats hawked over our heads. A jackal yipped somewhere in the darkness. No light could be seen anywhere. The sky was alive with a million stars. As we returned to the house we knew how privileged we were to be here.

We could hear hyena whooping in the night, the grunt of a distant lion, the call of night birds, the sawing of cicadas. We slept well.

🏛✕🏛✕🏛✕

We awoke to the sound of birds and to the smell of coffee. 'I suggest,' said Shrub, when we emerged from our quarters, 'that you have a cup of coffee, go to bleed the camels and then come back for breakfast, and then go on to the sheep boma. From there you can return to Nakuru via Rumuruti. It's shorter that way. Salim, my head camel man will show you the way to the camels. I won't come with you. Getting trampled by a camel isn't my idea of fun. I'll leave that pleasure to you.'

We swallowed our coffee and went outside. The sky was powder blue, the air crisp and sharp, but we knew that would not last. Soon it would be hot, dusty and we would be damp with sweat.

Salim was middle-aged, lean and very black with a hennaed beard, indicating that he had had made the haj to Mecca, and therefore, in his eyes, was in a superior class to the infidels who surrounded him. He was friendly but not garrulous.

Within a wooden stockade near the river the camels were gathered in a great mob of grunting, roaring, complaining beasts.

The great thing about camels is that, although they bellow and snarl, showing their ugly brown fangs, and will, on occasion, bite and kick, they are, on the whole, responsive to the word of command, unlike most other grazing domestic animals.

Clutching our bottles and syringes, we climbed the palisade and dropped down into mayhem. We flattened ourselves against the side of the stockade as the camel-men, mostly brawny Turkanas, haltered and hobbled the camels. Tapping their shins with a light stick, grunting 'Toh! Toh!,' they persuaded them to kneel. This the camels did with an exasperated groan and roar, jaws open to expose their formidable teeth. The Turkana would then seize the camel by its lower lip, drag its head towards him while I would quickly throw a thin rope around its neck, raise the prominent jugular vein, insert needle and syringe and draw off the required volume of blood.

The Turkanas, little more than uncircumcised slaves in Salim's Islamic eyes, were marvellously agile and totally unafraid of their enormous charges. They laughed and joked as they darted between the head-high legs and snapping teeth on the end of snake like necks. We respected and admired them for their expertise and for the way they honoured their responsibilities. They did not abuse their animals as the Kikuyus frequently did. Kikuyus, usually arrogant work-shy youths, would often flog their harness-sored donkeys as they forced them to pull grossly overloaded carts, or if the cart was empty, whipped them into a desperate gallop on hoof-wrecking tarmac roads as they stood upright on the boards, whooping like demented Roman charioteers. Another cruelty was to harness three donkeys abreast, in the manner of a Russian troika, but done in such a way that the outer animals had to lean inwards to maintain balance and so were in constant risk of collapse.

The Turkanas might kill their enemies, but they did not beat their donkeys.

By the time we returned to the Shrub residence, we had bled 157 camels and the cool early freshness was long gone. The air shimmered with heat. The kopje, which last night had seemed to tower blackly over the house, now seemed to have receded and shrunk, its mighty boulders mere pebbles, faded and pale, cowering beneath the quivering sun. The only signs of life were a few scuttling lizards and Shrub himself, just in from his rounds.

We breakfasted on the verandah, looking across to the plain, where a solitary Grant's gazelle slowly made its way towards the waterhole.

'Right,' said Shrub, as we polished our plates, 'the sheep are in a boma beside the road to Rumuruti. Instead of going back to the bridge, take the track over the plains for four miles. When you come to a tree, it's the only one, bear left for another mile. My chap will be waiting for you. He's a Samburu called Lempurkel, a bit of a rogue, but then they all are!' He gave a mirthless laugh.

'Bear left at the tree?' said Berna as we trundled slowly across a dun coloured expanse of savanna.

'That's what he said,' I replied, 'so keep your eyes skinned.'

I drove slowly. The track was not good. But we drove slowly as we wished to absorb the beauty of the landscape, the rocky hills on the right, the spire of Mukenya ahead of us, the plain, long grass bent by the wind, a group of oryx, dust streaming behind them as they cantered out of sight. None of this was going to last. The country was changing. The population was huge and growing. Lines of enormous electricity pylons marched across the land where once there was nothing but pristine wilderness, hillsides once clothed in lovely thick forest were now sprinkled with hundreds of corrugated iron shacks, villages sprouted from nowhere, towns expanded, the roads were clogged with traffic, where once there were dirt tracks there were now two lane bitumen highways, along which thundered lorries, buses, matatus and droves of motorbikes, driven at breakneck speed by the worst drivers in the world.

The march of Progress was also the march to desecration and eventual oblivion. So we drove slowly, savouring what we knew future generations would be unable to savour.

'Look,' said Berna, 'there's the tree!'

So it was, a twisted, bent, gnarled old veteran of a thousand storms and winds, baking suns and lashing rain.

We bore left.

The sheep, black-headed Dorpers, the best by far for this marginal country, were waiting in a thorn-enclosed boma, close to a cattle crush.

Lempurkel was a short, stout, long-eared, brown man, with an unctuous smile. I wouldn't have trusted him with a box of matches. But we weren't here to pass judgement on his character.

Bleeding the sheep was a quick and easy job, and soon, with another dozen samples in our cool box, we turned onto the Rumuruti road and headed for home.

As we left I turned to Lempurkel, 'Do you think it's going to rain? Looks a bit black where we're going?'

'No, no,' he confidently assured us, 'that's just a passing shower over Loisaba. The road is smooth and dry all the way.'

Twenty minutes later, after having eased our way down a lumpy escarpment, we saw a vehicle coming towards us. It was a smallish 4WD driven by a middle-aged European woman. As we passed I gave her a cheery wave. She did not respond. I glanced at her. Grim, stony-faced, flinty-eyed, she glared straight ahead. 'Hell,' I said, 'what's wrong with her?'

We soon found out.

A mile further on, the road, without warning, degenerated into a series of enormous wallows and gullies. Heavy stone lorries, carrying material from a quarry, had been here, and the road surface, designed to carry only light traffic, had collapsed. In and out of the craters and ravines we inched our torturous way. Then it began to rain. When it rains in Kenya it comes down like a waterfall. There is no such thing as a light, gauzy, refreshing misty mizzle such as implied by that villain Lempurkel. Within seconds, if you go out, you will be drenched, to the skin. Now the enormous craters were brimming over, while a brown torrent rushed pell-mell down each sides of the road. With wipers and sweating driver working overtime we struggled on. Ahead of us we knew was the narrow bridge over the Ewaso Narok, the Black River, whose approaches would require careful negotiation if we were to avoid spending the night in the ditch.

Praying that we would not find a lorry embedded in the mire and blocking our passage, we slithered down to the bridge. It was empty. So we stopped and looked down at the water rushing northwards to join its sister stream, the Ewaso Nyiro. The rain had ceased and the sun was coming out and steam was rising from the mud. On a slender twig sat an aquamarine kingfisher, eyeing the turbid water. 'Surely it can't see anything,' I said, 'the water's totally opaque.'

But it could, for it darted down, a blue flash, and returned a second later with a small fish in its beak.' 'Got better eyes than you, Mr Cran,' said Berna. It certainly had. But I did see the rather bigger herd of elephants which wandered out of the bush a few miles further on. Seeing these great, peaceful, inoffensive, family-loving animals made one wonder why it was that only the human species waged war against itself. One never saw elephants or gorillas or aardvarks engaged in inter-species mass extermination pogroms. It often struck me that we were too clever by far for our own good. As Frederick the Great once said, 'The more I see of humanity the more I love my dog' – and for dog one might substitute elephant.

Churning on through dub and mire, the shacks of Kinamba were drawing nigh, where, to plagiarize Robert Burns, whores and bandits nightly ply. But it was daylight and sadly none were in evidence and we were past and soon on the Maralal Rumuruti turnpike, which, being rocky and stony, as opposed to being deep in mud, should, we hoped, allow us free passage to terra firma.

We were on the home straight. 'Only 20 miles to the tarmac!' I exulted. Past Ol Maisor, where Japper Evans ran his 40,000 acre ranch with an attractive nonconformist hand. Crash over a small stream and now a nice long semi-moist section with the euphorbia-clad bluff of Bobong (an enclave of Ol Maisor) approaching on our right.

'There's someone on the road,' said Berna, 'waving his arms.'

'Probably the local nutter,' I replied, 'I'll just slow down, and creep past him.'

But the man seemed to be adamant that we stop. He was waving a piece of paper, which, when I ground to a reluctant halt, he thrust at me. It was a fragment of an aged, yellowing *Daily Nation* and on it was scrawled 'Please come. Camel bitten by lion. John.' John was John Perrett, whose house topped the bluff. A snake-like track of intimidating steepness led up to John's abode which he shared with his wife Amanda, Japper's daughter. We turned right and crept and crashed our way to the summit, where John, lean, almost cadaverous, with a humorous smile, stick-like legs emerging from knee-length shorts and descending into battered sockless tackies, awaited our arrival.

'Hello Berna, hello Huge [his nickname for me]. Sorry to stop you but one of my camels had a bit of a tussle with a lion last night. Lion took a chunk out of his backside. But the lion didn't have time to eat it. The camel kicked its head in and it died.'

'Well that's gratifying,' I said, 'but how did you know we were around?'

'Ah, the native grapevine. Jungle drums and all that!' He grinned. 'Saw your note.'

'Yes, meant to send it in a forked stick, but I used the last one to pin down a nine foot cobra which came into the house, and in the fracas it broke.'

'What happened to the cobra?'

'Shot it with my twelve bore. Did no end of damage to the furniture.'

We told John that this was probably no bad thing, in that it would add an additional element of personality to an already highly idiosyncratic household.

He laughed.

'Right, where's the patient?'

The camel, surrounded by a motley crew of Turkanas and Samburu, sat, a look of intense irritation on its long curved face, within a small stone-walled paddock. At John's command, the men swiftly lashed the camel's legs together and rolled it onto its side. This did not please the animal and it bared its long brown teeth and bellowed in anger.

The lion, before it had been kicked in the head, had removed about a kilo of prime steak from the camel's hindquarters. Now there was a deep square hole and a large area of skin was missing. Total repair was impossible.

'I'll do my best, John,' I said, 'but most of this will have to heal by second intention as it's called. First intention is when the wound is closed and it heals cleanly.

'Third intention? Probably death. Let's hope that's not the case here. Lions are not noted for their dental hygiene, but we'll go ahead and then give a massive shot of antibiotic when we've finished.'

For an hour I cobbled and trimmed and tied and knotted.

'OK,' I said, 'that's the best I can do, so digits crossed.'

The ropes were untied and the camel rose with a groan and a belch and staggered off.

'By the way John, weren't you once munched by a lion.'

'Yep, lioness jumped on me from a bush. Did a bit of damage. But I just shoved a couple of intra-mammary mastitis tubes into the holes and they healed up rather nicely. Annoying in a way. Now, if I'd gone to the quack and he'd stitched me up I'd have some interesting scars to show people. As it is I've got none.'

'What happened?'

'Well, there were three lions, all brothers.'

'A bit like the billy goats gruff?'

'Yes, sort of. Anyway, they had a routine run from Sosian Ranch, to Gilfrid Powys' ranch Suyian, to us here, killing and eating the fattest cattle they could find. Gilfrid lost patience after they ate his best bull so he shot one. He also shot away one toe of one of the other two and when we saw his – the lion's not Gilfrid's – pugmarks in the dust or mud we knew they were back. When they killed two of our dairy cows we decided to sit up at night over the remains. I was in one hide with my headman and Japper was in the other with his girlfriend, Debbie. We were on high alert. Not sure how much attention Japper was paying to anything outside his hide. We were armed with shotguns, more suitable to downing pigeons and sandgrouse than a lion. Japper had a rifle.

'A lion came to our cow and the headman let loose with his shotgun and hit him in the chest and he took off. Japper later claimed that his cow was unvisited.

'In the morning the headman and I followed up the tracks of the lion. When the headman came rushing back past me at about 100 miles per hour I knew something was up. Next thing the lion erupted out of the bush and landed on top of me. I'd just time to pull the trigger and then I was on my back cuddling up to a lot of lion. The rest is a bit of a blur. The gun went flying, the lion bit my left arm, clawed my chest and then he was gone.

'I staggered to my feet and picked up my gun with my good right hand.

'Japper appeared from his love nest, having heard the shot.

'What happened?,' he asked.

'The lion's in that bush over there,' I replied.

'I can't see anything. Where? Where?'

He handed me his rifle, which I promptly dropped.

'What are you doing, boy?' he expostulated, 'that's my best rifle, boy, handed down to me by my father and grandfather. Look at it, boy! All covered in mud!'

'Sorry Japper, but the lion bit my left arm.'

'Oh,' he said.

'Look,' I said, 'you see that white thing in the bush? Just fire one inch in front of it.'

'He did. The lion leapt into the air and fell down dead. It was a perfect brain shot. The white thing was the lion's ear.

'Luckily, being still early in the morning and chilly, I was wearing a leather jacket, or I might not have got off so lightly. And I fell on my back, so maybe the lion thought I was in a submissive posture. Who knows?'

John and Amanda were laid back to the point of being horizontal. The word panic was not in their lexicon. Keep calm and carry on was. Nothing seemed to faze them.

Once, we were with them at the southern end of Lake Rudolf, miles from any road. We had followed John in our own vehicle over the Barrier, which separates the lake from the Suguta Valley. John had omitted to tell us that some parts of the track were near vertical.

John was going there to meet Amanda. She had led a group of elderly, enterprising Americans who had walked with the Perrett camels to the lake to raise funds for a school in Makindu, on the Mombasa road, where they had, in their distant youth, worked as Peace Corps volunteers, probably in order to avoid being drafted into their lost Vietnam war.

Two days later, having explored the barren wastes, camels all gone, Yankees all gone in a lorry, there were just our two lone vehicles left.

We climbed into ours, ready to depart.

'John,' I shouted, 'you go ahead. You know the way.'

John turned the key in his ancient, overloaded Land Cruiser. Nothing. Totally dead. John hopped out and lifted the bonnet and checked the battery, checked the terminals, tapped here, tapped there.

'Battery's croaked,' he informed us.

'Right, we'd better jump start it.'

'OK, let me get my jump leads,' said John.

'What on earth are those?' said Berna, as John emerged from the crammed interior of his Land Cruiser, carrying a pair of long bare tangled wires.

'These,' said John, proudly, 'are my jump leads. No one knows what they are, so they won't get stolen, unlike your pansy, fancy, pistol grip jobs!'

Pansy grips our pistol grips might have been but at least, unlike John's, they worked. We connected the two batteries, I started my engine, and we were away.

We knew that had we not been there and had the Perretts not been able to start their vehicle, they would not have panicked. They would have calmly sat down, cracked open a beer, contemplated the slippery waters of the Jade Sea and formulated a Plan.

Then there was the time, when, accompanied by an unsuspecting Belgian, John had been tasked with ferrying a consignment of beer in a light aircraft from Yei in the southern Sudan to a camp at Yambio some 150 miles to the west. John spread a Michelin road map of Central Africa on his knees, gunned the engine into life and took off.

As they droned westwards John studied the map and noticed that when they came over a significant river on their flight plan this would indicate that they were near their destination. Sure enough, there it was, a sinuous welcoming wriggle, bounded by a attractive green line of trees. Following the river John looked at the compass, which indicated 'south.' Hmm. Well, it will probably bear west in a minute or two. It didn't. After 20 minutes a touch of concern. But look, there's an airstrip! That must be it! So down we go. Land. No camp, but, hello, soldiers, holding guns. Uh oh!

John did not turn off the engine. Telling the Belgian to put his foot on the brake, he opened the throttle and opened his door and strolled across to the welcoming party.

'Bonjour, patron! Bonjour! Bienvenue au Congo!'

'Bonjour!' said John. John's French was limited. 'Ahh, ah, je suis desolé. J'ai oublié…' and he darted back to the plane, jumped in, told the Belgian to release the brake, and took off. North. Another 20 minutes and they were over the camp.

If you look at the map you will see that there is, for seemingly no accountable mapable reason, a triangular-shaped projection of the Congo jutting into the southern Sudan and, irritatingly, impeding a direct flight from Yei to Yambio.

John took this aeronautical incident in his stride. Most people in the north were like that.

Dilly Anderson lived at Kalacha, on the northern edge of the Chalbi Desert. Dilly was an American missionary and with his English wife Ruth had lived among the Gabra for decades. Indeed, members of the Anderson family seemed to have dwelt in the northern deserts since the time of the Flood. Unlike most missionaries Dilly's mission was not to proselytize but to help. He was a water engineer, digging wells, and providing water for the people. Unlike many missionaries he was no thin, pale-faced, bog-eyed fanatic, full of righteous zeal to dress the natives in long trousers and mother hubbards. With his bald brown head gleaming in the sun, built like an all-in wrestler, he exuded confidence and dependability.

Dilly's son-in-law Jonathan was cast in similar mould, although physically quite different, being larch pole tall, whereas Dilly was more like one of the ancient, squat cycads of his northern hills. Spending two days in a thicket repairing his broken down Land Rover was, for Jonathan, nothing worth writing home about. We had been on several character-forming expeditions together.

◈I◈I◈I◈I◈

On one occasion we, together with our respective spouses and offspring, were camped in the Horr Valley. Dilly, towing a drilling rig, was coming from Kalacha, in order to repair a well. He would be late, as one of his vehicles had been shot up by bandits the day before and he would be following an alternative route to get to us. Job done, he would take Berna, his daughter Carolyn and the kids back to Kalacha, while Jonathan and I climbed the 9,000 foot Mt. Nyiro on the opposite side of the valley. In the meantime we limbered up on Supuko on the Ol Doinyo Mara range, returning parched and dehydrated to meet Dilly and his rig.

The following morning, while Dilly set to work, we, with a Samburu guide, crossed the valley and began the 7,000 foot ascent, arriving on the summit shortly before dusk. We carried no tent, hoping to find a friendly manyatta on the summit plateau. We were in luck. There was one, only one, and the only occupants were children, mother having descended to Tum on the west and father to Kurungu to the east. We were welcomed into the fold and the entrance was barred with heavy logs. We crawled into the lozenge-shaped hut on all fours, congratulating ourselves on our good fortune. The guide lit a fire, we brewed up some soup, all the dormant insect life was stirred into activity and we settled down to an all-night scratch. At 9,000 feet the temperature quickly falls. Jonathan had brought a sleeping bag but no karrimat so he was warm but uncomfortable. I had brought a karrimat but no sleeping bag so I was comfortable but cold, very cold. In the morning we did not tarry and before dawn we were in the forest and plunging down to the distant valley.

While we were nearing the summit the evening before, Dilly, still towing his drilling rig, his vehicle full of women, children, and one reformed ex-convict called Bodyfiller, was approaching the southern margin of the Chalbi. Bodyfiller had long languished in Kisumu jail, where he had been taught the useful trade of bodyfilling damaged vehicles. Although there was little call for bodyfilling in the Chalbi Desert it did hold more promise than French knitting, embroidery, tapestry making and other abstruse penal pursuits. Bodyfiller had been called Bodyfiller for so long that his real name was long since lost in the mists of antiquity. He was an eager, active terrier of a man, forever smiling and offering to help. To his credit he did not belong to the widespread Dishonourable Brigade of Non-volunteers. He was a valuable member of the Team. Leaving the desolate village of Kargi, which existed only because of its numerous wells, Dilly swung the wheel north into the bare desert. Almost immediately trouble loomed. It had rained and the surface, normally bone dry and hard, was now soft and yielding in a worrying way. It was soon dark. There was no road. You just followed the tracks which you had made before and hoped for the best. They ploughed on but by 9pm they were well and truly bogged.

Everyone except Dilly got out to lighten the load, and immediately sank up their ankles in the mud. Twenty minutes later they were still stuck fast.

'What do we do, Dilly?' asked Berna.

'Well,' replied Dilly, slowly and precisely 'we assess the situation.'

'Well, I've assessed the situation and we're stuck.'

'We may have to unhitch.'

'What about light?'

'We have light,' said Dilly calmly, pointing upwards to the moon. Berna knew there was no need to worry. She and the rest were in safe hands.

Finally, by dint of careful forwarding and reversing, extraction was achieved. But there were still many miles of soggy desert to be traversed before landfall was gained. Dilly called up his wife Ruth on his two-way radio. She was in no way concerned at the predicament of the bemired travellers. 'I'll see you when I see you,' she chirped cheerily, 'got a big pot of chowder ready for you when you arrive.' Over and out.

Dilly consulted with Bodyfiller as to the best way forwards. Bodyfiller pointed out where Gabra cattle had been driven across the desert towards grazing and water. The cattle would have taken the driest way and so by following the trail of cow dung it should be possible to make progress. It worked, although it did involve a good deal of tacking from side to side. Finally, at 11 pm, after an epic eight hour drive they rolled into Kalacha ready to sample Ruth's chowder.

The following day, which was now thankfully hot and dry, Jonathan and I arrived at the scene of the bogging. Here was where the vehicle had sunk into the mire and it was surrounded by dozens of footprints, as though it had been encircled by a gang of marauding hostiles. But we noticed that the prints were small and that the feet had been bare. No self-respecting tribesperson in the north walks barefoot. Everyone wears sandals as a protection against the rocks, the heat, the thorns, the snakes and scorpions. These prints were those of our children, pounding about in the mud, as they waited for Dilly to get them out of their predicament.

We arrived at Kalacha, and after a pleasant night in a real bed, surfeited with chowder, and with a hearty breakfast of Gabra grits under our belts, we set off on the two-day return drive back to Nakuru. For the first 150 miles we saw only two other vehicles.

One welcome highlight was the appearance of a large cheetah in the Hedad, the wilderness between Kargi and Mt. Nyiro. Another was less welcome.

With Berna riding shotgun, kids lounging like Turkish pashas on a mattress in the back of our elderly Trooper, we were halfway between Baragoi and Merti, a notorious nest of ne'er do wells, footpads, and cut-throats. As we trundled along my attention was on the road, which was pitted with potholes, rocks and other impedimenta. Something made me look up. Seven men, all armed with rifles, the one at the rear also carrying what resembled a telephone pole, stepped out of the bush. All were clad in short black wrap-arounds, from waist to mid-thigh. Pokot bandits.

The leader raised his hand, rather in the authoritarian manner of an autocratic policeman stopping the traffic at a busy intersection. But his timing was all wrong. His sudden appearance gave me no time for either thought or warning of danger. Without breaking stride I returned his salute in a sort of '*nos morituri te salutant*' fashion and we were past them before they had time to close their sagging jaws or raise their weapons to their shoulders. In the rear mirror I could see them staring at us as we drew away, half expecting to hear the crack of gunfire and the hiss of deflating tyres. But nothing happened. With forethought the fellow with the log should have been at the front, ready to throw it down and block the road.

Better luck next time, chaps!

'Right, John,' I said, 'we'd better hit the road. Looks a bit black over Rumuruti.'

'Yes, that streamlet just this side can be a problem at times.'

The 'problem' was waiting for us as we slithered down the road to Rumuruti.

A few hundred yards ahead of us were the town buildings, the slaughterhouse, the prison, and, just beyond, tarmac. But on this side we could see a knot of people gathered at the bank of what was normally a dry, insignificant watercourse, and which was now a wide, foaming torrent. A large 4WD was halted on the edge, seemingly contemplating the situation. Waist deep in the flood, a young man was beckoning it to follow where he indicated it was safe to cross. A moment's hesitation, then, rather like a wary wildebeest making a leap into a river which might contain lurking crocodiles, the vehicle plunged into the stream. The exhaust was the first to vanish beneath the surface, then the rear bumper, now the water was half way up the doors. We watched with a sense of personal involvement. Our turn was next. Retreat was not on the agenda. Neither was the prospect of being swept downstream into the foetid fastness of the Rumuruti swamp into which this unwelcome freshet debouched. The vehicle swayed, tilted, sank, and then rose up the further bank, streaming water like a breaching whale. At once it was surrounded by those drenched helpers who had guided it across. Money well spent I thought.

Now it was our turn. Engage four wheel drive, low ratio, first gear, keep the engine running whatever happens. Water sucked into the exhaust spells curtains. In we go, watch the guide. If the water is waist deep or less, we're OK. If shoulder high we're both in serious trouble. Whoops! The back end swung round, pulled by the current, careful now, a judicious touch of the throttle, don't want to get dug in. Watch the guide. Ah, can feel rocks under the wheels. Almost there. A final surge, a scrabble up the steep bank, and stop to distribute largesse. Drive for a few hundred yards with foot on the brakes to dry them out, then it's 'Home James! And don't spare the horses!' 'Home! Home to Tara!'

Now we were on the home straight, which, if not really straight, was at least on tarmac, of sorts. Through Nyahururu, formerly Thomson's Falls, down the Subukia Escarpment, and into Bahati with the crater of Menengai straight ahead.

'We've just got to nip into Charlie Stubbs' place to check on that lame horse I saw last week,' I said. 'Shouldn't take more than a few minutes.'

Pio Pio Farm was only a couple of clicks off the tarmac and in no time we were rattling up the track to the gate. As I slowed down I saw a wisp of smoke appearing from below the bonnet. The stables were only a few yards beyond. 'Aagh,' I thought, 'I'll check it when we get there.' The gate was locked, so I turned off the engine, hooted and waited for the askari to open it. He came running. I switched on the engine and as I did so dense clouds of smoke came belching out from below the bonnet. The askari opened the gate and I shot forwards to the stables, leapt out and wrenched open the bonnet.

'Hell's bells and buckets of blood!' The engine was on fire! Flames were leaping into the air. Fortuitously a syce was watering the horses. 'Lete maji!' 'Bring water!' I bellowed. He did and threw a full bucket onto the flames. And another. And another. Hearing the racket, Charlie appeared. Charlie could be kindly described as portly, but he came at a quick canter. 'Hello,' he said, 'what's the issue?' 'A bit of a conflagration in the engine,' I replied. Charlie peered into the blackened innards. 'Hmm, looks like a wire had come loose and made contact with another and sparked and run back up the wiring. Been on a rough road eh? We'll have to replace the wiring. No way can you drive any further in this today.'

I looked. All the wiring was now bare, the rubber all gone. We were lucky the whole vehicle hadn't gone up in flames.

'Not to worry,' said Charlie, we've got a spare vehicle here. Leave yours here.

We'll fix it and you use ours until yours is ready.' 'Yes, no problem,' said Claire, Charlie's wife, who had appeared.

And there wasn't. I examined the lame horse, we had a cup of coffee, loaded our things into our new vehicle and we were on our way home again.

Four days later, we collected our car which had been re-wired and was as good as new. Up-country Kenyans – salt of the earth. No one like them. I sent the blood samples from the sheep and camels to the lab and the result confirmed that Q Fever was present on Mpala ranch. Q Fever or Query Fever, presumably because the first researchers in Australia were at a loss to know what they were dealing with. It is caused by a bacterium called Coxiella burnetii. Mostly found in sheep, goats, cattle and other ruminants, it is highly infectious and spread by inhalation, ingestion or direct contact with birth fluids or placenta. Due to its high rate of infectivity, stability, and potential for aerosol dispersion, it has been considered as a possible bio-terrorism agent.

As a result it is a notifiable disease in humans in the USA. When I relayed the result to Shrub he told me that the American student had also tested positive. I told him that segregation of infected animals and burning or burying of reproductive offal were some methods of control and that ticks could also be involved in transmission. The organism could also be shed in milk, urine and faeces and could be spread by wind-borne dust.

'And no available vaccine,' I said.

'Par for the course,' growled Shrub.

Chapter Seventeen

A STROLL IN SAMBURU-LAND

Monday 22nd July. Police Dog Unit – stitch flank stab wound caused by thief. Fate of thief unknown but if apprehended, not a situation I would like to be in. Visit Madrugada Ltd, vaccinate 12 horses with African Horse Sickness and rabies vaccine, and examine and treat sick steer – Madrugada means dawn in Spanish. The owner had farmed for a while in Argentina at the foot of the Andes and presumably had been entranced by the morning sun rising over the pampas to illuminate the eastern ramparts with its rosy rays. To Gogar Farms to treat three sick cows. Peter White – operate on bull terrier, remove cancerous skin lesions. Mweta Security, vomiting and scouring pup. Kenana Farm, stitch dog. To Muya Stables horse remove stitches. Wet and cold. Finish after dark.

Tuesday 23rd July. To Mweiga Estate 100 miles away, Beardsall swab mare, Mike Prettejohn horse with oesophageal impaction, stomach tube and administer liquid paraffin, recovered, Nicholson Nanyuki dog infected scrotum, Hessel Ngobit check pup, several dogs to see on return. Allen, dog infected ear. Emerich, dog kidney infection. Mweta Security, give pup one litre IV fluids etc. Finish after dark.

Wednesday 24th July. To Kenana Farm, rectal examine 40 cows and 15 mares – freezing cold and wet – everyone bar me bundled up warm and snug, damn their eyes. On to Turi, Gohil, German Shepherd skin condition. To St. Andrew's School vaccinate three cats then down bloody awful 'road' to Gogar Farms examine labrador with swelling on neck, treat with antibiotic and corticosteroid. On to Kiruto Farm, owned by one Samwell Benson Mugo, former Catholic priest turned farmer. His ecclesiastical vocation, sadly, does not extend to expertise in the realm of animal husbandry as I discover as I intone 'not in calf', 'not in calf' as I pregnancy-test his animals. Perhaps, I thought, as I shoved my arm up the next non-pregnant animal he was, having been called to the celibacy, unaware of the finer, or indeed coarser, details of the procreative process. I quickly dismiss these thoughts. After all, weren't the local papers full of lurid reports of priests impregnating girls, compromising under-age youths and molesting children? I suggest that, instead of relying on his unreliable workers to detect and report when cows come into season, when they had obviously better things to do such as boozing and whoring, he purchase an active, virile Boran bull and let him get on with the job. Unscientific perhaps, but I knew from experience that it would be effective. The offspring might be crossbreds but better that than nothing. He nods his great fat head and I go on my way, wondering if he would follow my advice. On to Madrugada again to vaccinate three more horses. But what's that smell? I trace it to the wheels. Tentatively I touch the rims. Shit! They're red hot! Smoking! Hoping they don't seize I drive to the surgery where several dogs are waiting. Including one owned by Shah from Colorsonic with nicotine poisoning. Fed raw native tumbaco by some youths. Respiratory distress, froth, foam and blood from the lungs and dies after ten minutes. A call from Milgo, Technology Farm, heifer stuck calving. 360 degree torsion of the uterus. Now dark. Op Caesar, calf dead, heifer up and owner happy. Home at 9pm.

Thursday 25th July. To the Solai Valley to Milmet and Teremuka Estates to pregnancy test more cattle – results better than those at Kiruto Farm – well, they could hardly be worse, could they? To Linda

Allen's place to vaccinate four dogs. Back to the surgery: Staffordshire bull terrier owned by the top-heavy and ever flamboyant and exuberant Shirley Luckhurst – anaemic, lethargic, enlarged spleen, feverish (the dog, not Shirley) – check blood smears – tick fever. More dogs to see and treat. 6pm call from Marcus Russell at Kongoni Farm Naivasha, 60 miles away, a female captive cheetah with her half-grown cubs had escaped from her enclosure. Arrive at 7.30pm. No hope of darting the mother. Total Nubian darkness. More likely to dart one of the cordon of Africans through which she broke. But then, amazingly, one of the cheetah youngsters ran into a fence and became entangled. I rushed up with ketamine and xylazine and shot what I hoped wasn't a lethal dose into its backside. In no time, out cold. So cold in fact that for a while the chilly breeze of anxiety began to play across my furrowed brow. But the anaesthetic is safe, isn't? We place the young cheetah in a box trap and cover it with dry grass. When it wakes up it will call for its mother who will come back into the enclosure. That's the theory. To Marcus' camp for a coffee. He has a delightful Cape Clawless Otter munching on fish and crayfish. I leave at 10pm and am home by midnight. Marcus phoned next morning to say that the cub played its part, and the mother and the rest of the cubs came back and so all was well. He was very pleased – as was I.

Friday 26th July. Daniel Espira from Kakamega rocks up with two bitches both of which, having been dosed with medroxyprogesterone acetate, to postpone heat, now have the most colossal pyometras (uteri) full of pus. So operate: one uterus weighs in at 10.5lbs, the other 6.5lbs. A call to the farm of Gideon Moi, son of El Presidente, to examine a horse with wind galls. Road awful. Why, why, do they grade roads when it's wet? So onto the newly graded dirt road, slippery as hell, like driving on grease, car all over the place, for 10 white-knuckle miles to the dismal dorp of Elementaita. Then beyond onto the ungraded section where the ruts are so deep you lose sight of the horizon. Damned difficult to find the way and now it's raining behind us. So quickly examine the horse, give the benefit of the Cran expertise and make a rapid retreat via Soysambu, Lord Delamere's 50,000-acre pad, to Gilgil where Fritz Zimmermann, yet another former wearer of the holy cloth (lots of them around it seems) and now conjugally joined with coal-black Christabel, has reported that he has a heifer having difficulties in giving birth. By this time the light has gone and it is now similarly dark so examining the crow-coloured animal in the funereal gloom does nothing to raise the sombre declining spirits. Two and a half hours later, having quadricepted the long-dead calf and with my left shoulder joint all but dislocated, I depart, getting back to the family hearth at 10.30 pm.

Saturday 27th July. A dark and rainy night and an ideal one for uninvited guests to break part of the main gate and make away with two chairs, a sofa and a camp table from our verandah, all without disturbing our dogs, or the slumbering night watchman. Obvious professionals. I phone the local flatfeet, telling the halfwit on duty exactly where I am located. He appears to speak no known language, but finally I gather that he has no idea where I am situated and furthermore the cop vehicle has no fuel. So I drive to get him. On arrival he looks around and declares that he will arrest one Jacob Mwathi by evening. I return him to his station and hear no more. Not a good start to the day. To the surgery. Someone from Baraka Convent Molo brings in a rabid dog tied up in a sack, snarling and biting at the sack. Euthanase and advise. A frantic call from Kenana Farm re a mare with colic. I rush out. Pulse rate 85 and rising. Conjunctivae brick red, stomach contents at nostrils, pass stomach tube to release pressure but prognosis very poor. Died three hours later. Post mortem: ruptured stomach due to blockage of gut by a pedunculated lipoma (fatty tumour). Back to the surgery where a dog, owned by our landlady, whose grim persona makes strong men wilt and quail, is brought in. Suspected strychnine poisoning: violent jerkings and spasms. So anaesthetize with pentobarbitone and give IV hydrocortisone. Later in the day, as the anaesthetic lightens, the spasms recur so re-anaesthetise. I tell the hovering harpy that the prognosis is poor-to-hopeless. She grimaces, sniffs and grunts. Next day the dog is still out cold but during the day improves very slowly, but is unable to see. The owner complains that a blind dog is a useless animal. Luckily she cannot read my thoughts, which include musings on red hot pokers, fundaments, females of the canine species and a variety of four letter words. The following day the dog has completely recovered. At the end of the month we receive notification that our rent is to be increased by 25%.

※ ※ ※ ※ ※

After a few weeks of such veterinary vicissitudes I decided that a break from dealing with the public, unwashed and otherwise, and their unfortunate charges, was called for. A mountain safari was what I am looking for, in an area where the terrain is rugged and hostile and the sparse inhabitants welcoming to the infrequent strangers who make an effort to visit their home patch. I scrutinize my maps in search of a character-forming summit. My short-list has shrunk to a remote few. I had climbed everything worth climbing in the southern part of the country, as well as in northern Tanzania, so my attention was now inexorably drawn to the distant summits of northern Kenya, where actually getting to the base of one's chosen mountain was, in many instances, as hard as the actual foot work. I had topped all of the peaks of the Mathews Range, bar one.

I had been up Ololokwe, Warges, where our guide had lost his way in the forest, Tipito – an excellent summit this, full of birds, cycads, buffalo, lion, with a superb castellated summit gained by a narrow rocky drawbridge, and with us was the legendary spear-throwing Dorobo, Lepasian.

Then there had been Mathews South where our 'guide' sat down, declaring 'Kichwa nauma mimi! Akila napotea! – My head hurts! My wits have deserted me!' In true British fashion we gave him short shrift, told him to elevate his shorts, and get moving. He did.

Mathews Main Peak was tackled from a rather run down camp sited in the valley of the River Ngeng, whose headwaters rose from the base of the mountain. Irritatingly, the owners appeared to have some sort of personal proprietorship over the valley. Accordingly, we were obliged to billet ourselves in this over-priced chummery, where the grub was of the lorry park variety, the beds lumpy and the staff surly. The place was a blot on the lovely surroundings of river, forest and mountain, the home of myriads of birds, elephant, buffalo, and, it was reputed, rhino. The river was full of tiny fish and a delight to the eye, and to our daughters, who spent hours with a makeshift rod and bent pin in vain efforts to catch one. At night we heard elephants trumpeting in the woods across the river. In the morning, we, myself, friend Peter McCarter, a rather morose Dorobo armed with an assegai, and a game scout, set off up the valley. As we departed, a sour faced female guest at the camp, seeing us leave, said to Berna – 'I saw your husband leaving to climb the mountain, and saying to you –"we'll be back in time for tea" – well, he hasn't a hope!' Berna said nothing. The river was low, which was in our favour, as we had to cross and re-cross it many times. Many parties had been turned back when the water was high. We moved fast, reached the headwaters, rested on a soft rock for ten minutes, traversed upwards along a very steep incline, descended a thousand feet to a col, and made the final ascent to the lofty summit, crowned by enormous trees. We reached the camp at 5.30, in time for a latish tea.

Mathews North was a different proposition. No roads led to it. Studying the map and Paul Clarke's Guidebook to the Mountains of Kenya suggested that the best approach might be from the Milgis Lugga, the wide sand river which separated the Mathews Range from the Ndotos to the north. The guide book also said, rather ominously, that no one had been up it for at least ten years. I contacted friend Jonathan Moss, partner on a number of previous character-forming forays, where both body, clothing and constitution had been put to the test and asked him if he was up for it. Without apparent thought he said yes. He would come with his wife Carolyn and young son Nick as support crew. Berna would support me, but being at school and in the throes of trying to instil knowledge and wisdom into the unreceptive skulls of a gaggle of pre-pubescent pupils, she didn't know it yet.

I suggested that we could pitch our tents in the lugga, but Jonathan said that there was a camp run by a middle-aged Kenya-born woman sited nearby, which might serve and save us the trouble of carting all of our own gear and also allow the ladies some peace and quiet while we were away mortifying the flesh. If there were people in the area, Samburu, they might be attracted to our camp site and any privacy would go out of the window. Usually they meant no harm, but having a gaggle of armed painted warriors and beaded giggling maidens and withered beldames with dugs hanging to their knees squatting a few yards away and watching your every move, could, after a few hours, become a trifle irritating. And if we were gone for more than a day then things would get a bit more complicated. We didn't really go for camps, where you were 'entertained' by fake tribesmen and tribeswomen, dolled up in red blankets and festooned with beads made in Manchester or somewhere, and who leapt up and down, jiggling their jewels and ululating just when you were trying to decide whether the glob on your plate was a pale French pancake or a warm refreshing napkin. Either way, both tasted the same. So, we would have preferred to camp, but hey, let's give this place a shot.

It appeared that the lady owner had had some sort of childhood trauma, in that she had an apparently irrational phobia towards teachers. Of course many of us disliked certain teachers while we were at school, but few of us carry this dislike into our middle years. In addition to this curious foible, she regarded the local area as her own private fiefdom, and what with the setting up of dispensaries and indeed, schools, with, Heaven forbid!, teachers, the dubious assets of civilization were insidiously eroding the ancient culture of the indigenous inhabitants. I could see that we would have to tread carefully here – a bit like Agag in the bible, I thought. But after he was pardoned by Saul, wasn't he killed by Samuel? Hmm.

I contacted the owner, whose name was Penelope. Penelope? This was a name I always associated with dreamy, be-spectacled, virginal, prayerful, blue-stockinged, ineffectual maidens. To add to my illusions, for years, never having met a live Penelope, I had always thought the name was pronounced as Penny Lope. For the life of me I could not imagine a Penelope running a camp in the bush. Well, we would see. We agreed on prices and dates and prepared ourselves.

Berna's half term break arrived and we set off, compass pointing north. After a night camped on a ranch on Laikipia we drove east along the dirt road towards Wamba. Bypassing Wamba, we took the road which ran north to Barsaloi which lay at the very western edge of the Milgis Lugga. The road was rough, but worse, much worse was to come. We arrived at the Seiya Lugga which seemed to be about half a mile wide and, although dry, was deep in soft sand. So, stop, engage the four wheel drive, low ratio, second gear and go, no stopping or you'll sink, get it up to third and plough through until you reach the other side and climb the bank onto terra firma. After that it was all rock and boulder and the odd welcome stretch of gravel to lighten the driving. As we drove up a steep section we came across a small Samburu manyatta where some youths took advantage of the ubiquitous boulders to hurl some at our two vehicles. This was unusual. Most Samburu are friendly and wave as you trundle by. Perhaps a previous truck had run down a couple of their goats and they were taking it out on the next ones that came along.

The road flattened out and for a brief light-hearted 20 minutes we bowled along, revelling in this arterial bonus. Lumpy hills appeared on our right. We had been told that when we had passed the last of these, a faint track would appear and that we should take this and follow it to our destination. Faint it was, so much so it was hard to decide whether it was man-made, goat-made or one of those mysterious natural phenomena only clearly visible from outer space. Penelope apparently never drove to her own camp. She had a plane and flew in to her airstrip carved out of a nearby hillside. We soon found out why. In no time at all, the track had vanished. It was obvious that no one had been this way in months, if not years. Luckily I had a map and by keeping the rocky mass of the hill called Mukerbin to our south, and the curiously named Loonchipiship Range to our east, we felt our way across country until we picked up the track again. Still, it was not as bad as the time when another local 'expert' advised that we follow *his* 'well-worn track' for seven kilometres up a sandy lugga to *his* cunningly hidden camp, which we foolishly did. 'Well-worn track' my ass! After a couple of hundred yards it vanished entirely. The sand deepened and deepened, until our four wheel drive broke with a horrid and expensive mechanical crunch of sundered metal. It turned out that if we had followed our noses and the designated road, we could have avoided the lugga altogether, apart for a very brief crossing. But some 'Kenya cowboys' like to prove their fragile manhood with the biggest Land Cruisers that money can buy and, by fitting them with oversized tyres and spotlights and bull-bars, show the peasantry just how manly they are by taking them where no vehicle was meant to go. Not that they would ever think of getting out and hoofing it. That's for the natives and eccentrics such as ourselves. Meanwhile, we inched our way across a thorn-covered plateau, until far to the north we could espy the southern foothills of the Ndotos, while to the east the noble outline of Mathews North appeared. The scenery was so sublime it almost made us forget how awful the 'road' was. Slowly we began to descend until far below us we could see the welcome wriggle of the Milgis Lugga. Lurching from boulder to boulder we eased our exhausted steeds down an ever-steepening incline until finally we descried evidence of habitation, something we had not seen since our stoning by the irritated Samburu delinquents.

A whitewashed rock indicated the proximity of Penelope's camp, which was sited on a small wooded bluff, overlooking a tiny stream, which fed a small pool. The camp proved to be small and unpretentious. As we drove up, a gaily bedecked Samburu warrior wearing a red toga and a ridge of plastic feathers in his ochered hair welcomed us. He looked like a human cockerel. For a member of such a bellicose tribe, we thought him to be rather portly, if the size of the gut straining against his tunic was anything to go by. But that's what comes of dining on camp scoff and standing around all day preening your plumage.

'Karibuni! Karibuni!' he said. 'Welcome! Welcome!'

We stiffly descended, covered in dust and anticipation.

'Well, hello there,' a low husky voice said. We turned and our jaws sagged.

'You must be Penelope,' I found myself saying to the advancing stunner who had just appeared. I almost said Penny Lope but stopped myself just in time. She was clad in an intriguing blend of Samburu and western garb, all jingling bangles and bracelets, neck chokers and beaded sandals. My, my, she didn't look anything like her reported 50 years: flawless honeyed skin, smooth unlined forehead, straight nose, finely carved lips with just a delicate trace of rouge, high cheekbones and a dazzling snow white smile. She was nothing like the Penelope of my imagination. She shimmered towards us like a sunlit Greek goddess.

'Yes, but call me Penny,' she insisted. Thank God for that, I thought. 'Welcome to my little camp. Karibu! We'll do our best to make you comfortable.'

The overweight tribal warrior now advanced, proffering a tray bearing goblets of some indefinable juice, the standard procedure at all lodges and camps – a bit like Eskimos offering you their wives for the night, or veiled Tourags preparing to sacrifice their best camel for the honoured guest – albeit on a smaller scale. But you knew it was just a cheap gimmick to put you off your guard before you found out that the beds were lumpy, that the shower didn't work, the toilet didn't flush and that the electrics were dodgy to the point of being downright dangerous. And that you had been overcharged.

Penny showed us to our tents. She moved with a curious, sinuous motion, rather like an octopus gliding over the sea bed. As she smilingly showed how to zip and unzip the tents, how to turn on the taps in the basic shower room and where to stow our clothes – all things which obviously demanded a higher qualification, like a PhD for example – we sensed that below the warmth, there was something rather hotter, a simmering fire, which threatened to burst into flames at any moment. The teacher thing, perhaps?

The view from the bluff was immense. To the north from the yellow bed of the huge lugga the forested foothills of the Ndotos rose into the clouds now obscuring the distant summit of Manmanet, the most southerly of the range. To our east Mathews North, our objective, was seen in convenient outline and we could see that from base to apex was a very long way. A night on the bare mountain looked inevitable. The summit was heavily forested. Our gaze drifted downwards and in an opening of the bush at the base we could see a number of grey shapes moving in a slow line towards the lugga where we knew there was water. Elephant. And in the lugga itself we could see, through binoculars, signs of human activity. Good, we thought. Here we would find someone familiar with the mountain.

Night fell. The stars came out. The air was warm and balmy, soft and gentle. A nightjar trilled in the dark. Crickets buzzed. A jackal barked in the distance.

Over the evening repast, served by more tribal warriors in an al fresco setting, lit by guttering moth-attracting candles, with just enough light to see your plate but not enough to identify what was on it, we told Penny of our plans for the following day. No, she hadn't been up Mathews North and knew of no one who had. It was very far, and would take many hours to climb, and would probably involve a night out. All these things we knew. She seemed to be almost put out by the fact that we might be stealing a march on her, intruding into 'her' territory, going somewhere she hadn't been. She offered the services of a couple of her staff, but we declined. If the butterball guarding the gates was anything to go by we would rather take our chances with a couple of passing nomads, keen for the chance to earn a few shillings in return for accompanying a pair of harmless lunatics up the mountain.

Meal over, I negotiated my way in the inky darkness to the kitchen to fill up our water bottles in preparation for an early start the following day. Here I met the cook, an ancient Meru, a toothless, garrulous old goat, but a positive mine of gossip, innuendo and rumour regarding his employer. I felt a bit like the wedding guest mesmerized by the Ancient Mariner as the old boy transfixed me with his rheumy eye. It seemed that she had two teenage children by a former professional hunter, who had forsaken her for the arms of a smouldering Somali beauty – at least we, both the cook and I, assumed her to be a smouldering Somali beauty, or otherwise why would he have left the lovely Penny? Something to think about as we toiled uphill on the morrow. There's nothing like a good bit of old fashioned conjecture and speculation to pass the time. The minutes flash by as you ferret and dissect, probe and analyse, in an attempt to sift fact from fiction.

Later, in the arms of my own Irish beauty, I imparted these salient nuggets for her delectation. She, having studied psychology at university, would be more at home in this area of interest than me. She told me that she would mull over the case while I was away in the wilds and in the meantime we hadn't come here to discuss Penelope's Freudian problems had we....? The alarm went off at 5.30. As I tiptoed out of the tent, Berna turned sleepily over in bed. 'Go, my warrior!' she pronounced. I went.

After a spartan breakfast we climbed into Jonathan's sturdy Land Rover and drove for several kilometres down the lugga, until we were opposite our proposed route, parked the vehicle under a large fig tree and girded our loins. Samburu women were collecting water from a number of wells dug in the sandy bed of the lugga. Sitting in the shade were a number of men, watching the proceedings. One had what looked like a 303 rifle. They came across to greet us. 'Soba' we said. 'Eba,' they replied. We told them that we had come to climb the mountain and that we required two men to come with us and show us the way.

Mountains in Kenya are not like those in Europe, where there are often well-marked paths indicating the way to the summit. Many mountains in Kenya are surrounded by dense bush or forest or thickets of thorn through which penetration can be extremely difficult. Beckoning paths made by game may confuse the stranger by leading him in a myriad of different directions until he is hopelessly lost. Once lost and out of water, your chips may be up. On Mt. Kenya several people, mostly rash and foolish Westerners have died, when attempting to thread their way through the forest. Some, stupid to the point of imbecility, reluctant to pay the national park entry fees, circumvented the entry gate, became totally lost, and either perished a miserable death from starvation, drowned in one of the many narrow torrents in an effort to obtain water, or met a buffalo going about its lawful business.

Most of the mountains in the country were remote, seldom visited and rarely climbed. Which is how we liked it. Only by getting out and walking through the country could you get to really appreciate its beauty, diversity and wildness. Driving through it was not the same. You saw it, but did not feel it. You did not feel the rocks under your feet, the sand as you crossed a dry river bed, the thorns as you negotiated a patch of bush, the exquisite coolness of a few square feet of shade, the welcoming breeze drying your sweat as you breasted a ridge above the baking plains. A fleeting glimpse of a bushbuck slipping away as you approached, the crash of retreating buffalo in the forest, the trumpet of an unseen elephant, remained in the mind's eye and ear, long after all the animals seen through the window of vehicle had vanished from memory.

By engaging with the local people you were showing your interest in them and putting a little into their limited economy and sharing a little of their way of life. Once you were on the mountain they would rarely, if ever, let you down. There was the usual bargaining and negotiating before you set off, but once on the march you could relax, which is probably not the correct operative word for plodding uphill, dodging the rocks and thorns, behind a pair of stick-thin, bony black legs shod in a pair of sandals, and whose owner is smoking a cigarette and chewing khat and talking nineteen to the dozen with his equally thin tribal brother. But when you rested under a tree, watching an iridescent sunbird flitting from flower to flower, or listening to the soporific rookete-coo of a dove in the branches, and got to the summit and marvelled at the view and descended in the dusk, purple mountains on all sides, and heard the far off tinkle of goat bells and caught the scent of woodsmoke, even as you staggered exhausted to your distant tent, dehydrated and wiped out, you knew it was all worth it.

The Samburu with the rifle was called Lolkerra. Yes, he said, he knew the way, as did his friend, Leboo. And, he said, we did not need to carry too much water, as there was plenty of water up there – 'Maji mingi, na mtoni safi sana' – 'lots of water and beautiful streams.' This was good news indeed. Humping five litres of water on your back, together with all your other stuff was to be avoided at all costs. In my mind's eye and ear I could already see and hear gurgling brooks running over clean gravel beds, savour musical waterfalls and discern delicately patterned fish hovering in shady, fern-fringed pools. Who knows, perhaps we might be dining on freshly caught trout tonight? Lolkerra spoke Swahili and a little English. Leboo only spoke Samburu, which is basically the same as Maa, the language of the Maasai, to whom the Samburu are closely related. Lolkerra proudly told us that his name, Lolkerra, meant 'owner of many goats.' He laughed. 'Leboo means 'born in the bush'!' 'Then,' I said, 'he sounds like the right man for us.' Our men went to their manyatta to collect some posho (mealie-meal), sugar, salt and tea, for, they told us, we would have to spend a night out.

Once, while on safari in West Pokot, near the Uganda border, a Kalenjin with us, called Joel Korir, exclaimed when he saw the Pokot, 'Eh! They are *so* black, they are glittering!' Our Samburu were not quite like that. They were a dark, honey chestnut brown, with narrow, fine-boned features, thin noses, and classically chiselled lips – in fact not unlike a male version of the fair Penelope. They carried not an ounce of fat on their lean, muscular bodies, and moved with an easy, unforced grace. They seemed to us to be perfectly adapted and attuned to their harsh environment. We could not imagine any other race, European or Asian, who so beautifully enhanced their background. Lolkerra and Leboo returned with their supplies together with a couple of pots in which to cook their meal. Both were clad in red shukas and little else. Neither, we were glad to see, had flowers or feathers in their hair.

We crossed the lugga. After a few hundred yards Leboo told us that he wanted to pay his respects to the grave of his father, who had died a few months previously. We peeled off into a wooded grove, where a mound of boulders indicated where Leboo's late dad had been laid to rest. We stood respectfully while Leboo recited a few murmured prayers over the grave. The dappled shade, the softly twittering birds, a few goats quietly pottering about, nibbling at the sparse greenery, the atmosphere was as reverent as that of the most hallowed cathedral. Compared to the grimy, soot-encrusted cemeteries seen from the train as you travel into London, this was a sylvan shrine worthy of the Gods. I made a mental note to tell my Beloved, that, when the time came for me to Hand in my Pail, this was the sort of place to which I wished my mortal remains to be brought. Once, when descending Porr, an isolated hill on the eastern shore of Lake Rudolf, we had come across the intact skeleton of a Turkana, seated upon a rock and gazing out forever over the surrounding desert. That would be a suitable alternative. A sort of skeletal immortality.

Now began a long slow ascent up a thorn-covered hillside. Lolkerra stopped to point out the pug marks of a lion on the path. They were fresh. I wondered what that lion had had for breakfast, or indeed, when he, or she, had last eaten. We hadn't seen anything bigger than a dik dik in days. Perhaps he, or she, was, even now, watching us, a pair of sinewy Samburu and a couple of scrawny palefaces, as we plodded uphill and wondering if we were worth the effort.

This was the sort of thing which made climbing mountains in Kenya and elsewhere in Africa so interesting. You never really knew what, or who, you were going to meet next. Not everyone does or is partial to coming face to face with an irritated buffalo or an aggressive tribal elder onto whose sacred ground you have just inadvertently trespassed. But hell, isn't that what you came to Africa for? To see and experience a bit of Africa that was, and is almost no more, and if the population increase and the do-gooders and the aid agencies and the misguided conservationists have their way – which they will – will soon be utterly no more, and everyone will barking into their smart phones and glaring at their tablets, the men will all be wearing long trousers and the women will be in spangled halter tops and everyone will be tooling around on Chinese motorbikes. OK if you like that sort of thing. We didn't.

The gradient steepened. We were now on a narrow gravelly ridge with a vertical drop into a gully on our left, choked with thick bush. Leboo hissed and pointed. A pair of spiralled horns, a white chevron between the eyes, a tufted brisket, a clatter of hooves, a rattle of stones and the greater kudu was gone.

It was hot, even as we got higher. But we knew, or at least, Lolkerra knew, that up ahead, we would find water, clear cool water in refreshing abundance. So, as the views widened, and the levels in our water bottles dropped ever lower, we powered on, in the sure and certain knowledge that we would soon be lolling beside cool Siloam's shady rill, enjoying our sandwiches, washed down by great invigorating draughts of what I normally only drank with whisky. But needs must etc…

Arriving breathlessly at a col, we gazed around in eager anticipation. A promising forested valley opened up on our right. This must be it. We cocked our ears for the sound of running water, the babbling of a brook, the gurgling of a small rapid. All was silent. Even the birds had ceased to sing. A short fruitless foray up the valley found none of the trout streams of which I had been dreaming for the past several waterless hours. There was no water here. Not a drop.

'Lolkerra,' I said sternly, 'wapi maji?' 'Where's the water?'

He looked embarrassed. It was the same old story. Neither had been as high as this before. Both had assumed that we, being weak and weedy wazungu, would have thrown in the sponge and given up and gone down long before we reached the col. And they had assumed, again wrongly, that if we had got that high, there would be water.

Many locals, living at the base of these mountains, have never been to their summits. What is the point? they might well say. So, although familiar with the paths and approaches lower down, often, once you drew near to the top, confidence evaporated, and you would be told – 'this is the top' – when any fool could see that you still had another thousand feet or so to go.

Suitably chastened, L and L fanned out in search of H_2O.

Leboo was soon back. 'Lipata,' he said. 'I've found it. 'It' turned out to be a pit, about three feet deep, at the bottom of which was a minuscule seepage of a dark, tarry fluid. The earth around the pit was embedded with the footprints of a cross section of the local fauna – we identified baboon, hyena, bush pig, buffalo and bushbuck. Plus a couple we were unable to name. It was obviously well frequented, which was hardly surprising in view of the paucity of water in the vicinity. Some of the prints were fresh, others old. This was where the friends of the forest came to slake their thirst. Now it was our turn. The water looked disgusting. And how were we to get it into our bottles?

Jonathan, with his PhD, was the brains of the party. By contrast the rest of us were unlettered oafs. 'What we do,' said Jonathan, 'is to use your plastic mug to scoop up the fluid as it seeps out of the ground, and then sieve the contents into our water bottles. Now, what shall we use as a sieve?' 'My shirt?' I offered. 'No, no! Too sweaty! I'm not drinking your revolting sweat.' 'OK, what about..?' and we both looked at Lolkerra's shuka. Forty five minutes later, our bottles were replenished with a bilious, beige fluid in which floated numerous indefinable bits and pieces. It was difficult to tell if they were alive or dead. I thought 'If we don't get typhoid or typhus or the galloping trots after this we never will – I'm going to take a sample back and get it cultured, in the interests of science.'

We hoisted our packs onto our shoulders, ready to tackle the last vertiginous section to the summit. As we did so, from the forest depths there came the shrill trumpet blast of an elephant. It did not sound overly friendly. But time was passing and we had no time to stand and stare, far less await the arrival of one of the forest's lawful inhabitants.

The shadows were lengthening as we breasted the lip of the final push. The summit was clothed with enormous trees, set well apart. The great soaring trunks were like the pillars of a huge temple. It was, as some Americans might say, awesome.

To the north the mountain dropped away to the Milgis Lugga, from which the timbered heights of Manmanet rose in the velvet blue distance. It was a view to die for.

Another cliché but appropriate. We stopped and had a pow wow, and decided that we could doss down here in the shelter of the trees. But before we did that I said, 'I say chaps, before we do so, let's have a shufti and see if there is an equally fine view towards the south. Perhaps on the other side of that thicket over there.' 'Good idea,' said Jonathan.

'Let's go while there's still a reasonable amount of light.'

So it was with a song on our lips, and with light hearts, having done the hard bit, reached the summit, and knowing that it was all downhill from now on, that we ambled through the solemn wooded aisles to the thicket, on the other side of which, we hoped to be confronted with yet another clichéd view to die for. Lolkerra went first, rifle at high port, for you never knew, did you, what you might encounter in these wild parts, followed by Leboo, toting his cooking pots, while we took up the rear. In no time the two Samburu had been swallowed up by the greenery.

But not for long.

An ear-splitting elephantine scream rent the peace of parting day, the foliage was torn asunder and first Lolkerra, and then Leboo, shot past us like two competing Olympic sprinters. Hard on their flying heels was an elephant and its intent was immediately apparent. A mountain of grey, preceded by two impressive tusks, erupted from the thicket. Jonathan and I did not stand upon the order of our going.

We went at once. We turned and high-tailed it in different directions. I did not look back but I could almost feel the juggernaut's breath on the nape of my neck. Then I tripped on something metallic and almost went base over apex, even arse over tip, tumbling forwards at forty five degrees and all but nose diving into the summit loam. Recovering with an almighty staggering rush I realised that Leboo had abandoned the pots he had carried all this way.

I did not stop but the elephant did. He – or she – we never did discover the brute's gender, trumpeted in either fury or triumph. In moments like this you're in no state to analyse your pursuer's vocab. According to Lolkerra, sheltering behind a large tree, the beast performed what can best be described as a clog dance on the unfortunate utensils, seizing them in its trunk, tossing them into the air before stomping on them. While our pursuer was thus engaged I bolted for the non-existent cover and took refuge behind a suitable tree. All of the trees on the summit were large and smooth trunked, with no branches lower that 20 feet above ground. They were widely separated with no vegetation between them, a bit like an English park, in fact. We felt very exposed.

As we burrowed behind our respective trees we hoped that once the pot pulverizing was over the beast would shove off.

It didn't. Instead it came looking for us.

Elephants have poor vision in the bright light of day, but it improves as the light fades. It was fading now. This was bad enough, but their sense of smell and hearing are both hyper-acute. They can hear up to distances of two and a half miles and smell water up to 12 miles. We were only 50 yards away.

I could hear it moving, then there was silence. What was it doing? Was it standing stock still, listening? Had it gone? Where was it?

Very, very carefully and slowly, I peered round the trunk of my tree.

'Shit!' It was there, a mere 25 yards away, trunk outstretched, sniffing the air like a great dog, weaving from side to side. Elephants, according to the experts, have a limited range of vision of only 25 feet, so it probably couldn't see me.

Scarcely daring to breathe, I watched. For about fifteen minutes the great beast remained in the same spot, immobile, seemingly trying to figure out where we had gone. I was getting stiff from trying to impersonate that chap in Pompeii who has been frozen in time ever since Vesuvius blew its top. Then, slowly, ever so slowly, reluctantly, the elephant turned away and began to amble back into the forest.

That was the moment I felt a tickle in my nose. I was going to sneeze. I scrunched up my proboscis, I curled my lips, I held my breath – well, I had been holding that for about half an hour – it was no good, something had to come out. And it did, with a muffled snort.

The elephant whirled round as on a sixpence, gave an almighty high pitched scream and charged, and almost simultaneously Lolkerra fired two shots over its head.

With a furious trumpet the elephant wheeled to the left and stampeded back into the forest and was gone. We rose somewhat stiffly to our feet. It was now almost dark, but soon the moon would rise and we decided that, if our four-legged friend did return, it would be safer to bivouac on the steep final rise than on the flatter summit. So there we spent the night. Leboo retrieved his battered pots, bashed them into some sort of shape, lit a fire, and with the revolting water from the pit, cooked a meal of sorts for himself and Lolkerra.

Jonathan and I spent a night of little comfort and less sleep on our respective ledges. A meal of cold baked beans washed down as fast as possible with what looked like horse piss, and probably tasted much the same, formed the basis of our evening repast.

Some people might think this was a penance: 'sunbeams scorching all the day, chilly dewdrops nightly shed, prowling beasts about thy way, stones thy pillow, earth thy bed' as the hymn has it but that was not how we saw it. To us this was better than any lodge or tented camp, where the wilderness was conveniently kept at bay and the only locals you met were receptionists, waiters and drivers, all keen to butter you up and persuade you to part with the expected pourboire, pandering to the post-colonial guilt complex, so engrained in the minds of the unwashed public from the never-ending pontificating on the media by left wing apologists, bleating about the iniquities of Empire. Looking back at history is necessary and essential but the past is the past and if you spend all your time peering over your shoulder, sooner or later you'll trip over your shoelaces.

No such feeling of guilt troubled us as we reclined on our mountainside, listening to the soft wind in the trees behind us, the quiet murmur of the Samburu as they crouched over their fire, the wind brush of a passing night bird, and watched the moon, a huge incandescent disc, rise above the forested ramparts of Manmanet. As it climbed higher and higher it became a shimmering alabaster globe, shedding a silvery light over our resting place.

I awoke once, to the distant trumpeting of an elephant. An owl hooted. A comet streaked across the night sky. I slept again.

'Night's candles are burnt out, and jocund day
Stands tiptoe on the misty mountain tops.'
'Awake! For Morning in the Bowl of night
Has flung the Stone that puts the Stars to Flight.'

Jonathan was the sort of chap who was forever reciting great chunks of Paradise Lost and Tennyson and bits of Latin as we plunged through bush and ploughed across boulder fields – '*iacta alea est* – the die is cast,' 'made weak by time and fate but strong in will. To strive, to seek, to find and not to yield,' 'to boldly go where no man has gone before' and so on. You know the sort of stuff:

> '*Up lad, 'tis late for lying,*
> *Hear the drums of morning play.*'

I stirred on my earthy bed. Jonathan was upright, nobly declaiming to the new-born day. The sun was rising and bright rays were lighting the opposite side of the valley. It was time to descend.

Down we went, pausing only to collect a suitable sample from the reeking pit. Fresh baboon and hyena prints were dotted around its puddled edge. Some of the drinkers had thoughtlessly voided their bowels in the immediate area. I looked forward to the results with scientific interest.

By mid-morning we had reached the lugga, paid off the troops and were in the Land Rover and heading back to Penelope's camp. We fairly tore up the lugga, flags flying and bugles blaring, little knowing that this sort of behaviour was something that was guaranteed to enrage the fair Penelope, who regarded the whole area as her personal kingdom with herself as monarch of everything she surveyed. From an eyrie above her camp, with a pair of powerful binoculars, she kept close watch of both subjects and unwelcome interlopers alike, and there was little doubt into which category we fell.

So when we drove up to the camp, giving the fleshy, befeathered janitor a cheery wave as we passed, our welcome from the proprietrix was rather less than effusive. The winning smile was gone. With flashing eyes and looking as though she had been dragged through a hedge backwards, she advanced upon us, Medusa locks in tangled disarray. Perseus at least, I thought, had had the benefit of his mirrored shield to protect himself from such stony orbs.

We were facing them head on and it was a damned unnerving sight. I could see that this was the sort of female, who, in the Middle Ages, if she had the power, would have no compunction about stringing you up by your thumbs, or getting her minions to rack you to death. So play it easy, was what went through my mind.

'Hi there Penny!' I greeted her. 'How's it all going?'

'It was all going fine until I heard you roaring up the lugga like an invading army, destroying the peace and tranquillity I have so carefully cultivated over the years.

An American called Jake or Jesse, or something equally barbaric, used to live in a valley off the lugga and just like you he would come howling along the lugga with a bloody great Stars and Stripes flag flapping from the roof of his buggy. Drove me bloody well mad!'

Well we could see that all right. She gave us a hard look.

'We're terribly sorry, old thing,' said Jonathan, 'for any inconvenience we may have caused you.' The wrong thing to say. Penelope went white at the gills. 'I am *not* your old thing, as you put it!' she retorted.

But Berna and Carolyn and son Nick had had a glorious time in such wonderful surroundings and were well catered for. They were glad to see us, as we arrived, bloody as usual after such jaunts, but unbowed. Now it was time to leave and make our slow way back to civilization and work.

We thanked Penny for her care, hospitality and expertise in such a remote location and she responded graciously and modestly. She seemed to have calmed down after her earlier outburst and was positively radiant. She had brushed her hair, touched up those lovely kissable lips, donned a fresh kaftan and from her beaded sandals peeped ten painted toes. I made my expected entry in the Visitors' Book, which, as usual, was filled with the obligatory rapturous comments by previous visitors. With perfumed Penny at my elbow I wrote a brief synopsis of our experiences. 'Now,' she said, 'what have you written? Mmm.

'Superb location. Wonderful experience. Camp staff friendly and helpful. Spent night out on mountain.' I told you so. 'No water.' 'What did you expect? Hot baths?' 'Charged by elephant.' Happens all the time – nothing to write home about. Anyway I must dash. Clients flying in! Mustn't keep them waiting!' And she was gone. 'So,' said

Berna, 'it would seem that she didn't get all dolled up for our sakes!' 'No indeed! The clients are probably loaded and she wants to look her best. But at least we know where we stand, which is always a good thing.' 'Funny there's been no mention of teachers while we've been here. She must know that I'm one.' 'Yes, that's odd. From what I was told I gathered she loathed their very guts.'

We decided that, as the road we had followed in to the camp was so awful, we would return by driving up the Milgis Lugga, meet the road to Barsaloi, and then veer left via the Operoi valley to Maralal, where we would join the main dirt road to Rumuruti and Nakuru.

Before we set off Berna asked Jonathan, who as our Man in the North was an expert in such things, a perfectly reasonable question: 'What do we do if we meet water flowing down the lugga?' 'Well,' said Jonathan, 'we hope we can take avoiding action by scaling the bank.'

This reply did not fill us with an abundance of optimism. Driving up a narrowing lugga with the possibility that at any moment flood water might come surging down towards you is akin to flying a light aircraft into a box canyon. You might be lucky, but then again you might not, and many people have been in vehicles washed away when without due thought they drove in bald headed and full of light-hearted optimism. It is the same with camping. Never camp in a lugga. Rain falling many miles away may result in a midnight flood able to wash you and your tent and vehicle to oblivion. There's a sudden roar and a whoosh, you are up to your armpits in a brown flood and then it's good night sweet prince, or princess.

After about an hour we paused for a bush break.

'I say, Jonathan,' said Berna, 'what's that coming down the lugga?' 'If I'm not mistaken,' replied Jonathan, 'it's water.'

So it was. Not much, but perhaps an indicator of things to come. We pushed on, tacking from side to side across the narrowing stream in an effort to drive on the diminishing fringe of shingle and sand. Both banks were now steep and getting steeper, and were covered with dense thickets of acacia, wild sisal and cactus, hardly conducive to easy riding. One day, I thought, there'll be a tarmac highway through here, with laybys full of day trippers and ice cream parlours, filling stations, pizza palaces and brothels, so enjoy it before the rot, which has already begun, sets in.

The passage narrowed until we were driving in running water up a narrow gully barely wide enough for our vehicles. Now we're for it I thought, if water comes down.

Turning round was now impossible. Then, suddenly, ahead of us was a bridge – the road to Barsaloi, and miraculously, there was a ramp up which we barrelled and onto the highway, such as it was. Now it would be all plain sailing. The road was rough, unsurfaced and rocky but when we turned off left towards Operoi it became smooth and sandy, running through lovely stands of tall acacia trees. Hornbills swooped in front of us, a go-away bird shouted a warning, goats were grazing, the air was cool, it was idyllic. We arrived at Operoi village, a line of shacks beside a river on the left, a Catholic church on the right, and that was it.

'So much for Operoi,' said Berna. But for all that it was such a dump it was not long before we wished we were back there and that we had paid more attention to the go-away bird. The 'road' was diabolical. For the first few miles the 'road' consisted of a succession of gigantic rocks over which one had to ease one's groaning vehicle, using four wheel drive, low ratio, first gear.

At times our Trooper was tilted over at such an angle I was afraid that it might fall on its side. I've driven on a few hairy roads in Kenya but this one took the biscuit. During the wet season it was impassable and today it has been abandoned to the forces of Nature. Now Operoi is accessed from Maralal via a new reasonably well-maintained Cresta Run type road further north. Meanwhile we ground our jolting way over the massive rocks, skirted a quaking bog, and inched ourselves up a narrow tunnel through the forest, praying that we wouldn't meet anyone coming downhill. Not that there was much chance of that. Only certified lunatics and those of unsound mind would of their own volition embark on such a venture. But once committed there was no turning back, as Macbeth so eloquently stated in Act Three Scene Four – look it up. So we crept ever upwards through the forest and despite everything were glad to do so, because further north all the woods had been felled for charcoal and timber for urban sawmills, leaving nothing but bare-stumped hills. Once chopped down, the pristine forest never returns despite every noble effort at regeneration. We turned a corner and there, standing astonished and immobile in the road, was a beautiful female bushbuck. She stared, unbelieving, and then, with a graceful bound, leapt into the forest and was gone, as though she had never been. We stopped to allow our vehicles let off steam. The track was very steep. A fluttering in the bushes and an exquisite paradise flycatcher was flitting from twig to twig. The forest was silent, the woods 'lovely, dark and deep,' in Robert Frost's words. But for how long before the rasp of the buzz saw and the roar of the timber lorry breaks into that pristine silence? A Frenchman called Karr came up with the fatuous epigram – 'plus ca change, c'est la meme chose' – 'the more things change, the more they stay the same'. What utter rot, I thought. Once these trees are felled, that's it. There will be no going back or staying the same. In the distance a baboon barked – 'be gone!' We left.

Finally we emerged from the forest and there, a few miles on our right, lay Maralal, tin-roofed houses scattered across the hillsides, the town lower down. We trundled along the rather attractive, tree-shaded main street, passing knots of colourfully clad, non-touristic Samburu, until we came to a grateful stop outside the Hard Rock café. This unpretentious eatery was sited hard by the famous garage owned by the Bhola family, to which on previous forays to the north we had, on a number of occasions, been obliged to repair to seek help when various parts of our vehicle failed or fell off. Here, also, we had met Wilfred Thesiger, the famous explorer and traveller, who resided in the town. He came strolling up the street, clad in Harris Tweed jacket, Oxford bags, polished brogues and flat cap, trailed by a coterie of Samburu youths. Siddiq Bhola, kindness personified, had set aside a room above his garage for Thesiger's use and often fed him as well.

Food was also on our minds as we pushed our way through the beaded curtain into the Hard Rock café. The place was full, heaving with African humanity, the air full of aromatic incense and sensuous pentatonic Somali music. As we stood hesitating, a Somali matron, whom I judged to be in the upper welterweight division, slid, as though on castors, towards us. Heavy-hipped and full-bosomed, she regarded us with a roguish eye, a slow, amused smile on her full lips. She beckoned us with a hennaed finger and we followed her through the packed room and out to a tiny, shady patio, where she sat us down at a moderately clean table. 'My name,' she said, 'is Barkhado. In English it means 'Sunshine.' And when she laughed and showed her snowy teeth and threw back her head-scarfed head it did seem that her smile, beaming down upon us, was like a personal ray of sunshine to rival that streaming from the firmament. 'You are most welcome.' Then she plied us with delicious, hot, crispy samosas, and scalding ginger tea, poured from a huge vacuum flask. Tiny birds twittered and cheeped in a little tree. It was all very peaceful.

Whenever we went on our modest excursions to the remoter parts of the land we would make a point of stopping at a Somali tea house – in Baragoi, Laisamis or Lokori – where we would be welcomed and refreshed and be given the latest news of stock raids, security and local mayhem.

Soon we were rattling along the rutted road across the Laikipia plateau to Rumuruti and so back to Nakuru.

Once back we dispatched the water sample collected from the mountain pit to the lab for analysis, plus a modestly framed enquiry to the fair Penelope raising a question regarding costs for staying at her wilderness retreat. These had risen to a degree since booking which demanded an answer.

Within a few short days we had our answers. Neither made for bedtime reading.

The one from the lab was basically as expected. It was short, brief and to the point. The water was hissing with Animal E.coli and the report came with the stark warning that it was 'totally unfit for human consumption'. A bit too late for that.

The one from Penelope stretched to seven pages of rank foolscap. They were not perfumed. Neither were they embossed, nor were they on the headed expensive notepaper with which lodges and camps use to attract custom from potential or current 'guests'. The seven pages looked as though they had been ripped violently from some random notepad. The writing was large and wild and heavily indentated suggesting that writer had been firmly in the grip of unbridled rage and passion.

A raw nerve had obviously been severely irritated.

In this diatribe we were advised in terms that brooked no doubt as to the writer's fevered view: we had done her a grave disservice by even hinting that we had been overcharged. On the contrary. We had, we were told, been given 'special rates,' water had been hauled from distant wells for our personal ablutions, askaris had been hired for our protection, the costs involved in maintaining a camp in such a remote area were astronomic and so on and on. Only once before had her rates ever been questioned – and at this point things began to get personal. And that person – 'guess what!' – 'had been a teacher!'

The rant continued with almost obscene references to beach boys and comparisons between coastal hotels and her pristine establishment. All directed seemingly at Berna to whom as a teacher and female, Penelope seemed to be venting her pent-up spleen and offloading her underlying psychoses. This astonishing document of invective obviously did not deserve a reply but was worthy of preservation if only to demonstrate how true were the words of King Duncan in Macbeth – yes, back to Macbeth again! – 'there's no art to find the mind's construction in the face,' – 'and,' said Berna, 'in future let's doss down in the lugga and to hell with all camps and their Lady Macbeths!' With which sentiment I most heartily agreed.

Chapter Eighteen

OPEN WIDE

Big booming Mike Sugden was on the blower.

'That you, Hugh?' His Yorkshire accent was as strong as it had been when he came to Kenya Colony all those years ago. 'Can ye coom out double quick tae see one of ma fillies? Bloody syces took them oot for canter an' when they come back do they unsaddle and water them?' 'No,' I replied, having also served time in the country, 'I don't suppose they did.' 'Too bloody right they didn't! Nae, them boogers just shoved them into stable as they were, stirrups dangling and go and sit on their haunches to discuss my various deficiencies. So one filly has damaged its mouth biting at stirrup. So coom as quick as ye can!'

I piled into my Peugeot and took off at high speed.

Mike was one of a dying breed, a Kenya character, big-hearted and big-mouthed at the same time, kind yet firm, warm and generous, unafraid to speak his mind, he stood out from the crowd. He had been married to, or closely associated with, a sequence of African women, with whom he had several children and whose languages he spoke fluently and to effect. Known by his African neighbours as arap Maina, he was a larger than life character. Nowadays there are few like him. Nonconformists are rare. They have been replaced by grey men in grey suits. Eccentrics, for which

Kenya was notorious, made the country stand out and gave the place its unique character. Whatever your views, there is no doubt that it was the Kenya settler who lit the spark and fanned the flame of international interest in the country. When you think of some other African countries, such as little worm-shaped Malawi, flat empty Zambia or even flatter, emptier Botswana, the mind goes blank. Picturesque they may be, lovely game-full National Parks they may have but as far as character is concerned they fall at the first fence.

Then there are the others, blood-soaked and wrecked: the Congo, Somalia, Liberia, whose history is nothing but a litany of failure, human misery and despair. Countries to shy away from. Of course Kenya's record is anything but squeaky clean – Mau Mau, post-election violence and killings, massive corruption, police brutality, tribalism, but on the whole a darn sight better than most of its neighbours. And the people are friendly and warm towards visitors. Tourists come to see wildlife of course, but also, possibly without thinking about it, because of the country's history – British East, Kenya Colony, the Lunatic Line – and its association with the former colonial power, Britain, and tales of explorers, white hunters, Happy Valley and aristocratic scandal. All that is in the past and with population growth, erosion of wildlife habitat, the steady dwindling of the last remnants of true wilderness, the country is inexorably losing its former individuality in the face of 'progress' and is in danger of becoming just another warm weather destination where, if you are lucky, you may see a couple of elephant in the distance or a brace of lions lured to your mini-van by a zebra steak, and where you may loll, with others, gin and tonic at your elbow, on your lounger by the Indian Ocean, while container ships steam by, instead of dhows and dugout canoes.

But Mike was still with us, growing ever larger, his voice undiminished. When he came to see me at my surgery in Club Lane, he would dispatch his driver to summon me to his car window. This was because, with his belly the size it had become, getting into his car was difficult enough, but getting out was well-nigh impossible. But he still, with an effort, was able to lever himself up the Club steps and into the Men's Bar.

I arrived at his farm, wondering what I was going to see this time. I passed the sign board – 'Aren't we Hall' – more evidence of Mike's eccentricity.

I stopped at the stables where head syce Kosgei, a Nandi, was standing, looking rather nervous, probably because he had just had a bollocking from his master. 'Jambo, Kosgei,' I greeted him, 'where's the patient?' He jerked his head towards the first stable. 'What happened?' I asked. 'Sijui – I don't know,' he replied. The stock response from a guilty party. Well, I had a jolly good idea what had happened.

I examined the filly, which was standing, head lowered, blood dripping from her open mouth, obviously in considerable pain. I lifted her head to try and estimate the degree of damage. She wasn't having any of that. She whinnied loudly, reared and backed away.

Sedation was required. I had a choice. Xylazine, or detomidine, trade name Domosedan. I decided on the latter. More expensive and not so good when used when anaesthetising horses, its effect as a sedative was predictable, lasted longer than xylazine and the sedated animal tended to stand without swaying or staggering.

I returned to the car, arranged a few instruments on a tray, wolf teeth extractors, tooth forceps, suture material, needle holders, local anaesthetic.

As I slipped the needle into the filly's jugular I heard Mike's heavy breathing as he staggered into the stable behind me.

'So what's the damage?'

'I'll know in a minute, when the sedative takes effect. But I do know what must have happened. In biting at the dangling stirrup her lower jaw got caught where you put your foot and in trying to free it she must have reared backwards and this is the result.'

Mike said something in Nandi to Kosgei who flinched. Thanks to his symbiotic relationship with a succession of Nandi ladies he spoke the language fluently. Whatever he said was not complimentary.

The filly's head is now drooping and she is standing with both forelegs spread. I ask Kosgei to lift her head. 'Ndiyo Bwana, ndiyo,' he says eager to atone for his previous neglect. Do I smell booze? I am not sure, but I see Mike, head up, nostrils dilated, snuffing the air like a questing buffalo.

I push a hand-held mouth gag between the molars on the left side of the filly's mouth. The heavy metal dental gag is no good here as the injury is all at the front in the incisor area. 'Mike,' I say, 'can you grab that torch and shine it into her mouth. Ah, now we can see the damage. Looks pretty extensive. From what I can see, several incisors have been dislodged from their positions and jammed backwards into the mouth and there's a plate of bone from the upper jaw which appears to have been unshipped from its moorings. It's going to be a bit tricky repairing this mess. But nothing venture, nothing gain. I'll need an extra pair of hands. Can you summon a couple of syces to assist?'

Mike had a voice whose volume was such that, had he been aboard a ship nosing its way up the English Channel in thick fog, he would have out-bellowed the most powerful foghorn in existence. He used it now. A pair of hadada ibis, quietly and unconcernedly prodding the greensward for their daily sustenance, rose in sudden alarm, venting their fright with loud calls of distress. The required grooms came at a quick gallop. They knew that their jobs, if not their very existence, were on the line.

I gave one the tray of instruments to hold. The other was to ensure that the gag did not slip. The job was going to be hard enough without having my fingers bifurcated by what was left of the filly's teeth.

'Right, Kosgei, my man,' I said, your task is to support the filly's head on your manly shoulder, while I do what I have to do. In the course of my undistinguished career in the service of this benighted land, my back has been broken and buggered beyond redemption and spending the next couple of hours bent over like Quasimodo is not something I intend to do. Hence your vital role in the proceedings.'

The weight of an average horse's head is 10% of its bodyweight. The filly weighed about 1,000lbs, ergo her head weighed about 100lbs. Kosgei did not look tremendously overjoyed when he received his instructions but with Mike wheezing and glowering in the background like an upright elephant seal he hoisted the mass of equine cranium onto his shoulder. Portable horse head supports, as used in more advanced countries, were not something I toted around in my car, even if I had access to them.

With a fine needle I infiltrated the gum and palate with local anaesthetic, and set to work, removing teeth which had been irreparably damaged, straightening others, wiring the opposing lower canines with stainless steel wire and finally, with considerable difficulty because of its position, suturing the hard palate to the gum. By the time I had finished, after what seemed like hours, I was quite light-headed, having had to stitch with my skull turned upside down. Plus, as time passed, Kosgei's ability to hold the filly's head upright perceptibly dwindled, so by the time I inserted the last stitch I was almost on my long-suffering knees.

Kosgei, having supported the filly's head on his shoulder for the past couple of hours, was now visibly wilting and beginning to sway from side to side. Whether this was from fatigue or from whatever he might have drunk while discussing the undoubted defects of his master's character, was difficult to tell. But, having trimmed the final suture and told him that he could now depart, he tottered off like the proverbial drunken sailor.

The two other syces grinned. Kosgei, unlike them had drawn the short straw.

Mike was less judgemental. 'Kosgei is a good man,' he grunted, 'good with horses, damn shame he's too fond of the booze.'

'OK Mike,' I said, 'I've done my best. Keep her inside on soft food for the next ten days or so. Nothing hard or fibrous. Don't want to dislodge those stitches. But most mouth wounds usually heal well, given half a chance. Saliva has anti-bacterial properties you know.' 'I didn't,' said Mike, 'but if you come down to the house you can salivate while I pour you a snort.'

I did. The filly's mouth healed well.

Of course not all problems with animals' mouths end so well. Canine mouth cancers, if malignant, such as the dreaded squamous cell carcinoma, carry a very poor prognosis. But most conditions, if diagnosed early and treated correctly, respond well and give a good outcome, due in part to the rich blood supply to the area. Fortunately, the average owner, at the sight of their dog or cat slobbering or salivating, will start hunting for a vet's phone number. And quite rightly so. The problem may be due to poisoning, or, in East Africa, to rabies, or, if in a cow or sheep, to foot and mouth disease. Diagnosis is the key from which everything else follows. Dogs would not infrequently get bones stuck transversely across their mouths. Often the dog would be unable to close its jaws so that they would hang open, resulting in salivation. But these symptoms mimic those of rabies and more than one owner spent unwise time rooting around in a rabid dog's mouth with an ungloved hand searching for a non-existent bone. The interesting thing was that it was often the highly educated owners who indulged in such actual, and indeed potential, madness, reinforcing the fact, once again, that intelligence is not the same as common sense.

During my long career I had seen numerous cases of rabies – in dogs and cats, sheep, cattle and horses, and I could tell if a dog had rabies almost as soon as I saw it. The glazed look, the hanging jaw, the frequent semi-paralysis of a limb, a sudden snap at a non-existent fly, the dilated pupils

None of these symptoms would be evident in a dog with a foreign body stuck in its mouth. But to be on the safe side I always wore gloves when opening such dogs' mouths and I had been vaccinated many times against rabies. Removal of such foreign bodies was easy: sedate, insert a gag, and remove with long forceps and you had a relieved dog and owner.

Then there were the things which, to a layman, appeared alarming, such as viral warts in young dogs and young horses. Sometime the whole mouth, tongue and gums seemed to be covered with these grey growths. Usually they were small in size, but on occasion could be quite large. I knew that they would resolve spontaneously, given time. So I had to encourage patience, something some owners did not possess.

Then there was a benign tumour-like mass called an epulis, found on the gum of dogs. The name comes from the Greek 'epi' and 'ulon' meaning 'on the gingiva.' I liked to impress the more pedantic and academic of my clients with such obscure and useless snippets of information. Caught early these growths were easily and successfully removed, with rare recurrence.

I was always impressed by the abilities of animals to cope with what seemed, at first sight, to be life-threatening events. A dog bitten on the tongue by a puff adder. The whole mouth swelled up. The dog could scarcely breathe. I gave IV snake bite anti-venom and IV corticosteroids, fully expecting imminent death. Slowly the swelling subsided and the dog began to drink water. But the tongue turned black and hard and finally most of it sloughed off leaving a pathetic remnant at the back of the throat. But the dog, amazingly, coped with its situation and learned to eat. As did a cow I was called to see on a farm near Naivasha, which had somehow or other, managed to tear most of its tongue in half.

It was a Sunday – most emergencies seemed to happen either on the Sabbath or at night – and as we arrived, a storm of major proportions was about to break. The anterior half of the tongue was hanging by a thread, so I cut it off with a pair of scissors. We slalomed our way through the mud back to the main road. Later we heard that the cow did well and ate normally. As did a goose whose upper beak was bitten off by a dog. On a routine visit along the south shore of Lake Naivasha I was asked to look at a German Shepherd dog which had been bitten on the face by a puff adder several days previously. Why, I asked, not unreasonably, had help been not sought earlier? The owner was a hard-bitten, bull-necked Dutch South African, called Pikkie van der Merwe. At that time Kenya was awash with jokes about the mythical Van der Merwe, the archetypical bone-headed Afrikaner, so I had to be careful not to allow my features break into a smile as I remembered one of many of the choice witticisms concerning Van and his innumerable faux pas. This Afrikaner was not the sort of chap with which to bandy ribald reflections on his fellow countryman. 'Ach, man,' he said, 'it's just a dog. In Africa you must take your chances, the rough with the smooth, eh? You live or you die.' I wondered what he himself might have done if he had been bitten on the face by a puff adder. The side of the dog's face where the bite had occurred was now totally devoid of skin and muscle. All had sloughed away following the bite, leaving exposed bare bone and teeth. There was nothing to be done. The dog did not appear to be in any distress or pain and was able to eat normally. Six weeks later the whole area was covered with healthy tissue and after another month you would have had to peer closely to detect any puff adder input.

'There you are,' said Pikkie, in his broad Suid Afrikaans accent, 'let Nature take its course, man. Ja, all this bloody reliance on drugs is just spitting in her face.'

He was right of course. The trick is to know when to use drugs and when not to. Many conditions will resolve in spite of treatment, not because of it. In the West, and nowadays in the so-called developing countries, drugs are used with gay abandon, so much so that the planet is faced with a major antibiotic resistance crisis. Divine retribution, some might say. My own armoury of drugs was niggardly in the extreme. Many farmers, due to the easy availability of over-the-counter drugs, sold willy nilly with zero checks, held veritable pharmacopoeias of antibiotics, valid and expired, and various nostrums of dubious validity, far in excess of my own. The market is now flooded with sub-standard Chinese drugs, so the problem, unless governments intervene, will only get worse. Intervention, due to the stranglehold China has on many African countries, is unlikely.

❖❘❖❘❖❘❖❘❖

So, when Peter Faull phoned from Laikipia, saying that he had a cheetah with a broken jaw, I knew that, apart from the necessary anaesthetic drugs, the rest would, I hoped, be a matter of basic drug-less veterinary carpentry.

Peter and his wife Rosalie lived and worked on a large ranch on the northern edge of the Laikipia plateau. They also owned a small farm at Poror, north of Maralal, at about 8,000 feet in the aromatic cedar forest, on the rim of the great escarpment which drops in a mighty sweep into the baking Suguta Valley. To the north the land fell away more gradually, until finally, far, far from the cool forest, it slid into the slippery waters of the Jade Sea – Lake Rudolf.

Here among the great, moss-covered trees, from whose branches wisps of old man's beard fluttered in the breeze, they grew pyrethrum and ran mule safaris into the surrounding hills. Peter had been a professional hunter and he bore on his chest the scars from a too close encounter with a lion, wounded by his client in the Lake Magadi area of southern Kenya, close to the Tanzanian border. Peter had a dicky heart and had had one of his valves replaced with one from a non-volunteer donor pig. This required renewal every ten years or so. The new valve performed its function admirably, but with a distinctly audible clicking sound, such that, when Peter came to the door of the surgery, and if there happened to be a blessed break in the diabolical drumming by the blind beggar in the street outside or if the iron-lunged resident preacher paused for breath between Exodus and Leviticus, it sounded as if he had a clock or a ticking time bomb within his chest. This did not prevent Peter from indulging in frequent buffalo hunts on the ranch, accompanied by his favourite Staffordshire bull terrier, Pok, whose neck was encircled by a wide, heavy, leather collar embedded with formidable brass studs to protect him during his frequent sanguinary encounters with the local baboons.

Rosalie supervised a plantation of miraa, or khat, a stimulant drug, on the ranch, a plant whose growth she monitored with almost parental devotion. Every afternoon, the harvested crop, packed in manageable bunches, would be rushed at high speed, either to Maralal for local consumption, or to Nanyuki or Nairobi, to be flown to Mogadishu in Somalia in order to narcotize the male population. Speed of transport was of the essence.

The stuff had to arrive and be within the recipient's masticating jaws within 48 hours in order to achieve maximum effect. Hence Rosalie's single-minded dedication to her chosen mission. Many countries have banned the use of miraa, but it may not be any more dangerous to health than some people's curious habit of drinking several strong cups of coffee daily.

As far as I knew neither Peter nor Rosalie chewed miraa, but moderate smoking and drinking was not off the menu. Life was there to be enjoyed and if what you enjoyed doing shortened it then so be it. When I heard that so-and-so had died falling off a mountain and people groaned and said 'ah, what a waste of a life' I had to disagree. He – it was usually a he – had died doing what he liked best and what better end could there be than that? Nick Nowicki was a good friend of ours. He was Polish, born before World War II during which his father was murdered by the Russians in Katyn Forest. Driven from Poland by both the Russians and the Germans, he ended up a refugee in Siberia, eventually making his way to India and finally to Mombasa where he disembarked. He trained as a motor mechanic and rose to become manager of the Peugeot franchise in Nakuru. He had had such a hard life in his youth, surviving on starvation rations, that he determined to make up for lost time, never stinting on the vodka or good food, and during all of his time in Kenya he worked hard at his job and on enjoying himself and being a friend to others. Plus winning the East African Safari Rally in 1963 and 1968 when, on both occasions, due to atrocious weather conditions, only seven cars finished. Nick drove a standard Peugot 404, a triumph never equalled. Present-day rallies in Kenya are tame, milksop affairs by comparison. Peter and Rosalie were cut from the same stalwart cloth.

The cheetah, which was semi-tame, duly arrived at my surgery in Club Lane. Confined within a large box trap, it was male and large and was more than a little agitated by a journey lasting over four hours and by his strange surroundings. As the trap was carried into the surgery, a large and excited crowd gathered to watch the proceedings. All of this added to the cheetah's state of anxiety. Fortunately Peter had come with his gun bearer, a Kamba named Muyambu, which means lion, and he behaved like one when the crowd surged up to the door of the surgery. He bared his filed teeth and snarled at the mob to stand back.

The cheetah was a magnificent animal, with his spotted pelt, his long black-tipped tail, his wonderful golden eyes and black tear-marks on his face, so marked to allow this fastest animal on four legs to focus on fleeing, jinking prey. I estimated his weight to be about 65 kilos.

We carried the box trap into the surgery and closed the door against the excited mob, whose frustration at being denied further excitement was manifested by groans and sighs of disappointment. Anaesthetic options were limited to the xylazine/ketamine combo, and glad I was to have them. In the '60s and '70s I would have been hard pressed to anaesthetise a fully-grown cheetah in the prime of life. Giving an intravenous injection of sodium pentobarbitone to a non-compliant wild cat would have been out of the question, as would the use of ether or chloroform. So I blessed the chemists who first formulated the current intramuscular anaesthetics. Present day vets, with their extraordinary expertise and knowledge, far in excess of my own, have little idea of the limitations under which their forebears , and indeed, some of their still extant stone age colleagues, laboured – and yet, despite all, came up with the goods.

So I computed the dosage – one mg per kg of xylazine, followed ten minutes later by 8mg per kg of ketamine, given into the muscles of the hind leg. Now the problem was how to administer the injection. Darting in such a confined space was inadvisable.

Muyambu came to the rescue.

Peter explained that the cheetah, named Zorro, found as a tiny cub in the bush beside his dead mother and equally dead sister, had been hand reared by Muyambu. Now fully grown, he was venturing further and further from his enclosure on the ranch and attempting to run down game. But, not having been taught that zebra are beyond the capabilities of even the most experienced cheetah, he took one on and paid the price by being kicked in the face.

'Muyambu is the only one who can handle him,' said Peter.

I was glad to hear it.

Muyambu opened the trap. Zorro shot out, Muyambu grabbed him round the neck and I shot the xylazine into his hind leg. Ten minutes later, with Zorro now recumbent and half asleep, I administered the ketamine.

Very soon he was out cold. We lifted him onto the table.

I examined his jaw. He had a compound fracture of the left

mandible and the symphysis – the join at the front of the jaw where left and right mandible meet – was split apart.

'Right, Peter,' I said, 'what we have to do is to drive a stainless steel pin through the intact right mandible below the tongue and through the fractured left mandible, making sure that the fractured site is properly aligned. Then we will wire both canines together and finally stitch that tear in the skin. Oh and place a couple of corks onto the sharp ends of the pins.'

'Sounds complicated,' said Peter. 'Not really,' I said, 'it's mostly a matter of getting the alignment right plus controlled force. Anyway, let's see how we get on.'

I shaved and sterilized a small area of skin on both mandibles posterior to the fracture site, and marked the entry and exit of the pin with a marker pen. I selected a suitably-sized pin, trimmed it for length and sharpened the cut end. Using a brace and bit I slowly began to drive the pin through the sound mandible. Slowly, because too fast would create heat and make the grip on the bone less secure. Ah, a sudden lessening in the opposing force. We are through! Now, carefully, carefully, align the pin on the mark on the fracture side and drive the pin through until about an inch on both sides is protruding.

Now, thread a wire round the lower canines, first making a groove at their base to ensure the tightened wire doesn't slip. And finally, stitch the rent in the skin where the zebra's hoof had impacted the jaw.

'Right, Peter old son,' I said, 'that's it. Alignment is excellent. Solid as the Rock of Gibraltar. Let's put on the corks. Those ends are sharp. It'll take a while before he comes round. Maybe another two or three hours. Takes longer than in dogs, cats or horses. Better wait and let him come round here rather than have him bashing himself against the side of the trap on the way back. I'll wait here with Muyambu while you go across the Club for a snort before you leave.'

'Jolly good idea,' said Peter with his customary grin.

Six weeks later I removed the pin and wire. Zorro's jaw healed well without incident and he was soon back hunting. And he left zebra strictly alone.

Chapter Nineteen

A TRIP TO THE COAST

Gurmit Singh was on his way to the coast. He had spent the night at the Sikh temple at Makindu, halfway between Nairobi and Mombasa, where he had enjoyed an evening carousing with his friends. The temple was open to all bona fide travellers of any race, hue or religion, and was free, only requesting on departure a donation to keep it so. We had spent the odd night there, and found the atmosphere and the fare to be rather more congenial than in the chicken-and-chips joints in places such as Mtito Andei and Voi, further down the line.

The Sikhs are a hospitable bunch, friendly, hard-working and open, and seem, fortunately, to have forgotten the reverses they suffered at the hands of the brutal Brits during the battles of Sobraon, Chillianwallah and Gujerat during the 1st and 2nd Sikh Wars. They are a proud martial race, and, like the British before the rot set in, sure and confident of their status in the world.

Gurmit was looking forward to spending time with his coastal mistress, Amina, a spellbinding Swahili half caste, who had him in her thrall, and whose ravishing beauty and physical charms were renowned from Lamu to Lungalunga. Mentally savouring the awaiting erotic delights, imagination in full flow, Gurmit stepped on the gas.

Through Tsavo he roared. Baobab trees flashed by. Ambling elephants were ignored. The resident baboons at Tsavo Bridge scampered for safety as he shot over the notorious landmark where some of his former fellow compatriots may have become lion lunch during the construction of the Lunatic Line from Mombasa to Lake Vic. There were no man-eating lions to hinder the present-day Chinese in the construction of their space age line so why did it take them longer to get from Mombasa to Nairobi with all their sophisticated gear than did the Brits, Africans and Indians with pick and shovel to do twice the distance? Now, in direct competition with the rightful elephant owners of the land, there was another elephantine intruder, only this one was white.

The long downhill stretch to Voi was a direct invitation to do the ton. The Merc responded like a stallion to the touch of the spur. It leapt forwards, eager to obey its master's imperious command. Too late, Gurmit saw the traffic cop's imperative upraised arm.

He slowed and pulled off the road.

The policeman, following his well-filled paunch, came up to Gurmit's window.

'Wewe, Muhindi – you, Indian! – you are breaking the speed limit. Here it is 80kph. You were doing 140! Our machine, it does not lie! So, you must go to cot and there will be a big fine. Now we will go to the station for you to be charged.'

The cop moved round to the passenger side and made to get into the car. This was illegal and Gurmit knew it, so he kept the door closed. The cop came back. 'Hand me yo license,' he barked. This was also illegal. The police can look at your license, but do not have the authority to take it out from your hand.

Gurmit knew that he had broken the speed limit and that he would be charged and fined. But he also knew that what the cop really wanted was not to take him to the Police Station to be charged. If he did that there would be nothing in it for him. What he wanted was 'chai' – 'tea' – in plain words, a financial inducement to let Gurmit go.

So Gurmit waited.

The cop leant his fleshy person over Gurmit's window.

'You see that flat grey rock over there? The one with that big red-headed lizard sitting on it? Go across there as though you are going for a short call, lift the rock and put...' he lifted four fat fingers, 'under it. Then come back here – na sikia? You understand? I will be watching you.'

Gurmit nodded, got out of the car and strolled across to the rock. He could feel the cop's eyes watching him.

He reached the rock.

At that moment he heard the high pitched whine of another car approaching at the speed of sound. He turned his head. Once again the Guardian of the Law uplifted his admonitory arm. The car, a BMW this time, stopped. It was driven by a chauffeur. The rear window slid down, revealing a portly African gentleman, whose shaven skull gleamed like a polished football in the mid-morning sunshine. Words were exchanged, followed by a smart salute from the uniformed gendarme. This was obviously what is known in Francophone West Africa as 'un grand' – a 'big man'.

Gurmit turned his attention to the grey rock. He turned it over. His eyes widened. Below the rock, in a hollowed out space, lay hundreds of banknotes of all denominations. He even spotted a couple of US greenbacks and a UK pound amid the pile: the night and morning's takings. The cop and the big man were still conversationally engaged. Gurmit hesitated, but only for a moment. Then he stooped and scooped up the notes, stuffing them into his pockets, into his socks and inside his shirt. He replaced the grey rock and, heart beating with excitement and apprehension, sauntered back to his Merc, pretending to be innocently buttoning his flies. The cop looked up from the BMW. Gurmit gave him a conspiratorial grin and a thumbs up, got into his car, started the engine and gently, gently, so as not to arouse suspicion, eased the Merc back onto the tarmac and in slo-mo cruised away. In his rear view mirror he could see the cop looking at his retreating rear. 'Too late, mate!' he thought to himself. Once out of sight he gunned the engine. Two hours later palm trees and the blue Indian Ocean filled his windscreen and the soft soporific air of the coast wafted through his open windows.

Gurmit knew that the cop would not report him for having taken what he himself had illegally acquired, and that if Gurmit took the cash to the nearest cop shop the situation would become even more complex as the police were all in it together. A swindicate. And returning the cash to their original owners? Out of the question. They were party to bribery and corruption. The money was untraceable. Gurmit threw back his head and laughed, turned up the stereo, and sang along with the Soggy Bottom Boys. Lady Luck had smiled upon him today and he intended to enjoy the bounty.

Gurmit spent rather more time with the lovely Amina than he had originally intended. Together they went deep sea fishing, they went on dhow trips, they ate in expensive restaurants. Never, thought, Gurmit, was money better spent. He lavished Amina with perfume, jewel-encrusted bracelets, coral necklaces and silver sandals. When he told her how he had come into the money she clapped her hands and laughed until the tears ran down her golden cheeks – 'Aie mapenzi wangu! – oh my darling! – when I think of that fat cop's face when he found his hidey hole empty! Everything gone and nothing he could do about it!' – and off she went again in peals of merriment, slapping her thighs, that famous bosom jumping until her flimsy kanga was in imminent danger of being unhitched from its precarious moorings.

Finally it was time for Gurmit to return to the world of work and drudgery in the capital. Not wishing to encounter the bloated Bow Street Runner, who might have GBH on his mind should he recognize him, an alternative route was advisable. This would be longer and rougher, but more picturesque and less frequented, with the possibility of encountering four – as opposed to two legged – predators. This would involve a sharp left turn before Voi, at Maungu, thence to the Kasigau Gate into the southern part of Tsavo West, a remote entry whose main claim to fame lay in the fact that if you wished to lay your hands on some illegally-mined rubies, this was where to come. When Berna and I came this way we were the first visitors to pass through the gate for a month, but sure enough, out of the bush crept a couple of ruby sellers. And the unkempt and unmaintained track across the bush which Gurmit would follow to far Lake Jipe was one of those guaranteed to unseat your exhaust pipe from its attachments. So he would encounter no police here. From Lake Jipe he would cross the Taveta road, drive to Loitokitok at the Kenyan side of Kilimanjaro and from there follow the turnpike to Emali on the main Nairobi road. Home and dry.

But first a slight change in appearance was called for. Gurmit doffed his turban and tucked his long uncut hair inside a large baseball cap, which bore the dubious logo 'Prime Target' – chosen with care by Amina. He shaved off his beard but kept his moustache. Finally he bought a pair of clear horned-rimmed spectacles and his disguise was complete.

'Ready to go,' he told Amina, who had another paroxysm of mirth at his appearance. 'Kwa heri, macho ine! Goodbye, four eyes! Kwa heri Karasingha yangu! Goodbye my Sikh. Napenda wewe! I love you!' Her laughter followed him as he drove away. He smiled – for a long time. This had been a trip to remember. It is not recorded how Gurmit explained to his wife why his business trip to the coast had taken so long or why he had returned beard and turban-less.

Chapter Twenty

LA LUTA CONTINUA

'Daktari, can you come? Naweza kuja saidia? Can you come and help? We have a horse here, very sick. It cannot move. Natoa jasho mingi. It is sweating too much.

Kuja! Come!' Elijah, pronounced Eleejah, alias Kwanda, head syce on Kongoy Farm, was on the phone. It was 5pm, it would be dark in an hour or so, the farm was 35k away on the other side of the squalid collection of shacks which constituted the township of Nasokoi, at the end of a road where the potholes were so deep that you needed a periscope to see if there was any approaching traffic, which was unlikely as no one drove this way except in dire emergency. At least the weather was dry which meant that the problem might be foot-deep drifts of bull dust. On more than one occasion the gallant Peugeot had ground to an ignominious halt in the tropical equivalent of a snowdrift. Crows were making wing to the rooky wood along with pairs of loud-voiced hadada ibis and the light was decidedly thick by the time I reached the farm gate and the great-coated askari swung wide the portal.

Elijah was waiting. Like many other syces in Kenya, he was a Kipsigis by tribe, from the west, and like many of his compatriots, bore, in addition to his ancestral patronymic a biblical name – Daniel,

Jonah, Paul, Peter, and Isaac were rather more common in the country than exotics such as Tarquin, Peregrine, Giles and Reginald. But Elijah preferred his nickname Kwanda, which meant 'Boss,' the neopara or headman. I had known Kwanda for many years. Like most Kenyans he was always friendly, smiling and seemed ageless. Never lost his temper, unlike many Europeans, especially those new to the country who did not understand the dasturi, or customs of the land.

Kwanda led me to the stable in which the patient was housed. 'Don't go in,' he said, 'she can be dangerous if aroused.' So I looked through the opening from the next door stable. The horse was standing in a rigid position, immobile, ears stiff and erect, and she was covered with sweat. A door banged somewhere. The mare reacted as though she had been poked with an electric prod. She reared like a wooden marionette and staggered across the stable, hit the opposite wall with a crash, almost fell and ended up leaning, nostrils flared, against the wall, neck extended. 'What is wrong with her?' asked Kwanda, standing beside me. 'She's got tetanus,' I said, 'and she will die soon.' 'Haki ya Mungu – the will of God,' said Kwanda. 'Well,' I said, 'not exactly. She must have had a cut or a scratch, probably on a leg, which has let infection in.' 'Ndiyo, yes she caught her leg in wire two weeks ago. Just a small cut and after a week it had healed. I have never seen this before.' None of the 60-odd horses on the place had been vaccinated. The mare died during the night and next morning I returned and vaccinated the lot.

Tetanus in animals is not common in Kenya. The organism lives in the soil and the disease is more common in intensively farmed countries where the soil is frequently manured and turned over. The exception in Kenya may have been in the heavily populated agricultural lands of the Luo people adjacent to the fertile shores of Lake Victoria. Here it had been the custom for both men and women to have the lower six incisors removed. If a person was so unfortunate to contract lockjaw from tetanus, that person could be fluid-fed via a straw inserted through the dental gap. Perhaps the custom arose during an outbreak of the disease and then morphed into a coming of age ritual, rather like circumcision in other tribes. The Luos do not circumcise so perhaps they felt they had to have some personal mutilation in order to demonstrate to other tribes that they too were up there with the rest. The practice has fallen into abeyance and today only tribal ancients can give you that gap-toothed grin which identified the owner as a fully fledged paid up Luo.

Cases of tetanus in dogs and cats are rare – horses are the most susceptible species – but one day a dog was brought in by a tall, well-spoken Asian called Hassan. He cultivated a somewhat aggressive, male-dominant moustache, and an air of knowledge concerning canine ailments and gave the impression that he was consulting me under sufferance. Below the moustache the chin was weak and the lips loose and moist and Hassan's hair was, in view of his age, unnaturally black. 'Grecian 2,000, I bet,' I thought.

The dog was led in by a stocky African, whose bare feet suggested that he was not being overpaid by his employer. Hassan, being a Muslim and a Follower of the Prophet, would not touch the dog, which was used to guard his premises. 'Good afternoon, daktari, this is my dog, and he is refusing to walk and to do his job, despite my beating him. I suspect he is just being lazy but perhaps you can give him the once over before I decide what to do with him.' 'All right,' I replied, as the dog was placed on the table, 'how long has he been like this. What is his name, by the way?' 'About two days and no, he has no name. He is just a guard dog. Why would I want to give him a name? He is not my child!'

The nameless one stood on the table, immobile. His ears, normally drooping, stood erect and stiff. Lips were drawn back exposing the teeth. I took his temperature – normal. I tapped his head above his eyes. The nictitating membrane slid across the cornea. Conjunctival colour salmon pink. I lifted the dog and placed him on the floor and snapped my fingers and watched. He was, with difficulty able to shuffle sideways. At least he was able to move. Unlike a wretched donkey with tetanus, affected while I was away climbing some mountain or other. Recovery being impossible Berna had requested the stalwart Mike Sugden to put the poor animal out of its misery. He duly came and drew his revolver from his armpit where it nestled when not in use. Some children stood watching. 'Tell them totos to get out of way,' said Mike, 'I might miss!' He raised his revolver. Berna turned away. A shot. Berna turned back. The donkey was still standing, immobile. Mike was flabbergasted, stunned. He hadn't missed. He shot again and the donkey fell. But it had already been dead. Its legs were so stiff and standing with all legs straddled it remained upright like a wooden dummy. Hassan's dog was more fortunate. 'This is tetanus,' I told him. 'With luck, tetanus antitoxin (if we can get it) sedation, antibiotics and careful nursing, he may recover.' 'How much will it cost?' said Hassan. An understandable question, but I knew that what he really meant was 'how little?' After decades of study I could tell at a glance who would pay without demur and who would not. The ones at the bottom of the pile, scrabbling amid the detritus, the sans culotte, the hewers of wood and drawers of water, knowing that nothing in life is free, usually paid up without protest. These I charged according to their meagre means. The ones in the middle liked to chance their arm and tried their best to pay as little as possible, hinting how difficult times were, coming out with a sob story about the cost of living and then you looked out and saw that Mr Hassan had tooled up in a brand new state-of-the-art Land Cruiser and you knew full well that he lived in a marbled mansion on the Hill. The ones at the peak of the pyramid either coughed up promptly, or not at all. And there was little you could do about it. Hassan grudgingly agreed to pay.

Slowly the dog recovered, initially being able to lap water, then soup, and eventually to swallow soft meat. The dog was able to shuffle around and gradually became more mobile. The ears however, remained erect for many weeks.

At the end of this lengthy process, with the dog in full recovery mode, Mr Hassan announced that he had decided to have the dog 'put down,' having grown tired of its company and its uselessness as a guard and asked if I would do it.

'Certainly not!' I said, 'if you think that after all this effort and sweat and strain that I am going to kill this animal you are very much mistaken. Please pay up and get out!'

'You insufferable shit,' I thought. He paid up and left. I never did discover what happened to the dog.

In direct contrast to this soulless, humourless character was Andrew Raven. He was the sort of chap who made bad news sound like good. His personal positivity was in sharp contrast to the depressing negativity displayed by Mr Hassan. Andrew was a gifted photographer and naturalist, an expert on the freshwater fish of East Africa and a marvel at guiding prospective film-makers in the right direction when they came to the country to make documentaries or indeed movies of any kind. He was a white, country-born Kenyan. Only 0.1% of Kenya's population is white and so in many parts of the country there are children who have never seen a European and rush wildly for the safety of their mother's skirts when one of the pale-faced demons hoves in view. Of this 0.1% rather more than half are full blooded Kenya citizens. The paltry rest, mostly Brits, with a sprinkling of Americans, Australians and EU nationals are classed as either 'aliens' or 'foreigners', although in many cases their allegiance to the country is at least as strong as those holding the indigo passport. Indeed, many white Kenyans held, or hold, another passport, a back-up as an aid to overseas travel or in case the mythical balloon went up. The second passport was often that of Ireland, whose consul seemed at one time to dish them out like bannocks to anyone with even the most tenuous link to the Emerald Isle. With the advent of dual nationality, many white Kenyans have regained their former British Citizenship, a fairly straightforward process, unlike the case when Brits try to acquire Kenya Citizenship, a bureaucratic nightmare taking up to ten years – or never – and involving much palm greasing and shuffling of application papers and the mysterious vanishing of files at critical moments. About 25,000 British passport holders live in Kenya. Approximately 250,000 Kenyans live in the UK.

Andrew's wife Zelda had been a bold scuba diver and they together ran a campsite and home-stay for travellers and visitors on the farm where they lived. Their place was called Kinyonga Campsite after the numerous chameleons found in the area. Many Africans regard chameleons with fear and suspicion. With their goggling, independently swivelling eyes, like animated CCTV cameras, their slo-mo swaying gait, their prehensile tails, their ability to change colour and their body-length projectile tongues, it was little wonder to me why they were seen in African mythology as creatures of distrust and deceit. 'The leopard cannot change his spots nor the Aethiopian his dusky skin,' but here was a creature which seemingly could change its colour at will and could watch you at the same time without turning its head. It was not to be trusted.

Andrew could best be described as burly and hirsute, a Falstaff of the Highlands, a convivial host with an ever ready welcome and smile, a fount of local knowledge and wisdom on a vast range of subjects, from the abstruse to the mundane.

One subject, however, on which he tended to hesitate, was equestrianism or anything involving too close contact with horses. On the farm where he lived, the owner presided over a troop of over a hundred of horses and when he was away, the onus fell on Andrew to make urgent contact with me when the bolt fell, as it did with alarming frequency. Once, when the owner was cruising the Norwegian fiords, it was a yearling which ran into an inconveniently-sited tractor and trailer, tearing open its abdomen, creating a rent from which protruded a section of unwanted small intestine, blue and throbbing. As usual it was late in the day, the light was fading and the rain was sheeting down. So by torchlight in a stable, hunched over the anaesthetised patient like Quasimodo, much time was spent returning and repairing. I could have done with Esmeralda to lighten the tension. But thanks to Andrew's rapid reporting, the recovery was, as medical reports say, uneventful. Nothing irritates me more than being presented with an animal, which the owner has been ineffectually treating, or 'watching', for the past week or so and then expecting me to pluck their chestnuts from the fire. Telling them that the only thing that improves with age is wine, or that the Age of Miracles is past made little difference.

But I knew that Andrew was not one of these procrastinators. Despite his laid-back patina he was a man of action and not one to wait and watch while an animal declined into a state of irreversible bodily decay. I would tell people that when it came to animal health it was far better to over than to under-react. I would far rather arrive to find a horse reported with colic quietly grazing than to find it writhing on the ground in unrelenting agony because the owner decided to 'watch and wait.'

Andrew was on the phone now. 'Hugh,' he said, 'the Old Man's away,' (he always referred to the owner as 'the Old Man') 'and one of his yearling fillies is not right.'

'Not right?' I asked. 'Yes, not eating, sweating, got her neck stretched out in a funny way as though there might be something stuck in her throat, and her eyes look a bit odd.' 'OK,'I replied, 'let me come out and have a shufti.'

As I swerved to avoid an oncoming matatu barrelling towards me on the wrong side of the road, I cogitated on what this might be. Might be rabies, might be tetanus. Whatever this was it sounded like some sort of neurological condition and these I knew did not carry a favourable outcome. Another matatu howled past me bearing the thoughtful logo, 'even the poor laugh' – so they do.

During the major rabies outbreak in the '80s I was seeing rabies cases on a regular basis in dogs, horses, cattle, sheep and even cats, and I could tell if an animal had rabies within minutes of looking at it – the glazed, staring look in dogs, often accompanied by a paralysed lower jaw, the continual bellowing and straining in cattle, the unpredictable aggression in horses.

Over the weed-covered railway line to Kisumu and along the main street of Ikangu. At one time there had been a substantial heronry in a large tree along this street, where the birds were always seen roosting and nesting. No more. The tree had been cut down to make way for 'development.' Where had the birds gone? I noticed a few more hotels – The Plan B, The Overdose and The Liquids. Pass I thought.

Andrew was waiting at the stables. He was one of those fellows whose opinion was that time spent shaving and maintaining sartorial standards was time wasted, and better spent attending to the more important things in life, such as the study of wildlife, photography and the upkeep of his numerous cottages in preparation for incoming visitors. He was not one to spend hours in front of the mirror meticulously aligning the parting in his hair, dabbing on the aftershave, or ensuring that his socks matched. Unlike Henry Morton Stanley who, even as he struggled, fever-ridden, emaciated and light headed through the cannibal-infested forests of the Congo, insisted on shaving and sprucing himself up on a daily basis.

Andrew cared little about the opinion of others. He was an 'up and at 'em' sort of chap. So when I saw that Andrew was sporting a week-old beard, that his hair resembled a field of ripe wheat buffeted by a strong gale and that he was wearing a jumper which looked as though it had been retrieved from the back of a refuse wagon, I knew that he was in working mode.

'Hi Hugh,' he greeted me, 'well there she is,' pointing to a large chestnut filly, standing inside an open sided stable.

I walked across and looked. The first thing I noticed was a soiled bandage around her lower right hind leg. The filly was standing stock still, head and neck extended. Her flanks were black with sweat, and her nostrils were flared. I moved closer. She did not move or register my presence, as a normal horse would do. Her ears, which would have swivelled in my direction as I approached, remained rigidly upright.

I walked round to lift the pole barring entry to the stable.

'Chunga, bwana!' said Maritim, the attending syce, 'iko hatari!' 'Careful, bwana, she can be dangerous.'

Softly I moved closer. She did not move, but I felt that she was aware that I was nearby. The corneas of both eyes were covered by the protruding nictitating membranes and it seemed she was unable to see. Very gently I touched her neck. It was as hard as a plank of wood.

Suddenly, without warning, she had a wild, violent muscular spasm, rearing and staggering across the stable. I took sharp, appropriate avoiding action, narrowly missing being unpleasantly mashed against the woodwork.

Enough of that, I thought. 'OK,' I said to Maritim,' 'let's sedate her and take her outside.' So, very carefully and slowly, I gave her a low intravenous dose, and after a few minutes she relaxed sufficiently to allow us to lead her out into the paddock. But, almost at once she seemed to panic, rearing and staggering uncontrollably from side to side. The light seemed to have an alarming galvanizing effect.

'Right,' I said, 'back inside.'

I did a rectal. She was constipated.

Maritim plucked some fresh grass and offered it to the filly. It was obvious that she wanted to eat. She tried in vain to move her jaws, desperately trying to grip the tufts of greenery. It was no good. Her jaws were clamped shut, rigid, as though in a vice.

'Andrew,' I said, 'this is tetanus and her chances of recovery are close to zero.'

He nodded. 'We can try by giving a massive dose of penicillin, keeping her sedated, and in a darkened stable, but I don't hold out much hope. There isn't any antitoxin available locally and it's too late for the vaccine.'

I turned to Maritim, who told me that the filly had not been vaccinated against tetanus, and had cut her leg about two weeks previously, hence the bandage. She had not been given appropriate antibiotics at the time either.

'Well, Andrew,' I said, 'that's it. Looks like the Grim Reaper is waiting in the wings.'

As I spoke, a shadow passed overhead. We both looked up. A hamerkop, the lightning bird, harbinger of approaching death, on silent wings, flew over the stable. We all looked at each other.

The filly died the following day.

Chapter Twenty One

A SLIP AND A STING

To the south of Nakuru, now heaving with humanity, teeming with traffic, and overlain with a noxious pall of exhaust fumes and the gaseous exhalations of jerry-built factories, charcoal stoves and smoking refuse pits, lay Lake Nakuru. A gallant rear-guard of flamingos hung grimly to its alkaline shore, despite the pollutants being daily pumped into the water, their sole source of sustenance.

To the north rose the swelling bulk of Menengai, an extinct volcanic mass, whose caldera was reported to be the second most extensive in Africa, only pipped at the post by Ngorongoro in Tanzania. Menengai's once serene flanks, virginal and untouched by the lascivious hand of Man, were now pockmarked and defiled by countless tin roofed shacks and scored by a maze of tracks and water-scoured gullies. The forest was gone, the hillsides bare earth.

The caldera, however, remained inviolate, being waterless and inhospitable. Flows of black, razor sharp lava, unseen crevasses, sinister steam jets and an ominous and all-pervading silence kept people away. Apart from a troop of xenophobic cliff-dwelling baboons, a few rock hyrax, and the occasional steinbok, the place was lifeless. The ominous croak of a fan-tailed raven added to an atmosphere of unease.

There was good reason for this. Menengai has long been a place of ill omen. Here it was that a legion of the Ilaikipiak Maasai was slaughtered by their cousins the Ilpurko, and their bodies thrown over the crater walls. The numerous steam jets on the crater floor were believed to be the restless spirits of the dead trying to escape and attain heaven. The name Menengai means 'the dead' in Maa. And here in 1932 a young white settler, Charles Ross, a homicidal sadist, murdered two young European women, throwing one body into the crater. He was the first European to be hanged in Kenya. Some might wonder – if his victims had been black, would he have been executed? Peter Poole, in 1960, was the first European to be hanged for murdering an African, his servant, whom he shot for having thrown stones at his dogs. On Menengai there have been other murders, mostly unsolved. But it is also a spiritual place with people coming from afar to pray and meditate and in caves on the crater wall abstruse sects meet on Sundays to sing, drum and chant.

The walls of the crater were steep, mostly vertical, and in places were over a thousand feet high.

Ten o'clock at night, cold, moonless, windy, some rain. The phone rang. What would it be this time? A mare stuck foaling? A horse with colic? A dog run over? A British citizen picked up by the police? 'Hello? This is Madsen here, your Danish neighbour.' Leif Madsen was a missionary who lived a couple of kilometres away, a very short distance in Kenyan eyes, where a close neighbour might live 20 kilometres away. Dour on the surface, like many Danes, Leif was a good stick, and, beneath the John Knoxian exterior, lay a refined sense of humour. He lived with his attractive, fashion-conscious wife and teenage children in a suburb of Nakuru.

'I vonder if you can help me? I knew that you vere a climber. A friend of my son is in trouble in the crater. He only came to Kenya yesterday and he and my son and another young man went walking in the crater. As it was getting late they decided to try to climb out as it would take too long for them to return the way they had come. On the way up the boy slipped and fell and had badly damaged his knee and cannot move. My son is with him and we know where he is as the other boy walked out and raised the alarm.'

'Right,' I said, 'I'll phone a climbing friend who has a rope and also the War Memorial Hospital to see if we can borrow a stretcher. We'll need that.'

So I phoned Chris Drayton, a maths teacher at nearby Greensteds School and asked if he could help. Of course he would. Climbers are like that. It is part of the ethos of climbing. No hesitation. Someone's in trouble, you help.

We met at our house and set off for the crater. Berna brought flasks of hot tea, sandwiches, torches – and a ball of string. Berna never went anywhere without a torch, even in the blinding glare of mid-day. It stemmed from the time when, coming back from Nairobi at night – it was safe to drive at night then – we had a puncture on the escarpment.

In those days Berna always carried a candle, which indicates just how far behind the times we were. Berna was seven months pregnant at the time and it was raining and there was a howling gale. By the time the wheel was changed and we were soaking wet and the flickering candle had blown out about a hundred times she had sworn a mighty oath never, ever, to move anywhere without a torch. We collected the stretcher from the hospital and drove up the steep dirt road to the view point, the highest point on the crater rim. Here the drop was immense, probably 1500 feet.

A police Land Rover was parked beside a wooden sign indicating how far we were from London, Vladivostok, New York and Punta Arenas. We stepped out of the cars. A strong wind was blowing and it was cold. 'At least they'll be out of the wind down there and it'll be a bit warmer,' said Berna. I nodded. A sharp gust of rain smacked into us.

'This is where they are,' said Leif, 'the boy was quite clear on that.'

Chris uncoiled his 600 foot rope. There were no trees or rocks to provide an anchor. 'Damn,' said Chris. 'What about the police Land Rover?' said Berna. 'Good idea,' said Chris.

I went across and knocked on the window. No response. I peered inside. I could see nothing. Whoever was in there was either asleep or dead. 'Berna,' I said, 'can you bring me your Maglite.'

This torch could throw a beam for a hundred yards and sear the retinas at fifty. I gave the interior of the Land Rover a five second burst. There was a sudden eruption of blankets and greatcoats and a pair of dishevelled constables emerged, blinking and rubbing their eyes.

'I say,' I said, 'do you mind awfully if we use your Land Rover as an anchor to protect our friend here while he goes down on a rope to locate the injured party.'

They did not mind and edged their vehicle a bit closer to the edge. They said that they were waiting for the arrival of the Nakuru Fire Brigade and what else could they do but get a bit of shut-eye?

'Quite right,' I said, 'there was nothing else to do.'

So we secured to the rope to the vehicle and Chris, wearing a powerful head torch, vanished over the edge and disappeared into the darkness.

He was gone a long time. We could hear him shouting, but whether he was shouting for help or shouting to the beleaguered duo was impossible to tell.

Finally, he emerged over the lip of the crater, breathing heavily. 'Gad,' he panted, 'I got to within a couple of hundred feet of them. But I couldn't get any closer. It's all loose and crumbly down there. Some bits are vertical, others just near vertical. Everything comes away in your hand. There's absolutely nowhere to fix a safe belay. They seem OK though. On a sort of ledge. Boy's in some pain. Asking for pain killers, blankets and something to drink. What have we got?'

Berna, ever resourceful, replied. 'Yes. I brought Panadols, flasks of tea, sandwiches, a basket – and a ball of string! And we can take the blanket off the back seat of the car.' 'Great,' said Chris, 'I'll go back down and lower the things down to them.' So saying, once again he vanished into the darkness.

By the time Chris got back up it was 2 o'clock in the morning.

'Thanks, Chris,' I said, 'right, we'd better get home and get some sleep and come back as soon as it's light, walk in, and climb up with the stretcher and get him out. We'll need a couple of extra hands to help carry the stretcher. I'll roust out our gardener and the askari.

And we'll need your rope to lower him down to the crater floor. And bandages.'

Dawn, and we were pussy-footing down a steep path where there was a break in the cliffs, laden with all of our gear. We followed the path below the cliff until we could see the two figures about 500 feet above us.

Dragging the stretcher, we scrambled up the near vertical side of the crater. The two Danes were very glad to see us. But they were in good spirits. I examined the young man's damaged knee and I did not like what I saw. There was a long, deep, horizontal gash across the front and the interior of the joint was clearly visible. I bandaged and bound his leg and we strapped him into the stretcher and, with the help of our stout African helpers, began lowering him to the crater floor. This was a slow business, the sun was now up and soon our brows were beaded with honest sweat.

Once on the horizontal, we each took a corner of the stretcher and began the long walk out. Half way there, we heard a loud rattling noise. We looked up and a large black helicopter appeared, swooping over the rim of the crater. Leif had played his part. The machine landed and carefully we lifted the stretcher inside. His friend got in beside him. Before it took off I spoke to the injured boy – 'Look,' I said, 'if I were you, get yourself back to Denmark. That knee needs top class specialist treatment. Don't hang around. You may not get that here.'

The helicopter took him, landed at a nearby airstrip, picked up s nurse to hold the boy's hand and headed to Nairobi. Other counsel prevailed. He was taken to a hospital in Nairobi where the wound was closed. Complications ensued, and eventually remedial surgery in Denmark was required. A year later he was better, but still hobbling.

The next day we were gratified to read in the newspapers what a splendid job the Nakuru Fire Brigade had done in rescuing a young white foreigner who had fallen in Menengai Crater.

If I thought that our heroics in the crater had excused me, even briefly, from the daily tribulations of veterinary alarms and excursions and that, after our exertions, I was entitled to a short break. I was speedily disabused.

No sooner had I reached home before I heard the strident call of the phone.

'Damn you, Alexander Graham Bell!' I thought. It was Rosanna Steinkuller, a vivacious Zimbabwean, who lived on a farm near Njoro, where she schooled and trained a string of show jumpers and ponies.

She was in alarm mode and with good reason.

'Hugh!' she shrilled, 'can you come quickly! Bees! Bees have got into the stable and attacked my stallion, Dingaan, my pride and joy, and he's been badly stung.'

The farm was on the pipeline road, some 15 miles from town. I checked to see if I had enough dexamethasone, antihistamine and adrenaline and put the foot to the floor.

Swerving through a herd of tuk tuks I pulled onto the main street and headed out of town. In the past you could let your mind wander and ponder on the case in hand as you coasted along the near empty highway. No more. Your entire cerebral cortex was now focused on survival. Armies of motorbike taxis called boda bodas hurtled at death-defying speeds on all sides, overtaking on the right, on the left, cutting in and approaching head on with zero intention of giving way. The usual complement of riders was three to a bike, but often four, and five was nothing to write home about. Extraordinary loads were carried. Once I saw a sofa on the back of one bike with a large lady sitting, regally, in the centre – well, she had to sit there in order to maintain balance. Massive, weighty sacks of charcoal, piled sky high, would force a motorbike rider forwards so that he was sitting on the fuel tank, chest nuzzling the handlebars, upon which was often perilously perched a helmet-less toddler. Crash helmets were a mark of the weak and effeminate. And Heaven help you if you were so unfortunate as to have an accident with one of these motorbike fiends. At once scores of fellow motorbikers in full attack mode would appear and surround your vehicle like the swarm of bees who had attacked poor Dingaan.

Onto the highway, a matatu in front signalling left. You know it is quite likely that he will turn right. There he goes. Off to the right. And what does that mysterious logo 'Liquid Biopsy' convey to the travelling public?

Watch out! – a lorry heading towards me on my side of the road. Pull onto the hard shoulder and he roars past. I take note of his logo – 'Pulverizer' – it figures. It always intrigued me how people, 99% of them male, when walking around on their hind legs, would behave in a perfectly normal, friendly, civilized way, but put them behind a wheel or handle bars and a Jekyll and Hyde transformation would immediately take place. The sight of a pedestrian trying to cross the road would induce a feeling of irrational rage. Any vehicle ahead had to be overtaken, no matter how, on the right, on the left, see how close you can cut in. If there was an oncoming vehicle, the challenge was to see how close you could get bar a head-on collision. The overwhelming mantra of driving in Africa is that attack is the best form of defence.

Half way to the farm. Buses and heavy long-distance trucks on the road. The former go like the wind and only stop to pick up passengers and to slow down for the police in order to hand over the expected pecuniary offering. I slalomed into the yard in a cloud of dust. Rosanna was there with head syce Kahugu, both trying to hold Dingaan, who was staggering from side to side and neighing in distress. Dingaan lurched backwards, crashed into wooden railings, nose-dived forwards, fell to his knees, and then, with a mighty effort, clambered to his feet and stood, breathing heavily. His eyes were flickering from side to side. I could see that giving an IV injection here could be a bit tricky. Dingaan was a big animal, clocking in at about 700 kilos. The prick of a needle might well precipitate an almighty eruption and I had a good idea who might be in the line of fire.

Dingaan was covered from nose to tail in thousands of bee stings and a few moribund bees were still attached to his once glossy hide. Angry bees were zooming in all directions, so trying to concentrate on the task in hand was difficult.

'He was trapped in his stable,' said Rosanna between sobs, 'all the other horses managed to break out, but, because he is a stallion, the door to his stable is high and solid. We couldn't get anywhere near him. He went mad in there. Finally I covered myself in a big plastic gunny bag and rushed out and opened the door and he came out like a rocket.'

'Well,' I said, 'we're going to have to give him a sedative in order to be able to handle him and to try and treat him and remove those stings.' This was easier said than done, what with bees dive-bombing us and Dingaan in a state of physical and mental derangement. What was needed was just enough sedative to calm him down but not so much that he could not move. We had to get him as far from the stables as possible. Xylazine was the drug of choice. Get it into a vein and the effect was a predictable and reliable state of relaxation. Under normal circumstances it acted within two minutes. These were decidedly not normal circumstances.

The African bee, although smaller than the European honey bee, is considerably more defensive and aggressive and will pursue targets for up to half a kilometre. So run away! And don't think that diving into water will help you, because the bees will wait until you emerge. Unlike wasps and hornets, whose sting is smooth, and makes them capable of inflicting multiple insertions, that of the bee is unwisely barbed so it sticks in mammalian skin and cannot be removed. It's a one-off job, and the bee dies in a particularly gruesome manner. The wretched insect is disembowelled as it tears itself loose from its sting, which remains impaled in the skin, pumping venom into the victim in a rather sinister fashion. And as it breathes its last the dying bee emits alarm pheromones which attract other bees. And to add to this seemingly bizarre scenario, all of the attack stinging bees are female – an airborne army of female cannon fodder bent on self-destruction in a combination of kamikaze and hara kiri . The sting is a modified ovipositor. So once again chaps, the female of the species appears to be more deadly than the male. But, hang on a moment – those brave females are prepared to die to save the hive – dulce et decorum est pro patria mori – while the boys just potter about back at base, sitting around, eating honey and thinking about having sex with the queen. Sounds familiar?

271

Some Africans are rather proud that their bees are so aggressive. 'Kumbe!' they will say, 'Behold! Our black bees are the bravest in the world! They never hesitate to defend what's theirs. Your white bees are soft and fat.' But they run like stags when they hear a swarm approaching – as Dingaan would have done, were he not locked in his stable.

Dingaan stood trembling, but from his demeanour I could tell that at any moment he was going to have another 'episode.' With experience you know when an animal is on the point of reacting in a violent manner. When doing rectal examinations for pregnancy in the mare – it's all done remotely these days – if the horse begins to lean backward on the bar behind its rump, look out. It's time to withdraw your arm, because she is just about to give a convulsive leap and start lashing out in your direction and if your arm is still inside, serious mischief to your person may ensue.

So I had to act fast. Luckily I had a vial of 10% xylazine, so the required volume would be small – about 3ml. Select a fine needle, draw up the requisite amount, fingers in the jugular furrow, raise the vein, a short silent prayer, push in the needle, press the plunger. Wait. No reaction! Ah, a slight drooping of the head, but then a sudden sideways staggering rush, knocking Kahugu off his feet, trampling him under hoof, towing Rosanna through the dust as she tries to maintain hold of the head rope. Dingaan struck a post and stood, snorting, chest heaving. The syce, brave fellow, scrambled to his feet and seizing the bridle, dragged the stallion through a gate and into an open field. There, thanks to the sedative, he was just about manageable.

With a stiff floor brush we scrubbed his hide in an effort to remove all of the stingers. I injected him with anti-histamine, dexamethasone and adrenaline. I auscultated his heart: 95 beats to the minute. Anything over 80, in a pathological situation, as this was, is an indication that recovery is unlikely and that the end is nigh. The pathology of bee stings is either the direct result of the injected toxin, mainly a protein called melittin, or due to anaphylaxis. In Dingaan's case it was obviously the former and everything was shutting down.

Now the effects of the sedative were lightening and he was growing restless. I gave him a half dose and he settled down, but only briefly.

Without warning, Dingaan reared, toppled over backwards, landed with a fearful crash, and went into a series of violent convulsions, legs thrashing, smashing his noble head on the ground, until there was foam bubbling from his nostrils and blood running from his eyes.

I turned to Rosanna, who was standing distraught, staring in disbelief at what was happening to her beloved stallion. The syce was also staring, bog-eyed, horrified.

'Rosanna,' I said, 'this is the end. But the end may be prolonged and we cannot leave him like this. We have to put him down. I don't carry my humane killer with me in the car, and giving an IV injection of pentobarbitone while he's convulsing like this may be impossible, so we will have to shoot him. Who is there in the area with a gun?'

Rosanna was so upset she could barely speak. Then she said – 'I think Ollie Nightingale has a shotgun.' I phoned Ollie. He came within 20 minutes and shot Dingaan.

Chapter Twenty Two

WEDDING BELLS

Jimmy Simpson was getting married.

Jimmy was a teacher at a prep school, which catered for the children of expatriates, and those of Asian businessmen and wealthy Africans. Here Berna had taught before she was swept off her feet by a handsome young Scots vet (me!) and up the aisle of St Christopher's Church in Nakuru. We knew Jimmy well. He was an affable individual, a rising star in the school with a keen sense of his own importance. He would have risen even higher but for the fateful day when, during the half-term break, he fell off his motorbike and onto his head.

When Jimmy failed to turn up for work the headmaster instituted a search party to scour the town for his whereabouts. Police stations, hospitals, hotels and houses of ill repute were visited in an effort to track Jimmy down, all to no avail. Then someone happened to be driving past the Government General Hospital and saw, sitting on a bench, sunning himself, clad in a pair of hideously striped purple pyjamas, a rather unkempt and unknown European. Enquiries were made at the hospital as to the identity of this individual and the answer was that they didn't know who he was as he was unable to tell them, and no identifying documents were found on his person. Closer

274

scrutiny by the Good Samaritan revealed, that, beneath the week old beard and scruffy appearance, lurked the form of Jimmy Simpson.

Jimmy was transferred from the dubious confines of the government hospital to the private War Memorial Hospital, where, cleaned and shaved, we visited him. After enquiring after his health, we asked him about the food on offer at the government hospital. He thought deeply for a long moment, and then said, 'it wasn't *so* bad. Every morning they gave me a big bowl of Cran.' This answer suggested that things were not quite as they should be in the top storey. But at least he had a vague idea of who we were.

It took Jimmy quite some time to recover from his accident. He had forgotten how to sign his name and had to go to the bank to explain to the manager why his signature now resembled that made by an ink drenched drunken spider staggering across the page.

Now Jimmy was getting married and would we come to the ceremony? We accepted with alacrity. Anything which broke the endless wheel of crisis and catastrophe was to be welcomed.

Jimmy had once been engaged to a well-favoured English maiden – at least we had charitably assumed that she was a maiden – but that liaison had sadly withered on the vine.

Now he was affianced to a comely African lady, of proven fertility, who, although certainly unable to be classified as a vestal virgin, had a quality distinctly lacking in the pale, chilly ice maiden from the North. To wit, she had charm. Miriam Rotich was cheerful, loquacious and friendly, with the warm smiling face of the South. Still young, she dressed well, in a way that showed her splendid figure to full advantage, one that many young urban African women possess, before the ravages of child bearing, age and a western diet transforms a Botticelli Venus into an amorphous gelatinous mass. But at the moment curvaceous Miriam was a feast for the eyes, with barely a straight line to be seen. She was a lovely person in all respects.

Sadly, Jimmy's blinkered, bigoted, colour conscious parents failed to appreciate her obvious qualities, seeing little other than that she was not like them and refused to attend the wedding.

The ceremony was to be held in the spacious school assembly hall, in the Great Hall of the Children, where assemblies, prize-giving and speeches were held.

We arrived on time at 2pm, attired in our finest and took our seats in the auditorium which was already full of expectant guests. The wedding was to take place on the stage, rather like a theatrical production. At the back of the hall stood a long wide table, laden with a wide range of alcoholic drinks – beer, whisky, gin, vodka, rum, you name it, it was all there – in readiness for the post wedding celebrations.

After 30 minutes there was no sign of significant activity on stage, apart from some furtive movement by a small scruffy individual whose role in the proceedings was unclear. After another 30 minutes there was a clank behind us and an empty beer bottle rolled under our seats and was kicked forwards to continue its irreverent way to the front. Then there came another and another. Soon the respectful expectant silence was replaced by the clinking of bottles and raucous laughter and the scraping of chairs as people rearranged themselves, the better to enjoy the free booze. By the time the bride and groom appeared on stage the congregation was well and truly oiled. A European couple, teachers newly arrived in the country, slipped into the chairs beside us. They were English, from Kent, they told us. They looked nervous. We were the only other white faces in a sea of intoxicated Africans. 'Are Kenyan weddings always like this?' they whispered. 'Oh yes,' we said, 'this is perfectly normal.' They paled. 'We see,' they continued, 'that the proceedings are to be conducted by a bishop! Bishop Ogongo – is that the correct pronunciation? Isn't that rather unusual? After all we're not even in a church!'

A sudden blast from a loud speaker cut short our conversation and momentarily hushed the congregation. It was the small weasely individual, who appeared to be some sort of electrician. 'Testing! Testing!' he bellowed into a microphone. Then he mouthed 'OK' and beckoned into the wings.

Onto the stage, splendid and regal in ecclesiastical robes, swept Bishop Ogongo, followed by a suited gent, whose gait and dishevelled attire suggested that he had refreshed himself prior to his entry. 'Who is that?' I asked an African sitting in front of us.

'That is Sammy Oluoch, the registrar, to make sure that everything is legal and above board,' I was informed. 'He looks pissed to me,' I replied. 'Yes, he is, but as long as he doesn't fall down, all he has to do is to be on hand to witness the ceremony.' The Kentish couple, who had overheard this, were appalled.

Bishop Ogongo was very big, very black and very shiny. Whether his shine was an inherent genetic trait or was a result of his having sipped rather too well at the bowl of sacerdotal wine we could not tell.

East Africa is awash with bishops, many of doubtful provenance. They are, in fact, ten a penny. You see them, striding the streets, clad in purple and yellow, cassocked and mitred, an enormous cross dangling on their bosoms, brandishing a pole-vault sized crozier in their right hands. And then there are the Prophets, who attract thousands with their promises of recovery from everything from cancer, paralysis and destitution, to death, and who make thousands in the process as they dupe and deceive the gullible public.

The bishop, a benign smile playing across his expansive features, took up his stance at a lectern with the mike and stood there for several minutes in silence, surveying the crowd, supporting himself on the improvised pulpit and swaying gently from side to side. Then, seeming to collect himself, he signalled to right and left and the bride and groom made their entrance onto the stage.

The crowd clapped and roared their approval. Miriam was a vision in white, a circlet of snowy flowers across her smooth ebony brow. She looked serene and lovely. Jimmy, rather less lovely, was in a muted dove grey suit, his tie slightly askew. They stood on either side of the bishop who now spoke for the first time. 'Brethren, dearly beloved, we are gathered here today in the sight of God, to join this two happy couples in....' His booming voice bellowing through the auditorium was suddenly cut short .We could see his lips moving but heard no sound. In the wings we could see the dwarfish electrician plunging about with bare wires in either hand, frantically trying to reignite the public address system. More shouting and whistling from the congregation as they waited for the wretched electrician to go up in flames. '....Holy Matrimony.' The bishop was back. Loud cheers. The Kentish duo looked on in stunned silence.

'Brother James, do you have the ring?'

Brother James did not respond. 'Brother James!' the bishop repeated, rather testily, we thought. Jimmy realised, with a start, that the bishop was referring to himself. He delved, first into one pocket and then into the other. We could see him mouthing 'Oh shit!' He looked around as though searching for his non-existent best man. Then he darted off the stage.

He was gone a long time. As far as the assembled guests were concerned it was not time wasted as they applied themselves with renewed vigour to the alcoholic beverages on tap. When Jimmy returned it was with a lurch and a stagger, but he had the ring. With a thumbs up he held it aloft to an approving gallery, who roared their approval. The bishop resumed.

'Sister Miriam, do you take this wedded man to be your lawful husband, to honour and obey, in this world and the next, and do you, Brother James, do you take this woman to be your lawful life, in sickness and health, as long as ye both shall live, till Death do you part, so help you God?' Both answered in the affirmative. Miriam remained dignified and calm. Jimmy wore an inane grin, suggesting that his prolonged absence in search of the missing ring had been spent in other pursuits.

'Brother James,' the bishop now proclaimed, 'you may now kiss the bride and on her finger place the ring.' Jimmy lurched across the stage. He seemed to have considerable difficulty in threading the ring onto the correct finger. So much so that some unkind members of the congregation started a rhythmic clapping. Any moment now, I thought, there'll be a Mexican wave.

At last he succeeded and, clasping Miriam to his thorax, gave her a resounding kiss and led her down into the body of the kirk and towards the now much depleted bar. Raising a brimming beaker he proposed a toast -'to Miriam and may God bless all who sail in her!' 'To Miriam!' we, along with the rest of the inebriated mob, bawled.

We looked around for our Kentish friends. They had, like the Arabs in Longfellow's poem, folded their tents and had silently stolen away. They were wrong to do so. Jimmy's toast marked the beginning of a memorable party.

Chapter Twenty Three

BRAIN AND BRAWN

After Jimmy's nuptials it was almost a relief to get back to the 'normality' of veterinary chaos.

In the West the advance of 'Civilization and Progress' coupled with rampant urbanization and industrial farming has had the result that many interesting animal diseases are no longer on display. The same is happening in Africa. As forests are felled and the bush is cleared, the hosts and carriers of intriguing maladies such as trypanosomiasis (the tsetse fly) Bovine Petechial Fever (the bushbuck) and Corridor Disease (the buffalo) are deprived of areas in which to breed and survive. Even the nematode worm *Spirocerca lupi*, which resides in nodules in the walls of the oesophagus and aorta of dogs, is now a rarity, because the intermediate host, the humble and hard-working dung beetle, has been driven to the edge of extinction by pesticides and modern industrial farming. And a good thing too, many in the West and Africa might say. We must eliminate all those nasty infringements on our daily lives so that we can cultivate our crops safely on huge monocultured fields, drip fed from vast centre pivots, tilled and fertilized and cleared of all irritating outside interferences by a bewildering array of pesticides and herbicides. And we must rear our animals in safe, sterile conditions, preferably under cover and protected from that unpleasant outside environment. And we can now do it all remotely! No more need to get soil underneath our fingernails or having to clump around in heavy dung-encrusted hobnail boots, like backward medieval peasants. And then, fingernail clean, we can go home in our air-conditioned cars to our air-conditioned homes with their astro-turfed lawns, and punch the remote and watch a bit of another First World induced carnage in the Third World. Oh happy day!

Even in Kenya the times were changing. The days when one might meet aardvark, porcupine, civet, jackal or even lion on the outskirts of Nakuru were long gone. As was being able to drive, as we once did one Sunday, 1,075 kilometres to and from Taita Ranch, next to the Tanzanian border, to investigate an outbreak of disease in the cattle, have lunch with a twitchy, gone troppo Greek, diagnose trypanosomiasis and return by 9pm. The traffic nightmare has put paid to such light-hearted jaunts.

But, although the incidence of some diseases had dwindled, we were not, thank goodness, at the stage in some European countries, including the UK, where vets spent their working hours dealing with lame and infertile cattle, thanks to the beastly conditions in which many of the wretched animals were kept, ditto horses or equids as they now like to call them, and counselling psychotic pets and their psychotic owners. It was no wonder that so many vets needed counselling themselves.

Things were moving that way in Kenya, but not yet, dear Lord, not yet.

The incidence of rabies had declined, thanks to the widespread vaccination of domestic dogs. No longer was I seeing two or three cases a day, as I was in the 1980s, in dogs, cattle, sheep and horses. Now I was lucky if I saw two or three cases a year. So when Tristan Voorspuy phoned saying that he had a safari horse acting oddly, my ears pricked up.

After the usual skirmish with the traffic I arrived to find Tristan in a state of mild anxiety. 'Ah, Hugh,' he said, 'glad to see you. Seem to have a spot of problem with Pot Luck. Wonder if you can cast your eye over him.' Pot Luck was a large, chestnut gelding, the survivor of one particularly nasty bout of biliary fever and most recently an attack by a lion in the Mara which had left him with a couple of impressive tramline scars on his rump. 'He's in the top field next to the stables. Let's walk up and have a look at him.'

We stumbled up the track to the stables. The sky was blue, the birds were singing, a pair of black and white casqued hornbills flew overhead, lizards scuttled in the undergrowth – it was difficult to imagine anything untoward here.

'Pot bit the syce this morning,' said Tristan, as he negotiated a bouldery section of the path, 'out of the blue, zero provocation. He's normally as quiet as a lamb and then he had a go at the stable door. Munched a great chunk out of the woodwork. We've let him out into the field. Safer there. Don't want a dead syce on our hands.'

Pot Luck was standing by himself in the middle of a large grassy field. A normal horse would have had his head down, hard at work filling his stomach. Pot seemed to be staring abstractedly into the middle distance. Suddenly he snapped his jaws and began biting in a frenzy at his chest, drawing blood. Then he started trotting aimlessly around the field. Every now and again he would stumble, stop and fall, and then get up and repeat the process. Now he came surging towards us, lurching, twitching and jerking, teeth bared, foam dripping from his lips. 'Time to take avoiding action, I think,' I said to Tristan. We retired behind a closed gate while Pot Luck continued his erratic progress.

'Well Tristan,' I said, 'this looks like rabies. I saw a rabid donkey once, biting itself like that – disembowelled itself and didn't stop there. Not a pleasant sight.'

'Yes, I thought about rabies myself,' replied Tristan, 'the horse has never been vaccinated. That's bad enough, but we had an American client riding him only two days ago and now he's back in the States! So slight panic.'

'Could be a brain tumour, I said, 'I saw a horse once behave a bit like this and it turned out to be due to a tumour in its frontal cortex; or it could be crotalaria poisoning, but rabies is much more likely. We need to get Pot's brain down to the lab in Kabete as soon as possible to get this diagnosed. But first of all we need to euthanase him without messing up his brain. Giving him a lethal IV injection is out of the question at the moment.

He will collapse eventually and then I could do it but we need to get an immediate diagnosis, so that the sooner everyone involved, including your American client, can be

protected the better. A humane heart shot is what is required.'

'Right, I'll get my 375. That should do the trick.' 'By the way,' I said, 'this Yank. Is he one of those litigious sorts? 'No thank God. He's a good bloke and would be perfectly amenable to being gored to death by a buffalo or tusked to infinity by an elephant – a sort of heroic finale – but he might well draw the line at ending up as a gibbering idiot dying from rabies.' 'Well, send him a wire pronto. Tell him to start a course of injections immediately while we wait for an answer. In the meantime let's blot poor Pot and put him out of his misery.'

Tristan returned with his 375 and with one shot dropped Pot in his stumbling tracks. His sufferings were over. 'Now, we've got to remove his head. I've been vaccinated many times so I'll do that if you can get some gunny sacks.' I pulled on a pair of shoulder-length disposable gloves and set to with my bush knife. By the time Tristan came back I had done the deed and lowered the head into sack number one. A horse's head weighs about 10% of its bodyweight. Pot Luck had been in life about 600 kilos so it was no featherweight. We added a couple more sacks and finally put the lot inside a thick plastic bag. A tractor came and dragged Pot's carcase away to be lowered into a freshly-dug pit.

'Now,' I said to Tristan, 'we have to get the head to Kabete as soon as possible. Wait! Berna's going to Nairobi tomorrow for a school fixture. I wonder...?'

It was gathering dusk when I reached home.

'Hello my love!' I caroled as I breezed into the house, 'I've got a little something in the boot which I want to pop into the freezer for you to take to Kabete when you go to Nairobi tomorrow.'

'What is it?' Berna was instantly on her guard. 'It's a horse's head in fact. Probably rabid.'

'Whaaat?'

'Yes, but it's ok, it's well wrapped up, totally secure, no risk to anyone.' Berna by this time was reasonably well inured to this sort of thing. The head was so large that we had to virtually empty the freezer in order to get it in. Our middle daughter Sophie wandered in as we were lowering Pot's skull into the deep freeze. 'What's that?' she asked. Most kids would be appalled to be told that Mummy and Daddy were storing a horse's head among the ice cream and sausages. Not ours. They were so used to a daily diet of blood and gore that nothing fazed them. 'Just a horse's head, dear,' said Berna. 'Oh,' replied Sophie and tottered off.

Sophie knew her animal anatomy from a very early age. On one occasion Dick Crawford came to the house with a cat which had died in his kennels. He wanted me to do a post mortem which I did on the veranda. I found that the cat had died of toxaemia due to a blocked urethra as a result of longstanding rock-hard constipation. Unable to urinate, kidney failure had ensued. Sophie, beady-eyed, stood watching while I opened up the body. Later Dick phoned to find out the cause of death. He was never one to wait and watch while one of his beloved inmates was being eviscerated.

I was not on hand to answer the call but Sophie, aged about four, was. She lifted the phone. 'Is your dad there?' asked Dick, 'I'd like to know what killed the cat.' 'No, he's not,' said Sophie, 'but I can tell you. It's quite simple really. The poo pipe had blocked off the wee bag.' 'Thank you very much,' replied Dick.

Sophie was not quite so hot on her ornithology. A client brought a large turkey to the surgery for examination. Sophie, in great excitement, told her mother, 'Mum, Mum! Dad's got a great big vulture in the surgery!'

Next day Berna took the head to the lab at Kabete. She was somewhat disappointed when, on arrival at the lab, the attending technician exhibited no surprise at being presented with a horse's head by a young and attractive European woman.

'I was a bit miffed,' Berna told me. 'He just hoisted it onto his shoulder and marched away.'

The result came back – positive for rabies – but all in-contacts, including the American, had been vaccinated and no one developed symptoms. All in all a successful outcome – except for Pot Luck of course.

><><><><><

For years we staved off having a television set, being of the view that staring at the infernal box would have a retrograde effect on our girls' intellectual development. And for years they made their own entertainment, both inside and outside, and were the better for it. At friends' houses they were often exposed to the usual inane infantile offerings on the screen. They were so mesmerized by the flickering rubbish on offer that they got to the stage where they built their own set out of cardboard and lay on the carpet, staring at it. Of course there was nothing to be seen with the naked eye but imagination is a wonderful thing and from out of that pathetic box sprang all sorts of amazing things which have stood the poor watchers in good stead to this day.

We ourselves, together with a small handful of the cerebrally deprived, would, once a week, repair to the Club to watch a video session on an enlarged screen, leaving house girl Esther at home to make sure the infants did not get up to any mischief, such as raiding the drinks cabinet, during our absence. The usual offerings were usually fairly benign. On this occasion the programme in question was *The Jewel in the Crown*, the television series adapted from the novels by Paul Scott based around the death throes of the British Raj.

The majority of the small audience were staid elderly couples and the odd widow, all rather conservative in their tastes. They out-aged us by several decades. At the rear of the hall was a table on which were laid piles of cups, plates and saucers, glasses and cutlery in readiness for the following day's breakfast. The club secretary was Jock Rutherford, a lean, leathery, hard drinking, politically incorrect remnant of Empire, ably assisted in his task by Lopez, his Goan assistant. Two different characters could hardly be imagined. Lopez was politeness personified, self-effacing and a gentleman in every sense of the word.

Jock was none of these. We liked them both and they seemed to like us.

The episode was drawing to a close. The beastly Ronald Merrick had beaten the shit out of poor Hari Kumar, falsely accusing him of having deflowered the saintly Daphne Manners in the Bibighar Gardens and the audience seemed to be silently digesting these portentous and harrowing events when there was the most ear-splitting crash of breaking crockery at our backs. At the same moment the lights came on and every head, including our own, turned. There, sitting on the floor, surrounded by piles of fractured plates, broken cups, shattered saucers and smashed bottles of tomato ketchup, sat Jock, a benign and ever so slightly embarrassed grin on his rugged features. He made a futile attempt to get his feet and failed, floundering ineffectually like a beached salmon. Hearing the crash two waiters rushed in and lifted the inebriated Jock to his feet. Coming in at the end of the performance he had leaned back against the table, the better to stabilize himself, lost his footing, grabbed the tablecloth in a futile effort to remain upright, failed, and brought the whole lot thundering to the ground around him. The old bokkies in the audience gazed on at this disgraceful exhibition with haughty disapproval. We could barely contain our mirth and grinned back at Jock. We did not grin for long. A club servant approached us bearing a note. In all my time in Africa I kept hoping that one day I might receive a message borne in a cleft stick held aloft by a panting runner. I never did and neither did I on this occasion. It appeared that Esther, our house help – to call her by the now politically incorrect term house-girl would, in view of her advancing age and spreading bulk, be no longer appropriate – had received a call, and, knowing that we were at the Club, had forwarded it to the front desk.

I read the message with foreboding – 'heifer stuck calving for three days at Kiboko Farm, South Lake Naivasha, owner been trying to pull calf out since 2pm. Please come.' I glanced at my watch – 10pm. The traffic might be lighter at this time of night but it would still take us an hour and a half to get to the farm. And driving at night was not without its hazards – vehicles with only one headlight, or none, lorries with no rear lights, invisible cyclists clad in black, verge-grazing zebra, police road blocks lit by a single guttering tilly lamp and manned by unwelcoming well-armed gendarmes. No wonder the British High Commission forbade its well-paid employees from driving at night.

Girding our loins we set off. There was no moon and it felt like rain. On our right as we passed Lake Elementaita dark clouds were massing over the distant Mau Escarpment. It was eleven as we motored through Gilgil, half way to our destination. The town was quiet, apart from Chez Yvonne, a night-club cum brothel at the corner of the road leading to Ol Kalou. Even with our car windows closed we were almost deafened by the booming cacophony emanating from its interior where strobe lights flashed and the beat of jungle drums echoed into the night. A drunk staggered across the street. A tightly skirted tart waved an invitation. We knew we would be given a warm welcome and were sorely tempted, knowing what well might be awaiting us when we arrived at our destination. We pressed on, leaving the bright lights of Gilgil in our wake.

One police road block, one broken-down lorry, a car in the ditch, was that a body in the drain or someone sleeping it off or a ruse to get you to stop before hijacking you? and we were through Naivasha and on the South Lake road. Most of the big fever trees had gone, making way for the vast polythene greenhouses growing flowers and vegetables for the European markets. The lake was now polluted, tainted by the run-off from these hideous monstrosities, despite the protestations of innocence by their obscenely wealthy owners. The wildlife was dwindling and how the diminishing hippo population survived was a mystery.

Past the drive to the house where Joan Root had been murdered for opposing illegal fishing on the lake and not far to go now. A patter of rain on the windscreen. A sudden downpour and now the rain was thundering down. On with the wipers and – shit! – the wiper on my side slipped its moorings and flew off into outer darkness, gone without trace. The rain was now battering on the windscreen and only by leaning across to Berna's side of the car could I see where I was going. Forward motion now slowed to a pitiful crawl. Twenty minutes later and the midnight hour was chiming as we slithered into the farmyard. The rain had eased but that was our only consolation. The field we were in was a sea of mud and peering through the rain bespattered windscreen I could see that our patient was recumbent: always a bad sign.

I hooted the horn and a glow worm-like pinprick of light appeared in the darkness. Not wishing to become embedded in the mire I waited as the light approached. It seemed to be all over the place. 'Whoever's holding that torch,' said Berna, 'is either drunk or up to his knees in mud.' 'It'll be the latter,' I replied, 'Foxy Reynard, the owner of this place, is far too mean to spend money on booze. I don't come here very often – the bugger's far too tight fisted – more likely to have a go himself and when that fails, call me, just like now. I have told him time without number that the Age of Miracles is past but it was wasted breath. Shine your Mini Maglite on him.'

She did so and lurching towards us was a thin bearded individual, a hatchet shaped nose protruding from a mass of ragged foliage. It reminded me of the rather unkind description of Bruce Mackenzie, Kenya Minister of Agriculture under Jomo Kenyatta's government, and who was killed when flying back from Idi Amin's Uganda by a bomb placed in his plane. His facial growth was such that some wag described him as looking like a weasel peering out of a bear's arse. But Mackenzie was a big, burly individual. This chap looked positively anorexic, even to the extent of having no eyebrows. I just hoped he wouldn't be similarly inclined when it came to payment.

'Morning Foxy,' I greeted him, 'here we are. Can we get the patient into the crush? Her present position may make examination a bit difficult. Can she stand?'

'Yes, she can but I don't think you can get your car any closer. It's been sheeting down here for hours.'

Great, I thought, just great. 'Can you summon some assistance and bring some water and soap.' Foxy staggered away, shouting in Swahili. 'Right,' I said, 'on with the gumboots.' I couldn't find them anywhere. 'Berna,' I said, 'are the boots on your side of the car?' They weren't. We searched in the boot. Nothing. One of the few simple basic tasks assigned to my assistant was to keep the car stocked up with drugs and to clean my boots and ensure that they and my waterproof apron were where I expected them to be, especially in the middle of the night. He at this moment was either fast asleep or carousing in some tavern, the minor vicissitudes of his employer far from mind. Berna, ever resourceful, produced, as if from nowhere, a pair of plastic bags. These I drew over my normal footwear, tied them round my ankles with some binder twine, wrapped a towel round my midriff to protect my person from the inevitable backwardly projected uterine effusions and we were ready for action. Berna, not wishing to ruin her dainty pumps, opted to go barefoot. We floundered after Foxy, using Berna's torch to light our way. Berna slipped in the goo and let rip with an unladylike oath. We arrived at the spot where the heifer, a Friesan, lay in the mud. Protruding from her vulva was a pair of calf's legs to which was attached a couple of filthy, frayed ropes. I touched the legs. They were cold. One was broken.

'Well,' I said, 'these bright sparks must have been pulling away here for hours. The calf must be dead and Heaven knows what we'll find inside.'

I nudged the heifer in the ribs and to my relief, she stood up. There's nothing worse than trying to extricate a long-dead calf from a recumbent heifer in the dark, in the mud and in the rain.

A group of shadowy figures emerged from the outer into the inner darkness. Most appeared to be wearing black greatcoats and in the stygian gloom they were almost invisible. From their guttural talk I could tell that they were Turkanas, the tall, lean, iron hard men from the north west. Lurking in the background was the runt-like figure of Foxy.

'So, Foxy,' I said, 'it would appear that your brawny mess mates have been hard at work at the capstan bars.'

Foxy seemed to be unaware of this early morning nautical irony. 'Oh yes,' he replied, 'we've been hauling away for hours. I was just about to hitch up the Toyota when I decided to call you.'

'Thank you very much,' I said, 'now would you be a good chap and bring me that bucket of hot water and a bar of soap and not the stuff you use to scrub the floors. I want the one you use to sterilize your revolting armpits.'

After what seemed like a couple of hours – so does time crawl by when you're standing ankle deep in cold mud, with more rain in the offing, at an hour when life is at its lowest ebb and knowing that very soon it may be considerably lower – Foxy reappeared, followed by a minion carrying a largish bucket at the bottom of which was a kettle-full of tepid water.

I sighed. One does a lot of sighing in Africa. Shouting and losing your temper gets you nowhere. Not that sighing does either. But it does keep you out of trouble.

We moved the patient into a crush. I soaped my arm and inserted it into the vagina. It was as I expected. The calf was dead and not recently, the tissues were dry and swollen. I poured in a couple of litres of obstetrical lubricant and tried again. The calf's head was large and bulbous and so big that there was barely enough room for my arm in there. 'Let's try pulling the head out, cutting it off and see if it's possible to use the embryotome to try to remove the calf in sections.'

I squelched my way back to the car, assembled the embryotome, retrieved the eye hooks from the gumboot-less boot and trudged back to the scene of action. A light rain began to fall.

After the usual contortions I got the hooks firmly embedded in the calf's eye sockets, poured in some more lubricant, and gave the attached ropes to one of the weaker looking Turks, a difficult identification to make in the abominable darkness. I didn't want one of the hulking great bravos doing any more damage to the poor animal. So I told the chosen one to exert a steady pull under my direction with no tribal jerkings or wrenchings.

Slowly, ever so slowly, the head emerged, together with some more of the legs. And that was it. Impasse. Any more pulling meant that we were pulling both calf and uterus. The calf was too big, the heifer was too small and the tissues too swollen. I gave the order to cease pulling. With a sharp knife I removed the head, pushed everything back inside, re-lubricated the tract and reassessed the situation with my left arm and what was left of my overstretched brain. I always used my left arm for obstetrical procedures like this and for pregnancy testing cows and mares. Having pregnancy tested thousands of cattle and hundreds of mares and calved thousands of cattle and foaled scores of mares, my left arm was now like one of the eight arms of the octopus, a brain acting independently of my cerebral cortex. It now told me that any further digging and delving would be futile, and would exhaust both me and the heifer, so put away your embryotome and get out your scalpel because that is the only way you are going to be able to extract this calf. 'Foxy?' I spoke into the Nubian darkness, 'I'm going to have to do a Caesar here in order to get this calf out. Not ideal in view of the fact that the calf is dead and has been so for a day or so, but the only other option is slaughter. What do you say?'

For several minutes Foxy said nothing. I could imagine him screwing up his piggy eyes and wrestling with what passed for his conscience. Then I heard something, but I could not tell if it was an amorous cricket, Foxy's brain cogs turning over or whether he was tapping at the pocket calculator he always carried in order to ensure that he wasn't being diddled by the locals. Finally he spoke – 'How much?' I gave him a modest estimate. More silence. The rain increased in strength. Foxy and his native cohort were warmly clad. We were not. 'All right. Go ahead.'

Back through the bog, and hump my well-filled surgical bag, an array of sutures, ropes, syringes and a few bottles of local anaesthetic through the deepening swamp to where Foxy had switched off his miserable torch in order to save on batteries. Thank God Berna had her Maglite. Many Africans seem to be able to see in total darkness, aptly demonstrated by the number of lorries and buses which thunder along the Kenyan, and presumably many other sub-Saharan roads, at night, without any headlights whatsoever.

A handy throwback to the Halcyon pre-colonial days when life was dictated by the sun and the moon and not by the white man's intrusive and objectionable electrical gadgetry. But in the meantime we weak westerners, Berna and I, had to cope with our feeble orbs and get on with it. 'Toa mtama kwa mananda,' – 'take the heifer out of the crush,' I instructed the invisible Turkanas, 'na lalisha yeye kando' –

'and lay her down.' 'Foxy, can you bring a bale of hay or straw to act as a table? Quickly please before I croak from hypothermia.'

The Turks were as keen as we were to get the job over and done with and get back to whatever they were doing before we arrived, which, knowing them, was probably either boozing or whoring, or both at the same time. They almost lifted the heifer out of the crush and laid her gently on her right side. Caesarian sections in ruminants are always carried out via the left flank. The intestines nestle on the right side of the ruminant abdomen so if you are one of those persons (and they do exist) who doesn't know their right from their left, and if you do go in on the wrong side you're in for a nasty surprise as yards of guts hasten to the exit and trying to replace them, far less carry out the operation, makes threading the proverbial camel through the eye of a needle child's play by comparison. So through the left flank it is.

By the time we had lashed the heifer's legs, shaved the operational area and injected local anaesthetic, a feeble glimmer of light indicated the arrival of the lord of the manor, accompanied by a serf toting a bale of straw. I laid out my instruments and, with Berna acting as assistant, set to, with her directing her Maglite. With a light drizzle pattering on my naked back this was no time for pussy-footing around. A bold incision through the skin, then the subcutaneous tissue, three layers of muscle, some bleeding, but that would soon stop, now the filmy peritoneal lining of the abdomen hoves into view. Nick that with the point of the scalpel and enlarge the opening with a pair of surgical scissors. In with the stout left arm and locate the uterus. Sweep the hand over the gravid womb and identify a hind leg. But the calf is big and swollen so getting a hand round a hock is not easy. My manly thorax, bent over the opened abdomen, is preventing the rain from entering this vital cavity, but it's time to get this business over. A supreme effort and I get the hock up and out of the incision, but now in order to keep it there I have to use my other hand to hold it there. 'Berna,' I grunt, 'get the scalpel and cut the uterus between my hands.' 'Where, where,' she gasps, directing her torch. 'There, there!' I point with my nose, rather like a desperate ibis stabbing the ground with its beak for worms or beetles.' More gasping. 'Come on woman! Don't prod or poke! The calf can't feel anything! It's already dead! That's better. Don't cut my bloody finger off! Shove the knife in so I can get a grip on the leg.' A four-inch incision, big enough so I can grab the uterine wall, hold it and insert my hand and seize the leg. Hoist the hock into the chilly night air, now cup a hand round the hoof so it doesn't tear the uterus and carefully lever the whole leg through the incision. Repeat with leg number two. Now both hind legs are out.

I bark an order to one of the goggling Turkanas to hold the leg and pull upwards, gently. He grabs the leg and, being as strong as the proverbial ox, is able to lift the rear end of the calf up to the incision, which I enlarge, as an incision cut with a scalpel is easier to repair than an uncontrolled tear. 'Sasa, mguu ingine' – 'now the other leg.' So, by alternately pulling one leg and then the other, the pelvis is slid diagonally out of the uterus. The rest of the calf follows easily. I grab the uterine wall to prevent any of its contents from spilling into the abdominal cavity and pull it out as far as I can, and clamp it with strong forceps. The dead calf is dragged away and I wonder if the Turkanas will have it for breakfast. I fish inside the now empty uterus and carefully remove the placenta.

Now I can relax. All I have to do now is to sew her up. Half way through the proceedings, needle poised to transfix the external oblique, I had the feeling that we had company. I looked up, and there, outlined against the scudding clouds, was a cove with a video camera! 'Who the devil are you?' I exclaimed. 'Me, I am Fritz, from Bremerhaven, in Chermany, unt I am overlander, camping next door mit meine Helga. I cannot sleep. I hear voices talking so I arise unt I see you unt your so lovely lady do ze operation and I have taken film. I am hoping you do not mind that I did not ask your permissions.' 'Join the party Fritz,' I said, 'all are welcome. No exceptions. By the way, did you see a small dwarfish chap with a beard in the vicinity?' 'Nein, I am seeing no one.' 'OK,' I said and bent once again to my task

The final thank God stitch inserted, we undid the ropes and rolled the heifer onto her chest, at which point she rose to her feet and strolled off without a thank you or backward glance. This was reassuring. She would be ok.

By the time I had straightened up, half of the Turkanas had drifted away. 'I wonder what's happened to Foxy,' I said. 'Here he comes,' said Berna and sure enough the man himself was at my elbow. A half-moon was now rising and in its silvery light I could see that Foxy was wearing a kikoi – a coastal sarong – below a shapeless rumpled jersey. He saw my glance and thinly disguised frown – he gave a guilty snigger – 'felt a bit tired, been a long day, went for a bit of a lie down, knew I wouldn't be much use here..,' he tailed off. Well, mate, I thought, you're right about the last bit. 'Everything went all right then?' he asked. 'Yup,' I replied, 'she should be fine. Stitches out in two week's time – ok?' Foxy looked troubled, mentally totting up the bawbees. 'Er, does that mean you've got to come back to do that?' 'Oh yes,' I said cheerfully, 'we wouldn't want some incompetent ass undoing all my good work, would we?' 'No I suppose not.' And with a Scrooge-like look on his ferrety features he turned and vanished whence he came.

'Miserable old sod,' said Berna, 'not a word of thanks, no offer of tea, food, or even a dry bun and glass of water. Will he even pay?' 'Probably, but he'll take his time about it.'

By now everyone but us had gone. We carried our things back to the car. The rain had stopped, the moon had risen, and from the distant lake we could hear the grunting of hippos. Crickets were in full voice. A nightjar churred. An owl floated by on silent, velvet wings. The operation had gone well, no thanks to that half-wit Foxy, who, like many others like him, had no conception, and probably cared less, about what was involved in doing a Caesarian section virtually single-handed in almost total darkness, in the rain, as long as he benefitted and forked out the bare minimum.

The homeward drive was on a blessedly empty road. On our right dark clouds were massing over the Aberdares, but as we descended the escarpment beyond Gilgil a silvery sheen gilded the surface of Lake Elementaita. I woke Berna, who had been enjoying a spot of well-earned slumber after our nocturnal trials. She gazed at the lovely sight, so peaceful in the moonlight. 'I wonder,' she said sleepily, 'what the next episode of *The Jewel in the Crown* will bring.'

Chapter Twenty Four

A LITTLE BIT OF THIS
A LITTLE BIT OF THAT

People in the UK often ask us why we live in Africa. 'Isn't is dangerous?' they ask. 'It's full of disease, it's dirty and corrupt, isn't it?' 'It's all of those things,' we reply, 'dozens of people we know have met violent ends, we've had malaria several times, had tick typhus, hepatitis, Rift Valley Fever, brucellosis, giardia, septicaemia, broken bones, the lot. But the place is also full of life and colour, it's vibrant, the people, of all races, are for the most part open and friendly, the wildlife is still there, the weather is good, it's warm, there are mountains to climb and the coast is fabulous. And for a vet it's ideal. You don't make any money – at least I didn't – but every day you see conditions most vets in the UK would give their eye teeth to see. I probably see a greater variety of animal diseases in a day than most vets in the UK see in a month. In addition to all the maladies seen in Europe we have a whole host of wonderful tropical diseases – African Horse Sickness, Rift Valley Fever, rabies, East Coast Fever, Corridor Disease, redwater, Anaplasmosis, trypanosomiasis, camel pox, three-day sickness, sweating sickness, lumpy skin disease, snake bites; plus animals being gored, bitten and gouged by buffalo, lion, leopard, warthog and crocodile. Truly glorious territory for an enthusiast such as myself.'

People ask, 'Do you regret going to Africa? After all, if you'd stayed here you would be long retired by now, living in a nice house in some leafy suburb, or in the Cotswolds or in Bognor Regis.' 'The trouble is that I read too much Rider Haggard, Conrad, Stanley and *Tales from the Outposts* as a boy. Wanted a life of hazard and adventure.' 'And did you get it?' 'With knobs on.' 'You must be mad.'

But I came to Africa just in time, before the twin ravages of population growth and climate change altered things forever. Now no future generation will see the Mountains of the Moon as they used to be, silent and unvisited, with their now-vanished glaciers and enormous snowfields, hanging cornices and feet long icicles, or Maasai women with their arms and legs bound from ankle to knee and from wrist to elbow with circlets of silver, or spear-carrying moran trotting across the plains, or Kikuyu women with their shaven heads and huge pink ear-rings toting back-breaking loads of firewood.

The naked Pokot are now in long trousers and roaring around on motorbikes. Even as late as the mid-60s there were, in the Nakuru area, apart from the main highway to Uganda, only two tarred roads, and they were a mere ten miles in length. Now the country is criss-crossed with hundreds of miles of bitumen, towns are springing up where there once was nothing but the odd passing tribesman, or woman, and apart from the sigh of the wind, and the twittering of birds, as peaceful as a Sunday afternoon. The roar of passing traffic and the din of ghetto blasters has broken that age long silence.

But this is still Africa, where anything might happen. And it does. In spades.

Murray Roberts was brought up on the soporific shores of Lake Baringo, where he lived in his cliff-topped eyrie with his lovely wife Elizabeth. The house was still cliff-topped but the problem now was that most of the cliff was under water, due to a combination of unseasonable rains, removal of top soil, silting, deforestation and dark rumours of shifting Rift Valley tectonic plates. With an extra 40 feet of water in the lake, getting to Murray's house by land was no longer an option and access was only possible by canoe. To some this may sound romantic, with images of Sanders of the River and loyal chanting paddlers conveying the white bwana and his pale memsahib to their distant destination, but when the waters are lapping at your front door the romance begins to fade. And there are other irritants. Creatures which live at a lower altitude to your own are flushed from their homes and forced to flit to higher ground. And when that includes your house and those creatures include snakes, scorpions, centipedes and three-foot monitor lizards, things can get a bit tiresome. Both Murray and Elizabeth were cast in stoical mould. Murray was a highly skilled and dedicated environmentalist, growing trees and helping the local people to better their lot. Elizabeth had lived for many years among the Pokot, spoke their language fluently and ran an essential dispensary.

They kept brindle Staffordshire bull terriers, tough, hardy, immensely strong, friendly dogs. Their strength was often their salvation when they came into too close contact with monkeys, local dogs and baboons.

The lake continued to rise. Shoreline shambas, houses, lodges and hotels vanished beneath the water. The three storey house of Betty, Murry's mother, had long since collapsed and disappeared.

Rasta the bull terrier pottered out of the house in the early morning. Samson the odd job man watched him as the dog walked to where the water was gently lapping at the top of the cliff. The nightly chorus of chirping frogs and sawing cicadas had fallen silent. A heron stood motionless in nearby reeds. An egret, a floodlit study in ivory, meditated on a rock. A flight of surface-skimming cormorants flew past. A fish jumped. The sun was rising over the Mukutan Gorge on the eastern side of the lake, shining like a searchlight into the eyes of Rasta and Samson. But it was not shining into the eyes of a crocodile which lay, still and silent, a few yards offshore, watching the dog as he approached to slake his thirst. Rasta bent his head to drink. With a watery rush the crocodile lunged at Rasta, seizing him by the neck. The heron and egret rose in alarm. Rasta, being Rasta, fought back, fought hard, biting at the iron hard, scaly jaw which held him in its terrifying grip.

Hearing the commotion, Samson, realizing what was happening, grabbed a length of wood lying by the house, and sprinted to the water's edge and, without thought, but with all his strength, smashed the croc on the nose. With a horrid swirl the crocodile submerged, taking Rasta with him.

Samson stood, looking at the dark waters, still heaving like a pot on the boil, small fresh waves arriving at his feet. He was on the point of turning away to convey his grim early morning tidings to his master and mistress, when the crocodile suddenly erupted from the deep, Rasta still clamped in his reptilian jaws. Once again Samson raised his baton and gave the croc what-for on the snout. But this time fortune favoured both Samson and Rasta. To the astonishment of both the great jaws relaxed. Rasta struggled free, fell into the shallows, staggered up the bank and collapsed, gasping and wheezing, in the shade of a friendly bush. Whether Samson's blow had struck a sensitive nerve was something on which he did not linger to ponder as he rushed the punctured and waterlogged Rasta to the house where Murray and Elizabeth had been roused by Samson's vocalizations as he laid into the croc.

Murray and Elizabeth gently placed Rasta into their canoe, started the outboard motor and steered to shore, where their Land Rover was parked, and drove the 70 miles to my surgery in Nakuru.

Any other dog would have died by the time he reached me. Rasta was certainly not in good shape, but my experience of Staffies gave me hope. He was punctured in several places – his neck, chest and hind leg – and I knew that these wounds would probably suppurate. Crocodiles, not known for tooth brushing and with their penchant for storing their prey in an under-water larder until it is nice and rotten and ready for the table have teeth laden with pathogens. One of Rasta's own canines was sticking out at right angles, a result of biting the armour-clad neck of his oppressor. As it appeared to still have a reasonable blood supply, rather than remove it, I decided to try to lever it back into position. I looked up at Murray. Murray is a largish chap and he loomed over me.

'Murray,' I said, 'Rasta will be unable to eat with his tooth like this, so we either take it out or lever it back. We will have to give a sedative but it's safe so I suggest we give it a try.' 'Go for it,' said Murray. The reply I expected. But before I went for it I listened to Rasta's chest. He had spent some involuntary time under water and I suspected he had inhaled water and who knew what else. The waters of Lake Baringo were far from clear and were full of particulate matter and the bottom to which Rasta had been taken was deep in mud. Rasta's lungs did not sound great. In fact they sounded pretty awful. It sounded as if he was breathing through a hosepipe. 'Murray,' I said, 'let's stand him on his forelegs and see what comes out.' So we did and about a pint of brown Baringo water poured out of Rasta's mouth and nose. 'That's better,' I said, 'now we can proceed.' The sedative drug xylazine is very safe but on one occasion I did have to ask Murray if Rasta was still breathing at his end. But all went well and a few minutes of deft manipulation saw the displaced canine back in its socket, and there it remained.

Then it was a matter of treating the several bite wounds and the aspiration pneumonia. This took rather longer, several weeks in fact. In the end Rasta made a full recovery. But he remained forever nervous about going anywhere near water's edge.

When Mel Gibson/aka William Wallace, was, on the orders of the English king Edward, the Hammer of the Scots, disembowelled in the closing sequences of the biopic 'Braveheart', he took it on his stubbly chin with little more than a manly antipodean grimace, as though his only problem was a segment of trapped wind, and not the untimely terminal exteriorization of his entrails. In real life things are rather different.

When your guts are out of the safe, warm haven of your abdominal cavity, and exposed to the unfriendly outdoor world, your survival time can be, unless swift remedial action is taken, measured in a matter of hours. Then it's goodnight sweet prince in rather unpleasant fashion. Shock and blood loss finish you off in short order.

So, when I received a call to attend to a camel, gored in the abdomen by a buffalo, on Soysambu, Lord Delamere's ranch, I prepared myself for the worst. You go half hoping that the animal will be already dead by the time you arrive, so that you don't have to shoot it, or have to spend hours pushing its guts back inside, stitching it up, and then have it die anyway from shock and septicaemia. The camel, a female, was lying in the middle of an open plain and looking very depressed, as well she might be. Her entire length of intestine was lying beside her, covered with dirt, dung and flies, and the ground was soaked in blood and stomach contents. As I walked towards her, the camel gave a long despairing groan and sank onto her side.

I turned to the herdsman standing at my side. 'Hawezi pona. Ta kufa. Mzuri ku-ua yeye sasa' – she can't recover. She's going to die. It's best if we put her down now.' He nodded in agreement. At that moment Donno Dunn, who lived on the ranch, drove up. A professional crop sprayer, he was also an honorary game warden and had his 475 in his Land Cruiser. At my request, he shot the camel. Her sufferings were over. Donno told me that two other camels had been killed by buffalo in the past month, possibly by the same animal, as the Kenya Wildlife Services had shot and wounded a buffalo suspected of having been responsible for both deaths. So now we had a wounded, very angry, camel-killing buffalo to deal with and next time, he, or she, might target a schoolchild, a woman going to fetch water or a shepherd herding his flock.

Then there was the German Shepherd police dog.

It was mid-winter and I was somewhere in the frozen steppe in Central Asia. I was in a richly-caparisoned yurt. Outside snow was thickly falling but the yurt was pleasantly overheated and made more so, as local custom dictated, by the deft personal attentions of a pair of slant-eyed beauties, whose only garb was a pair of fur-lined boots. Suddenly, at a pre-climactic moment, my anticipatory pleasure was rudely disrupted by the arrival, outside the yurt, of a fire engine, which commenced to sound its ear-splitting horn at full volume. On and on it bellowed its klaxon. The doe-eyed darlings appeared to pay no attention to the hideous din. 'Are they deaf?' I wondered. Then the whole yurt started to shake. An earthquake! I staggered to the door of the yurt and out into the snowy wastes. 'Wake up! Wake up, Hugh! The phone's ringing!' Berna was shaking my shoulder. My delightful Mongolian idyll was over. Which unfeeling bastard was responsible for thrusting me back into the cruel world? Grabbing a phone in total darkness when my technicoloured dream was still vivid reality was not easy. Where the hell is the bloody thing? I find the bedside light switch. Ye gods! 3.35am! I grab the phone – 'Yes? Who is it?' 'Police,' barks a voice at the other end. 'Oh shit!' I think, scrolling down all the latent possibilities: that time I crossed the central reservation outside State House and failed to notice the upraised constabulary arm; the time one night I ran over a police bollard and again failed to notice a flashing torch, requesting an explanatory pull-over and who knew what else? 'Dog Section! Daktari! One of our dogs has been stabbed by a thief. Please attend!' Qualified relief. I threw on some clothes and got to the surgery in short order and arrived panting. Always show that you are eager and willing. It may get you off the Wanted List. The police Land Rover was parked in the street outside the surgery.

'Aiya,' I said to the waiting sergeant, 'lete ndani.' 'OK, bring him in.'

The dog did not walk in, a bad sign. A large German Shepherd, he was laid on the table. I quickly checked his vital signs. Rapid heart-beat, ivory coloured gums and conjunctiva, gasping respirations, enlarged abdomen, in the centre of which was a two inch long gash, the entry site of the knife. It did not look long enough to account for the critical, life-threatening symptoms. Filling the wound was a section of gut. Using a blunt spatula, I gently moved the gut to one side, trying to assess the extent of the damage. Suddenly, there was a trickle, then a stream and finally a tidal wave of blood, pouring from the wound, litres of it, rushing across the table and onto the floor. I clapped a wad of cotton wool over the red tsunami. I might have been Canute on the beach for all the good I did. I grabbed a scalpel and enlarged the wound and stuck my hand in, rooting around, searching for the origin of the flood. The dog was too far gone to require an anaesthetic. By the time

I found the source of supply – a puncture in the posterior vena cava the diameter of my finger, it was too late. The dog's mouth opened, he gasped, his head bent backwards and he was gone.

The posterior vena cava is the largest vein in the rear part of the body, draining the legs, and basically everything behind the heart. Unstoppable haemorrhage is the depressing outcome of sharp trauma to this vein.

I turned to the sergeant. I hadn't paid much attention to him until now, being focused on the German Shepherd. My, he was a big chap. My head barely reached his chest. A great football of a head rested on massive shoulders and his cranium, shaven and shining, gleamed and twinkled as though one of his underlings had spent a good half hour polishing his master's skull. Small, cunning, boot-black eyes were almost hidden in fleshy folds of facial fat. At the back of his skull there was a deep horizontal cleft where his cerebellum met his spinal cord. He was not a pretty sight. Further down a prosperous abdomen jutted out into the limited confines of my consulting room. At home he was probably a charming family man, going to church on Sundays, patting urchins on the head and donating to the poor and needy. Here he was an object of threat and menace.

After explaining in layman's terms why the dog had succumbed so quickly I asked, 'What happened to the thief?' The sergeant grinned. 'He did not escape!' A hovering constable laughed.

While they carried the dead dog away, I was left to clean up the blood and ponder, once again, on the daily complexities of life in Africa – the violence, the friendly smiling people, the corruption, the generosity of ordinary folk, the underlying tension, the wildlife, the poaching, vast landscapes and vile slums.

'Well, how did it go then?' asked wide-awake Berna when I returned. 'No survivors,' I replied.

But occasionally there was the odd exception. On the game-rich country between Gilgil and Naivasha, north of the Nakuru/Nairobi highway, lived Chris and Christine Campbell-Clause. The similarity of their names, together with their double-barrelled surname, was something which was regarded without comment in Kenya, where eccentricity was an indication that you were a fully fledged member of up country society. The plains adjacent to the Campbell-Clause's house were full of wildlife: impala, Tommy, jackal, buffalo and warthog, which trotted across the veldt, tails erect, rooting and burrowing with impunity, as, apart from the odd leopard, they had no predators. Having no predators they grew bold and lost their fear, including that of the Campbell-Clause's dogs.

One day, when the dogs, including one large ridgeback called Fisi – hyena – were taken out for a walk, a family of warthog, including massive, razor-tusked daddy, crossed their path. Small-brained Fisi, cerebral cortex whipped into a lather of frenzied excitement, rushed forwards in wild pursuit. The warthogs turned and ran, tails upstanding like flagstaffs. The ridgeback seemed to be on the point of overtaking and seizing the last piglet when the paterfamilias whipped round, lowered his head and drove his tusks into Fisi's abdomen, zipping him open from sternum to pubis, spilling his guts onto the ground.

The Cambell-Clauses ran up. The warthogs had gone. Fisi lay on the ground, intestines lying in a smoking heap beside him. Chris did not hesitate. He knew what to do if he was to save Fisi from a horrible end. He whipped off his shirt, gently lifted Fisi's exteriorized entrails and wrapped them carefully within its folds. Chris and Christine lifted the ridgeback and rushed back to the house, piled into the Land Cruiser and, with Christine holding Fisi, making sure that the intestines remained well wrapped, drove to Club Lane in Nakuru, where I was waiting.

Alerted to their arrival, I was in preparation mode. Assistant Kip had laid out the instruments. Half an hour later, his master and mistress having broken both the speed limit and the record time from Gilgil to Nakuru, Fisi was carried into the surgery, guts still suspended within Chris's shirt. Passers by goggled at shirtless Chris, manly torso bedaubed with canine gore, as he bore Fisi through the batwing doors and into the surgery.

There was no time to waste. Estimating his weight at 35kgs, I zapped in a dose of xylazine, waited the requisite 10 minutes and then shot in a dose of ketamine. Fisi was now out cold and we lifted him onto the table, removed Chris's shirt and inspected the damage.

To my relief the intestines were all intact, had a good colour and the arteries were pulsating nicely.

'Looks good, Chris. Fisi's young, strong and healthy so let's go. First we'll wash the intestines with warm saline to remove any bits of dirt and the odd ant or beetle which might be nestling in there. Then we'll try to shove everything back in and stitch him up. There's always a risk he'll die from shock, now or later, but that's a chance we'll have to take.'

A discreet cough behind us. 'Excuse me gentlemen,' said Christine, 'but if you don't mind I'll leave you to it while I powder my nose in the Club. All that blood and guts is making me feel quite faint.' 'Well don't you faint Chris,' I said, 'we need all hands to the pumps.' 'Come back in a couple of hours, Christine,' I called as she left.

I knew that I didn't need Chris to be on hand as together Kip and I could manage perfectly well, but sometimes it does the client good to see what is involved and that the bill presented is justified and that it's not all nail clipping and vaccinating sweet little puppies.

In fact it took us three hours before the job was done. Returning a mess of guts whence they came requires a certain degree of care. Handling intestines roughly can easily lead to shock which may be terminal. Finally the last stitch was inserted.

'Now,' I said, 'we'll run in some IV fluids, together with some antibiotic and with a bit of luck Fisi will be back to chasing anything but warthogs in a week or so.' And he was.

🏛✕🏛✕🏛✕

Margaret Mwende was waiting when I walked into my surgery. Margaret lived at Dundori, about 10 miles from Nakuru, on the eastern flanks of the Rift Valley. Dundori was high, about 8,000 feet above sea level, and was always cool and green, even during times of drought when the plains below were biscuit brown and the sun scorched the land and dust devils rose into the shimmering air.

In a cardboard box at her feet crouched a rather depressed dog. Middle-aged Margaret had brought it in on the back of a boda boda (a motorbike taxi) and was now hoping that I could help.

She told me that her dog, a bitch, had given birth to three pups seven days previously, all three had died and now her abdomen was bloated and she was not eating. Margaret had taken her to a local vet, who advised her to have the dog put down – 'but I didn't want to.'

We lifted the dog, which was unable to stand, onto the table. Her abdomen was enormously distended, tense and painful. I tapped it – the medical term is the rather curious word ballottement – derived, typically, from the French and Italian and meaning to slosh – and felt a wave of fluid rather like a mini tidal wave flow from one side to the other. But why, if she had already given birth? Don a surgical glove, lubricate a digit and insert it through the vulva into the vagina. Bingo! A long-dead pup lodged in the passage, a finger in the gynaecological dyke.

Carefully hook a finger under the pup and attempt to draw it out. Careful – the pup is in danger of imminent disintegration. Slowly now, and out it comes, and the dam is breached and a great rush of bloody, uterine fluid pours out, across the table, onto the floor and over my boots, and spreads like a neap tide over the cement, followed by a litre of retained urine. The dog is now deflated and I give a shot of oxytocin to contract the uterus, some antibiotic, and Margaret packs her dog back into its cardboard box, swings her leg over the motorbike, balances the box on her lap and sets off for home.

Next day Margaret phoned up. The bitch is up and walking and she is delighted, telling me that her dog has fully recovered.

◈❙◈❙◈❙◈❙◈

A few days later Rose Kemboi rushed in holding an adult Japanese Spitz which was having convulsions. I anaesthetized the dog with xylazine and ketamine, hoping that this would do the trick. It didn't. As soon as the anaesthetic began to lighten, the convulsions returned, with the dog cartwheeling and jerking and twitching all over its kennel. At this point Rose came rushing back with another Spitz having convulsions. When you have a dog having fits or convulsions, the standard procedure is to give IV pentobarbitone, none of which was available in Kenya. But – hang on a mo! What about EuthaNaze, triple strength non-sterile pentobarbitone, normally used for euthanasing animals, small and large? I had that. The Royal College might not approve of its use in this way, but what the hell, they're 4,000 miles away and this is an emergency.

I calculated the dose, divided it by three, and because it was so small, diluted it with sterile water. Then, with Kip, raising the vein, I slowly injected the pentobarbitone into the cephalic vein until anaesthesia was attained.

As we began to deal with dog number two, in rushed Rose's son, with convulsing dog number three.

With the solution already made up, it was only as matter of moments to slip the drug into the vein.

Now all three dogs were out cold and it was just a matter of time and waiting to see what would happen when they came round. This would take several hours. I went home.

Next morning all three dogs were up and bouncing around. What caused the convulsions remained yet another of life's innumerable unsolved mysteries.

⚜⚜⚜⚜⚜

Margaret was obviously poor and bereft of funds. Rose Kemboi less so. But compared to prices charged in the UK, what I could reasonably charge my African clients and retain their custom was ludicrously small. This was Africa, where one had to charge within people's means, or they would not come at all, and the affected animal would suffer. The comparison between the 'West' and Africa could be stark. A miniature dachshund, having eaten some dark chocolate, was presented, out of hours, to a veterinary practice in Somerset, given an emetic to make it vomit and discharged. The client was presented with a bill for £250. This equates to double the average Kenyan's monthly salary. To charge anything like this in Nakuru would act as a permanent disincentive to any future visits.

I did not run an appointment system. Open house was my motto. Anyone passing by was free to come in, ask for advice, bring their animals – dogs, cats, sheep, goats – sell their fruit and vegetables, their roasted peanuts, or just pass the time of day. Africa is the land of the open door, the ready smile, the friendly greeting, the helping hand, and also the AK47 and the glowering policeman, the humble peasant and the arrogant politician. A land of surprising contradictions.

$$\text{\textasciitilde} \text{\textasciitilde} \text{\textasciitilde} \text{\textasciitilde} \text{\textasciitilde}$$

'M'sieu Cran?' I knew a French voice when I heard one so I replied in like vein – 'Ah oui.'

'My name is Jean-Luc Dessin and I am a film director based in Nairobi. I have been asked to film pelicans in flight for a film about migrating birds. Now these pelicans are rather special. They were hatched in France, trained to follow a micro-light in Senegal and I have been filming them, close-up, down at Magadi. But now that the filming is over they have to go back to France and the authorities there require a vet certificate stating that they are healthy and free from disease. Can you do that for me?'

'Bien sur,' I replied. Magadi was about 180 miles from Nakuru, in the Rift Valley, just north of the Tanzanian border, close by the lake of the same name, and at the foot of the extinct volcano Shompole, of less than sacred memory, on which several personal attempts on what has been described as the most unpleasant mountain in Kenya, had finally resulted in success.

'Yes,' I said, 'we can do that, as long as it's on a Sunday so that my wife Benadette can come along and also being on a Sunday it won't interfere with my daily work.'

'Ah Bernadette, quel joli nom!' exclaimed Jean-Luc.

'Francais typique!' I thought, imagining a Jean-Belmondo type, Gauloise drooping from lower lip, eyes half closed against the curl of smoke and a slow half smile wreathing continental lips.

When we later met him it was to discover that he was nothing like that. He wasn't even wearing a beret and he was a non-smoker.

So on Sunday we drove to Magadi. We left early, the weather was good, the road was dry and we made good time. As we drove between Gilgil and Naivasha, the sun, a red glowing globe, rose above the crest of the dark Aberdares on our left, shafts of soft light picking out groups of grazing zebra. A warthog, tail erect, trotted through the bush. At the toll station a herd of buffalo stood, black and motionless, waiting for the sun to warm their backs. A pair of Egyptian geese flew overhead, heading for Lake Naivasha. The new road now bypassed Naivasha town and rose gradually along the eastern wall of the Rift Valley. Far away to our right the steam jets at Ol Karia, white plumes against their sombre background, rose into the still morning air. Now we were opposite Longonot, the sharply summited extinct volcano, its crater clearly delineated in the crystalline air.

And now we were at almost 9,000 feet with the great swoop of the valley opening up, the yellow plains stretching away, volcanic Suswa in the middle ground, and far, far away, the forested heights of the western wall of the Rift. One of the great sights of Africa and one which never ceases to lift the heart. Now the road began to descend towards Nairobi. This was all Kikuyu country, cool, green, fertile, heavily cultivated and thickly populated. Through the affluent suburbs of Karen and Langata, where grand houses inhabited by aid 'workers', highly paid expats, languid diplomats and wealthy African elite lined quiet leafy lanes. Well-treed plantations screened the select and privileged from the noisome nearby treeless slums of Kibera. Kibera bears the unwelcome title of being the biggest slum in Africa and as such was unlikely to be the destination of anyone living in Karen or Langata. I had been there and it was like being in an urban maze – steep, narrow, winding dirt tracks, often ending without warning in a vertical drop into a ditch or stream, houses and shacks so crammed together that if you so wished you could walk on the roofs from one side of the slum to the other without touching the ground, no signs to tell you where you were, people everywhere, friendly for the most part although sometimes you heard the word 'tajiri' – rich man – muttered as you tried vainly to find the exit. And, compared to the people living here, you were a 'tajiri.' Although it was a slum it was also a close knit community and many of its inhabitants would rather stay there than be moved to the soulless flats being built on Kibera's periphery.

Soon we were rounding the high southern end of the Ngong Hills, the hills so beloved by Karen Blixen. We had climbed steeply, through open grassy uplands, a strong wind buffeting the car, hawks hovering, sheep and cattle grazing, the odd herdsman lifting his hand in salute, until we reached Corner Baridi – Cold Corner – the highest point and prepared to descend back into the Rift Valley. Here there was a view point, where tourists were sometimes ferried out from Nairobi so that they could take photos of several hundred square miles of bush and be able to tell the folks back home that they had been in the African 'wilderness.' The place was deserted but we knew that this was where, if you weren't hassled by trinket-selling Maasai 'warriors' and their beaded women folk, there was always the chance of being held up and robbed by one or other of the local footpads and cutpurses. So we did not linger but set off down the steepening incline.

As we descended so did the temperature rise, and we rejoiced exceedingly. Decades in Africa had thinned our blood and we were now warm weather fiends. We could easily understand why creatures like snakes and lizards slowed down when the temperature dropped. They preferred heat and so did we. The country was now dry and stony. A deep ravine on our left held some pools of brown water where a herd of cattle was being watered by a solitary Maasai. Eastwards stood Oloolkisaile, a notoriously bouldery mountain, the haunt of reedbuck and eland, and one best avoided by anyone with suspect joints.

The road rose to a pass between two hills and there, in the distance was Lake Magadi, a baking shimmering expanse of gleaming white soda flats. Jean-Luc had told us to meet him near the golf course, private links for the express use of members of the Magadi Club, which in turn was for the express use of the upper echelons of the Lake Magadi Soda Company, which mined the lake, no peasants need apply. Golfers expecting smooth fairways, manicured greens, raked bunkers and a stately clubhouse would not have been impressed by the Magadi Golf Course. Here none of those effete facilities existed. The entire nine hole course was composed of gravel. Not a blade of grass was to be seen anywhere. The rough was the adjacent boulder field. There was no shade anywhere and there were no caddies, and no clubhouse and as far as we could see, no golfers either. We were not surprised and it suited our purpose admirably.

We found Jean-Luc standing outside a grass roofed structure, a couple of kilometres before the golf course and just beyond the outskirts of Magadi village, which slumbered in late morning torpor. A minibus was parked nearby. 'Bonjour, bienvenue!' he greeted us. Jean-Luc was a compact individual, fit looking, lantern jawed and he exuded an air of quiet competence. 'Come and meet my pilots and then you can meet the stars of the show.' The two pilots were Marcel and Erik. Marcel, tall and lean, was from France, Erik, who was small, saturnine, dark and bearded, lived in Senegal. Erik had once flown his microlight from France to Senegal following and filming migrating birds. Jean-Luc explained that the pelicans regarded the microlight as one of their flock and once it was airborne they would take off and follow it. Like many birds, such as geese, pelicans in a flock fly in a V formation, following a leader. The leader is not always the same. When the leader tires and falls back, another bird take his or her place. Likewise with the microlight. If the pilot throttles back, one of the pelicans will take its place as the microlight joins the back of the queue.

'Come and meet the birds,' said Jean-Luc, leading us to the square hut and opening the door. The interior was light and airy and inside, facing us like a classroom of expectant children, were the pelicans, staring with bright eager eyes at the newcomers. And, like school children at break time, they stampeded towards us, beaks open. Jean-Luc had a bag full of fish, and he tossed one into each gaping maw. But the pelicans were not just pleased to be fed. They seemed to be genuinely glad to see us. They came crowding forwards, beaks open, demanding that we scratch the inside of their massive beaks. With their immaculate snowy plumage, black-tipped wings, questing obsidian eyes and lemon yellow pouch and bill, they were splendid birds.

'Scooby doo! Scooby doo! Viens ici!' called Jean-Luc, and one massive pelican, with a great whoosh of its enormous wings, launched itself into the air, barrelled over our heads, crash landed on the Frenchman's shoulder and began to gently nibble his ear. We were suitably impressed. But I remembered that I was here to carry out health checks on the birds prior to their return to France. So we caught and examined each of the twelve pelicans, from Aristide to Zola, from Camille to Scooby Doo. We opened their beaks, peered down their throats, lifted their wings, checked for parasites, examined their webbed feet, shone a torch into their eyes, auscultated their lungs and hearts, lifted their tails, scrutinized their fundaments and watched them as they pottered about, prodding at our footwear or just staring up at us, a scrutinising look of avian curiosity on their long white faces.

'Right, Jean-Luc, that's OK. Now if they were horses I would ask to have them trotted up to check for lameness, so the equivalent in this case is for me to see them flying.'

'D'accord,' said Jean-Luc. ' The micro-lights are ready at the first fairway. Marcel can go up in the first micro-light, the birds will follow, you can see them take off and if you wish, your wife, the so attractive Bernadette, can go with Erik in number two.' 'Sounds just the job,' I said. Jean-Luc opened the door of the shed and out the pelicans waddled. The back door of the mini-bus was open and the seats had been removed. 'Au camion! Au camion!' said Jean-Luc and in they all hopped. Pelicans are not noted for their ability to walk long distances. We also hopped into the camion and Jean-Luc drove to the first fairway which was long and hard. Here he stopped. All the pelicans hopped out and waited expectantly while the micro-lights were prepared for take-off.

Jean-Luc explained that Marcel would take off, circle and do a low run over the fairway at which point the pelicans would launch themselves into the air and follow him and at the same time Erik would also launch himself and passenger and follow the flock. The microlight's pilot sat in front. Behind him at a slightly higher altitude sat the passenger, who might also be doing any filming and behind the passenger was a sort of chicken mesh wire cage to protect him or her from what looked like a giant fan which propelled the machine. There was no canopy or windscreen and only a flimsy lap belt to prevent any inadvertent exit. Jean-Luc, being French and therefore well versed in the seductive arts, turned to Berna and with a bow and a winning smile asked her if she would like to accompany Erik.'Enchanté,' replied Berna, hiding any nervousness she might have felt. 'You,' Jean-Luc said, turning to me, 'can go up next, after you have seen how ze birds fly.' Berna clambered into the rear seat and fastened what appeared to be a rather flimsy seat belt. Erik handed her a headset before climbing into the front seat. 'Excuse me,' asked Berna, ' you have the controls to hang on to. What do I hang on to?' Erick grinned. 'You can 'old on to ze shoulders of ze pilote!'

Marcel started his engine, gunned the motor and within seconds was airborne and rising rapidly. Soon he was a tiny buzzing dot in the cloudless sky. He banked, turned to the left, descended and turned again until he was flying low over us. I watched the pelicans, and as Marcel passed slowly overhead, they gathered themselves and running clumsily forwards to gain momentum, opened their enormous wings and were airborne, following Marcel. Erick followed suit, Berna gave me a wave and very soon the sky was empty. I turned to Jean-Luc. 'They've all passed with flying colours!' Fifteen minutes later Marcel appeared, followed by his little flock. Marcel's landing was expert and professional with a very short landing run of a few yards. Pelicans are used to landing on water so their landing was amateurish and chaotic with more than one nosedive and somersault. But they all scrambled to their feet and gathered around Jean-Luc for a fish treat.

'How was it?' I asked Berna as she climbed down. 'Wonderful! Eye-wateringly wonderful.' And so it was when it was my turn. Erick was skilful and bold. Take-off run, a spurt of a few yards and we were airborne, climbing fast, head set muffling the racket of the propeller at my back. No cabin, no windscreen, no restricting harness, just the rush of invigorating air, two thousand feet to the baking soda flats of Lake Magadi to the north, Lake Natron to the south in Tanzania, west to the forested heights of the Nguruman Escarpment, where Berna and I had hired donkeys from a Maasai manyatta, drunk milky tea, chatted with the elders and their wives and gone off up into the hills where we camped and met ochered moran and saw cheetah and oryx and baboons, bathed in crystal clear streams and listened to the birds. To the east was the brooding mass of Shompole, the long extinct volcano, steep, sharp ridges choked with wild sisal, cactus and elephant grass on which five attempts were made before the summit was finally attained, largely on hands and knees. Lions grunting in the swamp below, eagles soaring on the thermals above. God, I thought, what wonderful country! Life here is real and electric, sharp and bonefine, no softness, no round corners, but clean cut and hard and unforgiving and marvellous.

''allo! 'allo!' Erick was in the intercom. 'zere are some wildebeests on the edge of ze river and one looks an albino. Shall we go down and 'ave a look?' 'Go for it,' I bellowed back. So down we went in one great swooping curve, until we were less than a hundred feet over the galloping herd as they followed the line of the curving river. And sure enough one animal was white, quite unlike the rest which were their normal slate grey with black tufty tails. We followed them for a while before they wheeled in a half circle and doubled back in the opposite direction. Erick pulled back on the stick until we were up at a thousand feet. On the edge of Lake Magadi we could see a pink drift of flamingos. Erick banked sharply to avoid a circling vulture, so close I could look into the sharp, penetrating eyes as it turned its long snake-like neck to give us the drop-dead look of the professional scavenger.

We were now directly over the golf course. Far below I could see the mini-bus with a pair of tiny figures standing beside it. 'Right,' said Erick, 'down we go,' and cut the engine. We dropped like a falling leaf, in slow, sharp circles, in silence. This wasn't like spinning an aircraft when you suddenly drop and turn with adrenalin pumping speed, knowing that if you don't correct that spin in good time it's going to be bodybag time in short order. The microlight's big canopy acted like a parachute and compared to a plane the microlight was very light so our descent was slow and controlled. Erick brought the microlight into line with the fairway and touched down. We rolled a few yards and stopped.

It was time to go. I wrote a report indicating that the pelicans were fit to travel. We shook hands with Jean-Luc, Marcel and Erick, waved to the birds, climbed into the Peugeot and set off on the long drive back to Nakuru. Dust hung in the air, softening the harsh landscape. As we approached the ravine we had passed on the way down, an old Maasai shuffling along the road flagged us down. We stopped. 'Soba,' I said. 'Eba,' he replied. 'Dagunyo,' I responded, to which he gave the ritual answer 'Igo.' Preliminaries over, he made his expected request – 'Naweza saidia kubeba mimi paka Ngong? – Can you give me a lift as far as Ngong?' 'Sawa, ingia,' I said 'OK, get in.' He gave us a snaggle toothed grin. There were certain rules we followed when giving lifts to unknown pedestrians – a single woman or a woman and child, no problem, a single man probably OK, but make sure he is out in the open with no hidden companion lurking hidden in a nearby bush, a single man with a spear OK, with a gun no, more than one no go. The same probably goes for other parts of the world.

Out in the sticks, or the 'bundu' as we call it in Kenya, people not uncommonly wave you down, asking for water, which, if you have a surplus, you may feel pressed to give and you may, but carefully, or you may be overwhelmed by the sudden rush of an impi of the desperate and thirsty, who have failed in their forward thinking to carry sufficient for their requirements. This I discovered on many a mountain foray in which I would end up watering our 'guides' to my own detriment when they failed to carry enough for their own needs. How my kidneys have survived this long I do not know. In terms of giving lifts in other African countries such as the Congo, Nigeria and even South Africa, it is probably wiser to step on the gas and ignore any dubious entreaties to stop.

But our old Maasai was a rural gentleman of the old school. Down in the ravine flocks of sheep and goats were being driven homewards by small boys. We could hear the tinkle of goat bells and a cacophony of bleating as the animals scaled paths out of the ravine, led by a large imperious bellwether goat. The small boys appeared and, being polite Maasai boys, came across and, recognizing us as elders, bent their heads so that we could lay a kindly hand upon them, rather like a country priest blessing his flock. In the adjacent bush we could hear the accelerating coo coo coos of the wonderfully named emerald spotted wood dove. Late afternoon and the land was at rest, bathed in a benign, but deceptive and temporary peace. Come darkness and nocturnal carnivores, two and four-legged, would emerge to search, to find and to feed. In the main, most, including Man, were merely following their natural instincts. Only in Man, did these instincts ever overcome natural rational sense. Which was why, when unthinking, ignorant oafs referred to criminals and child molesters as 'animals' I would protest. No 'wild' animal would ever act in such a way.

We set off up the long hill towards Corner Baridi. On the way we chatted to our passenger – about his family, his cattle, the grazing, the lack of rain, the lions and hyenas eating the stock and what was the serikali (govt.) going to do about it? He was clad in an old red blanket, his ears were looped and laden with copper ornaments, and on his feet he had worn leather sandals. A warm earthy, bovine, milky aroma enveloped him and made us think of family, friends and a welcoming homestead. An old chum of ours, long resident in Kenya and now exiled in chilly England once wrote during an especially inclement winter that he longed for the smell of the Maasai and the reek of the Naivasha drains! Such are the senses which bring memories to vivid breathing life. At Ngong we dropped off our aged passenger, who expressed his deep gratitude. Closing both his hands he said 'Mungu awabariki! God bless you!' which was like receiving a benediction. Kenya is a deeply religious country and such expressions are common, but no less deeply meant and, whether expressed in the vernacular, in English or in Arabic – 'baraka Allahu fik' – they always left one feeling, whether a believer or not, humbled and singled out and personally protected by the guardian angels summoned by the speaker.

On the old dirt road to Mogotio. Morning. Sky blue. Warm breeze. A flash of black and white and out of an overhead acacia zooms a great sparrowhawk, whips an unsuspecting pigeon off the branch on which it was quietly dozing and lands in the verge beside the car, prey gripped in its talons. The bird glares at us, furious and raging at our presence. We can see a flutter of grey feathers as its doomed meal struggles to free itself from the hawk's razor sharp grip. I remember sitting on my veranda having breakfast when a great sparrowhawk shot by, a struggling chicken held fast in one taloned foot. I almost cheered. Unkind, perhaps, but it is always gratifying when you see something done well, especially in the fast diminishing natural world where the domestic normally outguns the wild. We watch the pigeon-pouncing raptor. I put the car in gear. The bird still stares as us, unblinking, with ferocious concentration, willing us to leave. We do.

I was on the way to a Greek-owned sisal estate to examine some goats which the owner had recently bought at an auction at Marigat near Lake Baringo. Once a year the President, who came from the area, held a huge auction there of sheep and goats, which were then taken by their buyers to all corners of the country. It seemed that none of these animals were ever inspected prior to sale to determine that they were free of disease and sure enough every year after the auction there were outbreaks of infections far and wide, usually of Contagious Caprine Pleuro-pneumonia in the goats. It was almost guaranteed. So when the owner, one Christof Yarinakis, told me that his recent acquisitions were coughing and dying in large numbers I had a pretty good idea of what to expect.

The road was rough, deep in dust, pitted with potholes and washboarded with corrugations. Progress was slow. We skirted the unlovely outskirts of Mogotio where unwashed infants howled at us as we passed, where fat mamas presided over mountains of water melons, where women beat laundry to death on the rocky banks of the Molo River and where men squatted in the shade watching the world and us go by. The road followed the line of the river as it wound its way towards distant Lake Baringo. On our right spiky green rows of sisal stretched south to the foot of Menengai Crater and encircled the swamp of Ol Punyata. The growing of sisal in East Africa was a preserve of the Greek community, as sawmills and timber were that of the Sikhs.

We turned onto the estate track. I had been on this track before, on the way to treat sick cattle. On that occasion over the brow of a small hill, at full tilt, had come what appeared to be a reincarnation of Erwin Rommel, in full Afrika Corps gear. The vehicle, a stripped down jeep, had no doors or windscreen, it was battered beyond belief, it was covered in mud and dust, the exhaust gave out a throaty roar, and seated behind the steering wheel was a lean, desperate-looking individual, wearing a pair of huge Teutonic goggles, clad in well worn field khaki and with sinewy arms the colour of hundred year old teak. The jeep screeched to a stop raising a huge cloud of dust.

When it finally cleared I was able to identify the driver as no less than Mr John Perrett, friend of long standing and whom those readers who have got this far, will have met. 'John,' I said, 'what are you doing here?' 'Working for the old Greek. Talking to the plants in a quiet encouraging voice in an effort to make them grow. Putting in time before we move up to Rumuruti to make our fortune from camels and rabbits.' 'Rabbits?' I said. 'Yes,' replied John, 'there's a market out there for rabbit meat and rabbit skins. The watu will gobble them up. We're building a rabbitoreum as we speak. Come down to my shack and have a Tusker and I'll tell you all about it.'

I did, the cold Tusker was just what I needed after a couple of hours in the sun looking at the old Greek's cattle, but the rabbits failed to prosper and the rabbitoreum remained, a bizarre, honey-combed structure, beside the Rumuruti Maralal road, yet another monument to a well meant wheeze to tap into the local market. All across Africa you will come across these reminders that what may do perfectly well in Europe or America may not, and in many cases, certainly will not, work in Africa. Use, possibly adapt, what has been there for millennia, and you won't go far wrong.

Christof, who turned out to be a young, compact, well-fleshed Greek, was waiting in the yards as we drove up. Behind him in a bone dry paddock was a flock of white and brown goats. Christof and I shook leathery hands. 'So,' I said,' when did you buy these goats and how many did you buy?' 'Got them ten days ago and almost before I got them here they were coughing and now seven have turned up their toes out of the forty I bought. There were hundreds, maybe thousands, of goats for sale and Mzee (the President) was there himself, supervising the whole thing' 'OK,' I said, 'Let's have a look and pm a couple.' The affected animals were standing around in a listless fashion, some had a nasal catarrh while others were coughing. Goats have an innate curiosity to investigate their surroundings but these animals were thin and dull and apathetic. I listened to their lungs and in many I could hear little. It seemed as though no air was getting into the chest. 'Right,' I said, ' let's post mortem a couple.'

I had bought a flick knife off a chap in Nakuru's main street and was keen to try it out. I zipped open the carcases from sternum to pubis – the knife passed muster – and knelt down in the warm dust to have a closer look. The lungs in all animals were swimming in a sea of clear yellow fluid, there were deposits of straw-coloured material covering parts of the lungs and there were adhesions between lung and chest wall. 'So,' I grunted, 'let's take a lung out and have a closer shufti.' I removed one and cut across it. My new knife was razor sharp but this was like sawing through an old cabbage. It was hard and consolidated. 'This,' I said the Christof, 'is CCPP and these goats were infected before you ever bought them. The incubation period is 3-4 weeks so no way could they have been infected on your premises. And being got from an auction run by the President you've got no come back. So all we can do is to inject all the rest with Tylosin Tartrate and hope for the best. Too late for any vaccination. This is what I suspected so I brought the dawa with me. So let's get on with it.' 'What about my sheep?' asked Christof. 'No, no, this infection only targets goats. You can house sheep and infected goats together. The sheep will remain healthy.'

So we injected all of the goats. 'Repeat daily for three days and keep me in the picture.' 'Ah many thanks, doctor, now before you take that arduous journey back to Nakuru join me in a glass of ouzu, please. My wife, she is in Greece, visiting her mama so I am here all alone. So, please!' I glanced at my watch, 4pm. Just a glass, no harm in that. None whatsoever. 'Well, many thanks.' By the time Christof had produced his bouzuki, did his Zorba the Greek impersonation, more than one glass of the national drink had been tossed down the little red road and I was beginning to see double and the room to sway from side to side in rather pleasing rocking fashion. I closed my eyes and when I opened them Christof appeared to have two heads. 'Time to go, old chap,' I said and lurched from my seat to the upright position. Christof was now standing at the top of a steep incline peering down at me with an anxious expression on his two faces. In slo-mo I crept carefully towards him. By the time I reached him he had only one head. I grasped his hand, wrung it fervently, thanked him profusely and stepping gingerly towards my car, got in, waved and drove away. Kip, who had been waiting while I caroused with Christof, gave me what I regarded as an unwarranted searching look. I ignored him.

The drive of 45 minutes on rough dirt road to the tarmac was in my favour. By the time we rolled onto semi-smooth bitumen I was almost sober. The last few miles had been a bit of a trial as it had begun to rain and as is usual in Africa when it rains it really means it and it comes down full force accompanied by peals of deafening thunder and vivid forks of lightning. So I was all over the place as I fought to stay out of the ditch. But having a pint of neat ouzu in circulation had its definite benefits. I was really relaxed. No tensing up or expostulating when we went into what seemed an unstoppable skid or slide into a bottomless pit. A gentle twitch on the wheel and we were again on course.

But as we approached Nakuru the storm grew ever more violent, until I could barely see where I was going. The rain thundered down. On either side fields of ripe maize were being flattened. Wipers going full time I crawled along. The windscreen misted up. I opened my side window to help clear it and was almost instantly soaked. 'Look out!' yelled Kip. A tree came crashing down, just off the road. Then it began to hail. The noise of the hailstones on the roof of the car was deafening. We snaked into town, aiming for the surgery. Open mouthed we stared at drifts of hail floating down Kenyatta Avenue. On the pavements the hail lay six inches deep. The storm was easing and people were out gazing in amazement at the sight. In the Club opposite the surgery trees were down and the surgery itself was flooded. Took us an hour to sweep out the water.

One morning later that week the phone rang. It was Kwanda from Kongoy farm. 'Jambo, daktari, habari ya asubuhi?' Good morning doctor, how are you?' 'Mzuri sana,' I replied – 'Very well.' No matter how bad you might feel, no matter how awful the situation might be, one always said 'mzuri sana.' It wasn't form to transfer your woes to another party – they had enough of their own to deal with. But it is also a fact that Africans on the whole are innately optimistic, smiling, rarely complaining and accepting many of life's calamities as the will of God, Kismet, Inshallah. 'Fisi liua farasi wawili usiku na likula yeye. Naweza kuja kuandika barua ya insurance?' Hyenas have killed and eaten two horses during the night. Can you come and sign their insurance papers?' 'Yes,' I said and put the phone down.

A few minutes later the phone rang again. 'Dr Cran? Inspector Macharia from CID here.' Oh shit. I thought. What now? 'I understand you are a representative of the British High Commission. Well, we have one of your parishioners here at the Central Police Station. Please come.'

'What's the problem?'

'You just come.'

So I went. The Central Police Station, or indeed any other police station in Kenya, was not a place I relished visiting. Outside were dozens of wrecked vehicles rusting and rotting in the sun. On the steps were lounging constables toting an array of weaponry, everything from pistols to rifles to submachine guns. Knots of ragged petitioners stood, gathered to discover what had happened to friends and relations arrested or incarcerated. No one paid you any attention. Inside, the prevailing impression was one of gloom and an all-pervading atmosphere of threat. Bare bulbs hung from the ceiling. Formerly whitewashed walls were now a dirty grey. On a low bench sat a despondent row of manacled prisoners. They had reason for their despondency. From time to time one would be frogmarched into a nearby room and the door closed. Thumps, shouts and screams followed entry. I took my place at the high desk for attention along with several other nervous-looking applicants. Finally, a bulbous policewoman with three pips on her sleeve caught my eye – 'Wewe, mzungu, nataka nini hapa?' You, whiteman, what do you want here?' Politely I informed her that I had come to see Inspector Macharia. 'You wait,' she said. A few minutes later a smartly uniformed officer appeared. He looked out of place in his dilapidated surroundings. 'Dr Cran? Please follow me.'

As we walked along dingy corridors and down broken flights of stairs he told me why he had phoned me. His story was long and involved. An Englishman, one John Stallard, had arrived in the country and had been living with friends, the Niederbachers, Franz and Monica, at Gilgil, where his brother had left his Discovery Land Rover. John had fallen into bad company and in his cups had promised to sell the Discovery, without authority, to an army officer based at Gilgil barracks and had accepted a substantial deposit. When he failed to produce the vehicle on demand he fled to Nakuru where he holed up in Bondeni, a slum area abutting the lake.

Here he dwelt with one Mary Macgregor. My ears pricked up. This must be the half-caste daughter of Roddy, whom I had known well, before he was killed when he drove one night into the back of an unlit tractor when returning to his farm near Turi. 'Mmm,' I said, 'I know the Niederbachers, clients of mine, and I knew Mary's father. What next?'

'The army officer contacted the police. One evening a constable tracked Mr Stallard to his house in Bondeni and knocked on the door. The officer was wearing spectacles. Mr Stallard opened the door. When the constable informed Mr Stallard the reason for his presence Mr Stallard punched him in the face, breaking his specs and cutting his cheek. Stallard was arrested, charged with assault and battery on a police officer, resisting arrest, theft, and deceit on an officer of the Kenya Army. He has been remanded in custody.'

By this time we were at the bottom of the stairs and in a basement below the police station. We entered a long dark cavern with a passageway running along the middle. The place stank of shit, sweat and stale urine. The cells on either side were packed with bodies. Arms reached out to us through the bars. The inspector wielded his swagger stick to good effect, cracking fingers and wrists. I searched amid the sea of heaving heads for sign of a European. Then I saw a thin white arm raised above the mob. 'Stallard!' I shouted. A figure struggled through the mob and clasped the bars with bony fingers.

Stallard did not look in good shape. He was unshaven and on his forehead glistened a thin film of sweat.

'You've got to get me out of here,' he gasped.

'Well,' said the inspector, 'I'll leave you to it.'

'How long have you been in here?' I asked. 'Ten days and it feels like ten years.

I hear that they are threatening to send me up to the prison. I'll never survive that. It's bad enough in here. The food, if you can call it that, is awful, we have to sleep on the floor – I haven't had a wink for days, and don't mention the toilet facilities because there are none.

But at least the cops keep an eye on you. It won't be the same up there. My case comes up next week. So, please help. I know I've been a fool, but it wasn't premeditated.'

'Well,' I said, 'I'll see what I can do.' As I walked out, dodging the clawing fingers, I thought of all the other cases in which I had been involved since I had rather rashly volunteered to be a Consular Warden for the British High Commission in Nairobi. Apart from all the routine stuff like registering all the Brits resident in my area, which stretched from Nakuru to the Ethiopian border, there were suicides to deal with, broken bodies to identify in the local mortuary (a place which stank like a sewer and was manned by leering, drunken, rapacious ghouls) visiting the sick in hospital, whether ancient senile locals or tourists injured in road accidents, burials at the decrepit cemetery, cremations on the burning ghats down by the lake to be arranged and attended – I lost count of the number of corpses I saw go up in smoke – and keeping tabs on the local security situation and liaising with Nairobi. In return I received a yearly invitation to a Queen's Birthday bash at the High Commissioner's stately residence at Muthaiga and the occasional rap over the knuckles for exceeding my remit. You must never ever put yourself in harm's way, I was told. Really? I put myself in harm's way every time I turned onto the tarmac from where I lived. And another thing. Whatever you do – do not give advice. You are not trained to do that. We don't know the answers either, but we will direct people to the relevant website so they can sort things out for themselves while we make arrangements for our next diplomatic beano. The stock pavlovian response to virtually any query was to 'refer to the website.' It drove me mad.

I took a great lungful of polluted Nakuru air as I emerged from the copshop. It was polluted with the smoke from thousands of charcoal stoves, from the diesel emissions from the trucks as they barrelled through on their way to Uganda, the Congo and Rwanda, and from the exhalations of the slums eating their way south to the shores of the lake, but it was cleaner than the foetid atmosphere within the police station.

I contacted a friendly lawyer and he gave some helpful advice. I next phoned the British High Commission and gave them chapter and verse, including the fact that Stallard had a return ticket back to the UK, a valid passport and a sister willing to help, the brother having washed his hands of him. I also spoke to a couple of influential Africans. So by dint of subtle pressure, a phone call from the Consul and a light oiling of the requisite palms, Stallard was released on bail and told to report to the police station on a daily basis. His sister in the UK was a royal pain. She phoned me on an infuriatingly regular basis, wanting to know how her brother was and when he would be allowed to return. All very well, except that she was seemingly ignorant of the fact that from October till March Kenya is three hours ahead of Hounslow or Slough or whatever ghastly place she had decided to set down roots. So when she decided that 11pm was an appropriate time to call me, it was 2am in my bed in Nakuru. Why she deemed that this was a reasonable time to call was not revealed. This went on for weeks. Finally a settlement, mostly financial, was reached. Its intricacies were complex and Machiavellian, but the various parties, apart from the brother, seemed to be satisfied. Stallard was fined and deported, the army officer was placated both financially and materially, and both judge and constable benefitted according to rank.

But long before this came to pass, I drove in the afternoon on day one to Kongoy to inspect the remains of the horses eaten by the hyenas. I met Kwanda at the stable yard and told him the reason why I was so late. 'Hakuna maneno,' he said. No problem. He smiled his toothy grin. The horses, both old, had been grazing high on the farm, and were not stabled at night. We found the bodies next to a ravine, an ideal place for hyenas to hole up. The carcases had been eaten clean. There was no smell. A fresh breeze bent the tall yellow grass, small birds rose fluttering into the air, a steinbok bounded away, in the far distance I could see the lake and, behind, the town and the rounded mass of Menengai. This had once been all Maasai land. But they had never lingered here. They knew that cattle grazed on the seemingly lush pastures did not thrive. Their land was appropriated by the red strangers from the north. The new owners wondered why their stock failed to put on weight, not knowing that the land between the lakes Nakuru and Elementaita was deficient in copper and cobalt. I could imagine the Maasai watching from where I stood, leaning on their spears, eyes narrowed against the sun, their women holding their laden donkeys, as the first white settlers encroached onto what had been theirs for centuries, before moving on, away from the future and the unwelcome intruders. My own heart ached for what had been lost. In my mind's eye I could see the vast yellow plain, dotted with zebra and antelope and giraffe, scattered thorn trees, not a house not a fence not a road to be seen, a small manyatta in the far distance, all backdropped by the dark forested wall of the Rift Valley.

A few weeks later I was called to a large farm on the north shore of Lake Naivasha. Coming towards me as I drove in was a span of oxen drawing a long heavy cart. The oxen were of different colours – black, brindle, cream, chestnut and grey. Walking beside the cart, holding a long heavy whip trailing in the dust, was an old African, a battered slouch hat on his grizzled head. As he approached I realized that he was calling to the oxen in Afrikaans. 'Ach! Koos!' crack went his whip. 'Maak gou, Vlooi!' Again his whip cracked. I stopped. He stopped. 'Gouie dag, baas!' 'Good morning, sir.' We spoke in Swahili. He was very old, so old he told me that he had no idea when he had been born. Except that it was when the fierce settlers from South Africa still lived and farmed near Eldoret and had taught him how to break and train oxen to plough and draw carts. He was a fine old fellow. We talked while the oxen stood patiently in the manner of oxen. 'Kwa heri, mzee,' goodbye old man. 'Totsiens baas.' Goodbye, sir.

We shall not see his like again.

Chapter Twenty Five

'AND NICANOR LAY DEAD IN HIS HARNESS'

On my occasional trips to the UK there were a couple of things which always took me by surprise. After living so long in Africa surrounded by Africans and sometimes going for days and weeks without seeing another European I was always surprised on landing in London to discover just how many white people were left in the world. I had got to the stage where I was under the impression that we had become yet another Endangered Species. Seemingly not so. I was, and remain, undecided whether this was a good thing or not.

The other thing which intrigued me was the number of old, grey and white haired people around, hobbling, leaning on walking sticks, poling themselves along with trekking tools, supporting themselves on Zimmer frames, zipping along on powered buggies, nestling in wheelchairs and, very occasionally, moving under their own steam. There seemed to an endless supply of these apparently live, aged and infirm ancients of either sex. Upon reflection I realized that, in Africa, your chances of sprouting grey hairs were poor to middling. After all, if the average life span in a country is, say, 45, then only the very odd exception would appear tonsured in grey and they would be regarded as being as old as Methuselah. The average lifespan in Kenya was about 60, so a good deal less than that in the 'west.' No, the reason you didn't see many old people was due to the fact that the majority had handed in their pails at a relatively young age.

Many of our European friends in Africa had bitten the dust before their expected time. There had been no drawn-out lingering, no aimless pottering in the garden in Tunbridge Wells waiting for the Grim Reaper to come knocking. And of those who were still alive, many were only so by the grace of God, having had as many close shaves as we had had. Cancer and disease had removed a few but for many the end was violent and quick. The same went for Africans, who died from infections such as malaria, AIDS, and TB but also from road accidents, cattle raids and criminal violence. In the General Hospital in Nakuru one ward was entirely devoted to treating victims of motorbike accidents. When driving on Kenya's roads to come across an accident with a body still lying warm and motionless on the road was nothing unusual. Once I was driving behind a pick-up in which a number of people were seated. Suddenly, without warning, a woman stood up and stepped off. She hit the tarmac with hideous force. Her head split open, spilling blood and brains behind her as her body skated across the road.

In a relatively small population of Europeans in Kenya, the number known to us who had not died in their beds was extraordinarily high. Everyone has heard of how George Adamson was murdered in Kora National Reserve, how his wife Joy was murdered in Shaba, Julie Ward in the Mara and Joan Root at Naivasha. But there were many more, good friends of ours. Both Rick Hopcraft and Simon Combes, the former had been a professional hunter, the latter a world renowned painter of wildlife, had been killed by buffalo. Gilfrid Powys had been killed on his ranch on Laikipia by an elephant. Marco Villa, one-armed and hunting alone in the swamps surrounding Lake Naivasha, had been killed by a buffalo. Howard Henley had been killed by a hippo while duck shooting in the swamps of Lake Ol Bolossat. He was only 18. All of these would have accepted the risks and agreeed that, if the worse came to the worst, this was an honourable way to go.

Not so if you were done to death by some pombe-smelling thug wielding an axe or panga. Gentle, artistic Hobo Swift was one morning, while painting a canvas in his studio in Subukia, cut down by an axe and died a few days later. Dick Crawford was one evening hacked to the floor by an intruder armed with a panga. Sliced on the head he did not die immediately but might as well have done as he remained brain damaged and demented until he died, praying for death, a few years later. Charlie Stonewigg crossed the line by dallying with a female member of his house staff. Early one morning the husband, armed with the ubiquitous agricultural panga, murdered him as he lay in his bed in Gilgil. In none of these cases was anyone brought to book.

A little higher up the scale was death by the bullet. Cleaner, more surgical and, one hoped, less disfiguring. Johnny D'Olier was shot dead by Maasai bandits in the Masai Mara Game Reserve. Others in the party were winged and wounded. Tristan Voorspuy and his horse were shot by a Pokot raider on his ranch on Laikipia during the 2017 land invasions. Mike Javens was shot dead during a break-in at Kericho on the tea estate he was managing. Peter Jackson, aged 19, was killed during a Turkana raid on a Pokot homestead where he had spent the night. A woman and child were also killed. Peter had not been the target but happened to be in the path of a retaliatory raid.

To be killed in a plane crash was a tragedy but was regarded as being higher in the rankings than a car crash in that in most cases either you were personally responsible for your death by making some cardinal error of judgement, or that you were overcome by the forces of Nature or struck down by a Supreme Being. So perished David Francombe while flying a spray plane in a storm over the jungles of the Congo, Tiger Tim from Timau who vanished into the dark forests of the Aberdares, likewise the father of Mike Vaughn-Ryall, and George Aggett from Rumuruti, whose plane crashed and burned on take-off at Naivasha.

Both of our friends Mike Hughes and Ian Napier were killed in car accidents.

And of course there were others, less well known to us – Joanna Stutchbury, environmentalist, shot in Nairobi, Esmond Bradley

Martin, passionate campaigner for the rhino and elephant, stabbed to death in Nairobi. And then there is the mysterious murder of Tonio Trzebinski, shot in the suburb of Karen in Nairobi, and still unsolved after 21 years.

The newly appointed head of Greensteds School, on the outskirts of Nakuru, was stunned to learn that his son, currently visiting the island of Lamu, had been stabbed to death while on the beach near Shela. He immediately resigned and returned whence he came. Alf Gould, valiant veteran of conflicts in Palestine and Somalia, had a small farm at Gilgil. He had had some sort of trivial argument with his tractor driver over a piece of land. The following day the tractor driver attempted to run Alf over. Alf, no longer in his prime, managed to jump out of the way. The next day Alf suffered a heart attack and died.

John Elliot, another friend, lived with his wife Patty in a remote house on the banks of the Malewa River. John was a lovely chap, kind, hospitable, courteous and considerate to everyone, black and white. They had no children but owned a plethora of labradors as John was keen on bird shooting. One warm evening, mist rising from the river, nightjars churring, cicadas buzzing, frogs croaking in the reeds. Sudden silence. The sound of pounding feet, a rush at the door, which bursts open. Dogs bark. John tries to grab his shotgun to repel the intruders. There is a scuffle, a struggle, there is an explosion. John's lower jaw is blown off. The attackers flee. John survived to spend months in hospital, endured countless operations, but remained a sad deformed remnant of his former self. We were lucky, in that in all of our time in Africa we were never personally attacked or even threatened. Ironically, the only time I have been mugged was in Australia, where I was attacked by a gang of aborigines in the town of Bourke in western New South Wales.

In Africa people do not, on the whole, dwell on death, they do not spend days and weeks dissecting and probing the reasons why this or that happened. Death is accepted as part of life. 'His time was up.' 'It was God's will.' 'Shauri ya Mungu.' All the people we had known and who had been taken so precipitously had lived their lives to the full. There had been no time to rust or wither and decay. So for me they were always in their prime, no matter at what age they went. A friend taken like that is always a friend. He remains a friend. He cannot change. I can, as clear as day, see myself sitting in dear old Hobo's lounge with his wife Marian, the 'Ayatollah', having tea after pregnancy-testing their cattle at Subukia, I can hear Mike Hughes' booming laugh when he made a joke in the Men's Bar in the Rift and can see George Aggett pushing open the batwing doors of the surgery, a conspiratorial grin betokening a session putting the world to rights.

But, when I looked at Berna and our three daughters, or went to the supermarket to buy groceries and saw some lovely African girl, tall, narrow waisted, with huge eyelashes and long slender black fingers like a work of art, and looked around at all the other splendid Africans, honey-coloured, charcoal and matt, I prayed that God would stay His hand.

Chapter Twenty Six

ROMPING WITH THE RENDILLE

I had climbed in the Alps, the Andes and the Himalayas. I had been to Darfur in the far west of Sudan to climb Jebel Marra, to the Congo to scale Nyaragongo, to Uganda to climb Margherita, the highest peak in the Ruwenzoris, to Rwanda to nip up Karisimbi, to Tanzania to go the top of Kilimanjaro and to Ethiopia to trudge up Ras Dashan. Plus several others, mostly active volcanoes in the Indonesian archipelago. But for my mind the best by far were not these name-dropping monsters but the lower, mostly unknown, and little frequented, summits in Kenya's north.

To get to the summit of a high mountain is a personal achievement, but the higher you get, you realise, the less life there is. The scenery may be spectacular but something is missing. The slopes become more and more barren. A few hardy mammals and birds eke out a precarious existence. Rock hyrax in Africa and marmots in the Himalayas squeak at you as you toil upwards. Eagles and ravens peer down superciliously at your puny attempts to invade their domain. Once you reach the snowline on an ice mountain or the scree slopes on a volcano, your panting frame is likely to be the only life around and even more likely to be on the ebb.

But a lower mountain may be equally imposing and far more rewarding to climb. The vegetation may be more prolific, as may the wildlife. There is more likely to be water, with people living at the foot of the mountain. With the inevitable and inexorable creep of roads, schools, missions, government facilities, hospitals, filling stations, and police posts across the more accessible parts of what once had been 'wilderness', mountainous areas and remote deserts have become the only surviving remnants of what the land had once been, with people living a form of life long lost to the majority.

The setting up of national parks, conservation areas and game reserves and the exclusion of the former inhabitants is an admission of defeat. Population increase and 'progress' have won. Yes, they are there to protect the remnants of the species which once roamed a much greater area but their prime task is as much to keep Man, especially poor Man, out as to keep the animals in. Is it any wonder that they are regarded as irrelevant to many Africans, who are more likely to see a lion or an elephant on a television screen than in the 'wild'? And where Africans do live in proximity to game reserves, contact with large wild animals is more likely to be counter-productive then beneficial, with shambas being trashed by elephant and people killed by buffalo. There is insufficient room for both animals and Man; and Man will always win. In the long run most game parks and reserves will survive, but as exclusive enclaves, destinations for none but the super-rich, where the pampered few, clad in their 'safari' khaki, complete with pith helmets and attendant 'white hunter', will fly in to sip their gins and tonics and focus their zoom lenses on some bored lions and obese zebra.

But if you look hard enough and are prepared to forego the trappings of 'civilization' you can still find areas as yet unpolluted by the advancing emissaries of modernism. On the top of Poi, that huge rock monolith to the west of Ilaut, we found a lush green plateau of deep grass and a tiny Samburu manyatta. To the casual passer-by Poi looks utterly impregnable, surrounded by enormous 2,000 foot cliffs. But the Samburu had found a route, threading its way up the rear of the mountain to a veritable Shangri La for their sheep and goats to graze.

At Arsim, in the Ndotos, below the mountain Alimision, we had camped beneath a huge fig tree. The Samburu came and told us that while we stayed, this was our home. Children watched us quietly from a respectful distance. Beautiful women, all smiles and beads and necklaces, came and offered us milk and bracelets, blessing us. We were indeed blessed. The following night, benighted on the mountain without a tent, our two youthful Samburu guides, who actually knew almost as little about the route as we did, cut a grass bed for us, made sure we were well secured on the vertiginous slope, lit a fire and kept us as comfortable as it was possible to be under the circumstances. As dawn broke the sugar loaf mass of Poi was backlit by the rising sun. Small unseen birds twittered. Stiff, chilled and hungry, it did not take long to break camp. But you knew that in an hour or so it would be warm, even hot. As we slipped and slithered down to Arsim our two lads burst into song. Whether in expectation of an undeserved gratuity or that fact that they were going home, did not matter. They were happy and so were we.

At Cheblil, at the base of the Elgeyo-Marakwet Escarpment, we camped beside a clear stream falling from the plateau high above. A wedding party of Marakwet passed by. Next day was Christmas Eve. 'You must stay!' they insisted. 'We will slaughter a goat for you. Stay here with us for Christmas!' They were all smiles and laughter and their kindness was genuine and unforced. We were guests in their place and they honoured us. But, alas, the constraints of arrivals and departures, appointments and timetables, dictated that we depart. I wish that we had stayed.

In times of trouble the Ol Doinyo Mara range, east of the Horr Valley and to the south of Lake Rudolf, is a refuge for Samburu fleeing their age-old enemies, the Turkana. The Turkana, like the more effete Maasai to the south, are people of the plains. The Samburu seem to prefer the hills. My two brothers, one from Scotland and the other from Australia, had flown into the country and I decided that they should see a bit of unspoilt Kenya before the arrival of the bulldozers. We paused at the Somali tea shop in Baragoi to rehydrate and get the latest news. The news was that the Turkana had attacked the Samburu, killed a few and stolen their cattle, the Samburu had retaliated and now the rumour was that the Turkana were plotting yet another raid. In the past such raids did not do much harm as the combatants were armed with spears and simis. Now the AK47 was the weapon of choice and the death toll could be considerable. My brothers were concerned. I told them that apart from a slight risk of crossfire there was little to worry about. This was purely a tribal affair.

A night in South Horr and the following day saw us on the summit ridge of Mumusio at the southern end of Ol Doinyo Mara. We met a herdsman playing a solitary game of bao, the ancient board game found all over East Africa. The holes for the stones were cut in the rock on the ridge. He was playing against himself. His cattle were grazing nearby. A more spectacular site would be hard to find. In the far distance we could see the flash of water, Basso Narok, the Dark Lake, Rudolf, Lake Turkana, the Jade Sea. Across the Horr Valley rose the forested heights of Mt. Nyiro. Far below the eye was drawn to the green wriggle of the lugga and the streams which maintained the life of the valley. As we followed the line of the ridge and gazed over the wilderness to the east, our guide told us of an old man who lived in a manyatta – 'huuuko' – there! – pointing with his grizzled chin at a just visible thorn enclosure on a far distant barren hillside. Since he was born the old man had never left his home. There he had lived with his wives and children. He had never seen a European, set foot on tarmac or been to a city. I looked around me, saw the thorn-dotted hills, the yellow plains, the spiral of a dust devil, the misty far blue horizon, the vast sky and thought of a happy man, sitting amongst his sheep and goats, surrounded by his family, content with what he had, with utterly no need for the irrelevancies of the world beyond his view.

At the far end of the ridge there was an open plateau, dotted with Samburu cattle and their owners. We descended to South Horr by a steep, narrow path and met several armed men, moving with their stock to the higher pastures before the Turkana made their next move. We stopped to talk with them. All were friendly and willing to speak. My brother from Australia was taken aback by their openness and frank demeanour, so unlike, he said, that of his sad, repressed, depressed Aboriginal contacts.

A few weeks after we had left the Government decided that it was time to teach the Turkana a lesson. A contingent of newly-fledged police recruits, smartly clad in freshly ironed fatigues, wearing heavy brightly polished boots, weapons at the ready, descended on Baragoi. This would be a swift surgical operation, designed to bring those impudent savages to heel. A local Turkana was pressed into service to lead the lads to the locality of the hostiles. As this would be a short smart punitive strike, no need to burden ourselves with heavy water bottles. The Turkana, lightly clad in shuka and sandals, strode ahead. The squaddies stumbled behind. God, the sun is hot and my boots hurt. Seems a long way and where *are* those pesky Turks? I need a drink. We seem to be in some sort of valley with cliffs on either side, and where's that damned Turkana who's supposed to be showing us the way. Crack! Crack! Shit! Shit! We're under fire! No cover and where are they? At the top of those cliffs. Get back! Run away! Which is what they did. Over 40 police were killed, some by highly accurate long range sniper fire. Ambushed, most were mown down like rabbits. The wounded were finished off. Bodies were still being collected days later. The Turkanas melted away into the Suguta Valley.

血╳血╳血╳

About 10 miles north-west of the town of Laisamis a shark tooth of a mountain breaks the otherwise level plain. This is Holilogum Nder. I'd had it in my sights ever since we had passed it on the way back from climbing Poi. On that occasion we were in two vehicles, one of which had only one spare tyre. We had stopped to change the third of seven punctures, when two shots rang out. I looked at my companion, the redoubtable Graeme Watson. He looked at me. We both shrugged our shoulders. We were at the stage where if even if an impi had appeared from the bush we would have told them to go away and leave us alone. We had another 200 kilometres of corrugated track to cover before we hit the tarmac and were in no mood to deal with minor distractions.

But we both looked up at the mountain and decided that this would be a worthy objective. The summit was surrounded by vertical cliffs and look as we might we could see no easy route. Hours later, in darkness, we reached terra firma, the spare tyre had been beaten to death and the stricken vehicle limped into the frontier town of Isiolo on the bare rim.

A year later, coming back from Marsabit, where we had had the good fortune to see a hundred elephants at Lake Paradise, we came to a halt in Laisamis. Our vehicle was losing water. There was a mission at Laisamis. Berna, being a good Catholic, assured me that the good fathers there would tumble over each other in their efforts to render assistance to passing travellers. We also knew that these places usually have a workshop to service their vehicles. We drove up a rubbly track to the church on the hill. There was no sign of life. Wandering round the back we came across what we assumed to be the living quarters of the priests, a well-appointed red roofed house. I knocked on the door. No reply. Peering through a window I saw what I took to be an ecclesiast reclining in an armchair. Beside him was a small table on which stood a glass and a bottle. I tapped on the window. No response. I tapped harder. He looked up and very slowly raised himself and walked to the door, which he opened. He was short, but with his close cropped hair and pale skin he looked like a German or an Austrian.

He did not smile. Not a good sign.

'Good morning, father,' I said, 'I wonder if you can help us. Our vehicle is losing water...'

'No, no, nein! Help we cannot. We cannot help everzy passing tourist who comes here begging for help.' Tourist? What's he talking about? Do we look like tourists to this pallid pygmy? 'We are here to spread ze gospel to ze people.' I looked at the fleet of sparkling Land Cruisers parked in the mission garage and wondered what else was being done here to help ze local people, the Rendille, who anyway had their own religion to fall back on. Muttering, we trundled back down to the main plaza of Laisamis and parked, opened the bonnet and took stock of the small waterfall dripping onto the sand. Within a couple of minutes we were surrounded a crowd of the locals, some bedecked in gay apparel, others clad only in blanket and sandals, toddlers as bare as they were born, old hags with crusty eyes, giggling maidens. A few dogs slouched up to see what all the commotion was about. Crows hopped in the dust just out of range. Much advice and expertise were proffered. A few yards away was a large lorry emblazoned with the logo 'Marsabit Moran', although it had actually come from Moyale on the Ethiopian border. Protruding from under the lorry was a pair of oil stained be-trousered legs.

A few minutes later the owner of the legs, covered in dust and oil, eased himself out, rose to his feet and seeing us, came across to shake elbows. 'Habari! Harro! Do you have probrems? Me, I am mechanic and in dis lemote prace we mast all be helping each other. Eh?' Yes indeed I thought, thinking of the niggardly Teutonic divine squatting on his hill. 'Me my name is Samson and me I from West.' He meant Western Province so most likely he was a Luhya. 'So let us be rooking at de probrem.' While our new friend was sorting the probrem, a rather smartly dressed dude approached me, speaking excellent English, and introduced himself as Robert Dokhole. He was a Rendille and was working in a game conservancy near Isiolo. 'Robert,' I said, ' I want to climb Hololigum. Can you help? 'No problem,' he replied, no trouble with his Ls or Rs – 'My home is here in Laisamis, and the mountain is in Rendille land.'

As far as land was concerned the Rendille had drawn a short straw. Mostly desert stretching north from the Merille lugga to Marsabit, west to the Ndotos and north west to Lake Turkana, it is harsh, hot and windswept. Mountains are few. Only the low Losai Range, Moile, Baio and Hololigum rise above the desiccated plains. The Rendille are camel people, grazing their animals across the Kaisuit and Koroli Deserts, and the Korante Plain. They speak a language similar to Somali, although many can converse in Samburu. One theory is that the Rendille came from the north via the land of the Somalis from whom they separated and moved west. So the Somalis called them 'rertit' meaning rejected or separated. This name was misinterpreted by the colonial authorities who rendered it into 'Rendille.' There is a problem with this theory though, in that the word Rendille itself means the People of the Stick of God. What is certainly true is they have until recently rejected both Islam and to a certain extent, Christianity, worshipping a single god called Wakh, whose residence is the moon. Some of their customs are reminiscent of Jewish practices. It was all very confusing.

'My flend!' shouted Samson, 'me I have fixed de probrem. De water pipe from radiator to engine it was so split water it was leaking out. But now I have replaced pipe and you are fit to go.' I thanked him profusely, paid him for his services and asked him where we might get a beer. It was baking hot. 'Forrow me, my flend.' I beckoned to Robert and with Berna we entered a low fly-blown shack which advertised itself as the 'Online Hotel.' It was almost as hot inside as out but at least we were in the shade. We sat on a rickety wooden bench and drank our tepid beers and rested. By the time we were ready to go the four of us, had, without apparent effort, drunk the place dry.

We left, promising to return, relaxed and ready for the road and swearing eternal friendship. Return we did, not once but four times before the summit was attained. The road had by now been surfaced as far as the township of Merille on the lugga of the same name. Thereafter it was all dirt and corrugations, which in the vehicle destruction field were in the highest rank, being about a foot apart. When they are closer together you can, especially if you are not driving your own vehicle, rattle over them at high speed, ironing out the washboard effect. But these ones were so far apart that this was impossible. The 25 kilometres from Merille to Laisamis could take up to an hour as you wallowed in the troughs, breathing in your overtaking dust and praying that the Online still had some beer in stock.

Laisamis' claim to existence, like so many other settlements, was the presence of springs of water. The town lay at only 1,500 feet above sea level and as a result was always hot. So, although Holilogum Nder was only 4,657 feet in height and a mere dwarf compared to other mountains in Kenya, it was still over 3,000 feet above Laisamis, which lay in a hollow surrounded by rising land on all sides.

Round One saw Berna and me meeting Ronald in the main plaza. Compared to the languid lightly-clad strollers and flamboyant gents and ladies taking their ease in whatever shade was on offer, Ronald looked brisk and efficient and ready for action. He sported sharply ironed long trousers, a short sleeved shirt and smart trainers which put my battered old boots to shame. We shook hands. 'Ronald,' I said, 'we will need someone to look after the vehicle while we climb the mountain.' 'It is OK, no problem,' he said,' there is a manyatta near the bottom, we can find someone there, but maybe it might be a good idea to get some posho and chai and sugar.' This seemed a bit excessive to me, considering we were only planning on being here for two nights at most.

I walked into the nearest duka and bought a bag of number one posho, a kilo of sugar, a big packet of black tea and some tobacco and we drove towards the mountain. Small boys were herding camels, in a dry lugga women were digging for water, children with immensely long thin trimmed straight branches were knocking down tamarind pods for their goats which scrambled frantically to snap up every last morsel. On a thorny twig perched a tiny pygmy falcon, perfect in every miniature detail. Out of their holes in a dry bank white-throated bee-eaters were whirling in search of their favoured prey. Mad eyed goats stared as we drove past.

The road rose to a low pass between the Losai Range to the south and our mountain immediately to the north. We stopped and stared up at the beetling cliffs surrounding the summit. We could see no easy way to the top. A pair of ravens glided overhead. Their soft croaks seemed to mock us.

We drove on to the Rendille manyatta which lay a mile beyond the pass. The young men were all away with the herds of camels and small stock in search of grazing. We found only women, naked children and a few elderly dotards in residence. All looked thin and undernourished. These were Ronald's people. He knew their situation. We handed over the posho, maize flour, tea and sugar and he asked for one of the old men to come to our campsite that evening. The usual haggling followed but Ronald pointed to what we had just given them. One greybeard agreed to come. We gave him some tobacco and he gave us a gap-toothed grin.

We camped in the bush, well off the road. The sun, a blood orange, sank below the Ndotos to our west. The great sugarloaf of Poi stood outlined against a violet sky. A more dramatic landscape could scarcely be imagined. As the light dimmed the stars shone through the delicate tracery of the thorn trees. A jackal yipped. A hyena voiced its mournful *hooo yu* rising call. No other sound evokes the atmosphere of the African bush at night more than this. The moon began to rise, bathing everything in a soft silvery light. There were no mosquitos and we sat round our fire sipping our still cold beers, knowing that by morning they would be tepid, although they would still be welcome after our expected exertions on the hill which seemed to loom balefully over our tiny encampment. Mountains always look more intimidating and threatening at night.

In the pre-dawn dimness we struggled out of our sleeping bags, kicked the embers of the fire into life and brewed some tea. The old man, wrapped in his blanket, groaned and snored under his tree. Robert crawled out of his tent. With a justifiable grunt I shouldered my sack and followed Robert up the hill. He, wise man, did not, as most Europeans do, encumber himself with a mass of surplus and inessential impedimentia. A light stick for balance and prestige and he was ready to go. Why burden yourself with a back-breaking gallon of water when you knew that if you felt a bit dry-mouthed the well-meaning bwana would share his liquid load with you? Stumbling and cursing in the semi darkness we staggered upwards, tripping over stones and ripping shirts and shorts in the thorns. First blood was shed and it was barely daylight.

By mid-day we were below the summit ramparts and looking to Robert for further guidance and inspiration. 'So, Robert,' I said, 'what now?' 'This,' said Robert, 'is as far as we go. There is no way up from here.' Bollocks, I thought. Bloody well typical. You get to just below the summit and because your 'guide' hasn't been any higher you are told that this is it. No way my arse! From below I had seen what looked like a crack in the cliff wall which might be a gully leading to the top. 'Well,' I said, 'let me go a bit higher and have a look.' Berna wisely opted to rest in the non-existent shade of a stunted, gnarled and leafless tree. Much longer up here and we would all be gnarled and stunted. 'Back in a mo,' I said and scrambled on all fours up the near vertical slabs to the base of the overhanging cliffs. A traverse left below a large cave brought me into a thicket at the edge of the gully. I peered upwards. The gully was choked with huge smooth boulders and the angle looked to be not far short of eighty degrees. But the gully was deep and I reckoned that once into it, exposure to the vast stomach-churning drop below would be minimal. But without a rope it was not feasible.

I felt that I was being watched. Peering intently at me from clefts in the rock was a group of beady-eyed rock hyrax. What were they thinking, I wondered. Who was this ape-like creature clambering about in their personal space? I stared back into their inscrutable black eyes. They did not move. A baboon barked in annoyance from the top of the cliff. I looked up and the hyrax scuttled back into their rocks. The baboon barked again. I was not welcome here. A rush of air, a pair of swifts whistled overhead, almost parting my hair. I retreated.

'Well?' Berna enquired when I slithered back to where she and Robert were contemplating the view, 'did you get to the top?' 'I did not,' I replied, 'but I shall return.'

We sat on the hot rocks. Far below us the Losai Range lay puny and dwarfed. We drank some water, and ate our sandwiches and oranges. Rising out of the plain to the south was a thin spire. Robert saw me looking. 'That,' he said, 'is Moile, where the Rendille, so they say, burnt copies of the Koran, to show the Somalis that they wanted nothing to do with their religion. If you like we can go there tomorrow. My brother knows the way and he can show you.'

A pair of ravens circled and dropped onto a thorn tree and croaked at us. We went down.

Back in Laisamis we collected Robert's brother from the tea house where he had been taking his ease. His name was Aladi and he was small and thin and angular, and looked nothing like Robert who was tall and well nourished. Robert read my mind. 'Aladi, he is my cousin-brother.' Meaning that he was the son of one of his many uncles. Aladi, puffing on a cigarette, climbed aboard. A few minutes later he signalled me to stop opposite a roadside shack, into which he darted, returning a few minutes later clutching a large bunch of miraa. That evening, camped below Moile, Berna cooked us steak and potatoes. Robert did not hang back. Aladi dined on cigarettes and miraa. I wondered how he would fare on the morrow. I need not have worried. Wearing long past-their-date flip flops of different colours, his cheek bulging with a great wad of miraa, sucking on his fag, minus breakfast, Aladi's black reed-thin legs powered him up the crags of Moile like a mountain goat. I wheezed up the rocks in his wake. Near the summit we had to jump over a deep crevice from one slab to another, the further of which sloped downwards at an alarming angle, below which yawned a homicidal abyss. Aladi sprang across with caprine agility.

I was wearing heavy leather soled boots and I could see myself slipping on the lower rock and shooting off with fearful velocity to be terminally mashed on the metamorphic schist waiting to receive me. 'He who hesitates is lost,' I muttered. Well, I might be lost anyway so here goes and launched myself over the fissure, landing with a heart-stopping scrabble on the other side. The summit was a pile of rocks on the topmost of which was a large iron cross. This I assumed was the work of the priestly brethren in Laisamis. Although I had no aversion to crosses and other indicators of religious observation I was dismayed by the magnitude of this massive structure which seemed to me to be an intrusion and totally out of place on the top of this rarely climbed mountain. It seemed to shout arrogance and superiority, telling the poor benighted unbelievers on the plains below to forsake the moon and the stars and their heathen practices and to adopt or perish. How the iron for the great cross had been lugged up the mountain was something I did not care to think about. Porters urged on by fanatical priests or believers driven by their new faith?

Aladi was shouting something. 'Look,' he said. I looked. On the Marsabit road far below a lorry had overturned. We could see dead cattle lying on the sandy surface. Of the driver there was no sign. We both knew what had happened. The lorry, laden with cattle, going far too fast had skidded on the corrugations, the driver had lost control and the vehicle had overturned. Aladi laughed.

Round Two to Holilogum was, as far I was concerned, not a success. Jonathan Moss of Mathews North fame, accompanied by teenage daughter Naomi and eight-year-old son Nicolas and myself formed the party. In an effort to find an easier route we drove through the bush around the base of the mountain and camped. In the morning we struggled up through the bush only to find ourselves in the identical spot reached on the previous attempt. By this time Nicolas was exhausted. Jonathan and Naomi had gone ahead to investigate a previously unseen gully. So I remained behind with Nicolas.

This was just as well as a troupe of baboons, on seeing the small boy, began to approach in a rather menacing manner, barking and making rushes through the bushes. I threw stones at them and they reluctantly retreated, but if Nicolas had been alone the outcome might have been different.

The summit party returned, having reached the top. But it was getting late, so there was nothing for it but to descend. A greater kudu crashed away, scattering pebbles as it bounded downhill. A group of elephant drifted across our path and vanished like wraiths into the bush.

Round Three was a total washout. With my two brothers we had driven north full of high expectations of good weather and a straightforward climb. I had brought a rope, I knew the area, we had a good contact in Robert. It promised to be a doddle. We crossed the bridge over the wide, dry Merille lugga. People were digging for water in the sand and carting it away in wheelbarrows. The sun was shining. The omens looked good.

We drove to the Rendille manyatta near the base of the mountain to negotiate a fee for an askari. It very soon became obvious that the tentacles of the corporate world had extended even to this remote locality. This was not a conservancy but there were others to the south who knew how to charge the gullible and the post-colonial guilt stricken for non-existent facilities, to charge camping fees, conservancy fees for the protection of non-existent game, for security and so on and on. Here, whatever little game there was, was sparse and nervous. The scenery was magnificent, the birds were wonderful and you had the place to yourself and the local people were entitled to a fair cut, but by paying massively over the odds you set a precedent which would be hard to reverse. When John Hillaby walked through here in the 1960s and Teleki 70-odd years before him, the area was full of rhino and elephant. Teleki, an appalling marksman, shot, killed and wounded anything that moved on four, and sometimes two, legs. According to von Hohnel the Count had in 50 days 'killed with his own rifle, no less than 113 large animals, viz 10 elephants, 61 buffalos, 21 rhinoceroses, nine zebras, six hartebeest antelopes (kaama), four elands and two waterbucks,' in order to feed his men. As his epic journey of discovery from the Indian Ocean coast to Lake Rudolf and back, all on foot, present day adventurers please note, no phones, satellite, mobile or otherwise, took two years, the total wildlife carnage was immense. Now the elephant are few and those few are under pressure. There is no pressure on rhino because there aren't any. Once, when camped at Ngurinit, we came across the remnants of a rhino skeleton. A sad reminder of what once had been.

We bade farewell to our acquisitive friends and retired to Laisamis to camp. That night the grandfather of all storms fell upon us. Rain, when it falls in Africa, is not like Shakespeare's gentle rain falling upon the earth beneath. It comes down like a cataract, accompanied by ear-splitting booms of thunder and vivid flashes of lightning. Within seconds you are soaked to the skin, up to your shins in rushing brown water and trying to stay upright on a greasy muddy path. All night it thundered down and in the morning we struggled out of sopping sleeping bags into a waterlogged world. Clouds covered the mountain. Through binoculars we could see water pouring down the cliffs. It would be impossible to climb. Both we and the Rendille had lost out.

We had hoped to drive further north but the Milgis Lugga, a required crossing point, was in full flood. We retreated. At Merille the quarter-mile-wide lugga was in full spate, a roaring brown flood, bearing on its tossing surface trees, branches, here a dead goat, even a cow, turning and twisting in the current. The roofs of nearby dwellings poked above the coffee-coloured water.

Round four. Friend Peter McCarter, an agile forester, who had accompanied me on a number of character-forming forays, responded with worrying enthusiasm when I mooted the prospect of yet another attempt on the elusive summit. Peter was supremely fit and walked with enormous strides, vanishing over the horizon before I had even got my second wind. This was concerning. What was also concerning was Peter's seeming personal magnetism to near-death experiences when acting as a passenger in other people's vehicles. On one occasion when being driven to the airport in Nairobi in order to take wing to the UK he and his wife Julie were hijacked by armed gangsters, near Naivasha, narrowly escaped being shot and lost all of their luggage. A year later, when once again being driven with wife Julie by taxi to Nairobi to fly to the UK, a runaway saloon smashed into them, again near Naivasha. The taxi was written off, Peter suffered a fractured sternum and concussion. I drove very carefully and we arrived at the base of our mountain without major incident.

We picked up Robert in Laisamis and drove to the Rendille manyatta and found the people to be emollient and welcoming. Drought and lack of grazing made them appreciative of anything which might alleviate their hunger. We gave them some posho, sugar and salt and asked for a 'guide.' We knew that the guide would probably know as much about the route as we did but it is always best to engage the local people and to have them on your side in these areas. Once on the mountain they will never let you down and with their knowledge of medicinal plants and animals they are often a veritable walking encyclopaedia of information.

A rather weedy fellow wearing a knitted beanie appeared. He looked about fifteen, a mere stripling. When he removed the tea cosy from his skull he aged alarmingly. He was completely bald and must have been at least fifty. 'Jambo,' he said, 'mimi ni Akeno.' Robert told us that this name translated as 'he who brings good.' Excellent, we thought. Things are looking up. We asked Akeno to be ready to move off at dawn the following day. We did not really expect Akeno to be with us at dawn. Time is a fluid commodity in Africa. A few minutes, hours, even days, are not something to get worked up about. Some

Europeans, often those on massive salaries, fly into paroxysms of rage if kept waiting for more then a few minutes. This is not helpful. In Africa you have to adjust to a different mindset. Every evening as I was closing up, a group of friends would gather outside my surgery. They would bring chairs and bottles of beer and whisky and sit there chatting and drinking, sometimes for hours. When you see Africans sitting, alone, in pairs or in knots of three or four, they are not idle or lazy. They have perfected the art of utilizing time, something which has been lost in Europe and America. On the waterfront in Lamu, under a tree in Maasai-land, outside a shack in a slum in Nairobi, people gather to enjoy the end of the day. Instead of glaring at their 'devices' they are relating to each other. All this will change as the malignant mutating viruses of knowledge and technology submerge ancient tribal cultures and customs under a suffocating blanket of modernity and 'progress', but thankfully, not quite yet.

Akeno proved us wrong. At 6am, just as the sky was beginning to lighten in the east, and the first birds began to twitter, as the spidery web of the thorn trees showed against the lightening sky, there he was, polished stick in hand.

We gulped down a mug of tea, made sure we were carrying enough water for the day and set off. Akeno led the way, Peter went next, I took up the rear, carrying the all-important rope. The sun was rising and with it the temperature. But mostly we were in shade. After an hour we stopped for a rest and a drink. A lizard skittered away and vanished under a rock. A shadow passed overhead, some bird of prey checking to see what pickings there might be from these interlopers. A go-way bird landed in a tree, cackled derisively and flew off. We pressed on.

Now we were out from under the thin shade afforded by the thorn trees and approaching the beetling overhang. Trending left below a large cave we came to a dense thicket through which we had to force our way in order to enter the gully seen from far below. I was glad of this as the height and imperviousness of the vegetation hid that stomach-churning drop below. It was now fearfully hot and we had to get into the gully before we were fried alive.

Struggling like fish caught in a net, shedding blood and uttering fearful oaths we reached the edge of the tangled mat and peered into the cleft. It was deep and choked with huge, smooth, near-vertical boulders but there was the odd brave sapling here and there hanging on to life and adding a faint hint of hope to its otherwise barren features. Mungo Park, when struggling across some fearful desert in Africa, collapsed. But just where he fell, he noticed a tiny, delicate flower, surviving in the wilderness, and he knew that all was not lost. We were not quite in that category but the feeling was similar.

A few joint-dislocating moves and we were into the gully. It was refreshingly cool, even moist, with the lightest of breezes gently evaporating the honest sweat from our feverish brows. Reclining on the rocks, we took stock of our situation. Akeno looked up. 'Hapana! Hapana!' he said, 'hakuna njia hapa! Hakuna.' 'No, no, there is no way here!' He shook his beanied head with the most emphatic and positive negativity. 'Have a drink, Akeno,' I said. 'Look, we have a rope, the gully is deep, there is no exposure, we cannot fall, and if we throw the rope over those little trees we can pull ourselves up over the boulders.'

Akeno was adamant. I tried another tack, talking bilge about the honour of the tribe, family pride, personal prestige, the usual sort of sentimental rot. No go. Akeno was the lightest member of the team and even more agile than Peter, the agile forester, and I envisioned sending him ahead with the rope and what's more we could hoist him on our shoulders to get over the tricky sections.

Last throw. A monetary bonus when we returned to base. That worked and we were on our way. Akeno only weighed about 50 kilos so we were able to give him a shoulder so that he could thread the rope around a convenient sapling. Then we were able to pull ourselves up to the base of the next obstacle and so on. Our route was marked by shed blood and fragments of epidermis, mostly mine.

It always irritated me that when a bush mountain climb was brought to a conclusion, others remained as pristine and as cool as when they began, while I returned, shirt and shorts in tatters and legs and arms torn, scratched and streaming with blood. I liked to think that this was because I had been at the pointed end of the foray, whereas it was probably because I was less skilful and careful.

We pulled ourselves up over slab after slab until suddenly we were there and we popped out onto the very summit itself. This was a first. On no other mountain was the top reached in such a dramatic way. On all sides the cliffs dropped away. Across the wriggling worm of the Milgis lugga rose the prow of Baio, the sugar loaf of Poi, truncated Illim and the deserts stretching to Marsabit and beyond. As I stood there with Akeno, who still carried his polished staff, and surveyed the wonderful landscape I knew that, wherever I might go and whatever might happen, this marvellous country would be forever remain embedded in my heart and bones.

We went down. We roped down the gully. We were now fully exposed to the full furnace blast of the sun and then Akeno went off route. Instead of trending right as he should have done he led us straight down until we were scrabbling about on dangerously loose rock directly above a vertical precipice. Much perspiration and time were lost as we crept fearfully towards firmer ground, boots slipping on unstable rubble, cascades of detritus tumbling over the lip of the yawning abyss. Heart thumping, I followed the others as they gained a respite below a rocky overhang. We stopped to rest and rehydrate. My water bottle was still half full, Peter's was almost empty, Akeno carried no water. I shared my water, but rationed it with care as there was still a long way to go. I offered Akeno a hard-boiled egg. He refused to touch it. It appears that the Rendille have some sort of taboo when it comes to eggs, a bit like the Jews and pork, but I never did discover the genesis for this peculiar prohibition.

The going was easier now but the heat intensified. The sun-blackened rocks shimmered and danced until it was difficult to focus. The spindly shrubs quivered and shook. Our halts became more frequent. Only Akeno appeared to be unaffected. I came round a corner to find him stretched out asleep in the shade on a low soft rock, his bald head gleaming like a polished football. It never ceased to surprise me how Africans are able to sleep on surfaces on which no European would be able to tolerate for a moment. Behind me

I heard a sort of strangled choking sound, rather what one might expect from a hapless buffalo being suffocated by a lion, and turned to find Peter pointing at his mouth. He looked like an adult version of the child in the film 'Walkabout' meeting the aborigine and asking for water. We stopped and I gave my flask to Peter to alleviate his obvious thirst. He seemed unable to speak. We slowly continued our downward stumble. Every now and again I allowed Peter a few sips from my water bottle, tearing it away after a few moments lest he finish it all.

Finally, finally, the tents appeared and there was Robert, reclining at ease in one of the camp chairs. We tottered, swaying from side to side, towards the cans of Tusker which we knew lay within those tents. Robert rose, read our minds and with admirable dispatch had the cans in our hands, opened and ready to be poured down our parched gullets.

Even Akeno appeared to be affected by the long march. He flopped down, drank the tea which Robert offered him and closed his eyes. Opening them he gave Robert chapter and verse, casting numerous glances in our direction. It was obvious that he thought we were both completely mad but then 'Aiee! Ile mzee!' 'That old man!' looking at me. 'Aiee!! Aiee!!' He shook his head. Old man indeed! Cheeky bugger! Our eyes met and we both laughed. I shook him by the hand, thanked him for his help and gave him what we had promised. He rose, stretched, waved and strolled away to his manyatta.

Peter and I drank another beer. There were no more beers. 'Peter,' I said after a moment's brief reflection, 'why don't we pack up and drive to Laisamis and spend the night in a hotel? That way we can kill two birds with one stone – one, we can leave early in the morning and two, and more importantly, I can see that you are in urgent need of immediate rehydration and medical opinion has it that beer is a far better rehydrant than plain water or tea as it is full of vital proteins, carbs and vitamins. Laisamis will have a supply of Tuskers. What do you say?'

Peter was full of enthusiasm as he croaked out his agreement

It was dark by the time we rolled into Laisamis.

Robert directed us to a hostelry of choice. There was no choice in Laisamis. We were at the stage where it mattered not if the beer was presented on starched white linen or on broken plastic. There was no white linen in Laisamis, but there was bottled Tusker. We drove into a darkened compound where we parked. We sat at a cracked plastic table lit by a Tilly lamp while a runner went off in search of beer. By the time he returned our need was desperate. He brought a dozen of the precious brown bottles. Sighing with relief we set to. The first two barely touched the sides. The next was sipped with the appreciation of a connoisseur. The last was drunk very slowly. Across the table I could see Peter, his head floating like a great disembodied balloon in the darkness. I could not see Robert at all. A shooting star zipped across the starry sky. It was all very peaceful.

'Time to hit the hammock,' I slurred and made to rise. I found this to be difficult. I seemed to have lost the ability to use my legs, whose rubbery constitution was quite inadequate to bear my weight. The same went for my tongue whose previous loquacity had been replaced by slobbering infantile inadequacies. Robert came to my aid and carefully guided me to my cell. Hostelries in Laiasmis did not go in for excesses such as wash basins, chairs, tables or even curtains. A bed, a tattered mosquito net, a concrete floor and that was your lot. What did you expect for a hundred shillings? In the morning I noticed that the holes in the net had been cobbled together with bits of sticking plaster. Not all had been closed.

Ten days later I was in London. It was snowing. I felt the first oily taste in the mouth, the deadly lethargy, the shakes, the coming fever and knew that I was in for a another go of malaria and that for the next week or so I would feel like death.

Some might wonder whether the sensations I felt on the summit of Holilogum Nder were worth the risk of death from a fall on the mountain or from the bite of a mosquito and the answer is an emphatic – yes, they were, and are.

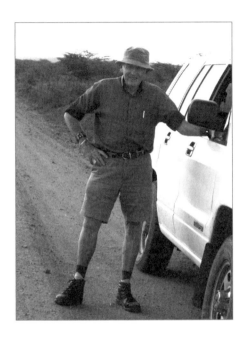

Hugh Cran qualified as a veterinary surgeon in Edinburgh in the early 1960s. In search of adventure and more sunshine than Aberdeen could offer, he answered a small ad. in 1966 to work in a rural practice in Kenya.

As well as working as a general vet in Nakuru, he kept diaries, and explored the wild mountains of Kenya. After a colourful and exhausting 50-year career in Africa he has just returned to the UK and now lives in Castle Carey, Somerset with his wife Berna.

Further Reading

And Miles to Go Before I Sleep Hugh Cran

Promises to Keep Hugh Cran

The Yellow Earl Douglas Sutherland

Man-eaters of Kumaon (with Sheppard illustrations) Jim Corbett

Hero of Kumaon Duff Hart-Davis

To Everything A Season Charles Moseley

Racing the Wind Patricia Nolan

Wild World Richard Barrett

Innocent Victims Catherine Buckle

The Hare Jill Mason

The Otter James Williams

The Rabbit Jill Mason

The Black Grouse Patrick Laurie

Living with Greys Tarquin Millington-Drake

The Byerley Turk Jeremy James

The Ride of My Life Michael Clayton

and many more countryside titles.

Full details of all our books are on

www.merlinunwin.co.uk